Economy and History

edited by

Michael Pammer, Mark Spoerer,
Ali Coskun Tuncer and Ulrich Woitek

1

Tomáš Cvrček

Schooling under control

The origins of public education in Imperial Austria 1769–1869

Mohr Siebeck

Tomáš Cvrček, born 1977; undergraduate studies at Charles University in Prague; Fulbright Scholar at Yale University; 2007 PhD at Vanderbilt University; since 2014 Lecturer in Economics at the UCL School of Slavonic and East European Studies in London, UK.
orcid.org/0000-0002-7311-758X

ISBN 978-3-16-159267-6 / eISBN 978-3-16-159268-3
DOI 10.1628/978-3-16-159268-3

ISSN 2700-2411 / eISSN 2700-242X (Economy and History)

The Deutsche Nationalbibliothek lists this publication in the Deutsche National-bibliographie; detailed bibliographic data are available at *http://dnb.dnb.de.*

The book was printed and bound on non-aging paper by Hubert & Co. in Göttingen. The cover was designed by Uli Gleis in Tübingen. Image: [Detail taken from] "Das Hauptschulgebäude". Lithography depicting the 1812 building of the major school Reichenberg/Liberec, from Anton Hoffmann, Geschichte der Haupt- und Mädchenschule in Reichenberg, Reichenberg: Anton Schöpfer, 1868.

Printed in Germany.

Preface

I first became interested in the history of the Theresian school reform in 2012. As I delved deeper into the statistical sources that the schooling authorities of the Austrian Empire generated over the decades and centuries, my fascination with the topic grew and so did the scale of the task before my eyes. Fortunately, from 2015 to 2019 I was able to rely on the support of two grants, one public and one private. The public one was a grant no. 15-16481S from the Grant Agency of the Czech Republic (Grantová agentura České republiky). The private was one was the Neuron Impulse grant no. 14/2015 awarded by Neuron Fund for Support of Science in Prague. Funds from these grants paid for the data collection without which there would be no book.

Throughout my work, I have benefitted greatly from the advice and comments of many colleagues, most of all Jeremy Atack, Diane Koenker, Michael Pammer, Ulrich Woitek and Thomas Lorman who have read drafts of every chapter, and also Tamás Vonyó, who read some, and Miroslav Zajíček, who started out as my collaborator in the whole project but whose professional path has since taken him elsewhere. To them I owe special thanks. I am also thankful for the comments I have received over the years from Jörg Baten, Howard Bodenhorn, David Chilosi, Rowena Gray, Tim Guinnane, Naomi Lamoreaux, Melinda Miller, David Mitch, Stefan Nikolic, Michael Pammer, Paul Wilson and anonymous referees at Explorations in Economic History and Cliometrica where papers dealing with various individual topics, covered in the book, have been published in the meantime. I owe a great debt of gratitude to all the members of the WEast network, and particularly those who participated in the network workshops in Budapest, Prague, London and Krakow, where drafts, working papers and finished chapters have also been presented. Those meetings have been a source of helpful suggestions, important corrections and (hopefully) improvements in the book.

I have benefited greatly from a strong research support by my home institution, the School of Slavonic and East European Studies (SSEES) at the University College London. I would not have been able to access many of the important documents cited in the book without the help of Andrea Zsubori at the SSEES library. I also thank my two most dedicated research assistants, Lukáš Jeníček and Tomáš Hanáček who transcribed, corrected and checked an inordinate amount of historical data. I also received great assistance from Mgr. Roman Kolek, the director of Státní okresní archiv Praha-východ, when I was searching for archival data on attendance.

Last but not least, I thank my wife Zuzana who has shown great patience and forbearance during the time when I worked on this book and who has heard more *curiosa* about the history of Austrian schooling over the last seven years than she ever bargained for.

In London, 1st December 2019

Table of Contents

Preface V
List of Tables VIII
List of Figures X

Introduction 1

Chapter 1 – The Policy 19

Chapter 2 – The Expansion 48

Chapter 3 – The Financing 88

Chapter 4 – The Teachers 125

Chapter 5 – The Pupils 163

Chapter 6 – The Learning 200

Chapter 7 – The Overhaul 233

Conclusion 264

Bibliography 281
Subject Index 294

List of Tables

Table 2.1: Distribution of school coverage by type of school, 1865 55
Table 2.2: Distribution of school coverage by extent of instruction, 1865 56
Table 2.3: Enrolment in Austrian school in Autumn 1780 59
Table 2.4: Number of children subject to compulsory schooling, 1865 65
Table 2.5: Estimated size of the school-age cohort in Lower Austria, 1865 67
Table 2.6: Determinants of enrolment in the diocese of České Budějovice: Results of a weighted OLS regression 82
Table 2.7: Paired t-tests for differences between Czechs and Germans in ethnically mixed schools 85
Table 3.1: Financing school construction in Bohnice, 1838–1839, in fl C. M. 92
Table 3.2: Average level of provision of school, 1865 94
Table 3.3: School patrons by type in selected dioceses in the early 1860s 96
Table 3.4: School quality by type of patron, 1865 101
Table 3.5: Physical infrastructure of schools by type of patron, 1865 102
Table 3.6: Compliance with regulation by type of patron, 1865 103
Table 3.7: Determinants of compliance – a probit model 105
Table 3.8: Probit model of classroom expansion 109
Table 3.9: Tuition fees across provinces, 1865 115
Table 3.10: Regression analysis of tuition fees 116
Table 3.11: Annual salary expenses by province, 1865 120
Table 4.1: Career progression among teachers in Lower Austria, 1852 129
Table 4.2: Composition of school staff by role, Lower Austria, 1852 132
Table 4.3: Places of birth and of work of Lower-Austrian teachers, 1852 133
Table 4.4: Male teachers' paths to Vienna, 1852 135
Table 4.5: Selected characteristics of school staff in Imperial Austria, 1865 136
Table 4.6: Characteristics of school staff across nationalities 138
Table 4.7: Determinants of staff and expenditure at German and non-German schools 142
Table 4.8: An example of a *Fassion*, 1861 146

Table 4.9: Teachers of Lviv Catholic diocese – descriptive statistics, 1844 149
Table 4.10: Determinants of teacher income in Lviv Catholic diocese (OLS) 151
Table 5.1: Enrolment and expected years of schooling, 1865 168
Table 5.2: Percentage of 5.0–15.0 year-olds enrolled in primary schools in European countries 174
Table 5.3: Gender gap in enrolment 176
Table 5.4: Causes of enrolment shortfall in selected provinces 178
Table 5.5: Schools in the "Attendance sample" 181
Table 5.6: Descriptive statistics of the "Attendance sample" 183
Table 5.7: Mean comparisons by gender and by location 185
Table 5.8: Determinants of attendance – Regression results 188
Table 5.9: Estimated total days of school attendance 190
Table 5.10: Annual earnings in selected occupations in Bohemia, 1852 191
Table 5.11: School absences and under-enrolment in the 1870–71 school year 196
Table 5.12: OLS results for school absences and under-enrolment 197
Table 6.1: Allocation of teaching time to various subjects according to *Allgemeine Schulordnung* of 1774 202
Table 6.2: Allocation of teaching time to various subjects according to *Politische Verfassung* of 1805 205
Table 6.3: Allocated total classroom hours over 6 years of schooling 207
Table 6.4: Estimated number of hours of unique lessons over 6 years of schooling 209
Table 6.5: Literacy estimation for Carinthia and Galicia 216
Table 6.6: Estimated and reported literacy of the 1850–59 birth cohort 218
Table 6.7: Quantity and quality of schooling in country and city, 1865 226
Table 6.8: Simultaneous equations estimation 229
Table 7.1: Schooling situation and reform implications in rural and urban electoral districts in 1865 249
Table 7.2: Probit model of voting on school reform, 1869 253
Table 7.3: Predicted probability of supporting the school reform, 1869 256
Table 7.4: Consequences of the school reform, 1865–1880 259

List of Figures

Figure 1.1: Adoption of *Realschule* in Imperial Austria, 1805–1870...............46
Figure 2.1: Schools in southern Moravia by year of establishment..................50
Figure 2.2: Number of major schools and of all schools, 1821–1868..............57
Figure 2.3: School coverage and enrolment ratio in Imperial Austria, 1818–1911..69
Figure 2.4: School coverage in various parts of Imperial Austria, 1807–1868..71
Figure 2.5: Difference in school coverage of girls and boys, 1821–1868........72
Figure 2.6: Number of schools by language of instruction in the Czech lands, 1808–1908..75
Figure 2.7: Number of schools by language of instruction in Carinthia, Styria, Carniola and the Austrian Littoral, 1817–1908..................76
Figure 2.8: Number of school by language of instruction in Tyrol, Vorarlberg, the Austrian Littoral and Dalmatia, 1818–1908..........78
Figure 2.9: Distribution of pupils by the time required to walk to school, 1862..80
Figure 2.10: Imputed percentage of 5.0–12.0 year-olds enrolled by type of school and distance to school, 1862.............................83
Figure 3.1: Imputed probability of classroom expansion In Lower Austria, 1851–1865...112
Figure 3.2: Distribution of pupils by annual tuition fee, 1865........................113
Figure 3.3: Expenditure on teacher salaries, 1828–1865...............................119
Figure 4.1: Age distribution of male lay teaching staff, Lower Austria, 1852..128
Figure 4.2: Distribution of annual earnings of rural teachers relative to unskilled labourers, 1865..144
Figure 4.3: Teachers in the Czech provinces, 1807–1868.............................159
Figure 4.4: Teachers in Galicia and Bukovina, 1818–1868............................160
Figure 5.1: Age profile of enrolment in selected provinces, 1865..................165
Figure 5.2: Enrolment ratio in the Czech provinces, 1775–1910...................171
Figure 5.3: Enrolment ratio in the Alpine provinces, 1775–1910..................172
Figure 5.4: Enrolment ratio in the Southern and Eastern provinces, 1775–1910...173
Figure 5.5: Enrolment of boys and girls, 1820–1910....................................175

Figure 5.6: Attendance profile by month and type of pupil............................184
Figure 6.1: Education creep among Carinthian men 213
Figure 6.2: Education creep among Galician women.....................................214
Figure 6.3: Enrolment-literacy scatterplot for the 1850–59 birth cohort........219
Figure 6.4: Scatterplot of expected years of schooling and literacy acquisition for the 1850–59 birth cohort.........................221
Figure 7.1: Electoral system of Imperial Austria, 1861–1867........................235

Introduction

The origins of mass schooling in Central Europe date back to the early modern era. Its rise is closely tied to active involvement of government: mass education was and is overwhelmingly public education in that its content, public access and financing are matters of detailed regulation.[1] The lands under the Habsburg sceptre were on the frontier of that development: how to refashion the empire's education had already become a prominent issue in the middle of the 18th century. The policy debate at the highest levels of the Habsburg court spanned the better part of two decades and coincided with a broader reform of the state, the aim of which was nothing less than transforming the motley Habsburg lands into a functional, unified modern great power. It swept across all levels of the education system but the sustained attention paid specifically to elementary schooling, hitherto the domain of the Church, was a first.[2] The fruit of this reform effort was a uniform institutional framework, whose underlying principles remained in force, unchanged, well into the 19th century. Here, then, was the moment when the government declared basic schooling too important to be left alone, assumed full control and has never let go of it to this day. Subsequent reforms restructured state control in various ways but changed little of the basic fact of it. This book is an analysis of the first incarnation of the system, bookended by the 1769 letter of bishop Firmian, which served as the immediate impulse for the policy, and the liberal educational reform of 1869, which marked a new departure in Austrian elementary education.

Few policies stay in place for a hundred years. If it makes any sense to pass judgment on a whole century of schooling policy, it is because the Austrian system retained the core of its original regulations throughout the period. These regulations made it fundamentally distinct from what existed before it and what came after it. Not even such upheavals as the Napoleonic Wars and the 1848 revolution could quite dislodge it. When the system final-

---

[1] In the words of Peter Lindert: "The history of mass primary and secondary schooling is dominated by the rise of public, not private, supply." See Lindert. *Growing Public: Social Spending and Economic Growth since the Eighteenth Century. Vol. 1.*, p. 88.

[2] Engelbrecht. *Geschichte des österreichischen Bildungswesens: Erziehung und Unterricht auf dem Boden Österreichs Vol. 3.*, p. 95–96; Veselá. *Vývoj české školy a učitelského vzdělávání*, p. 8.

ly died, it died by slow attrition, as its various components fell apart from the early 1850s onwards, before it was dealt a *coup de grace* by the reform laws of 1868–69. It is with this underlying unity of time, place and action in mind that this book seeks to answer its main question: was this, the first large-scale public schooling policy in the Habsburg realm, successful? Was it worth the trouble? But, successful at what? And whose "trouble" – whose effort and sacrifice to make it happen – was involved? On the point of the policy's success, my analysis leads me to a rather unambiguous and mostly pessimistic conclusion – perhaps more pessimistic than has been customary in the academic literature on this topic so far. This re-evaluation emerged from my examination of a hitherto underused source material – namely, the statistical data on the operation of the Austrian schooling system.

Until quite recently, these data, generated by the state's administrative apparatus in the process of operating the schooling system, were too vast and too scattered about to be effectively available for research. Advances in information technologies changed all that. Today, the sum total of the statistical material that I have collected for this book adds up to about 10 GB, which easily fits on a cheap flash drive. Twenty years ago, this would have required perhaps fifty 3½-inch floppy disks. Hundred and fifty years ago? The administration generated more data than any contemporary could have reasonably hoped to process. What this means, among other things, is that the statistics contain plenty of information that the school administrators did not even realize was actually embedded in them. That is my opening to say something new about the whole matter. Handled properly, the statistical analysis can be an important complement as well as corrective to past research into the more "literary", or non-numeric, evidence. Together, they yield a more accurate picture of what the Austrian schooling actually looked like and how it compared to what the Habsburg policy makers were trying to achieve.

Nations establish education systems for a variety of reasons. Modern discourse, especially among economists, has focused on the role of education as an engine of economic development. The school fulfils this role to the extent that it generates the necessary human capital, which then bears its proper return on the labour market. Skills such as literacy and numeracy are the most obvious examples of such human capital but one could just as well broaden the definition to cover general cognitive skills (the ability to learn) and social skills (the ability to effectively cooperate with others).[3] Historically, as industrialization unfolded and economies grew more complex, the demand for workers who could read blueprints and follow written instructions increased markedly.[4] Public schooling arose to meet that demand and it is for this rea-

---

[3] See Hanushek and Woessmann. "Do better schools lead to more growth? Cognitive skills, economic outcomes and causation."

[4] Mokyr. "Long term economic growth and the history of technology", p. 1159.

son that it has been called "the most profitable investment of public money" and "an important force in the escape from the Malthusian trap" of bare subsistence and slow growth, characteristic of all pre-modern economies.[5] But both of these quotes refer to education systems that arose in the late 19th century in the context of the Second Industrial Revolution, characterized by advanced sectors such as the chemical industry and electrical engineering. The farther back into the past one goes, the weaker the link between education and growth becomes. In the First Industrial Revolution, known for the development of textiles, iron making and machinery, the usefulness and effectiveness of schooling for economic development is a more dubious proposition. In fact, judging by evidence from England, it is plausible that the move from artisanal workshops to factories initially coincided with a trend towards de-skilling, as machines and production processes were made deliberately undemanding in terms of competence, so that ideally even a child could do it (and frequently did).[6] One consequence was that the dispersion of skills among workers actually increased, where the bulk of factory workers could be perfectly untouched by any formal schooling but they were supervised by, say, a skilled mechanic. The industrial workforce bifurcated: on the one side, a mass of illiterate lever-pullers; on the other, a fledgling cadre of technical staff who had more expertise (basic though it was) than had been customary in pre-industrial times. Still, the implication remains that even in the first phase of the Industrial Revolution, the economy undoubtedly offered a certain amount of jobs where literacy and numeracy were either outright indispensable or at least constituted a competitive edge when applying for the position.[7]

For rulers, at any rate, the economic advance of the masses mostly mattered not as an end in itself but as a way to increase the economic power of their realm, which in turn underpinned its military might. Here, the smoking gun (so to speak) is the frequently observed link between military rivalry and education reform. The argument is that public mass schooling inculcates in

---

[5] Lindert. *Growing Public Vol. 1,* p. 87; Galor. *Unified Growth Theory*, p. 46. The quote from Galor actually refers to a later incarnation of schooling, brought about by Second Industrial Revolution in the late 19th century. See also Easterlin. "Why isn't the whole world developed?"

[6] See Humphries. "Childhood and child labour in the British industrial revolution", p. 409; Mokyr and Voth. "Understanding growth in early modern Europe", p. 29; Mokyr, "Long term economic growth and the history of technology", p. 1160.

[7] One potential complication in making inferences from the English experience is that the situation of the technological leader, which England then was, may be fundamentally different from that of the rest of the world that was trying to catch up. It is plausible that follower nations saw fit to adopt mass schooling even during those stages, which England had completed without it, because their main pre-occupation was technological transfer, not new invention. See Becker, Hornung and Woessmann, "Catch Me If You Can: Education and Catch-up in the Industrial Revolution".

pupils a sense of national unity formed through a suitably nationalistic curriculum as well as the discipline and basic competence that makes for effective soldiers – loyalty and obedience, for short. Prussia usually serves as the defining example: Frederick II's resolve to reform his kingdom's schools crystallized while campaigning in the countryside during the Seven Years' War.[8] Some forty years later, the Prussians were again forced to think boldly about education reform, having been defeated by Napoleon in 1806. By the 1860s, with a string of prominent military victories under their belt, they were congratulating themselves that the reforms had indeed borne fruit on the battlefield.[9]

Similar narratives exist for other countries, too. In France, after the Bourbon restoration, schooling was long mired in a mostly unproductive tug-of-war between the conservative Catholic camp and the reform-minded republican camp. The defeat at Sedan in 1870 "tipped the scales in favour of the educational reformers", their efforts culminating in Jules Ferry's Laic Laws of 1881.[10] France then adopted a recognizably modern tax-based public schooling with compulsory attendance. Outside Europe, the Meiji reforms of Japan were motivated by a keenly felt military rivalry with the West and the desire to build up national strength across all sectors, not just education. After a brief civil war in 1868–69, the progressives in the Japanese government prevailed with their plans for a more mathematically and scientifically oriented curriculum and a new school system was introduced in the 1870s.[11] The United States, too, experienced an upswing in primary school spending in the wake of the First World War which was at least partially motivated by the anti-German sentiment arising from the recent conflict.[12]

---

[8] Melton. *Absolutism and the eighteenth-century origins of compulsory schooling in Prussia and Austria*, p. 172. Riedl argues that what spurred Frederick was that during the campaign he could not find enough literate men to fill the ranks of low-level army officers. See Riedl. *Zavádění povinné školní docházky na území současného jihomoravského kraje*, p. 8. For a general history of the development of the Prussian state apparatus and its reforms, see Clark. *Iron Kingdom: The Rise and Downfall of Prussia, 1600–1947.*

[9] At the battle of Sadová in 1866, as one newspaper put it, "the Prussian schoolteacher defeated the Austrian schoolteacher." The same argument resurfaced in France after the Prussian victory at Sedan in 1870, suggesting that it became a journalistic cliché by then. See Oscar Peschel. "Die Lehren der jüngsten Kriegsgeschichte." *Das Ausland: Ueberschau des neuesten Forschungen auf dem Gebiete der Natur-, Erd- und Völkerkunde* 29, 17th July 1866, p. 695; Moody. *French Education Since Napoleon*, p. 87.

[10] Lindert. *Growing Public Vol. 1,* p. 112.

[11] Aghion et al. "Education and Military Rivalry", p. 382–384.

[12] Schmick and Shertzer quote Fletcher Harper Swift, an early 20th century American professor and researcher of education, who argued that "every great war in which the United States has played a part has been followed by educational developments of supreme national importance". See Schmick and Shertzer. "The Impact of Early Investments in Urban School Systems in the United States." p. 2.

Not all national schooling histories followed this neat pattern, the most visible counterexample being Britain. The Parliament there passed numerous small education acts throughout the 19th century and then introduced a substantial reform of its elementary education in 1870 with no obvious recent military humiliation to pin it on.[13] However, one does not need to embrace the view that education is a continuation of war by other means to still appreciate that schools can serve an eminently political, state-building purpose. The military argument is only partly about battlefield prowess. More important was the effect of schooling on forging a united national identity that would provide the necessary cohesion in times of crisis.[14] The American example of post-First World War education expansion is a case in point: spending on schools increased particularly in areas with strong German minorities, who, it was felt, needed to be better integrated into the American body politic.[15] This was, by then, considered a tried and tested method, for already in the late 19th century, using similar rationale, many US states passed compulsory schooling laws so as to socialize immigrant children into the American way of life.[16] Europe was no different. Having won the many wars of unification, Germany came to view the school, together with the

[13] Lindert. *Growing Public Vol. 1*, p. 113. Instead, what disturbed the English complacency on education was that at the 1867 Paris World Exposition the country's manufacturing proved pre-eminent in "only" ten out of the 90 exhibition categories. Lyon Playfair, one of England's representatives among the jurors, hastened to point out, diagnosing immediately the main cause of England's disappointing performance, that "there was most unanimity of conviction [among other jurors] that France, Prussia, Austria, Belgium and Switzerland possess good systems of industrial education and that England possesses none." But as an indefatigable advocate of technical schooling, Playfair had an axe to grind, not to mention the talent to always stay on message, no matter the facts. Perhaps that was why he omitted to mention that at the Paris Expo Austria, with her allegedly superior technical schooling, scored just one Grand Prix across all categories and Prussia two, compared to England's "only" ten. See Green. *Education and State Formation: The Rise of Education Systems in England, France and the USA*, p. 296; Goñi. "Landed Elites and Education Provision in England: Evidence from School Boards, 1870–99", p. 10–11; Monaghan. "Some views on education and industrial progress a hundred years ago", p. 188; *Berichte über die allgemeine Ausstellung zu Paris im Jahre 1867. VII. Heft*, p. 553–587; K.k. Österreichische Central-Comité. *Bericht über die Welt-Ausstellung zu Paris im Jahre 1867. I. Band*, p. 357–359.

[14] See Ramirez and Boli. "The Political Construction of Mass Schooling: European Origins And Worldwide Institutionalization"; Soysal and Strang. "Construction of the First Mass Education Systems in Nineteenth-Century Europe."

[15] Schmick and Shertzer. "The Impact of Early Investments in Urban School Systems in the United States", p. 4–5.

[16] See Bandiera et al. "Nation-building Through Compulsory Schooling during the Age of Mass Migration." They were of doubtful effectiveness according to Landes and Solmon. "Compulsory Schooling Legislation: An Economic Analysis of Law and Social Change in the Nineteenth Century".

army, as the chief tool of national integration.[17] The newly created German Empire was even willing to go as far as to try to make Germans of the Poles within its borders. Ethnic Germans, too, received their share of indoctrination into proper loyalty to the *Reich*.[18] The Jules Ferry Laws in France operated from the premise of national unity also: towards elimination of local dialects in favour of standardized French and towards strengthening the republican values on which the Third Republic was built.[19] Of course, the usefulness of school for ideological purposes had been apparent long before the modern nation state: this was the reason why Protestant and Catholic Church alike so closely guarded their own role in schooling already in the pre-modern era.[20] It does not require all that much cynicism to argue that ideological propaganda is in fact the main *raison d' être* of modern mass schooling: the rulers' benign phrases about "welfare of the masses" cannot be taken at face value.[21] More often than not, the mass of the people was not so much the user of public education as its target.

The nation-building explanation of the rise of mass schooling has the advantage that it also accounts for why the educational build-up historically coincided with the invasion of the state into this sector, seizing control of its operation and crowding out – sometimes partially, sometimes entirely – church-based and private provision. Inculcation of belief, whether religious or ideological (e.g. patriotism, religious orthodoxy), differs from the simple teaching of skills in that beliefs are hard to verify externally whereas skills can, by and large, be tested for. People can fake ideological commitment or religious fervour to no end but for every skill there exists some more or less conclusive test that can reveal its true extent. Consequently, skill instruction can be contracted privately whereas inculcation in belief, especially if that belief is to be instilled in a third party (i.e. children), cannot.[22] Governments interested in shoring up their own legitimacy – whether a French republican one or a nationalist German one – could not but conclude that outsourcing such important task to the market was unreliable and promptly moved in and asserted their power. In terms of curriculum, this move usually also coincided with a shift in emphasis towards that kind of content that does not bear labour market return.

At the risk of certain oversimplification, then, the multitude of social forces and factors behind the rise of mass schooling can be said to fall under two

---

[17] Cinnirella and Schueler. "Nation building: The role of central spending in education."

[18] Ibid. section 3.2

[19] Lindert. *Growing Public Vol. 1*, p. 112–113; Aghion et al. p. 378

[20] Easterlin. "Why Isn't the Whole World Developed?" p. 10, 12–13.

[21] Lott. "Public Schooling, Indoctrination, and Totalitarianism".

[22] This argument has been most forcefully put forward by Pritchett and Viarengo, "The State, Socialisation, and Private Schooling: When Will Governments Support Alternative Producers?"

broad headings, the economic-developmental and the political-ideological. In real life, they were, of course, often intertwined: one strand of argument, for example, which puts the school's potential for indoctrination in the service of an economic goal, sees the historical task of public education as one of instilling in pupils discipline and punctuality that would prepare them for factory work.[23] But analytically, it is helpful to see these two headings as separate because each aligns with a distinct *modus operandi*. The economic-developmental one envisions the school as a locus of skill acquisition and predicts that the build-up of the school network should, at least partly, come "from below", (i.e. in response to popular demand informed by the growing sophistication of the labour market), allow ample room for private provision (whether charitable or based on tuition) and produce a diversity of types of schools with a variety of curricula of mostly practical orientation – depending on what the economy needs. Under the political-ideological heading, conversely, the school is a tool of social control, the impulse for its nationwide diffusion comes from the top, accompanied by a tight control of its operation, and the economic usefulness of the curriculum is of secondary importance.

Austria was not exempt from the forces that shaped schooling in all the other countries that have so far served as illustrations of the two paradigms. The "war theory" of school reform, for example, could fit the Austrian case well. Both the Theresian legislation of 1774 and the liberal reform of 1869 came in the wake of lost military conflicts. In the first instance, it was Austria's two-fold defeat at the hands of Prussia in 1740–48 and again in 1756–63. Swallowing their pride, the Catholic Habsburgs accepted the need to learn from the experiences and practices of the victorious Protestant power to their north.[24] In the second instance a century later, Austria's rising bourgeois politicians echoed the Prussian press in blaming the disaster of the Austro-Prussian War on, among other things, the lag of Austrian soldiers in education behind their Prussian counterparts. The embarrassing literacy rates of Austrian conscripts served as one of the cabinet's chief arguments in favour of a thorough modernization of the empire's schools.[25]

Certainly, there is plenty in the Austrian educational record that places it comfortably within the political-ideological paradigm. Ideological considera-

---

[23] See, for example, Field. "Economic and Demographic determinants of Educational Commitment: Massachusetts, 1855".

[24] Melton. *Absolutism*, p. 206.

[25] In the Austrian case, however, a conspicuous counterexample is the failure of Napoleonic defeats to inspire any education reform in a way that the humiliation at Jena led to a modernization of schools in Prussia. Neither Austerlitz (2nd December 1805), nor Wagram (6th July 1809) had any educational consequences, glorious defeats though they were. Perhaps bad timing was to blame: Austria had just completed a decade-long review of its educational policies in August 1805 and updated its schooling law in a manner that reinforced its conservative character – five months before the "Battle of the Three Emperors".

tions (about curriculum content, appropriate teacher training etc.) were of primary importance to policy makers, as was the uniformity of schools across the whole empire. This was arguably also the most effectively enforced part of the whole educational policy. Whether it achieved the aim of buttressing the legitimacy of the existing political regime is another matter. One of the aims of the Austrian policy was to use education to limit political change by discouraging popular participation. Yet, historically, the spread of education has often coincided with, and further fuelled, *increased* political participation.[26] It may well be that the complex issue of education caught the Habsburg rulers in an unresolvable paradox. Instituting ideologically loaded schooling so as to ensure that the political opinions of the masses are of the "right" kind amounted to an implicit admission that those opinions somehow mattered and that the masses were already a force on the political scene, even if the empire was as yet devoid of any of the usual trappings of democratic governance (e.g. suffrage). Needless to say, electoral politics and representative government eventually came to Austria anyway (1860) and a liberal school reform, which completely rewrote the curriculum, followed shortly thereafter.

In terms of the economic view, it would be anachronistic to look for the modern development-based, growth-oriented vocabulary in the 18th century documents inaugurating Austria's new educational policies. The best evidence of any awareness of the potential for schooling to improve the situation of the masses could perhaps be found in the grand words of the preamble, where empress Maria Theresa declared "education of youth of both sexes […] the most important grounds for the true welfare of the nations".[27] Judicious reading certainly demands a proper critical distance from such lofty phrases. After all, there is a reason why soaring rhetoric is usually reserved for the preambles: if it appeared in the body of the law, someone might try to actually enforce it.

Ultimately, the proof of the pudding is in the eating: whether a particular public education system could (even theoretically) be conducive to economic betterment or whether it effectively enforces ideological conformity will depend on how it operates and what it offers. It is inevitable that the two paradigms, outlined above, imply somewhat different standards of evaluation because they embody such different ideas of what a successful educational policy looks like. Fortunately, school systems created out of the political-ideological motives offer the modern researcher a relatively easy way out: the social and political elites driving the policy usually wrote their ideal schooling parameters right into the law. Surely, as a first pass, there is no harm in

---

[26] See Glaeser, Ponzetto and Shleifer. "Why does democracy need education?"

[27] See Allgemeine Schulordnung, 6th December 1774, TGB 1629/1774.

taking them at their word, which is what this book aims to do in the case of Austria.

I am not the first person to attempt such an evaluation. The writings on Austria's schooling system date back at least to the middle of the 19th century. The first broadly analytical publications on the topic were pamphlets and treatises of the revolutionary years 1848–1849, written by active teachers, where a critique of the existing system served as a pretext for various reform proposals. Modern academic historiography, informed by a clear research focus and a rigorous methodology, begins with Joseph A. Helfert's exhaustive work on the system's 18th century origins, published in 1861.[28] Helfert was not just an academic; he was also active in policy circles, serving as an undersecretary at Thun's Ministry of Education during the neo-absolutist era. Almost immediately after the publication of his book the baton of academic study passed into the hands of more liberal scholars, first among them Adolf Beer and Franz Hochegger, whose 1867 comparative study placed the Austrian system in the context of changing educational landscape of Europe and thereby sought to make the case for liberalization of schooling.[29] Further work in a similar vein, such as Adolf Ficker's in 1873 or Gustav Strakosch-Graßman's in 1905, continued to voice the liberal critique of the pre-1869 educational system.[30] By the turn of the century, more specialized, period-focused studies began to appear, such as Ferdinand Frank's retrospective of Austrian education since 1848 and Anton Weiss' analysis of the reformulation of the Theresian schooling under Francis I.[31] Weiss, a professor at the university in Graz and later Prague, was the first researcher to pay systematic attention to the statistical material produced by the schooling administration, even though statistical sciences of his time were not quite advanced enough to offer him tools for any sophisticated analysis beyond constructing basic descriptive tables.

It is arguably one of the regrettable side effects of the First World War that the new post-St Germain geopolitical realities of Central Europe impressed themselves so strongly into subsequent academic writing on education. From 1918 practically to this day, most monographs stay, so to speak, within their

[28] Helfert. *Die österreichische Volksschule. Geschichte, System, Statistik. I. Band – Die Gründung der österreichischen Volksschule durch Maria Theresia.*

[29] Beer and Hoechegger. *Die Fortschritte des Unterrichtswesens in den Culturstaaten Europas. I. Band.* Beer was actually directly involved in writing the reform law of 1869 under minister Hasner. See Aliprantis. "The afterlife of Enlightened Absolutism: commemoration of Maria Theresa and Joseph II and the politics of liberal reform in nineteenth-century imperial Austria", p. 314–315.

[30] Ficker. *Bericht über österreichisches Unterrichtswesen*; Strakosch-Grassmann. *Geschichte des österreichischen Unterrichtswesens.*

[31] Frank. *Die Österreichische Volksschule von 1848–1898*; Weiss. *Geschichte der österreichischen Volksschule 1792–1848.*

post-1918 borders, causing them to lose sight of the full amplitude of educational experiences associated with an empire-wide perspective. One can see Šafránek's two-volume work on the history of Czech schools as perhaps the first instance of this trend.[32] Though written during the last years of the Austrian Empire's existence, its geographic focus on Bohemia, accompanied by an even more pronounced national focus on the specifically Czech educational experience, made for a most auspiciously timed publication, when the second volume came out in barely established Czechoslovakia in January 1919, but also for one that was rather nationalistically one-sided. Subsequent Czechoslovak studies retained the country-based focus as did even foreign authors, such as Michail Kuzmin.[33] The self-enclosure into the new borders occurred on the Austrian side also.[34] A good example is the monumental work by Helmut Engelbrecht published in several volumes throughout the 1980s. As a comprehensive and exhaustive description of Austrian schooling across all epochs and educational levels, it arguably remains unsurpassed to this day. Yet perhaps as an inevitable trade-off of depth for breadth, it remained limited in its empirical focus to the area of the Austrian republic. This in no way diminishes the importance of his work as a source of insightful and often unique information on the shape of empire-wide policy or the inner workings of central government in educational matter. In fact, a similar observation can be readily extended to most other serious monographs with a country-specific focus: they usually cover the common ground of imperial legislation in good detail, even when they only assess its implementation within the limited confines of a single successor state. However, the cost of such approach is that, to use statistical jargon, it artificially limits the sample with inevitable consequences for accurate policy evaluation. After all, the Habsburg education system certainly looks much more robust and effective if the dismal records of Dalmatia, Bukovina and Galicia do not enter into the picture. In a further irony of history, when Galician educational data actually resurface in Polish national histories, written with the post-1921 or post-1945 borders in mind, suddenly even the subpar Galician school system – far below Bohemia or Lower Austria in all respects, but the most Pole-friendly across the three Partitions – looks rather good in contrast to the backwardness of Russian Poland and the merciless Germanizing pressures of Prussian Po-

[32] Šafránek. *Školy české I.svazek*, 1913; *II. svazek*, 1919.

[33] Kuzmin. *Vývoj školství a vzdělání v Československu.*; Jaroš and Job. *Rozvoj československého školství v číslech*; Veselá. *Vývoj české školy a učitelského vzdělávání.* After the Second World War, historians of the respective national educations also barely cited each other across borders, a fact no doubt caused in large part by the intellectual isolation of the Eastern bloc until 1989.

[34] See Battista, Ludwig. *Die österreichische Volksschule: ihr Werden, ihre äusseren Arbeitsbedingungen und ihre Erziehungs- und Bildungsarbeit*; Scheipl, Joseph and Helmut Seel. *Die Entwicklung des österreichischen Schulwesens, 1750–1936.*

land.[35] Complications and pitfalls like these are the reason why this book breaks with the country-specific approach and instead respects the borders of 1913.

The second half of the 20th century marked the time when historical research showed greater and more consistent interest in the statistical sources. Here, the trade-off between breadth and depth, inherent in a restricted geographic focus, turned out to have its virtues, as proved by a number of very insightful regional and local studies. As an early precursor, one could cite the other great monograph by Anton Weiss, a 1904–6 history of the Theresian school reform in Bohemia, which collected all the aggregate school statistics for the province, dating back to the 1780s.[36] From the 1970s onwards, in-depth investigations appeared for several former Habsburg provinces or even smaller geographical units: Wilhelm Pietsch's on Styria, Sebastian Hölzl's on Tyrol and Vorarlberg, Elmer Lechner's on Carinthia or Miroslav Riedl's on southern Moravia to name a few.[37] Through archival research, they unearthed data that did not make it into official statistical publications or that were swallowed up in empire-wide aggregates. For example, Miroslav Riedl, whose research probably ranks as the most thorough among the cited works, reconstructed the complete enrolment records for over 700 South-Moravian schools in 1787–1791. Combining the data with a first-hand knowledge of the region's geography, which allowed him to place each school in its local context, he presented an analysis of school enrolment, its determinants and its obstacles that was much deeper and more accurate than had been hitherto possible. As it turns out, seeing the high-flying imperial decrees land in the realities of a remote village school sharpens the contours of what was and was not achievable through a top-down reform in the late 18th century. That is why the authors of these regional researches often prove to be the most ambivalent about the success and effectiveness of the Austrian schooling policy.

Modern historiography has been further enriched by many excellent monographs that focus on issues that do not directly overlap with the research questions of this book. They are studies that, for example, address the nexus

---

[35] See, for example, Wandycz, Piotr. *The Lands of Partitioned Poland, 1795–1918*, p. 222–223, 270–271. Bukowski argues that even in the context of current Poland, the long-term legacy of the Austrian education system is positive relative the Russian and Prussian one. See Bukowski. "How history matters for student performance: lessons from the Partitions of Poland".

[36] Weiss. *Geschichte die Theresianische Schulreform in Bohmen*. The same data also appeared in Engliš. "Příspěvky ke statistice národního školství."

[37] Hölzl. "Studien zum Pflichtschulwesen in Tirol 1774–1806"; Lechner. "Die Revision des Reichsvolksschulgesetzes (1869) im Kronland Kärnten (1883). Meinungen und Maßnahmen."; Pietsch. *Die Theresianische Schulreform in der Steiermark (1775–1805)*; Riedl. *Zavádění povinné školní docházky na území současného Jihomoravského kraje.*

of education, culture and politics,[38] that are interested in the Austrian school as an example of practical pedagogy[39] or that focus on historical periods that only partially overlap with mine.[40] They, too, form a part of the background information on which I draw. Indeed, for all the undisputed usefulness of data, without a proper context they are not much more than just a pile of meaningless numbers but when actually placed in that context, they can speak powerfully, even decisively, on important questions.

That is, in fact, the agenda of this book: to let the reams of statistical material, produced by the schooling administration, speak. This kind of source is a useful complement and an illuminating corrective to the mostly qualitative assessments offered by other authors. My aim is to confront the official pronouncements, the decrees and policy guidelines with the realities of the school system as it developed throughout its first century. The basic parameters of the elementary school system, specified in the law, have been thoroughly documented and frequently cited in the literature. For example, almost any monograph on the topic mentions Joseph II's decree that a school be built wherever 90–100 pupils lived within a half-hour walk. This invites an obvious follow-up question: were schools actually built at this density? Was the system even close to complying with this stipulation? After all, the law can demand this, mandate that and forbid the other but whether and how much any of those provisions actually take root is another matter altogether.

The advantage of the Austrian case is that the data are quite abundant and conform to a uniform system of reporting. One of the consequences of the government's desire for tight control is that it mandated the collection of tremendous quantities of data on various aspects and these have not been used to their full potential. Like other forms of evidence, data have their own inbuilt checks for consistency and reliability: population shares need to add up to the whole, enrolment ratios should not exceed 100%, gender ratios need to be realistic etc. This means that internal inconsistencies, lacunae, outliers and mistakes can be quite easily spotted, if not always rectified. In this sense, numerical evidence can reveal things that other types of evidence might not. This is especially the case when the statistical material is analysed through methods that were not available to those who first produced it. Sometimes, even what is, by modern standards, a very simple check can reveal surprising (but profitably exploitable) deficiencies in the record. As an example, I was

---

[38] Zeps. *The Politics of Education in Austria: Church, State and the Reform of Education 1765–1962*; Voegler. *Liberalism and the Social Question in the Habsburg Hinterland: the Catholic Church in Upper Austria, 1850–1914.*

[39] Brezinka. *Pädagogik in Österreich. Die Geschichte des Fachs an den Universitäten vom 18. Jahrhundert bis zum Ende des 20. Jahrhunderts*; Veselá. *Vývoj české školy a učitelského vzdělávání.*

[40] Melton. *Absolutism and the eighteenth-century origins of compulsory schooling in Prussia and Austria.*

quite surprised by how many authors took the officially reported numbers of school-age children at face value, without seeing the need to confront the data produced by the school system with statistics on age structure rendered by the population census. I was then not at all surprised when it turned out that the educational authorities in many places severely undercounted the number of children who should have been in school. The statistical record offers many such instances. Whatever new revelations this book may bring, they will come from the confrontation of data with other data.

The backbone of my database is a collection of official published sources, from which I formed several distinct datasets. The main sources are the annual statistical publications that appeared from 1828 onwards: the *Tafeln zur Statistik der Oesterreichischen Monarchie* (TSOM), together with their precursors, and *Statistisches Jahrbuch der Oesterreichischen Monarchie* (SJOM).[41] After 1880, the Austrian Statistical Commission commenced a new series, the *Oesterreichische Statistik*, which mostly carried information on periods outside this book's focus but also include some useful retrospective data such as literacy rates for cohorts that went to school in the early part of the 19th century. Most of these publications contained relatively aggregated data, such as totals for the whole provinces, although smaller units were also occasionally cited. For a more disaggregated look, I relied primarily on the *Detail-Conscription*.[42] A most valuable resource, this was the first detailed, comprehensive, almost empire-wide survey of all elementary schools. It was conducted in the Spring 1865. Moreover, the survey results were published by school, offering a truly "micro" look into the structure of the system: this "school census" contains information on almost 11000 schools.[43] I rely on it so often throughout the book that I have come to refer to it by this shorthand title, *Detail-Conscription*, so as to spare the reader the repeated lengthy full citation. Fortunately, the practice of surveying all schools in quinquennial

---

[41] K. k. Handels-Ministerium. Statistisches Büro der Rechnungs-Kontrollbehörde. *Versuch einer Darstellung der Oesterreichischen Monarchie in Statistischen Tafeln. Iter Jahrgang. 1828*; K. k. Handels-Ministerium. Statistisches Büro der Rechnungs-Kontrollbehörde. *Darstellung der Österreichischen Monarchie in Statistische Tabellen. IIter Jahrgang. 1829*; K. k. Handels-Ministerium. Direktion der administrativen Statistik. *Tafeln zur Statistik der Österreichischen Monarchie 1830–1848*; –. *Tafeln zur Statistik der Österreichischen Monarchie. Vol. 1–5 Neue Folge*; K. k. Statistische Central-Commission. *Statistisches Jahrbuch der Österreichischen Monarchie für das Jahr 1863–1881.*

[42] The full citation is: K. k. Statistische Central-Commission. *Detail-Conscription der Volksschulen in den im Reichsrathe vertretenen Königreichen und Ländern nach dem Stande vom Ende des Schuljahres 1865.* Vienna: C. Ueberreuter'sche Buchdruckerei (M. Salzer). 1870.

[43] Sadly, the level of detail on schools in Galicia, Bukovina and Dalmatia was not as good as for all the other provinces. The *Detail-Conscription* still contains useful data on these three but wherever in the book the analysis goes all the way to the school level, these provinces had to be dropped.

intervals was incorporated into the school reform of 1869, in consequence of which we also have similar surveys for the school years 1870–71, 1874–75 and 1880–1881.

The official statistical yearbooks and special reports are supplemented by publications that were not necessary statistical in their original purpose but lent themselves easily to such manipulation. These included various teacher and school directories, such as the *Lehrer-Schema* published by Joseph Kaiser in 1852 for all of Lower Austria and by the Lviv Catholic Consistory in 1844.[44] Thanks to their standardized format of reporting and comprehensive coverage (within their areas), they could be converted into the teacher datasets, used in Chapter 4. Yet another summary list, this time of all parishes, though carrying a somewhat different set of variables, gave rise to the school coverage sample of the diocese of České Budějovice, analysed in Chapter 2.[45] Documents of this kind, although not always as rich and informative, were compiled in various years for other provinces also. None of them yielded as rich data as the Lower Austrian and the České Budějovice ones but they furnished useful information in a few detailed cases, which are noted in the text.

To these official publications, I added a few archival sources. One portion comes from the archives of northern and eastern Bohemia and includes data on the internal operation of rural schools during the school year 1864/65. They are the basis of the "Attendance sample" in Chapter 5. The other half of my archival sources are the Education Commission reports from the early years of the 19th century, before the official annual publications started, and they allow me to push the time series initially constructed from data in TSOM farther back into 1820s and 1810s. While these early reports were referred to in the works of Anton Weiss, they have not been, as far as I can tell, critically evaluated and used for a systematic statistical analysis until now.

Last but not least, as the list of primary sources in the bibliography makes clear, a good number of statistical data is actually not directly school-related but is necessary to place the educational statistics in a proper perspective. Most of them are of a demographic nature, such as population figures, fertility and mortality data, urbanization rates and so on, and come predominantly from the Austrian censuses and from the annual publications (TSOM and SJOM). For information of an economic nature, I made frequent use of reports published from the 1850s onwards by the then newly established Chambers of Commerce.

In organizing the book, it was not immediately clear whether the content and the argument lent itself better to a chronological arrangement or rather a

---

[44] See Kaiser. *Lehrer-Schema*; *Katalog des an den Volksschulen der Lemberger lat. Erzdiözese angestellten Lehrpersonals, für das Jahr 1844.*

[45] Trajer. *Historisch-statistische Beschreibung der Diöcese Budweis.*

thematic one. Eventually, I adopted a hybrid of the two: Chapter 1 presents an overview of the institutional structure in a chronological manner. Its purpose is to lay out the groundwork and to specify, by enumerating the most important policy parameters, the standards of implementation and provision to which their authors aspired. Having grounded the studied period within an appropriate chronological frame, the subsequent theme-based chapters fill in the specifics. In Chapter 2, I focus on the expansion of the school network, its density and reach. I introduce the concept of school coverage in order to measure the system's capacity as distinct from the enrolment ratio and the attendance rate, which measure its actual use. Most of the indicators I rely on are physical indicators, calculated in terms of both buildings and bodies, so as to assess the adequacy of the physical infrastructure vis-à-vis the pupil numbers that the government set out to school. Financial matters come into view in Chapter 3, which presents a good opportunity to analyse the political economy of schooling on the local level. Who paid and who gained, who sowed and who reaped (if anyone) are questions on which the existing literature has offered a number of hypotheses and on which a statistical analysis of the financial flows – "follow the money!" – may perhaps be best suited to offer an answer. Chapter 4 is about teachers – and in some sense that makes it, too, about money, since teaching staff usually represent the biggest expense in any schooling system.[46] But it is not only about money; it also considers the social situation of teachers, including their aspirations and frustrations, and the position that women teachers carved out for themselves on the educational labour market. Since, in the multinational empire, elementary education was inevitably prone to become a battleground of nationalisms, the chapter also discusses the national, or language, question, especially the fault line between German schools and all others. Pupils come to the foreground in Chapter 5 with a focus both on enrolment and on attendance. Attendance, especially, is one of the more elusive and intractable issues in research of historical schooling. My goal is to establish not only the extent of enrolment and regularity of attendance but also to identify its determinants. Here, I explore the economic situation of the rural families and attempt to assess the full cost – both out-of-pocket cost and opportunity cost – of schooling. In Chapter 6, I discuss the learning process. In its static sense, "learning" means a fixed amount of knowledge, coinciding with the content of the curriculum, i.e. what were the children learning? I look at the lesson plans and time allocation for each subject, providing an estimate of the number of total and of unique lessons that a pupil would be exposed to. In its dynamic sense, "learning" means the process of acquiring that knowledge which raises the question of the school's effectiveness, i.e. how educated, literate, skilled and knowledgeable did they become? Therefore, this chapter is where I investigate the

[46] Go and Lindert. "The uneven rise of American public schools to 1850", p. 11.

correlation between enrolment and literacy attainment. Chapter 7 then describes the final demise of the Theresian schooling system and offers another look at the political economy, this time of the liberal reform that ended it. Finally, I take the concluding section not just as the place to restate all the major findings of the previous seven chapters but rather as the moment to adopt a bird's eye view and, having studied what the Habsburg rulers did and where it led, to explore possible alternative paths that the empire's schooling could have taken. It is, admittedly, an exercise in counterfactual history to some extent but since much of the statistical analysis, e.g. a regression, involves an implicit counterfactual, I reasoned that I might as well openly acknowledge this and bring an outline of a possible alternative into broad daylight.

While many things receive attention, I should also be candid about areas and issues that this book does not discuss. First, geographically, it has nothing to say on the Hungarian part of the empire. The Lands of the Crown of St Stephen organized their schooling under its own law and they also formed a separate territory for statistical purposes.[47] Hence, Hungarian data do not have the same regularity, abundance and reliability as the Austrian data. A similar argument applies to the Italian provinces under the Habsburg sceptre, namely Lombardy and Venetia, which were acquired at the end of the Napoleonic Wars, retained much of their educational infrastructure and legislation from an earlier period and then left the Habsburg fold in 1859 and 1866. I do not include them in my analysis. Second, thematically, even with the relatively rich data that the Austrian sources supply, I am unable to answer certain questions that are customary to ask in connection with schooling. These include, for example, estimates of the return to schooling (on the individual, or microeconomic, level) or of the contribution of education to Austria's overall economic development (on the macroeconomic level). While I present some arguments on both issues, these arguments are based on qualitative evidence and not on data. The kind of dataset that such estimation requires, similar to one employed, for example, by Jason Long in the case of England, does not currently exist for the Habsburg monarchy.[48] Basically, any analysis that requires individual-level data linked across several years is something I found unfeasible at the present moment.

Let me close with a few necessary "points of order." Choosing the appropriate place names in an area so ethnically complex as the former empire of the Habsburgs is a tricky question. I make plenty of references to the region's major capitals and in those instances there is no reason to refrain from using their standard English names, like Vienna and Prague. The same applies to

---

[47] Hain. *Handbuch der Statistik des Österreichischen Kaiserstaates. I. Band.* p. 185.

[48] But see Klein. "Did Children's education matter?" for an example of this kind of analysis for late 19th century Austrian education.

provinces which all have well-established English names, from the Austrian Littoral to Galicia. But since my analysis also covers many obscure small places, whose 19th century German, Italian or even Polish names have fallen out of use, under which they could not be identified on a modern map, I decided to use in those instances their current names, with their 19th century (German) name mentioned in brackets on the place's first appearance in the text. And so Lemberg becomes Lviv, Reichenberg is Liberec and Budweis turns into České Budějovice.

Choosing an all-encompassing name for the sum-total of the territory analysed here is its own issue. I have mentioned above that Hungary and Italy are not in the database. The territory that I *do* cover is that motley collection of crown lands, stretching from Dalmatia to Bukovina, that, unfortunately, never shared a common name which one could consider accurate, official and widely recognized all at the same time. The official name was "Crown lands represented at the *Reichsrat*", which is a mouthful. A reasonably accurate name was "Cisleithania" but the expression is obscure to most people who are not intimately versed in the Habsburg constitutional history. Finally, there is "Austria" which enjoys certain common currency but is woefully inaccurate as it is stretched to cover areas belonging today to Romania, Ukraine, Italy, Montenegro and a host of other countries. For lack of a better word, I have settled on "Imperial Austria", which partakes in the popularity of "Austria" but has a qualifying adjective to emphasize that it is not identical to the modern-day Austrian republic. It is still inaccurate but it is the least bad option.

Regarding policy-related terms, I have tried to adhere to existing standard translations that have already appeared in other English-language works. The most frequently used is "trivial school" as a translation for the German *Trivialschule*. The phrase refers to *trivium*, the Latin expression for reading, writing and arithmetic. While in modern-day English, "trivial" carries certain pejorative connotations, denoting something that is insultingly simple, this pejorative meaning is in fact a derivative of the original one, as "something fit for elementary schooling". So, my phrase "trivial school" as a translation for *Trivialschule* is not used in its pejorative sense but in its original, technical sense: an elementary school teaching the three Rs. As for other expressions, I translate *Normalschule*, the kind of school that served as the norm for all the schools in a province, as "normal school" and I follow James van Horn Melton in translating *Hauptschule* as "major school".[49]

At the same time, I left many of the historical terms related to education in their original German. I retain, for example, the German expression *Realschule* for the lower-secondary practical school with a curriculum steeped in *realia*, because it was not worth creating a separate translation for the few

[49] See, for example, Melton. *Absolutism*, p. 212.

instances where it makes an appearance in the book. The same applies also to the two laws that informed Austrian schooling policy, the *Allgemeine Schulordnung* of 1774 and the *Politische Verfassung der deutschen Schulen* of 1805. The translation into English of each ("General School Ordinance" and "Political Constitution of German schools", respectively) does not add any value and, given the established meaning of words like "constitution" in general English parlance, it would only create confusion. For most German policy terms, I explain their meaning and translation on their first occurrence and then rely on the reader's good memory. Thus, overall, the place names are mostly modern while the policy jargon is mostly old. At first sight, that may seem inconsistent but I was guided by the consideration that, should an interested reader wish to retrace my analytical steps, he or she will likely search for the places in modern maps but search for the policy terms in old documents.

The emergence of mass schooling is one of the most consequential and impactful social events of the last three centuries. The question of how and why it happened is both interesting and important precisely because the public policy of universal education proved so transformative. Both advocates and detractors of schooling expansion had an inkling of its power, except one side welcomed it and the other feared it. The Austrian government eventually came down on the pro-expansion side and they certainly "thought big" when launching their school reform in 1774. But lacking a crystal ball, they were, in many ways, groping in the dark and inevitably took steps that, with the benefit of hindsight, proved a poor choice. The statistical analysis presented here attempts to discern how those policy decisions shaped the outcome and to what extent the policy makers bear the responsibility for it.

Chapter 1

The Policy

When Maria Theresa promulgated the *Allgemeine Schulordnung* (ASO) or General School Ordinance, in December 1774, it was an act of such impact that to this day all the Habsburg monarchy's successor states consider it the founding act of their modern public education.[1] It was a culmination of years of preparation and the beginning of a new era of mass schooling. Through this law, the Austrian state was setting out to implement an ambitious policy that would require extensive administrative and physical infrastructure, incur considerable expense and engender painful adjustments in many areas of life. The fruit of this endeavour, a system of universal elementary schooling, was to affect the ruler's every subject. The reform effort has since been described with many adjectives – "fundamental", "comprehensive", "outstanding", "foundational", "epochal" – but certainly not "trifling".[2] In undertaking a policy of such scale, the Habsburg state was responding to long-standing cultural, intellectual and economic forces which, since at least the second half of the 17th century, had been pushing school reform into the focus of top-level political agenda throughout the German-speaking world. These forces were not necessarily agreeable to the Habsburgs, but at some point during Maria Theresa's reign, it became clear that they could be neither beaten back nor altogether ignored.

Culturally, the first impetus for change was the emergence of pietism in the Protestant North in the 1660s with its emphasis on deep, inward faith bolstered by an individual's direct personal confrontation with the text of the

---

[1] Strictly speaking, the ASO only pertained to the western part of the monarchy. The lands of the Hungarian crown received their own schooling legislation in the form of *Ratio Educationis* in 1777. While a separate act formally speaking, it was part of the same reform effort as the ASO. See Helfert, Joseph Alexander. *Die österreichische Volksschule. Geschichte, System, Statistik. I. Band – Die Gründung der österreichischen Volksschule durch Maria Theresia*, p. 467.

[2] Ficker, Adolf. *Bericht über österreichisches Unterrichtswesen. Aus Anlass Der Weltausstellung 1873. I. Theil. Geschichte, Organisation und Statistik der österreichischen Unterrichtswesens*, p.18; Helfert. *Die österreichische Volksschule. Geschichte, System, Statistik. I. Band*, p. 118; Frank, Ferdinand. *Die Österreichische Volksschule von 1848 – 1898*, p. 2; Heiler, Bernhard and Rosa Lebmann. "Die Entwicklung der allgemeinbildenden Pflichtschulen in Österreich", p. 516. Beer, Adolf and Franz Hochegger. *Die Fortschritte des Unterrichtswesens in den Culturstaaten Europas*, p. 266.

Bible. Leading pietists proposed numerous ways to infuse daily life with such faith, including education. While Philip Jacob Spener, the "father of pietism", stressed university reform with a view to improve the preparation of preachers, his followers, most notably August H. Francke, came to appreciate the potential of lower-level schools in reaching the laity.[3] Appointed a preacher in a poor suburb of Halle in 1691, Francke encountered numerous orphans there who obviously could not acquire their faith the standard Protestant way – from their mothers. He founded a school for the poor in 1695 and over the course of the next three decades introduced numerous pedagogical features, designed to make instruction of large numbers of pupils as effective as possible: set lessons, separation of focused learning time from the intermission, the raising of one's hand when asking a question. Mass elementary schooling of young children thus gradually developed as natural means to achieve pietist aims because it could bring to the masses not only literacy but also direct inculcation of doctrine from an early age. By 1720s, Halle became the centre of school reform efforts because of its useful pedagogical knowhow, which was not only conveniently attuned to the pietist *Zeitgeist* but could also be readily replicated on a large scale.[4]

Outside the religious sphere, the question of mass schooling came to receive increasing attention from cameralism. As a system of thought, cameralism could be described as the intellectual vehicle for the transition from the feudal state of early modern Europe to the administrative state (*Beamtenstaat*) of the late 18th century. Its primary concern was how to organize the state so as to effectively raise revenue for the monarch.[5] Prussian authors, such as Justus Christoph Dithmar and Simon Peter Gasser, evaluated all institutions and regulations with a view to the control and utilization of a country's resources and this instrumental approach extended to religion. The stress that the Franckean school put on instilling diligence, obedience and other "Protestant virtues" in its pupils turned religion, in their eyes, into a potentially useful tool of social control.

These ideas spread south from Prussia, so that by the 1760s, the connection between schooling, religion, efficiency and control came to be appreciated by Austrian cameralists also.[6] One of the economic developments to which

---

[3] Spener, Philip Jacob. *Pia desideria*, p. 103–112.

[4] Melton, James Van Horn. *Absolutism and the eighteenth-century origins of compulsory schooling in Prussia and Austria*, Chapter 1.

[5] Tribe, Keith. "Cameralism and the Science of Government." *Journal of Modern History* 56 (1984): 264. See also Scheipl, Josef und Helmut Seel. *Die Entwicklung des österreichischen Schulwesens von 1750–1938*, p. 11–12.

[6] Kann cites the most prominent among Austrian cameralists, Joseph von Sonnenfels, in this context: "It is the concern of the Sovereign as the secular authority that his subjects should be well instructed in religious matters." See Kann, Robert A. *A Study in Austrian Intellectual History: From Late Baroque to Romanticism*, p. 173.

cameralist thought was trying to find a response was that, throughout the 18th century, the serfdom-based economy was showing increasing signs of strain. In Austria, where serfdom was more deeply entrenched than in Prussia, the pressure on serfs exerted by the landlords had been continually intensifying from the late 17th century onwards and the central authorities tried to counter this pressure by issuing edict after edict limiting the extent of the coerced labour service (*robota*).[7] This legislation proved ineffective and the second half of the 18th century saw an increase in rural unrest, culminating in the 1775 mass uprising in Bohemia. Such events highlighted how the coercive nature of serfdom undermined not only political stability by engendering social conflict but also the motivation to work in peasants. Cameralists proposed that instead of external coercion, discipline and diligence had to be internalized during childhood through schooling.[8]

In this context, mass schooling, while undoubtedly costly, could earn their endorsement – up to a point. In what James van Horn Melton called "a revealing paradox", the cameralist support of elementary education usually went hand in hand with opposition to the expansion of secondary and university education.[9] Far from being paradoxical, this stance was informed by the cameralist notion that the main purpose of schooling was internalizing work ethic, not acquisition of skill or knowledge. Given that, in their view, the main source of wealth of a state lay in its economically active population, an educational system that aroused in peasants an ambition to continue with their studies or perhaps to seek to put their newly acquired skills to use in the cities was decidedly undesirable because it reduced the agricultural labour force. Cameralists therefore trod a fine line on education – a nod to basic literacy supplemented by religious instruction was as far as they were willing to go.

Outside the cameralist milieu, however, the idea of mass literacy faced determined opposition for most of the 18th century because Austria, in contrast to Prussia, was a Catholic power. The 1713 papal bull *Unigenitus* explicitly rejected the notion of lay Bible reading and among Austrian Catholic clergy the practice was specifically associated with underground Protestantism. When a survey in 1752 revealed a disconcerting spread of crypto-Protestantism in the Styrian diocese of Seckau, its bishop, Leopold Ernst von Firmian, proposed to close all parish schools on the grounds that they were an

---

[7] In Bohemia, for example, edicts to such effects were introduced in 1680, 1717 and 1738. See Klein, Alexandr. "The Institutions of the 'Second Serfdom' and Economic Efficiency: Review of the Existing Evidence for Bohemia".

[8] As an example, see Johann Wiegand's 1772 treatise *Versuch unter dem Landvolke einzuführen, zu verbreiten, und allgemein zu machen* in which he supplemented his exhortations to diligence and thrift with his own proposed school ordinance.

[9] Melton. *Absolutism*, p. 214.

obvious conduit for "heresy".[10] The Catholicism of the Habsburg Counter-reformation had long preferred the stage play, the painting and the statuary to the book and the treatise as more direct ways of reaching the masses. Yet, from the middle of the 18th century, these non-literate methods were facing an intensifying competition from the printed word. By the 1760s, Vienna rose to rank third in book publishing among German cities, up from forty-sixth merely two decades earlier. Even without the domestic output, the fact that Austria was part of the German-speaking cultural sphere with its long-standing and lively literary tradition ensured that printed forms of expression were going to seep across the border from Germany.[11] Any notion of stemming this tide, even as technological improvements were making books ever cheaper, came to look less and less realistic. Thus, next to the cultural turn towards inward religion, spearheaded by pietists, and the emphasis on administrative and economic modernization, championed by cameralists, the proliferation of printed material was yet another force that neither the church hierarchy nor the state bureaucracy could beat and so they would have to join it.

It helped that they soon learned to appreciate that what was printed and therefore read was in some ways easier to control than the oral culture of country and town. Policymakers' views on the use of literacy and of mass education were changing in line with the recognition of the susceptibility of the printed word to censorship. When, in June 1760, Maria Theresa established a new administrative body in charge of all educational matters, she called it the Court Commission for Education and Book Censorship (*Studien- und Büchercensurs-Hofcommission*).[12] As its name suggested, its overarching task was both to promote and to prevent learning which illustrates how closely related schooling and ideological control were in the minds of Austria's leading lights on school reform. By May 1769, Leopold von Firmian, now promoted from Seckau to the prince-bishopric of Passau, was urging the empress in a memorandum to counter crypto-Protestantism not by shutting schools down but instead by establishing them.[13] In a revealing change of heart, he suggested that mass elementary schooling with a strong emphasis on instruction in the Catholic doctrine was an efficient tool in fighting heresy and ensuring religious conformity.

His memorandum served as the immediate impulse for the Austrian school reform. The underlying forces, operating in the background, had brought all the important players on board – church, state bureaucracy, landed aristocra-

---

[10] Melton. *Absolutism*, p. 60–61.

[11] Melton. *Absolutism*, p. 85.

[12] Ficker. *Bericht über österreichisches Unterrichtswesen*, p. 4; Pietsch, Walter. *Die Theresianische Schulreform in der Steiermark (1775–1805)*, p. 18. Throughout the book, I shorten the title to "Education Commission".

[13] Helfert. *Die österreichische Volksschule. Geschichte, System, Statistik. I. Band*, p. 617 cites the original letter in full.

cy – and from this point on the question was not whether but how. In resolving the various organizational issues, the Austrian bureaucracy could draw inspiration from the Prussian school reform, which had been taking place throughout the 1760s. King Frederick II's General Reglement for rural schools, promulgated in June 1763, dealt with many questions, including oversight, extent of curriculum and compulsory school age. Numerous aspects of the Prussian reform made it into Austrian law also. Already in 1771, a Normal School was established in Vienna, whose purpose (as the name indicates) was to serve as the template and norm for all future schools. Its organization and curriculum were modelled on the *Normalschule* founded by Ignaz Felbiger a few years earlier in the town of Sagan in Prussian Silesia. As an Augustinian abbot, Felbiger was instrumental in extending the Prussian school reform to the mostly Catholic areas of Silesia, which the Prussian king had annexed in the War of Austrian Succession. Many of the Viennese school reformers, such as Ignaz Parhammer, Josef Messmer and Philippides von Gaya, took their inspiration from Felbiger or even paid him a visit in Sagan and brought various parts of the knowhow to their *Normalschule* in Vienna, including the stress on teacher training, the separation of classroom from teacher's living quarters, group instruction and detailed time management of the school day.[14]

Still, given the difference in official religion between the two countries, Prussia could not be Austria's template for defining the rules of interaction between church and state. Even Frederick's treatment of his numerous Catholic subjects in Silesia could not quite serve as a blueprint: their schooling was arranged through a separate law, composed by Felbiger and enacted in 1765. Given that Lutheranism was Prussia's state religion, it obviously could not have been geared towards countering the spread of Protestantism and bolstering Catholic religiosity.

Austrian school reformers had to invent their own *modus vivendi* with the Catholic Church. Organizationally, Austria's pre-reform education system was in the hands of the Jesuit and Piarist orders[15] and the public law's distinction between "ecclesiasticum" (matters of the Catholic church) and "politicum" (matters of state) implied certain limits on how far the empress could intrude into "ecclesiastica", something which the Prussian king did not have to consider in his dealings with the state Lutheran church. In September 1770, Maria Theresa exploited a dispute between two ecclesiastical authorities over teachers' line of subordination as a pretext to declare schooling a "politicum", thereby claiming the right of teacher appointment for public authori-

---

[14] Melton. *Absolutism*, p. 203.

[15] Ficker. *Bericht über österreichisches Unterrichtswesen*, p. 17; Pietsch. *Die Theresianische Schulreform in der Steiermark, p.* 19.

ties. This precedent opened the door for the wholesale regulation of schools by the state and gave it the decisive policy initiative.[16]

With the state's many subsequent intrusions into what had been an ecclesiastical domain, the relationship between the state and the Catholic Church in matters of schooling did not find its new stable, long-term equilibrium for another thirty years as different stakeholders advocated different arrangements. The ideas, floated from time to time by various court advisors, ranged all over the spectrum and while the eventual solution, enacted in 1805, restored to the Church considerable powers of supervision and control, the debate in the 1770s unfolded from almost the exact opposite starting point. Formulated in 1771 in the wake of Maria Theresa's "politicum" declaration, the proposal of state councillor Count Pergen pushed the claims of the state even farther, assuming an almost complete elimination of the Catholic Church from education.[17] It was the first serious, comprehensive reform plan, considered by Maria Theresa. Pergen proposed to shut religious orders out of teaching positions entirely and allow parish clergy to teach only in cases of local shortage of secular teachers. He also entrusted supervision of content, teacher training and appointment exclusively to government bureaucracy. In terms of content, the school was to be strictly based on social class – *standesmässig* in contemporary parlance – and thus geared towards preventing any unwarranted social mobility. The proposal garnered enough support at court to prompt Maria Theresa to invite Pergen to submit names for the five-member directory, the supreme supervisory organ under his plan.

The Pergen plan ultimately foundered on two counts. One was its stance against religious orders. In a situation where secular teachers were yet to be trained, throwing away, wholesale, all the experienced pedagogues in the ranks of the Jesuits and Piarists seemed like unaffordable waste, especially since one secular teacher was more than three times costlier to maintain than a priestly one.[18] For Piarists, commitment to education being part of their vows, such exclusion would be liquidational and therefore engender strong opposition from the Catholic hierarchy.[19] The second strike against the Pergen plan was the proposed directory: after several months' search, Pergen nominated Abbot Felbiger and four Protestants. Entrusting the school reform, set in motion by bishop Firmian's dire warnings about the spread of Protes-

---

[16] Helfert. *Die österreichische Volksschule. I. Band*, p. 117–118.

[17] Helfert. *Die österreichische Volksschule. I. Band*, p. 196–213.

[18] Helfert. *Die österreichische Volksschule. I. Band*, p. 210.

[19] Founded in 1617 in Spain, the Order of Pious Schools, or Piarists, were the oldest Catholic order devoted primarily to offering free education to the poor. If the Pergen plan had succeeded, they would have largely lost all *raison d'etre* in Austria. For the historical importance of Piarist schools in the Czech lands, see Šafránek. *Školy české. I. svazek*, p. 110–115; for their role in Austria, see Engelbrecht. *Geschichte des österreichischen Bildungswesen Vol. 3*, p. 25–27.

tantism, to a committee dominated by Protestants was a bridge too far for the empress and in January 1772 the Pergen plan was shelved.[20]

The reform effort stalled somewhat after the Pergen fiasco, not least because it highlighted, incidentally, what an enormous and costly undertaking the school reform was. The debate over religious orders also clarified that the new school system would have to rely on the human resources of the Church, if it were to have any chance of success. In terms of cost, various new sources were proposed to be tapped throughout 1772, but none were found to be satisfactory.

Then, in a surprise turn of events, the financial aspect of the reform moved significantly closer to a workable solution when a papal bull issued in July 1773 announced the dissolution of the Jesuit order. The Pope conveniently ceded control of former Jesuit property in Austria to the Crown.[21] This included numerous former Latin Jesuit schools, ready with experienced staff and physical infrastructure in place, which could now be turned into state schools in line with the ideas of the reformers.[22] Instead of using the Jesuit property to prop up the general budget, it was used as a seed of a permanent fund, *Studienfond*, earmarked to support the schools.[23]

With this unexpected windfall, the work on the school reform swung back into high gear. In January 1774, Maria Theresa granted Felbiger full control over its details and implementation. By this time, Felbiger enjoyed quite some renown as a successful reformer and he possessed what to the Austrians was an attractive combination of traits: he was a Catholic with the Protestants' educational knowhow. He arrived in Vienna in May and by July drafted the law that would become the *Allgemeine Schulordnung*. It was made public in December 1774 and entered into force the following January.[24]

The law was rather uneven in its attention to various important aspects of the new school system.[25] Instead of focusing on administration and financing, its stipulations were disproportionately directed towards matters of instruction. Regulation of teaching content, teaching methods, textbooks used and types of schools had outsized priority. Article 2 split schools into three types, which varied in terms of location and curriculum. At the highest level, each province was to operate at least one *Normalschule*, modelled on the Viennese

---

[20] Melton. *Absolutism*, p. 207.

[21] Melton. *Absolutism*, p. 210.

[22] Helfert. *Die österreichische Volksschule. I. Band*, p. 296.

[23] Prausek, Vinzenz. *Die Verbesserung der Volksschule mit besonderer Rücksichtigung Österreichs*, p. 4.

[24] Melton. *Absolutism*, p. 212.

[25] The text of the laws discussed in this and other chapters comes from *ALEX: Historische Rechts- und Gesetzestexte Online* of the Österreichische Nationalbibliothek. See http:// http://alex.onb.ac.at.

one and located in each provincial capital, which would serve as the training grounds for new teachers. Next was the *Hauptschule*, or major school, which the law envisioned as operating in large cities or alongside monasteries that had the appropriate personnel to sustain the teaching of the content. Appendix B of the law specified that this type of school would have four grades. The lowest two grades were mostly focused on literacy-related subjects, with the first grade for the smallest children clearly serving as a most gradual introduction to education with a mere 14 hours of weekly instruction. In the third grade, pupils encountered arithmetic and religion, while in the fourth grade, other practical subjects such as geography and history were introduced. The *Hauptschule* was even supposed to be able to offer Latin as an elective in the fourth grade for those pupils who might be eligible for a further secondary education. The least sophisticated of the school types was the trivial school, *Trivialschule*, its name derived from the Latin expression for the three Rs, *trivium*. In specifying the content, the appendix made a distinction between urban and rural trivial schools, effectively creating a fourth type of school, with the urban trivial school offering a somewhat more extensive curriculum. It was designed to have only two grades and most of the time was to be spent acquiring literacy with religion and arithmetic coming second. Rural children were not getting any history or geography or Latin.

The stark difference between city and country in terms of content was a feature that remained embedded in the Austrian schooling legislation until the 1869 school reform. The same approach had been adopted by the Prussians. In both countries, the underlying rationale rested on the notion of *Standesmässigkeit*, or appropriateness of education to one's social station.[26] Country schools were not only offering fewer subjects than city schools but even in those subjects that they did offer, they were constrained to a lower standard of teaching relative to the city. The town schools taught the art of official correspondence; the zenith of country school literacy was correct grammar when writing to dictation. For reading, two separate reading books were published with somewhat different contents, one for country and one for city. In terms of numeracy, the major school curriculum progressed from simple arithmetic in the third grade to six weekly hours of home economics in the summer semester of the fourth grade. In the rural trivial schools, the instruction in arithmetic was not expected to move beyond the four elementary operations and basic *Regeldetri* (rule-of-three) and while some introduction to husbandry was mentioned in Article 5 as desirable, no explicit lesson time was allocated to it.

The country school timetable assumed that only one teacher would be available, imposing further limitations upon the teaching content even in subjects that were nominally identical across all types of schools: thus, both

[26] Melton. *Absolutism*, p. 187.

younger and older pupils would be taught in the same classroom at the same time, learning the same content. The timetable for the major school and even for a city-based trivial school, however, envisioned separate grades in separate classrooms, allowing for subjects such as arithmetic to be graduated in terms of difficulty across grades. Alternatively, the law allowed country schools to teach different age groups in different semesters: by Article 10, the older pupils, aged 9–13, were to attend primarily during the winter semester (from 1st December till the end of March), while the younger cohort, aged 6–8, would attend during the Spring semester (from Easter to end of September, with a three-week break during harvest time), when the older children were working in the fields.[27] In contrast to this, city pupils were all expected to come to school throughout the school year, which was set to start on 3rd November and end on 29th September, with a one-week break between semesters during Easter.

The law elaborated at length on the instruction of religion, its form and role spelled out in four separate paragraphs. The stress was on inculcation of morality and on behaviour that was proper to one's station. Instruction in religion was entrusted exclusively to priests but teachers were expected to sit in so that they could later review the content with the pupils (Art. 6). In contrast to the attention lavished on religion, the law listed writing, reading and arithmetic in one line, almost in passing. It is worth noting that even these subjects were to be infused with religion, particularly in the countryside. The law's four appendices contained detailed timetables for various types of school (see also Chapter 6 and Table 6.1 for detail). In rural trivial schools, for example, Bible reading was allocated separate classroom time, set apart from catechism, and even in lessons reserved for general reading, the approved readers mostly contained moralistic stories with religious content.[28]

The law left the teachers no room for experimentation or creativity in their method of instruction. Felbiger had been specifically invited to Vienna to implement his pedagogical method, which naturally became the only one sanctioned by the law. The normal schools in provincial capitals were to serve as the binding specimens of this new pedagogical norm and the teacher training courses attached to them were to ensure that all certified teachers of the realm would be apprised of it. Felbiger's *Methodenbuch* was one of the eight books approved for use in the school (the others being an instruction for house tutors and six textbooks) and Article 7 insisted that the teachers follow it to the letter, so as to ensure uniformity of teaching across the empire.

[27] At the same time, the law allowed parents in the country to send their children to school during both semesters, regardless of age, although they would have to reckon with the fact that teachers would target their lessons to whichever age group was predominant in each semester.

[28] See *Allgemeine Schulordnung*, Anhang – Litt D.

("More capable teachers", the law added, were allowed to peruse other, unlisted manuals "of similar content" but only for their own edification.) This comprehensive 500-page manual introduced teachers to the main aspects of Felbiger's pedagogy, such as the proper way to organize the class for group learning and his vaunted tabulation method of memorization, while also providing detailed instruction for the teaching of each subject. Not surprisingly, the manual reflected the law's main emphasis: religious instruction was treated most extensively and most carefully, followed by spelling, writing and reading. Felbiger's curriculum paid much less attention to arithmetic. Rural schools in particular were to focus on teaching literacy and only then, once reading has been mastered by the pupils, to move on to basic operations and rudimentary rule-of-three.[29] The method had its critics, who most of all objected to its tendency to teach by rote memorization, and it apparently became obsolete rather quickly.[30] Its fundamental tenets nonetheless remained, more or less, the building blocks of Austrian elementary education until the reform of 1869.

Next to content, the *Allgemeine Schulordnung* devoted ample space to administration and oversight. At the top of the new educational hierarchy stood the Education Commission. Each province would have its own provincial education commission, one of whose members was the director of the *Normalschule* in the provincial capital (Art. 1). Existing schools were to be converted to the "prescribed teaching method" under the commission's supervision before any further expansion of the school network took place (Art. 3). Each school was to have a local supervisor: Article 17 suggested that in villages, feudal lords appoint the local priest to this job, while in cities with a major school, the supervisory role fell first and foremost to the school director. Alternatively, the magistrate could appoint an active citizen with interest in school-related matters. Teachers were expected to fill out several forms every year, supplying the provincial education commissions with necessary data on the number of school-age children and on their enrolment and examination results (Art. 16). The exams were to be conducted twice yearly in the presence of the local priest, a magistrate and a representative of the feudal lord.

In contrast to the burdens laid on teachers and school administrators, the duties of other stakeholders received relatively brief mention in the law. The most important among them was the duty of parents and guardians to have their children, boys and girls, formally educated. For the vast majority, who

[29] Pacher, Lieselotte Maria. "Der elementare Rechenunterricht in deutschsprachigen Lehrbüchern Österreichs von Marie Theresia bis zum Ende der Monarchie", p. 63.

[30] Ficker. *Bericht über österreichisches Unterrichtswesen*, p. 25; Weiss, Anton. *Geschichte der österreichischen Volksschule 1792–1848. II. Band. Geschichte der österreichischen Volksschule unter Franz I. und Ferdinand I. 1792–1848*, 1904, p. 769–774; Pacher. "Der elementare Rechenunterricht", p. 67–71.

could not afford a private tutor, this meant sending children to school. Thus, "compulsory school attendance" is not the correct term for what the law instituted, technically speaking, but in practical terms that was exactly what it implied for the bottom 99% of the population. As with many other things, here, too, Austria was adopting the Prussian practice. It is worth noting that, outside the German-speaking world, making primary schooling compulsory did not catch on until the 19th century.[31] The first non-German state to adopt a policy of nationwide compulsory schooling was Denmark in 1814, followed by Greece in 1834.[32] In France, for example, compulsion was applied to children working in factories from 1841 onwards but a universally applicable legislation was not enacted until 1882. In England, primary school attendance became mandatory only in the 1880s. In the US, Massachusetts was the first state to legislate compulsory attendance in 1852 and it was not until the 1920s that all states had such a law.[33] In most of these instances, compulsion was introduced into school systems that had already been operating for decades, with varying but often quite high levels of voluntary enrolment. Prussia and Austria, on the other hand, chose to institute compulsion already at the inception of their reforms, undoubtedly hoping that this would boost the reach and use of the schools. The Austrian law, in fact, admitted to this motivation explicitly (Art. 13). Clearly, for all the lofty words in the law's preamble about the benefits of schooling for the edification of one's spirit, the empress did not trust her subjects to send their children to school of their own accord and instead relied on the force of the law. Magistrates in the cities and feudal authorities in the countryside were appointed to enforce the attendance mandate. Yet, it remained largely toothless, since no penalties or manner of enforcement were specified.[34] Moreover, the age range and duration of

[31] In Germany, in contrast, *Schulpflicht* was a standard feature of the general schooling law. Pfalz-Zweibrücken had such law already in 1592. Before long, almost all Protestant states introduced it. Bavaria instituted it first unsuccessfully in 1771, then again with greater effect in 1802. See also Kuzmin. *Vývoj školství a vzdělání v Československu*, p. 36.

[32] Soysal, Yasemin N. and David Strang. "Construction of the First Mass Education Systems in Nineteenth-Century Europe", p. 277–288.

[33] Maynes, Mary Jo. *Schooling for the people: comparative local studies of schooling history in France and Germany, 1750–1850,* p. 146; Mitch, David. *The Rise of Popular Literacy in Victorian England – The Influence of Private Choice and Public Policy.* p. 1–2; Clay, Karen; Lingwall, Jeff and Melvin Stephens Jr. "Do schooling laws matter? Evidence from the introduction of compulsory attendance laws in the United States"; Landes, William M. and Lewis C. Solmon "Compulsory Schooling Legislation: An Economic Analysis of Law and Social Change in the Nineteenth Century".

[34] Scheipl and Seel even go so far as to argue that the all the enrolment and attendance-related regulations were formulated "as a wish", as a mere desideratum, informed by the state's awareness of its limited means to effect a successful enforcement. Their implication is that the omission of any specific enforcement incentives was deliberate. This interpretation, however, clashes with numerous instances of strong (if ultimately ineffective) legal language

schooling were somewhat ambiguous: within one paragraph, the law demanded that children start school "without exception as soon as they commence their 6th year of life" (i.e. at age 5) only to concede, four lines below, that children may wait with school enrolment till age 6. Next, arguing that pupils will scarcely master the requisite content before age 12, the law demanded "at least 6 or 7 years" of attendance – but at the same time invited pupils to stay on beyond age 12 on a voluntary basis or to exit early from the school on condition that they pass all the necessary exams.[35] Parents could also withdraw their children from the public school altogether, as long as they hired a properly certified house tutor and the child sat the annual exams, just like the school-attending children.

The law was similarly vague on the duties of villages and towns to establish new schools. Article 3 mentioned the need to open new schools in places where the youth were too numerous to attend existing schools or where no school existed at all, but provided no further details. What is particularly astonishing, the law had practically nothing to say about financing. Indeed, this ambitious plan to bring new and improved schooling to the last village of the empire devoted none of its stipulations to funding matters: it contained no discussion of teacher salaries or their sources, it earmarked no particular tax revenue for the schools or specified any tuition fees. Article 3 merely noted that when new schools were being established, the villages and towns, who "draw immediate benefit" from them, were to bear the bulk of the cost, with some aid to be granted by feudal authorities, who stood to gain "well-behaved and useful serfs."

Several considerations informed this evasive approach. One was the aforementioned financial windfall from the abolition of the Jesuit order, which allowed the reformers to sidestep the issue of long-term financial footing of the schooling system for the moment. Another was the fact that the first wave of implementation of the law involved converting already existing schools to the new teaching method, whose income sources could be grandfathered into the new system. Yet another consideration was that introducing new taxes might make the school reform unpopular. At one point during the drafting of the law, a proposal was floated that feudal lords be forced to contribute construction materials and the serfs the labour to the establishment of a new school but Felbiger himself rejected it on the grounds that it would

in the pertinent articles, as well as in the law's demand to involve the magistracy and feudal administration in the matter. See Scheipl and Seel. *Die Entwicklung des österreichischen Schulwesens von 1750–1938*, p. 16.

[35] These ambiguities have led to some confusion among authors, some of whom argue that the school enrolment started at 5, others at 6. See Heiler and Lebmann. "Die Entwicklung der allgemeinbildenden Pflichtschulen in Österreich" for the latter and Ficker. *Bericht über österreichisches Unterrichtswesen* for the former.

burden the feudal lords too much.[36] As a result, the law, demanding the creation of a vast school network with thousands of new teaching staff to serve hundreds of thousands of pupils, offered no specific instruction on where the resources for the whole scheme were to come from.

After the *Allgemeine Schulordnung* entered into force in 1775, it became clear before long that its emphases and omissions – a reflection of the preferences of its main "sponsor", the Crown – would require a correction in the face of the realities "on the ground". These corrections pertained primarily to issues of financing and enforcement of attendance. Felbiger's comprehensive report from September 1780 claimed that less than a third of school age children were actually in schools. One immediately obvious way to address the problem was to empower the authorities to compel attendance through specific means that the original law lacked. A decree in October 1781 introduced fines and compulsory community service as punishments for parents of truant children. Poorer parents were also to be denied access to poor aid.[37] Joseph II, however, believed that parents kept their children away from schools also because of the tuition fee. He instructed the Education Commission to find ways to make schools free of charge.

Here, the issue of enrolment and attendance spilled directly into the issue of financing, for such a step would eliminate an important source of revenue right at the time when the Commission was also seeking ways to expand it. Apart from truancy, the second, more important reason for the low overall attendance rate was that the existing school network was insufficient to cover the whole population. Initial efforts to implement the reform focused on converting existing schools to the new form. By 1781, Joseph II was ready to progress towards the more daunting goal of making schooling truly universal.[38] This required setting down a sufficiently workable blueprint for how new schools would be established and then supported. Given the *Schulordnung*'s vagueness on this point, the authorities resorted to various methods to obtain funds – some standard, such as sale of the newly approved textbooks, some quite colourful, such as levies on theatre plays and masquerade balls.[39] By the early 1780s, the financial windfall from the Jesuit property was supplemented by assets seized by further closures of monasteries forced by Joseph II. The newly appointed head of the Education Commission, Gottfried van Swieten, even argued in favour of appropriating all of the monastic in-

---

[36] Ficker. *Bericht über österreichisches Unterrichtswesen*, p. 22; Helfert. *Die österreichische Volksschule. I. Band*, p. 328.

[37] K.k. Verordnung 135/1781, dated 20th October 1781; Ficker. *Bericht über österreichisches Unterrichtswesen*, p. 23.

[38] Wangermann, Ernst. *Aufklärung und staatsbürgerliche Erziehung: Gottfried van Swieten als Reformator des österreichischen Unterrichtswesens 1781–1791*, p. 42.

[39] Riegger, Joseph Anton von. *Materialien zur alten und neuen Statistik von Böhmen. X. Heft*, p. 234–235; Helfert. *Die österreichische Volksschule. I. Band*, p. 393–401.

come for schooling purposes.[40] These confiscations, while certainly helpful at their time, were nonetheless one-time gains and therefore scarcely a sustainable basis for an on-going, potentially decades-long task of building up the school network.

Under the arrangements that gradually took shape between August 1783 and October 1787, tuition fees remained in place as a source of teacher salary. This was to be further supplemented by income from the teacher's church duties.[41] The parish would supply the teacher's living quarters free of charge, which were to be separate from the classroom. New provisions also specified how dense the school network should be in the countryside: wherever 90–100 school-age children lived within half-hour of walking distance, a school was to be built with a teacher for every 100 pupils and a teaching assistant for any additional 50 pupils above that. The building costs as well as the operational costs of the school were to be shared between the village or parish, the feudal landlord and the local church patron, i.e. the party responsible for maintaining the church and entitled to appoint the priest.[42] This three-way cooperation, which came to be known as *Schulpatronat*, was adopted for lack of a better solution after much back and forth between the various government bureaus.[43] But once it was put in place, it became one of the most durable fixtures of the system. Despite much general dissatisfaction, it survived until the early 1860s. Incidentally, it was also quite similar to the arrangement that had been rejected by Felbiger back in 1775 when he was drafting the *Schulordnung*.

While the weak spots and loopholes of the original legislation were patched in the course of the 1780s, the law's main preoccupation with content, control and teaching method survived most challenges. The reasons why Felbiger's pedagogy, now enshrined in law, proved so impervious to change reveal for whose convenience and benefit the new schooling system worked. When Felbiger's successor but one, Joseph Anton Gall, proposed in 1786 to replace the tabulation method, which could degenerate into mechanistic memorization, with a "socratic" method that appealed to student's under-

[40] Wangermann. *Aufklärung und staatsbürgerliche Erziehung*, p. 51.

[41] One exception was the province of Tyrol, which requested an abolition of tuition fee for its pupils. This request was granted in 1788. See Wangermann. *Aufklärung und staatsbürgerliche Erziehung.* p. 53–54.

[42] Often, the church patron happened to be the local feudal lord, which somewhat simplified the negotiations usually accompanying the construction of a new school. Weiss. *Geschichte der österreichischen Volksschule 1792–1848. II. Band.* p. 764–768; Ficker. *Bericht über österreichisches Unterrichtswesen*, p. 23–24; Wangermann. *Aufklärung und staatsbürgerliche Erziehung.* p. 55.

[43] Numerous wildly divergent schemes were proposed and then rejected for their unfeasibility. See Wangermann. *Aufklärung und staatsbürgerliche Erziehung*, p. 42–50 for a more detailed discussion.

standing, his superiors in the Education Commission objected on three grounds.[44] The first was that teachers mostly lacked the skill and competence to let go of the fixed structure of Felbigerian lesson plans. Secondly, such liberalization of method would threaten the uniformity of curriculum across the empire, which would make the system difficult to administer. Moreover – the third reason – the reigning priority of the day was extending the school network, i.e. to focus on quantity, not quality.[45] The convenience of the administrators took precedence over the effectiveness of instruction. Gall was eventually able to push through a few changes, such as the elimination of group reading and the introduction of mental calculation in arithmetic.[46] For a brief period, Gall's socratic method was even introduced into the teaching of religion. But before long, the tide turned and the powers that be concluded that any interactive, question-and-answer format in religious instruction was outright destructive.[47] The forces of inertia were already at work a mere decade after the reform's start.

After the change on the throne in 1790, however, the challenge to the rigid, centralized, top-down structure came from the new emperor himself. Leopold II dissolved the Education Commission and instead appointed one of the leading lights of the Austrian Enlightenment, the legal scholar Karl Anton von Martini, to propose changes to modernize the school system. Among the new ideas was a measure of self-regulation by teachers as a professional body, which would have allowed for new impulses and initiative from below.[48] Yet, before any of these plans could come to pass, Leopold died and Austria became involved in a protracted war with France.

The idea of updating the school system did not die with Leopold but was diverted by emperor Francis in the opposite direction. All notions of self-regulation were abandoned; instead, Francis called for proper "school policing", a jarring term that conveys the extent and intensity of ideological control that he wished to see applied to pupils and teachers alike.[49] A revision commission, formed in 1795 under the leadership of conservative count Rottenhan, prepared a report specifying appropriate changes to the existing sys-

[44] For an example of the socratic method, see Seebauer, Renate. *Lehrerbildung in Porträts: von der Normalschule bis zur Gegenwart. Band 2. Schul- und Hochschulgeschichte*, p. 39–40.

[45] Weiss. *Geschichte der österreichischen Volksschule 1792–1848. II. Band.* p. 775–776.

[46] Ficker. *Bericht über österreichisches Unterrichtswesen*, p. 25.

[47] Engelbrecht Helmut. *Geschichte des österreichischen Bildungswesens: Erziehung und Unterricht auf dem Boden Österreichs, Vol. 3. Von der frühen Aufklärung bis zum Vormärz,* p. 223; Weiss, Anton. *Geschichte der österreichischen Volksschule 1792–1848. I. Band. Die Entstehungsgeschichte des Volksschul-Planes von 1804*, 1904. p. 3.

[48] Ficker. *Bericht über österreichisches Unterrichtswesen*, p. 5–6.

[49] Heiler and Lebmann. "Die Entwicklung der allgemeinbildenden Pflichtschulen in Österreich" p. 519.

tem: a stronger role for the Church in teacher supervision, a limitation of rural schools' curriculum to religion plus *trivium*, a renewed stress on *Standesmässigkeit* to counter the subversive influence of French ideas and a shift of financial responsibility for schools solely on the shoulders of local communities.[50] None of these ideas was a radical departure: at best, they represented a shift in emphasis within the existing parameters. The only conceptual innovation that the Rottenhan commission introduced was the *Realschule*, or technical school. As an owner of a north-Bohemian estate with some nascent manufacturing activity, Rottenhan was interested in nurturing a social stratum of technically skilled professionals through this new type of selective urban school for ambitious middle-class sons.[51] To that end, the commission proposed to redirect the income from assets of dissolved monasteries, which had hitherto been spent on salary subsidies for teachers, to pay for these *Realchulen*, of which there would be seventeen.[52] With this, Rottenhan's revision commission submitted its proposal and disbanded in 1799.

Since some of the suggested changes – not least the financial ones – encountered opposition at Court, the Rottenhan proposal went through one more round of review and rewriting in 1802–1804, during which the emperor readily embraced the reactionary aspects of the proposal, such as extensive supervision by the Church, while scaling back its progressive ideas, such as the *Realschule*. The resulting plan became the basis for a new comprehensive legislation, *Politische Verfassung der deutschen Schulen*, or Political Constitution of German Schools, which was approved in 1805.

This new law, which replaced the *Schulordnung* of 1774, was a veritable "school codex" of all-encompassing, exhaustive regulations of primary school matters down to the last detail.[53] In 478 pedantic articles, it specified matters as diverse and as incidental as the size of school desks (Article 356), pupils' attire on examination day (Art. 91), the maximum cost of classroom cleaning (Art. 170), and that children must not hide their hands in class (Art. 230). It was split into 23 sections, each dealing with a particular aspect of the system, starting with a new and expanded structure of oversight in Section 1. Here, in the "most fundamental" section of the whole law, the emperor made good on his "school policing" plans.[54] In line with the Rottenhan proposal, the law recruited the Church for this supervisory role to be performed at three separate levels. The parish priest was the most immediate overseer of the

---

[50] Engelbrecht Helmut. *Geschichte des österreichischen Bildungswesens: Erziehung und Unterricht auf dem Boden Österreichs, Vol. 3.* p. 223–224.

[51] Bidermann, Hermann Ignaz. *Die technische Bildung im Kaiserthume Oesterreich. Ein Betrag zur Geschichte der Industrie und des Handels*. Vienna: Carl Gerold und Sohn, 1854. p. 66.

[52] Weiss. *Geschichte der österreichischen Volksschule 1792–1848. I. Band.* p. 142.

[53] All the following citations from the law come from its ninth edition, published in 1847.

[54] Weiss. *Geschichte der österreichischen Volksschule 1792–1848. II. Band.* p. 8.

local school – intimately acquainted with its operation, not least because he was also obligated to serve as instructor of catechism. The parish clergy reported to the district overseer, appointed at the level of vicariate, whose duties involved an annual inspection visit at each school and compiling a report for the diocesan consistory, the third and highest level of church oversight.

Given the prodigious importance assigned to religious instruction, the law relied on the bishops to enforce Catholic orthodoxy and so the consistories were not only overseeing the parish clergy in their role as religious teachers but were also in charge of the teacher training courses and, by extension, of certification of teachers. Proper teacher training received extensive attention in the law. Compared to a single paragraph in the *Allgemeine Schulordnung*, the *Politische Verfassung* devoted the whole of Section 8 to mandate a three-month teaching course to all rural school teachers and 6-month course for all major school teachers. All clergy were also to be instructed in the approved teaching method as a pre-condition of their admission to the priesthood. With all the reporting, visitations, teacher training, certification and active participation in religious instruction, the Catholic Church's supervisory responsibilities were extensive.

Beyond the third and highest level, the oversight passed into the hands of provincial education commissions in each crown land and beyond that, of course, to a re-established Education Commission (*Studienhofkommission*) in Vienna. Thus, while the daunting day-to-day work was assigned to the Church, the final word in all matters rested with the state. On a local level, secular oversight was restricted to matters of physical infrastructure, i.e. to making sure that school buildings were up to code, contained in Section 19 of the law, and that local stakeholders were attending to necessary repairs.

The autonomy of teachers was constrained in numerous ways. Many of the earlier stipulations were carried over, such as the priority of memorization in teaching and learning, the ban on all unapproved textbooks (now supplemented by a procedure to report and deal with illicit books, should they appear among pupils) or the compulsory adherence to pre-approved lesson plans and teaching methods. But the new law went farther. A whole Section 11 was dedicated to specifying the duties and regulations pertaining to the teacher's job and personal conduct in 56 exacting paragraphs. These involved a requirement to monitor pupils' personal hygiene, regulation of permissible forms of physical punishment, rules for dealing with parents, prohibition against having a trade on the side and general exhortations to lead an unblemished, God-fearing life of sobriety and moderation. Numerous provisions were legislating the obvious: that teachers should know the subjects they were teaching, understand the textbooks they were using, keep abreast of regulation updates, keep the classroom appropriately heated and ventilated, teach during specified hours and not cut classes short and so forth. Between the minute instructions and the relentless supervision, the message was that teachers could not quite be trusted.[55] Even conducting the year-end exam was entrusted to the priest, who alone decided who passed and who failed.

A new addition to the law was the section on teacher qualifications incorporating a 1792 ordinance against illicit teachers. These *Winkellehrer*, perhaps best translated as teachers "on the sly", had a long history in the German-speaking world.[56] They did not have official permission or certification to teach and simply offered their services on the grounds that they could impart a particular skill or knowledge, such as literacy, at a better value-for-money and at the customer's convenience. They were the "black market" in education and, in fact, one of the motivations behind the school reform, going back to Maria Theresa, was to crowd these unsupervised peddlers of learning out of the market with the government's own, properly regulated alternative.[57] The *Allgemeine Schulordnung* had vaguely threatened a punishment against such teachers but the fact that the prohibition had to be reinforced in the 1790s and then further reiterated in the *Politische Verfassung* of 1805, suggests that the weeding out of these teachers had not been entirely successful. The penalties now grew markedly more specific and stiffer, including arrest. Any pupils of such *Winkellehrer* were also barred from applying for scholarships and would not be admitted to the *Gymnasium*, a secondary school.

In terms of curriculum, the law represented a step back from what had already been a rather narrow knowledge base, especially in the countryside. Article 28 declared it "a major error in public schooling" to introduce pupils to learning inappropriate to their station and since rural populations earned their livelihood through physical labour, country school curriculum did not need to extend beyond religion and *trivium*. Mental arithmetic remained but rule-of-three was now reserved only for third grade and higher, and therefore out of the sphere of rural two-grade schools. Pupils could expect to learn to write to dictation but almost no instruction in composition was provided for. Other potentially useful skills, such as introduction to husbandry, included in the 1774 law, found no mention in the new law either. The only subject that gained in emphasis was religion. It was deemed "the most important and most difficult subject of all" and mastering it was the sole precondition for progression to a higher grade (Art. 66). Echoing the cameralist ideas of the 18th century, its purpose in the curriculum was not to inspire faith or spiritual growth but to inculcate discipline and acquiescence to one's social status (Art. 41).

---

[55] Strakosch-Graßmann. *Geschichte des österreichischen Unterrichswesens*, p. 160.

[56] See Friedrichs, Christopher R. "Whose House of Learning? Some Thoughts on German Schools in Post-Reformation Germany."

[57] Melton. *Absolutism*, p. 12. Here, too, the motivation was partly religious as *Winkelschulen* were suspect, not without merit, of fostering underground Protestantism.

The curriculum in towns and cities, especially in major schools, was more extensive. The new law thus reconfirmed and even widened the gap between town and country schools. Subjects such as grammar, German composition and basic Latin (for those planning to progress on to a *Gymnasium*) were to be taught in the third grade, while drawing, geometry, geography, history, mechanics and biology would appear in the fourth grade.

New subjects also appeared in the newly introduced *Realschule*. Rottenhan had a curriculum proposal ready already in 1799, when he first floated the idea: it was put together by none other than Franz Josef Gerstner, one of the pre-eminent engineers of the monarchy and later the founding director of the Prague polytechnic. It envisioned the *Realschule* as a secondary school with a four-year course of study, comprising pure and applied mathematics, geometry, physics, mechanics, modern languages, introduction to business administration and even some commercial law. However, as the proposal made its way through the deliberation process at Court, it was gradually watered down and the *Realschule*, as eventually incorporated into the law, was a much-diluted derivative of the original idea.[58] The course of study was reduced to three years, with stress on accounting, husbandry, technical drawing and some natural sciences. Instead of the rigorous technical school Rottenhan desired, the law created a glorified major school, positioned at the apex of the existing primary school system.

The sections covering all these aspects – oversight, role of teachers and their training, reductions in the curriculum – were the main areas where the *Politische Verfassung* broke new ground, although in many ways it just formalized and intensified earlier trends in control and administration. In all other areas, the law was not much more than a compilation and reconfirmation of various ordinances and decrees that had accumulated since the promulgation of the *Allgemeine Schulordnung* in 1774 and that had therefore been in force for quite some time.[59] A good example is the system of financing. Despite the revision commission's lengthy discussion on the topic of teacher remuneration, Rottenhan was unable to push through his proposal to shift the financial responsibility for teacher salary solely onto local communities. In the absence of any other broadly acceptable solution, Section 10 of the law defaulted to endorsing the Josephinian arrangements, whereby teachers drew their support from tuition fees, from church duties (e.g. playing the organ and conducting the choir) and from various in-kind contributions paid either by pupils' parents or by feudal lords (firewood). Even the nominal values of minimum salaries – 130 fl. for a teacher and 70 fl. for a teaching assistant annually – were lifted straight from the pertinent 1785 decree. Teachers were now required to draw up itemized lists of all their income sources every year

[58] Ficker. *Bericht über österreichisches Unterrichtswesen*, p. 179–181.

[59] Weiss. *Geschichte der österreichischen Volksschule 1792–1848. II. Band.* p. 7–17.

and these would serve as the basis for levying requisite sums and contributions from liable parties.

Similarly, in matters of new school construction, the *Schulpatronat* established by Joseph II remained intact. Section 19 specified that feudal authorities were to supply the construction materials, school patrons would pay for all skilled labour, such as bricklayers and carpenters, while villages and towns provided the unskilled labour. The same division applied to repairs. In terms of the desired density of the school network, the law also let stand Joseph II's earlier decree requiring a new school for every 90–100 school-age children within half-hour of walking distance.

A few minor changes appeared in the organization of the school year, mainly in fixing free days and religious holidays. For the most part, however, earlier arrangements again were carried over into the new law: town schools started on 1st November while rural schools could vary their start date and end date as agricultural needs dictated. They could allocate vacations throughout the year for harvest, vintage and haymaking, as long as the combined vacation time did not exceed five weeks. Rural schools could even adjust the beginning of the school day to accommodate the rhythm of the agricultural workday. The law's uncharacteristic flexibility in scheduling was motivated by the desire to maximize enrolment and attendance in the countryside (Art. 82). All-day instruction, expected of town schools and desired in rural schools, involved four hours per day, five days per week. In major schools, this increased to 5 hours per day in 3rd grade and 6 hours in 4th grade. But rural schools, especially when overcrowded, could split the day into a two-hour session for the smaller children and a three-hour one for older children. Such half-day instruction subsequently proved to be a frequently used method to increase enrolment in the countryside, where teachers were scarce. Consequently, while Article 345 demanded that there be ideally no more than 80 pupils per teacher and per classroom and Article 346 mandated a construction of a new classroom and a hiring of an extra assistant whenever the number of school-age children crossed 100 per either, Article 350 specifically allowed that under half-day instruction all the prescribed pupil-teacher and pupil-classroom ratios count as double. These parameters had all been in force, in a slightly different formulation, since 1784.[60]

In numerous other organizational matters, the new legislation also brought no changes: the definition of the school age, treatment of tuition fees, the penalties for truancy, the reporting duties placed on teachers, the regulations pertaining to Jews and Protestants[61] – these had all been put in place at some point over the preceding three decades.

---

[60] See Wangermann. *Aufklärung und staatsbürgerliche Erziehung*, p. 48.

[61] Given the confessional nature of the Austrian school, these regulations were mainly concerned with specifying the rights of these non-Catholic religious communities to establish

The *Politische Verfassung* of 1805 was the first and last comprehensive reconsideration and revision of the whole school-related legislative framework until the liberal reform of 1869. It was an opportunity to plug the most conspicuous gaps in the original Theresian *Schulordnung* and to replace some of the subsequent ad-hoc fixes with more robust and durable solutions. On this score, however, the whole effort must be judged an almost perfect miss. Instead of complementing each other, the two laws shared the same obsessions and the same blind spots. Both laid great stress on control, on supervision, on fixing the right method of instruction and on specifying the content. Both also betrayed certain indifference to matters of financing and of further expansion of the school network. In the *Schulordnung*, this showed as the complete absence of any specifics, in the *Verfassung*, as a wholesale embrace of earlier decrees. Almost ten years of deliberations generated no new solutions on this score. In fact, far from searching for new ways to broaden the financial base of the whole schooling system, the Rottenhan commission's main preoccupation was to show that their proposed changes could be implemented at almost no extra cost.[62]

After the emperor approved the law in August 1805, the implementation stalled at first as Austria went through the most wrenching decade of the Napoleonic Wars. The defeat at Austerlitz (1805), the humiliating peace of Schönbrunn (1809), the state bankruptcy (1811) all relegated educational matters to an issue of second-order importance. The Congress of Vienna brought Austria not only peace but also the recovery of considerable territory that she had earlier lost to Napoleon, as well as a few new provinces in northern Italy. The re-acquired crown lands – Tyrol, Carniola, Dalmatia, Austrian Littoral, Salzburg, parts of Upper Austria and western half of Carinthia – were brought under the aegis of the school law gradually from 1816 onwards.[63] Carniola and Littoral started reporting to Vienna in 1817, Tyrol and Vorarlberg in 1818.[64] Lombardian and Venetian schooling operated under somewhat modified financial arrangements, which included neither *Schulpatronat* nor tuition fees, and instead relied on communal support. Dalmatia received its own regulation, modelled on the *Politische Verfsassung*, in 1822.[65]

Beyond these local adjustments, necessitated by the transitions in the newly acquired territories, the institutional framework of Austrian schooling remained substantially unchanged and unchallenged until 1848. New decrees by the Education Commission, when they appeared, served to clarify and

their own schools and the proper manner of their oversight.

[62] Weiss. *Geschichte der österreichischen Volksschule 1792–1848. I. Band.* p. 138–151.

[63] Engelbrecht. *Geschichte Des österreichischen Bildungswesens: Erziehung und Unterricht auf dem Boden Österreichs, Vol. 3.* p. 229.

[64] OeStA, Vienna: HHStA, Studienhofkomission fol. 1968/5–6.

[65] Ficker. *Bericht über österreichisches Unterrichtswesen*, p. 33.

strengthen existing regulations or to swat down unwelcome fads and novelties that could disturb the purity of mandated methods, content or lines of subordination. For example, in 1820, the Bell-Lancaster, or monitorial, system of teaching, then used with some success in Britain, was banned from the Austrian classroom.[66] The Education Commission also obstinately resisted calls to make teacher training more rigorous and longer, both because such "overeducation" was unnecessary, given the limited curriculum, and also because it could lead to demands for better pay.[67] Teacher periodicals and school libraries were non-existent.[68] Official policy relentlessly strove to solidify control e.g. by clamping down on the few extant private schools, by denying parents any say in school choice, by restricting literature permissible for school use, by banning foreigners from all teaching positions and by repeatedly re-emphasizing the importance of religion in the whole scheme of primary education. To that end, in 1816 a post-primary, follow-up instruction – a so-called *Wiederholungsschule*, or review school, which met every Sunday afternoon – was made compulsory for all youth under the age of 15.[69]

A new impulse for change only came with the upheavals of 1848. A modern Ministry of Education was established in March. Free choice of method of instruction was granted to teachers and instruction in one's mother tongue was guaranteed.[70] New textbooks appeared on the market. Teachers began to organize in professional associations while their training was extended at first to one year and, in 1849, to two years.[71] The demand for more extensive primary education in cities led to the creation of a new type of school, *Bürgerschule*, or civic school, out of the major school of the pre-1848 era.[72] Broader institutional changes of 1848 nevertheless brought new complications too, especially financial ones. The abolition of the patrimonial administration removed feudal obligations towards schools. The *Schulpatronat* itself was not expressly abolished but in the emerging new civil, bourgeois society, it looked ever more anachronistic. By 1849, many former feudal lords stopped supporting schools. Even collection of tuition fees, which the towns and villages were obliged to levy on behalf of the teacher, became

---

[66] *Politische Verfassung*, 1847, p. 24.

[67] Engelbrecht. *Geschichte Des österreichischen Bildungswesens: Erziehung und Unterricht auf dem Boden Österreichs, Vol. 3.* p. 232.

[68] Frank, Ferdinand. "Kurzer Überblick über die geschichtliche Entwicklung des österreichischen Volksschulwesens in den letzten fünfzig Jahren", p.65.

[69] Ficker. *Bericht über österreichisches Unterrichtswesen*, p. 31–33.

[70] M. Erlass 2. September 1848, RGB 110/1848.

[71] Engelbrecht, Helmut. *Geschichte Des österreichischen Bildungswesens: Erziehung und Unterricht auf dem Boden Österreichs, Vol. 4. Von 1848 Bis Zum Ende der Monarchie*, p. 108.

[72] Frank. *Die Österreichische Volksschule von 1848–1898*. p. 18–19.

patchy. Primary schooling was in need of a firmer financial footing, with clear new rules and earmarked sources.

However, given the defeat of the revolution in 1849, a wholesale educational reform did not come to pass. The neo-absolutist regime, ushered in with the accession of Francis Joseph I, acknowledged such changes as could not be reversed but did not intend to pursue the liberal agenda of 1848 further. For the next decade, progress in schooling matters took the form of gradual, modest alterations, one decree at a time. Consequently, the *Bürgerschule* stayed and its curriculum received an official sanction in 1851; the *Schulpatronat* was reduced in 1849 to an obligation to support a school's operational costs but not construction or extension costs; the professional teacher organizations continued but in 1853 their sphere of activity was constrained.[73] By 1855, the government tried to turn the clock back at least in matters of oversight and granted the control over teaching, content and even teacher appointments to the Catholic Church through a Concordat with the Holy See. This did not prove to have lasting impact, however, because the cultural hegemony of the Church had been irrevocably undermined by the events of 1848 and because the political constellation, underpinning the Concordat on the Austrian side, crumbled with yet another sudden political change, the abrupt arrival of the constitutional era in 1860.

The new political realities, embodied in the February Constitution of 1861, meant that the urban, bourgeois element gained greater say in all matters of policy, including schooling, through the newly formed and elected provincial assemblies. Within their first electoral term, these assemblies definitively abolished the *Schulpatronat*.[74] The financial responsibility for schools was unambiguously shifting towards municipalities and villages. Aided by the new law on municipal self-government of 1861, many cities, particularly large ones, seized the opportunity to exert greater control over their schools.[75] The rapid expansion of urban education strengthened calls for a fundamental modernization of existing legislation in the more liberal spirit of the times, as it had long been apparent that the *Politische Verfassung* was obsolete. Such reform indeed came in two parts in 1868–1869. The first part was a law on the secularization of Austrian schools. The influence of the Church shrank to the provision of religious instruction, which now became just one among several subjects. Teacher training, appointment and oversight from now on took place within the sphere of civil administration. The second part, called *Lex Hasner* after the education minister, newly defined the rights and respon-

---

[73] Frank. *Die Österreichische Volksschule von 1848–1898*. p. 12, 18, 22.

[74] Appropriate laws were passed in Istria and Silesia in 1863, in Bohemia, Gorica and Gradisca, Carinthia, Moravia, Lower and Upper Austria, Salzburg, Styria in 1864 and by Galicia in 1866.

[75] Frank, Ferdinand. "Kurzer Überblick über die geschichtliche Entwicklung des österreichischen Volksschulwesens", p. 15.

sibilities of teachers, reformed the curriculum and somewhat decentralized the administration of the whole system.[76]

This institutional overhaul of 1868–69 thus marked a definitive break with the way Austrian public schooling had been organized for a century. What came afterwards was an entirely new system, which retrospectively made the old one look like an abandoned, not altogether successful first try. If one should adopt a bird's eye view of that period, bracketed at one end by bishop Firmian's letter in 1769 and by Hasner's liberal reform of 1869 at the other, what, if any, were the enduring underlying principles or forces guiding education policy? It is tempting to view it, given its origin during the Enlightenment, through the prism of social reform, informed by Enlightenment ideals. But is there any evidence of such ideals in the policy itself? Even more provocatively, can the Austrian government – across the seven monarchs who reigned through public schooling's first century – be judged to have been *in favour* of education, given the shape and form of schooling they were promoting?

By the yardstick of the Kantian Enlightenment motto, *sapere aude* – "dare to know" – the answer is no. The authors of the education policy definitely did not want the masses to dare to know and sought to ensure that the thousands of village teachers, staffing the schools, would not dare to teach them too much. Count Rottenhan wrote as much in the policy statement he composed upon being appointed to lead the revision commission in 1795.[77] Much of this restrictive sentiment resurfaced in the *Politische Verfassung* in the anxious injunctions against unapproved additions to the curriculum, in the insistence on *Standesmässigkeit* or in the dire warnings against "undigested overlearning".[78] The outlook extended to matters of instruction method also, which is why Austria missed out on all the developments taking place in European pedagogy at the time. The Austrian school had no time for Pestalozzi or Herbart or Bell and Lancaster. Basedowian pedagogy, with its stress on open, less structured interaction between teacher and pupil and on pictorial, illustrative learning, made some inroads thanks to the efforts of Gall and his successor Spendou but the emphasis on memorization remained.[79]

---

[76] See Chapter 7 for a detailed analysis of the political economy of this reform.

[77] "It is therefore evident that the lower classes can only be schooled in such concepts, as do not interfere with their work and make them dissatisfied with their condition; rather, their whole system of thought should be restricted to the fulfillment of their moral duties and the wise and diligent fulfillment of their domestic and community obligations." The policy statement was published by his colleague and sometimes opponent Christian von Eggers in 1808. See Rottenhan, Heinrich Franz von. "Gutachten über den Gesichtspunkt und den Wirkungs-kreis der Studien-Revisions-Commission", p. 34.

[78] Articles 70 and 28 respectively.

[79] In pedagogical matters, Rottenhan saw his own proposal as a workable compromise between Basedow and Felbiger but warned against the "skepticism of Voltaire, Hume and

It would be a mistake, however, to blame the restrictive policy on Rottenhan's revision commission, as if its workings were extinguishing the presumed Enlightenment spirit of the earlier legislation.[80] There was considerable continuity between the *Schulordnung* of 1774 and the *Politische Verfassung* of 1805. The latter law's most important emendation was to tighten the screws of supervision while in most other matters it only sought to consolidate existing regulation.[81] Nor should this be a surprise, given that many of the people involved in fashioning the new law had already been around to contribute to the original one. Franz Karl Hägelin, who served on the revision commission under Rottenhan, had been an active member of the Lower-Austrian education commission already in the 1770s.[82] Johann Melchior von Birkenstock, another member of the commission, sat on Maria Theresa's School and Censorship Commission since 1771 and was a close collaborator of Pergen.[83] Joseph von Sonnenfels, also a member, had been active in policy circles at least since the 1760s.

Moreover, these men were not just some ranking policy advisors; they were among the most important and prominent representatives of the Enlightenment at the Viennese court and the guiding principle of constraining the masses' access to learning by limiting the curriculum was very much their idea.[84] Many leading figures of the Enlightenment throughout Europe shared this view and it was not limited to elementary schooling.[85] In 1771, for example, Sonnenfels himself argued against the proliferation of universities, echoing a sentiment that was widespread among leading policy thinkers of his time.[86] He got his wish, too: early in his reign, Joseph II abolished several

---

Helvetius etc." See Rottenhan. "Gutachten" p. 37, 48.

[80] Hölzl. "Studien zum Pflichtschulwesen in Tirol 1774–1806." p. 92 argues, for example, that Austrian schooling underwent a reactionary turn in the 1790s in response to the French Revolution. See also Engelbrecht. *Geschichte Des österreichischen Bildungswesens Vol. 3*, p. 228, Kuzmin. *Vývoj školství*, p. 67 and Scheipl and Seel. *Die Entwicklung des österreichischen Schulwesens*, 1750–1938, p. 24.

[81] Strakosch-Graßmann. *Geschichte des österreichischen Unterrichswesens.* p. 132.

[82] Helfert. *Die österreichische Volksschule. I. Band*, p. 141. Back in 1772, Hägelin was the author of the three-way split of elementary schools into normal schools, major schools and trivial schools. Engelbrecht. *Geschichte des österreichischen Bildungswesens.* Vol. 3, p. 103.

[83] Benedikt, Heinrich. "Birckenstock, Johann Melchior Edler von." Page 254 In: *Neue Deutsche Biographie. Band 2*; Helfert. *Die österreichische Volksschule. I. Band*, p. 247.

[84] Both Birkenstock and Sonnenfels were reputable scholars and connoisseurs. Sonnenfels, for example, taught cameralism at the University of Vienna since 1763 and contributed to the abolition of torture in Austria. Kann. *A Study in Austrian Intellectual History:* p. 181–189.

[85] Klingenstein, Grete. "Akademikerüberschuss als soziales Problem im Aufegklärten Absolutismus", p. 166.

[86] Sonnenfels, Joseph von. *Gesammelte Schriften: Reden. Achter Band.* Vienna: mit von Baumeisterischen Schriften. 1786. "Ueber den Nachtheil der vermehrten Universitäten."

institutions of higher learning on the grounds that they were superfluous.[87] A reform of secondary schooling of Austria, adopted in 1776, explicitly introduced a double standard for admission to a *Gymnasium*: aristocratic children were practically guaranteed a place whereas plebeian applicants needed to show knowledge of basic Latin.[88] Numerous secondary schools were closed down either upon the dissolution of the Jesuit order, which had run them, or during the Josephine era, when *Gymnasium* enrolment dropped by 25%.[89] The emperor even at one point planned to finance elementary school expansion by savings in secondary and tertiary education. When his Education Commission chairman, Gottfried van Swieten, disabused him of this plan, pointing out that even outright abolition of all post-elementary schooling would be no more than a drop in the bucket, tuition fees were introduced at both *Gymnasia* and universities.[90] This restrictive impulse did not disappear with Joseph II but continued well after the Napoleonic Wars with further constraints imposed on secondary and tertiary education in 1819–1824 leading to another decrease in student numbers.[91]

The two-pronged policy of concurrent expansion of elementary schooling and reduction of all other levels of education may, indeed, seem as "a central paradox of absolutist school reform"[92] – but only as long as one presumes that the ultimate aim of the reform was to raise the intellectual level of the population. A closer reading of the Austrian legislation in its cultural context reveals a more fitting principle underlying the policy: social control through tighter ideological control. The whole school reform, from the time of Maria Theresa at least until 1848, was not so much a movement to promote education, as it was a containment operation to make sure that it did not, in fact, get out of hand. In designing the new school system, the policy makers obviously had to accommodate the demands of certain constituencies, which here and there led them to introduce into the curriculum items that were not strictly speaking necessary from the ideological control point of view. Yet, even when such compromises were incorporated, the subsequent inclination was

---

[87] Wangermann. *Aufklärung und staatsbürgerliche Erziehung*. p. 19–22.

[88] Recall that Latin was excluded from the rural curriculum and even at major school in towns was only offered as a voluntary subject. The stipulation of Article 128 of *Politische Verfassung*, mentioned earlier, that all those found to have been instructed by the illegal uncertified teachers (*Winkellehrer*) would be barred from *Gymnasium*, indicates that this "black market" in education shifted by late 18th century precisely into this niche where aspiring commoner applicants received secret instruction in Latin in order to clear the admission bar put in their way by the restrictive reform.

[89] Melton. *Absolutism*, p. 214–217.

[90] Wangermann. *Aufklärung und staatsbürgerliche Erziehung*. p. 42 – 45.

[91] Ficker. *Bericht über österreichisches Unterrichtswesen*, p. 182; Jaroš and Job. *Rozvoj československého školství v číslech*, p. 25.

[92] Melton. *Absolutism*, p. 189.

still to brake the expansion of those branches of the system, where useful, practical knowledge could be acquired.

A telling example of this is the diffusion of Rottenhan's personal pet project, the *Realschule*, which was explicitly written into the law as an integral part of the system and thus seemed to enjoy, by all appearances, the imprimatur of official recognition. Figure 1.1 shows the spread of this type of school between 1805 and 1870. Far from achieving Rottenhan's initial aim of quickly establishing 17 such schools across the Habsburg lands, there were only eight of them as late as 1848. Even this count is overly rosy, since five of those schools (Vienna, Prague, Lviv, Graz and Trieste) were attached to polytechnics or other tertiary institutions and therefore served as their preparatory courses rather than as stand-alone lower-secondary schools that Rottenhan had envisioned. Only three *Realschulen* were founded independently of a polytechnic and they all faced strong headwinds from the centre. Already in 1804, a local businessman bequeathed what became the seed money for the *Realschule* in the rising north-Bohemian industrial centre of Liberec (Reichenberg). In 1816, the archbishop of Prague endowed a fund to pay teacher salaries both for this (as yet future) school and another one to be founded in Rakovník (Rakonic).[93] By 1826, the Liberec town council already secured a building and equipment for the school and yet the "final approval by the highest authorities" was still outstanding as of 1829.[94] This *Realschule* did not start teaching until 1837. The one in Rakovník fared marginally better, accepting first 14 students in 1833.[95] Even the *Realschule* attached to the Prague polytechnic faced bureaucratic opposition: first proposed in 1811, its draft statute went through several rounds of revisions and resubmissions, including one which took the Education Commission in Vienna seven years to consider and then reject. The school finally opened in October 1833.[96] Representatives from Tyrol and Carinthia repeatedly requested concessions to establish a *Realschule* but in vain.[97] Another such school, planned for the Moravian capital of Brno in 1811, never materialized.[98] Even already operating *Realschulen* established in Tyrol during the brief Bavarian rule in 1810–

[93] Both gifts are described in *Album. Herausgeben vom Lehrkörper der Oberrealschule in Reichenberg zur fünfundzwanzigjährigen Jubelfeier der Lehranstalt.* 1862, p. 39–45

[94] Czoernig. *Topographisch-historisch-statistische Beschreibung von Reichenberg*, p. 22.

[95] Sbor pro oslavu stoletého jubilea reálky rakovnické. *Sto let reálky rakovnické; památník vydaný k stému výročí založení reálky v Rakovníku. Díl 1. Dějiny, vzpomínky, význam*, p. 342–343.

[96] Jelinek, Carl. *Das ständisch-polytechnische Institut zu Prag. Programm zur fünfzigjährigen Erinnerungs-Feier an die Eröffnung des Institutes*, p. 53–77.

[97] Ficker. *Bericht über österreichisches Unterrichtswesen*, p. 182.

[98] Šišma, Pavel. *Matematika na německé technice v Brně*, p. 15.

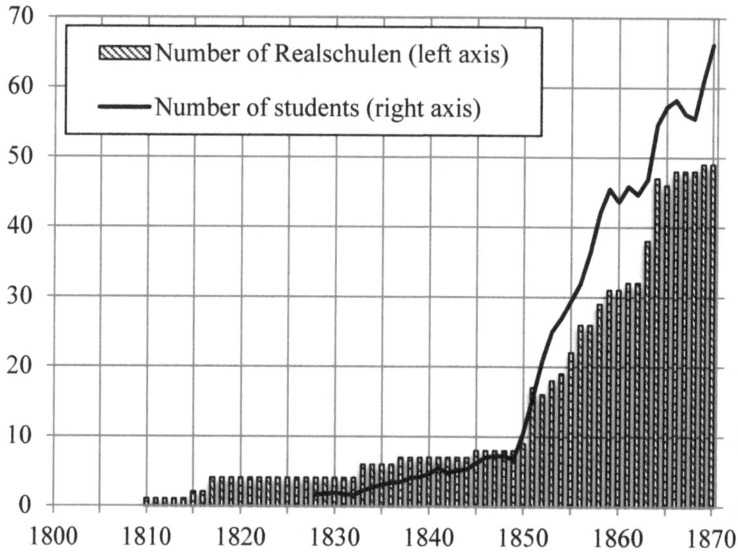

Figure 1.1: Adoption of *Realschule* in Imperial Austria, 1805–1870
Note: While the data regarding the number of these schools are complete and reliable, the student numbers, due to a few missing data points in the sources, had to be interpolated in a few instances: for the Viennese *Realschule* in 1839, 1840, 1845 and 1848, for the Trieste *Realschule* in 1845 and 1848, for the Prague *Realschule* in 1834 and for the Brody and Lviv *Realschulen* in 1845 and 1848.
Sources: Album. Herausgeben vom Lehrkörper der Oberrealschule in Reichenberg zur fünfundzwanzigjährigen Jubelfeier der Lehranstalt. p. 141; Austria. K. k. Handels-Ministerium. Statistisches Büro der Rechnungs-Kontrollbehörde. *Versuch einer Darstellung der Oesterreichischen Monarchie in Statistischen Tafeln. Iter Jahrgang. 1828.* Vienna, 1829; Austria K. k. Handels-Ministerium. Statistisches Büro der Rechnungs-Kontrollbehörde. *Darstellung der Österreichischen Monarchie in Statistische Tabellen. IIter Jahrgang. 1829.* Vienna, 1830; Exner, Franz Wilhelm. *Das k.k. polytechnische Institut in Wien, seine Gründung, seine Entwicklung und sein jetziger Zustand.* p. 46; Jelinek, Carl. *Das ständisch-polytechnische Institut zu Prag.* p. 157; Joanneum. *Jahresbericht des steiermärkisch-ständischen Joanneums zu Gratz für das Schuljahr 1846–1851*; Prechtl, Johann Joseph. "Geschichte des kaiserl. königl. polytechnischen Instituts." p. XIII; Sbor pro oslavu stoletého jubilea reálky rakovnické. *Sto let reálky rakovnické* p. 342–343; Schimmer. "Frenquenz der Lehranstalten Oesterreich's von 1841 bis 1876, in Vergleichung zur Bevölkerung", p. 60; *TSOM 1830–1865.*

1815 were abolished once the monarchy re-annexed the territory.[99] In spite of its fully legal status, unambiguously anchored in the *Politische Verfassung*, strong support from the aristocracy in the provinces and available financial

[99] Bidermann, Hermann Ignaz. *Die technische Bildung im Kaiserthume Oesterreich. Ein Betrag zur Geschichte der Industrie und des Handels*, p. 77.

patronage from both landed and commercial interests, the *Realschule* remained a marginal phenomenon and the total number of students at these schools never exceeded 1500 before 1848.

Such a meager tally was not due to lack of demand. The post-1848 explosion of both schools and student numbers in Figure 1.1 shows that the desire for decent practical and technically oriented education was widespread. The *Realschule* students increased in number from about 1454 in 1847 to 15622 in 1871. During this time, the *Gymnasium* students, with their focus on classical languages and liberal arts education, still outnumbered them – their totals fluctuated somewhat below 20000 before 1848, then grew to peak at 30629 in 1866 – but in terms of rate of change, there was no doubt, which of these two was the dynamic sector in the 1850s and 1860s. The contrast between the pre-1848 and post-1848 record suggests even more strongly than the testimonies of bureaucratic obstruction that in the first half of the 19th century (at least), the biggest obstacle to the spread of a certain type of real, practical education was the central government.

The case of the *Realschule*, while instructive, is ultimately but a small part of the whole picture. The other types of schools – the rural schools, the town schools, the major schools – formed a much bigger part of the system. But the same logic applied to them, too. The oft-quoted 1821 speech by emperor Francis I to the students of Ljubljana Lyceum, who were training to become teachers, aptly summarized what his government expected from the educational system:[100]

> "New ideas are in vogue these days, which I do not approve of and never will. Stay away from those ideas; focus on the positive. For I do not need learned men but honest, well-behaved subjects. It will be your job to educate youth to that end. Whoever serves me must teach what I command. Who cannot teach it or who comes to me with new ideas, can go away or I shall remove him."

The emperor's assertions reflected his confidence that the central government held all the cards: through the unsparing totality of the regulations, it designed the "product", it wielded the power to enforce its monopoly and it commanded the resources, financial and human, to diffuse it throughout the realm. But this forceful approach also foreordained the reception of the schooling policy among the "honest, well-behaved subjects" of his empire. It mattered greatly whether the people would be eager collaborators or passive resisters. This was the one aspect that was largely out of the government's hands. As the subsequent chapters will show, the government reaped what it had sowed.

---

[100] Allgemeine Zeitung, Nro. 38, 7th February 1821, p. 152.

Chapter 2

The Expansion

The concept of school coverage that I introduce in this chapter is distinct from school enrolment. Throughout most of the chapter, my goal is to assess how many school-age children were within reach of the school system as it expanded after 1774, regardless of whether they actually enrolled.[1] School coverage is therefore a measure of access to schooling, not of actual use. The distinction is helpful for parsing the attitudes and decisions of different actors in the whole system: low enrolment in places with low school coverage suggests slow diffusion of the school network, perhaps on account of lax work by local school authorities; on the other hand, low enrolment in the context of high – perhaps even full – coverage indicates reluctance of parents to send their children to schools that are available and within reach, weak enforcement of the compulsory attendance, or both. The distinction will also highlight the somewhat underappreciated fact that the mechanisms, which the Austrian educational authorities had in place to assess the extent of school coverage, were ill-equipped to provide an accurate and comprehensive picture. Consequently, the actual access and availability of schools was always worse – in some years markedly worse – than the officials believed.

At the time of Maria Theresa's reform, the Habsburg lands already had thousands of schools, some of long standing. Admittedly, most of them were quite unsophisticated. Teaching was often limited to winter and the level of instruction varied with the quality of staff. A 1769 report on the schools at the Imperial Estate of Kolín in Bohemia found two village teachers capable of teaching in both Czech and German and fully proficient in the *trivium* next to another five who could only speak Czech and were weak in arithmetic. Fifteen miles down the road from Kolín, however, in Sadská, a village that fancied itself a small town, a school with one teacher and two assistants offered not only the *trivium* in both Czech and German but also Latin and music, just like in neighbouring Poděbrady (an actual town).[2] In all rural schools, wherever they existed, reading and writing formed the irreducible core that was often, but not always, supplemented with arithmetic.

Putting together a more comprehensive picture of what the situation before 1774 looked like is not straightforward. No empire-wide statistics on this

[1] The question of enrolment receives its own treatment elsewhere, mostly in Chapter 5.
[2] Šafránek. *Školy české I. svazek*, p. 137–138.

matter have been preserved. Using the data for one region, southern Moravia, Figure 2.1 depicts what probably was a fairly typical dynamic, prevailing over the century before the reform. The source is a survey, undertaken by Moravian authorities in 1787–91, so as to take stock of the situation some decade and a half after the reform's introduction.[3] For each school in their area, they tabulated, among other things, the year of the school's establishment, which makes it possible to reconstruct a rare retrospective of the region's schooling situation before 1774.

Since the source has no information on schools that may have existed before 1787 but for whatever reason did not survive to the time of the survey, some caution is advisable in interpreting the figure. Strictly speaking, the black line denoting the "cumulative number of schools" does not capture how many schools there were in south Moravia in a given year but rather how many of the schools, still standing in 1791, the recently established schooling authorities "inherited" from that year and before. This introduces a downward bias to the reported pre-1791 school stock: if the figure shows a cumulative number of 168 schools for the year, say, 1751, it means that 168 schools of the 738 surveyed by the authorities in 1791 had already been around forty years earlier. The actual number of schools back in 1751 may have been higher – the difference being schools that closed in the meantime. At the same time, it is unlikely that the downward bias is large. For the figure to be markedly off, say, by an order of magnitude, it would require considerable "churn", i.e. many schools starting up and folding every year, each lasting but a short period. Instead, the graph implies that a considerable number of schools existed for decades, suggesting that village schools were a long-term undertaking. Furthermore, in the years before the school reform, village teachers often filled a number of other important roles in the community's daily life, such as scribe, church organist, market and court registrar – so much so that often the teaching role was not even his primary occupation.[4] These were further, strong incentives for making teacher appointments long-term. Thus, once a school was established, it probably lasted many years and more likely than not survived to the time of the survey. A few may have closed but that would not substantially alter the overall picture. The upshot is that the figure does not capture the pre-reform situation precisely but it is close enough.

It offers several interesting observations about the school network in those years. Already mentioned was the surprising durability of many of these places of learning. About one out of six of the surveyed schools dated back to before 1700, indicating that schools had been a fixture of village life long be-

[3] The data, collected by Miroslav Riedl, cover about half the province, roughly overlapping with the area of the diocese of Brno. See Riedl. *Zavádění povinné školní docházky*, p. 5.

[4] Engelbrecht. *Geschichte des österreichischen Bildungswesen Vol. 3*, p. 22–23.

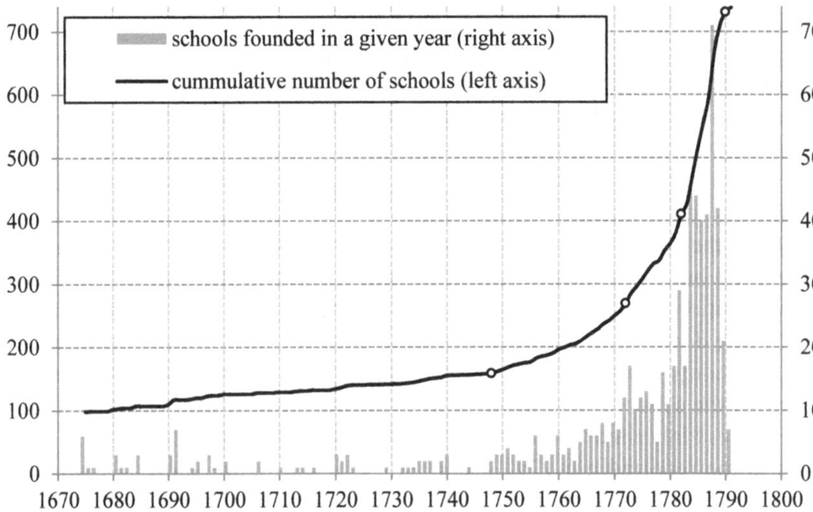

Figure 2.1: Schools in southern Moravia by year of establishment
Source: Riedl. *Zavádění povinné školní docházky*, p. 15–28.

fore the reform. This was not just a south-Moravian peculiarity: in the Alpine provinces, a school existed in every town and in every rural parish and their numbers grew further after 1700.[5] Speaking of growth, the grey bars in Figure 1 capture the number of schools established in a given year. The pattern of spurts and pauses in school launches correlates to some extent with years of war and peace: after a few establishments in the early 1680s, new foundations became rare during the three decades of warfare comprising the Great Turkish War (1683–1699) and the War of the Spanish Succession (1701–1714). Somewhat livelier activity resumed in the 1720s and 1730s but came again to a halt during the War of the Austrian Succession (1740–1748). From 1748 onwards, school founding became a regular occurrence in southern Moravia.[6] In the figure, I highlighted a few data points along the black cumulative curve that are potential candidates for breaks in the trend of school growth over the century. The year 1748 is the first of these, since from then on at least one school was launched every year. The next is 1772 when the number of new schools rose for the first time to double digits. It consistently stayed above ten with the exception of 1778, the year of the Potato War with Bavaria. The next break came in 1782, ushering in a decade of feverish launch activity, which ended in 1790 as abruptly as it had started eight years

[5] Ibid. p. 21. The Alpine provinces roughly correspond to modern-day Austrian republic.

[6] Admittedly, here the correlation with wars loses much of its potency: Seven Year's War (1756–63) seems to have had no dampening impact, despite its proximity to Moravia.

earlier. Of these four breaks, only the third can be said to be directly related to the new schooling policy, specifically, to Joseph II's 1781 decision to focus attention on expanding the school network, bolstered in 1784 by a regulation demanding a new school for every 90–100 school-age children living within the radius of a thirty-minute walking distance.[7] The halt in 1790 was caused partly by the impact of another Austro-Turkish War (1788–1791) and partly by the death, in February of that year, of the main driver of the expansion, the emperor himself.[8]

The south-Moravian record shows that elementary schooling, even in the less sophisticated countryside, had its own dynamic, quite apart from the official policy; that it experienced a persistent and accelerating expansion long before the reform; and that, when the *Allgemeine Schulordnung* came into force in January 1775, the educational administration found a relatively extensive school network already in place. While there were considerable differences in the level of development between the various parts of the empire, it is unlikely that the south-Moravian situation was exceptional or untypical. After all, the wars affected the whole empire and a similar pattern of ups and down can be detected in the available evidence from other provinces, too (although none as comprehensive as the south-Moravian data). Styria, for example, also saw record high numbers of new school constructions in the 1780s give way to almost nothing after 1790.[9]

The year of the reform itself, 1774/5, did not constitute a material break in trend. Given how many pre-reform schools were to be grandfathered into the new system, the initial focus of the reformers was to start by converting existing schools to the new method rather than to grow the school network. Article 3 of the law stressed the obligation of existing teachers to adopt the new method as soon as possible. Only in a follow-up paragraph did the article specify, in rather vague terms, where and when new schools should be established. In the first years after the passage, the focus was on bringing existing schools under the aegis of the new supervisory bodies and ensuring that they were limiting their teaching to the legally sanctioned method, using only approved textbooks. Numerous secondary schools, once belonging to various religious orders, were now turned into major schools, which also served as training grounds for teachers. In Moravia, for example, out of the existing 737 trivial schools, some 342 had been reformed in line with the new law by 1780, while the remaining 395 were still using old methods and textbooks.[10]

---

[7] Wangermann. *Aufklärung und staatsbüfgerliche Erziehung*, p. 47–49.

[8] Apparently, a ban on new school building construction was issued already in January 1789 so as to focus resources on winning the war. Pietsch. *Die Theresianische Schulreform in der Steiermark*, p. 122.

[9] Ibid. p. 120.

[10] Helfert. *Die österreichische Volksschule*, p. 583.

In Styria, about 113 out of 233 had been improved.[11] Tallying the data from all Habsburg provinces (except Hungary which had its own separate schooling law), Felbiger counted 3993 schools that conformed to the law as of September 1780 out of a total of 6197.[12]

Yet, Article 12 clearly mandated primary education for all school-age children of both sexes and, unless their parents hired a private tutor, those children "belonged in schools without exception." Conversion of existing schools was therefore only the beginning – the easy part. The more serious task, which came to the fore at about the same time as Joseph II became the sole ruler, was to make schooling truly universal. There were perhaps 1.5–1.6 million school-age children in all non-Hungarian crown lands in 1780 but only 208580 were enrolled in the 3993 reformed schools according to Felbiger's 1780 report.[13] Gerhart van Swieten, one of Joseph II's advisors in matters of education, estimated that some 18000 trained and certified teachers would be needed to educate all the children.[14]

The expansion of the school network progressed unevenly across the many Habsburg provinces. At one end of the spectrum were the success stories, such as Lower Austria and Bohemia. Starting from an already fairly dense school network, Lower Austria added about 150 new schools between 1781 and 1785, reaching a total of 999 schools.[15] Over the next eight decades, only 200 more schools were added, which amounted to little more than a simple adjustment to overall population growth. Bohemia started from a somewhat lower base but between 1777 and 1800, the number of schools grew by about 50%, reaching 2644 at the end of the century.[16] In Moravia and Silesia, the number of schools doubled between 1783 and 1808.[17] Joseph II's desire to achieve the greatest possible expansion in the shortest possible time meant that close attention was paid to the issues of school financing. The result was the establishment of the institution of school patronage (*Schulpatronat*), which provided a workable blueprint that could be effectively replicated in villages and towns across the provinces.

---

[11] Pietsch. *Die Theresianische Schulreform in der Steiermark*, p. 48

[12] Helfert. *Die österreichische Volksschule*, p. 583.

[13] The estimate of the number of school-age children is based on Goehlert's data for total population, assuming that the 5.0–12.0 age cohort constituted about 15% of the population. See Goehlert, J. Vincenz. "Häuser und Volkszahl sowie Viehstand Oesterreichs in der Regierungsperiode Kaiser Josef's II." *Statistische Monatschrift* V (1879): 405. The enrolment total comes from Helfert. *Die österreichische Volksschule*, p. 583. Felbiger himself estimated the number of school-age children at 735805, which was certainly too low. See Wangermann. *Aufklärung und staatsbürgerliche Erziehung*, p. 43.

[14] Wangermann. *Aufklärung und staatsbürgerliche Erziehung*, p. 43.

[15] Weiss. *Geschichte der österreichischen Volksschule 1792–1848. II. Band.* p. 763, 769.

[16] Engliš, Karel. "Příspěvky ke statistice národního školství." *Zprávy Zemského statistického úřadu království Českého* 7 (1905): XXIX

[17] Weiss. *Geschichte der österreichischen Volksschule 1792–1848. II. Band.* p. 871–874.

But the contrast of these dynamically growing provinces with the crown lands further to the South and East shows that a successful expansion was easier to jumpstart where a pre-existing critical mass of school infrastructure and staff numbers were already in place. Carniola reported to have 16 schools in 1781. By 1807, their number decreased to 12, which was negligible in a province of more than 300000 inhabitants.[18] Bukovina opened the first "regulation school" only in 1783 and by 1809 their total rose to 11.[19]

The initial expansion drive petered out in many places after Joseph II died and the French Wars started. Styria boosted the number of schools from 174 to 376 during the 1780s but added approximately only 30 schools between 1788 and 1808.[20] A similar fate befell southern Moravia: based on the 1787–91 surveys, the authorities estimated that they needed another 233 new schools to make good on Joseph's school density regulation. Of these, 102 were in operation by 1807, whereas the rest were either never founded or had to close after only a brief duration. Moreover, many of the recent 1780s foundations also proved unsustainable, so that the total net increase in the number of schools between 1788 and 1807 was just six.[21] The same was true for recently acquired Galicia, which made almost no progress between 1789 and 1815. In the South, from the Austrian Littoral to Dalmatia, a real boom in school establishment did not commence until the 1840s but it still took the rest of the 19th century before school coverage was anywhere close to full, i.e. offering a place to every child. Galicia and Bukovina registered several short-term spurts, such as in the 1830s and again in the 1850s, but the definitive effort to achieve complete coverage had to wait until after the liberal school reform of 1869. In short, the immediate achievement of the Theresian reform in terms of school expansion amounted to a spasm of frenetic activity in the 1780s, followed by a return either to stagnation or to the more steady but also more realistically grounded rate of growth that had prevailed before the reform's implementation.

In spite of such meager results across the empire, the assessment by the court authorities was relatively positive. During the discussions over the proposal of the *Politische Verfassung* in 1802, one of the emperor's chief advisors in matters of schooling, Martin Lorenz, argued that no further expansion in the number of schools was necessary, because the efforts inspired by Joseph II had worked and coverage was already quite complete.[22] In some places, in fact, Lorenz even saw a need to scale it down. It is hard to fathom how he reached this conclusion, since many provinces had barely started

[18] Weiss. *Geschichte der österreichischen Volksschule 1792–1848. II. Band.* p. 948.

[19] Ibid., p. 902.

[20] Ibid., p. 806–809.

[21] Riedl. *Zavádění povinné školní docházky*, p. 84–85.

[22] Weiss. *Geschichte der österreichischen Volksschule 1792–1848. I. Band.* p. 198.

building up their school network. Dalmatia, then recently acquired by Austria through the Treaty of Campo Formio, had in fact zero schools at the time (meaning schools that were compliant with Austrian law), as several officials were quick to point out.[23] Lorenz's concern regarding further expansion was that in remote mountainous villages, which were not served by a parish priest, schools could not be properly supervised and putting a teacher in such places could lead to some unauthorized, unsupervised imparting of literacy. This combination of complacency and caution lulled some provinces into protracted periods of stagnation throughout the first half of the 19th century. For example, in Salzburg province, which came to the Habsburg fold with an already developed school network, the number of schools fluctuated within a narrow range of 140–150, or about 1 per 1000 inhabitants, even though the mountainous terrain and the uneven distribution of the population across the province meant that schools were out of reach for about a quarter of the school-age children in the whole province.

While these aggregate numbers furnish a picture about the overall extent of schooling, they hide important differences in the quality and nature of schools catering to students in diverse locales. The largest towns and cities could afford to support a major school (*Hauptschule*), which had the broadest curriculum and was usually staffed by several teachers. Elsewhere, the standard was the *Trivialschule*, specified at length in the law. The teacher lived in the school building and supplied a full-year, all-day education five days a week in return for regularly paid tuition fees and a few other perks. Majority of schools were of this kind. But for smaller villages or in areas with scattered populations, such an arrangement could not be so easily implemented and sustained, which is why the locals, in tacit cooperation with district supervisors, sometimes had to bend the regulations. That inevitably compromised access.

Some of these measures, such as half-day teaching, were anticipated by the law. This was available in schools where pupil numbers outgrew the classroom and had to be split into a morning and afternoon group. Some schools operated only for one semester each year. In places with distances too long for children to traverse, the solution took the form of an *Excurrendo-Schule*, or branch school, where the teacher, serving in a particular trivial school, was required to itinerate around neighbouring villages, stopping in each on a particular day of the week to deliver his lessons. Frequently, teachers preferred to hire a substitute from among recent young teacher course graduates to do the itinerant teaching in their place. In the wake of the partial liberalization following the events of 1848, the Ministry of Education also legally recognized various other ad-hoc school types, which had developed over time. A provisional school (*Nothschule*) was a school that was allowed to operate in

[23] Ibid., p. 209–210.

Table 2.1: Distribution of school coverage by type of school, 1865

	Percentage of school-age (5.0–12.0) children covered by…				
	major school	trivial school	branch school	provisional school	no school
Lower Austria	20.7	51.7	2.2	3.9	21.5
Upper Austria	6.9	76.8	0.4	0.1	15.7
Salzburg	7.5	69.1	1.3	1.1	21.0
Styria	7.2	56.6	1.0	7.9	27.3
Carinthia	7.9	58.4	2.7	2.1	28.9
Carniola	7.6	48.1	1.7	7.1	35.6
Austrian Littoral	18.1	38.1	0.4	12.1	31.3
Tyrol & Vorarlberg	11.2	70.3	6.0	7.0	5.4
Bohemia	8.1	63.7	10.6	1.4	16.2
Moravia	7.9	73.8	4.6	0.9	12.8
Silesia	6.0	70.4	3.7	0.2	19.6
Total	11.3	62.1	2.8	4.1	19.7

Source: Detail-Conscription.

less than adequate classroom space – a concession to villages that did not have the necessary funds to establish a school in full compliance of the regulation. On the other hand, parish school (*Pfarr-schule*) was a trivial school, enhanced by the addition of a third grade to the curriculum.[24]

School-age children who lived in the vicinity of a school were administratively assigned to it and could not enrol in any other. But since school coverage was far from full, many children were not assigned to any school at all. Table 2.1 shows how access to schooling varied by region and type of school and it was clearly rather unequal. Almost a fifth of all children in the listed provinces had no access at all and almost 7% had only access to branch and provisional schools, that supplied less than the full extent of the curriculum.[25] The proportion varied widely between provinces, with high values reported either for mountainous provinces (Styria, Tyrol and the Bohemian borderlands), where such provisional fixes were necessitated by the dispersed population, or for poor southern provinces (Carniola and Littoral).[26] About three fifths of all pupils had access to the trivial school but here, too, the provinces displayed considerable variation.

Table 2.2 further shows how much school time was available to children who were assigned to a school. Most schools were teaching year-round and

[24] Frank. *Die Österreichische Volksschule von 1848–1898*. p. 21.

[25] Note that the table includes only provinces for which we could separate children by the type of school they were assigned to. For Galicia, Bukovina and Dalmatia such detailed data are not available, although we can estimate the overall extent of school coverage: it was 66%, 75% and 44% respectively. Including these three provinces in the total would increase the overall percentage of children with no access to any school from 19.7% to about 24%.

[26] Hölzl. "Studien zum Pflichtschulwesen in Tirol 1774–1806", p. 98.

Table 2.2: Distribution of school coverage by extent of instruction, 1865

	Percentage of children covered by a school teaching...			
	all-year, all-day	all-year, half-day	half-year, all-day	half-year, half-day
Lower Austria	61.5	38.3	0.1	0.1
Upper Austria	52.6	47.1	0.3	0.0
Salzburg	97.2	2.8	0.0	0.0
Styria	74.5	23.8	0.8	0.9
Carinthia	89.1	7.0	3.6	0.3
Carniola	71.9	20.9	1.3	5.9
Austrian Littoral	75.3	22.5	1.1	1.1
Tyrol & Vorarlberg	20.1	1.8	77.2	0.8
Bohemia	91.9	7.9	0.2	0.0
Moravia	89.8	10.0	0.2	0.0
Silesia	83.5	16.5	0.0	0.0
Total	78.6	15.6	5.5	0.3

Source: Detail-Conscription.

all day but such practice was far from common in several provinces. In Tyrol, in fact, only about a fifth of the children belonged to a school that taught all year, while in Upper Austria about half of all schools operated on a half- day basis. The purpose of these two tables is to illustrate that "access to a school" could and did mean markedly different things in different areas. In Tyrol, for example, almost every school-age child had access to a school but most of those schools closed down for the spring and summer. Bohemia and Upper Austria had comparable overall school coverage of about 84–85% but, once adjusted for the amount of school time, Upper Austrian children had access to markedly less schooling than their Bohemian counterparts.

The quick fixes and piecemeal arrangements that so many local communities adopted in place of a proper, "full-time" trivial school were a product of an even match between two forces pushing in opposite directions. Educational authorities desired as complete a coverage as possible and increasing the number of schools was obviously an integral part of that effort. But the policymakers were also aware of the accompanying burden, hence their anxious efforts to keep tuition fees low and to spread the costs of maintaining a school across several different sources, so that they would not all fall on the pupils' parents. At the same time, the trivial schools had relatively little to offer to the villagers and townsfolk on the ground. The curriculum was constrained and repetitive and sending children to school meant forgoing their labour. Unsurprisingly, the low-quality provisional and branch schools and the half-day teaching arose as an uneasy compromise in places where the powers that be wanted a school but the people on the ground not so much.[27]

[27] For a similar argument about the divergence between educational preferences of peasants and educational authorities in the context of 19th century Russia, see Eklof. *Russian*

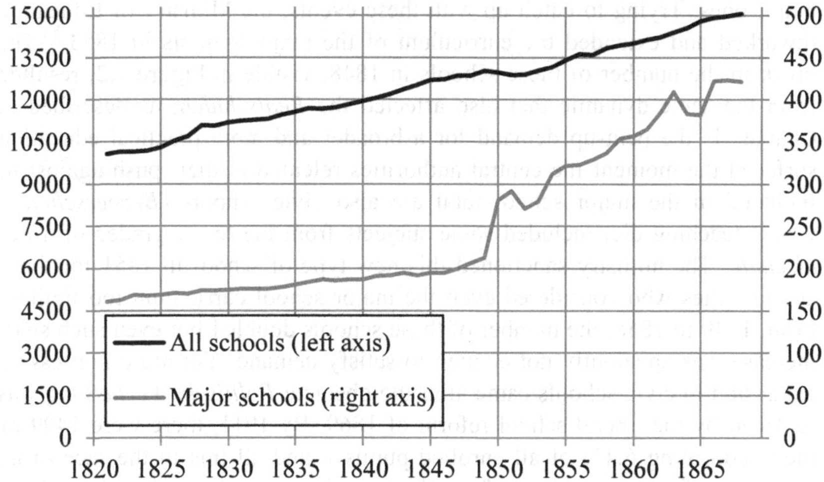

Figure 2.2: Number of major schools and of all schools, 1821–1868
Source: Versuch, Darstellung, TSOM, SJOM

At the other end of the quality spectrum, however, the roles were reversed. Table 2.1 showed that only a minority had access to the major schools, which were the best-appointed elementary schools the system could offer. They often had a teacher training course attached to them because their classroom practice was the norm and model for all other schools. Moreover, in contrast to the trivial schools, the major schools were financed from the *Studienfond*, a central school fund. The Education Commission therefore resisted converting trivial schools into major schools by extending the curriculum, lest it increase the claims made on the school fund.[28] To give an example, when the rising industrial town of Liberec in North Bohemia sought the elevation of the local trivial school to a major school in 1808, they had to show as part of their petition that the town was able to cover extra salary expenses from communal sources.[29] Figure 2.2 shows that the authorities' resistance to major schools was relatively successful: of the 10071 schools operating in 1821, only 163, or 1.6% were major schools and this proportion did not change much over the course of the next three decades, or until the late 1840s.

The growth of major schools was thus held back and their number grew at about the same rate as the overall number of schools until 1848. As the revolutionary events of that year loosened the grip of central authorities, many towns took their own initiative and started converting their trivial schools into

peasant schools: Officialdom, Village Culture and Popular Peagogy, 1861–1914, p. 251–282.

[28] Engelbrecht. *Geschichte Des österreichischen Bildungswesens Vol. 3*, p. 239.

[29] Hoffmann, *Geschichte der Haupt- und Mädchenschule in Reichenberg*, p. 60.

major ones. Trying to catch up with these events, the Ministry of Education reworked and extended the curriculum of the major schools in 1853.[30] The break in the number of these schools in 1848, visible in Figure 2.2, resulted from the same dynamic that also affected the *Realschulen*, as described in Chapter 1: the pent-up demand for a broader and more practical education surfaced the moment the central authorities relented in their push against it. Included in the major school total are also civic schools (*Bürgerschulen*) whose teaching diet included some subjects from the lower grades of a *Realschule*. The ministry sanctioned this new type of school in 1851 for those communities who considered even the major school curriculum too limited. From 1849 to 1868, the number of these schools doubled but even such swift increase was apparently not enough to satisfy demand. Yet more impressive expansion in civic schools came after the obsolete *Politische Verfassung* was replaced by the liberal school reform of 1869. By 1911, there were 1499 of them, educating 6.4% of all enrolled pupils – and all this in the face of an ever-intensifying competition from the booming secondary education whose curriculum overlapped with that of civic schools to some extent.[31]

All these experiences, sudden breaks, temporary reversals and retroactive fixes show that throughout the century preceding the 1869 liberal reform, school expansion was hemmed in by institutional obstacles of the government's own making. The state refused to allow enough freedom of education to let the citizenry decide how much and what kind of schooling they wanted; on the other hand, it was eager to extend to everyone a type of schooling that they did not want. The number of schools grew gradually – Figure 2.2 shows about a 50% increase over a period of not quite five decades – but it did not grow as fast as it could have and certainly not as much as it needed to grow to truly encompass all school-age children. It did not help that even the authorities themselves were scarcely in a position to form any precise idea of how many such children there were.

Given what we know about the number of schools, what was the proportion of school-age children who could reasonably have been able to enrol in them at any given moment? At the outset, the proportion was quite low, which is why Joseph II was so eager to expand the system, but even the 1781 report by Felbiger was overoptimistic about the status quo. Table 2.3 critically evaluates some of the data in Felbiger's overview – one of the earliest semi-comprehensive data points available – which is a good opportunity for an important clarification. Both contemporaries and subsequent historians have been interested in gauging the success of the Theresian school reform in

---

[30] Frank, *Die Österreichische Volksschule von 1848–1898*. p. 18–19.

[31] K.k. Statistische Zentralkomission. "2. Heft: Statistik der Unterrichtsanstalten in den im Reichsrate vertretenen Königreichen und Ländern für das Jahr 1910/1911." *Österreichische Statistik. Neue Folge. Vol. 8.* (1914): pp. 290–299.

Table 2.3: Enrolment in Austrian schools in Autumn 1780

Province	Number of children			Percent enrolled	
	enrolled in schools	reported school-bound	estimated cohort size	reported	estimated
Lower Austria	37686	94977	130000	39.7	29.0
Upper Austria	12559		83000		15.1
Styria	3785	75000	123000	5.0	3.1
Carniola	1104		58000		1.9
Tyrol	3711	61000	84000	6.1	4.4
Bohemia	88692	225583	440000	39.3	20.2
Moravia	22883	118437	215000	19.3	10.6
Silesia	4188	26800	58000	15.6	7.2
Galicia	5864		510000		1.1
Bukovina	0[a]		35000		0.0
Total	*180472*		*1742000*		*10.4*

Note: Data for Carinthia, Austrian Littoral and Vorarlberg are unavailable. Salzburg and Dalmatia were not yet under Habsburg rule. "Reported school-bound" refers to the number of children supposed to attend school, as counted by the teachers and administrators as of September 1780. "Estimated cohort size" provides an estimate, rounded to thousands, of the total number of children aged 5.0–12.0 on the basis of total population in each province.

[a]Refers to the number of pupils enrolled in the new post-reform type of schools. Wangermann, *Aufklärung und staatsbürgerliche Erziehung*, p. 60 notes that Bukovina did not have any such school until 1783.

Sources: For enrolment totals and reported number of school-bound children, see Weiss. *Geschichte der österreichischen Volksschule 1792–1848. II. Band*, p. 763–969; Hölzl. "Studien zum Pflichtschulwesen in Tirol 1774–1806", p. 137. For the way cohort size was estimated, see text. The underlying population data, on which these estimates come from the following sources: Demian, *Darstellung der Oesterreichischen Monarchie I. Band, 2te Abtheilung*, 23; Goehlert, "Die Ergebnisse der in Osterreich im vorigen Jahrhundert ausgefuhrten Volkszahlungen", p. 76–77; Goehlert "Häuser und Volkszahl sowie Viehstand Oesterreichs" p. 402–405; Goehlert, "Die Entwicklung der Bevölkerung von Tirol und Vorarlberg", p. 53; Hain, Joseph. *Handbuch der Statistik des Österreichischen Kaiserstaates. I. Band*, p. 489–491; Hassel, *Statistischer Abriss des Östreichschen Kaisertums*, p. 54; Liechtenstern, *Statistische Uebersicht des Oesterreichischen Kaiser-staats*; –. *Handbuch der neuesten Geographie des Österreichischen Kaiserstaates. I. Theil.* p. 121, 191; Kárníková, *Vývoj obyvatelstva v českých zemich, 1754–1914*. p. 329; –. *Archiv für Geographie und Statistik* 1 (1803), p. 204–392; "Ueber die Lage, Grösse, Bestandtheile und Bevölkerung der östrechischen Erb-Monarchie." *Archiv für Geographie und Statistik* 1 (1803), p. 25.

terms of the fraction of school-age children enrolled in elementary schools. The usual sources for such statistics were school reports that provincial school commissions compiled from the data supplied to them by individual teachers. The teachers were obligated by law to report every year the number of enrolled children (*schulbesuchende Kinder*) as well as the number of what the law called *schulfähige Kinder*. The latter expression literally means "children competent for school" but it referred to those children in a school's vicinity, who were of school age and therefore fell under the schooling mandate. It is easy to see that this manner of accounting for school-age children was open to bias: areas with no schools and no teachers to compile the list were omitted. When the provincial school commissions aggregated the teacher reports into provincial totals, they were inevitably obtaining biased numbers even if most teachers submitted full and accurate accounts of school age children in their particular school precinct. Given this omission, it would be misleading to interpret the reported *schulfähige Kinder* as "school-age children", because this statistic was not fit to capture the size of the school-age cohort, especially in provinces where the educational infrastructure was sparse. Consequently, I translate this expression as "school-bound children" – that is, children who must have made it onto some teacher's list somewhere and were therefore expected and supposed to enrol in the school where he was teaching.[32]

The undercount could be quite stark, as the example of Styria can illustrate. Thanks to one particularly detailed population survey in this Alpine duchy, dating from 1830, we have data on the age structure, which yields a somewhat precise estimate of the number of school-age children in Styria at that time.[33] The data were published, together with all kinds of other statistics including on schooling, in the Austrian government's recently introduced official annual statistical publication, *Tafeln zur Statistik der Oesterreichischen Monarchie* (TSOM). At this time, population surveys, which were not full-blown censuses, were conducted at regular intervals by the Austrian army with a view to establish the number of potential conscripts.[34] The military paid some attention to the age structure especially among boys and young men, so as to be able to predict recruiting numbers ahead of time. In spite of having the infrastructure, the manpower and the motivation to carry out this task, the army faced a real risk of potential undercount both of men (and boys), since feudal lords had an interest in limiting conscription of valuable workforce as much as possible, and also of women, since they were not as important to the army.[35] Fortunately, of all the population surveys conducted before Austria's first modern population census of 1857, the 1830

---

[32] I reserve the expression "school-age children" to refer to my estimates of the total size of the school-age cohort based on other, demographic data.

[33] K. k. Handels-Ministerium. Direktion der administrativen Statistik. *Tafeln zur Statistik der Österreichischen Monarchie 1830. Vol 3.* Table 7.

[34] Kárníková. *Vývoj obyvatelstva v českých zemích, 1754–1914*, p. 287–307.

[35] Bolognese-Leuchtenmüller, Birgit. *Bevölkerungsentwicklung und Berufsstruktur, Gesundheits- und Fürsorgwesen in Österreich 1750–1918*, p. 31; Goehlert estimated, for example, that the 1781 census, conducted by the army, resulted in about 5–6% undercount. See Goehlert. "Die Ergebnisse der in Osterreich im vorigen Jahrhundert ausgefuhrten Volkszahlungen im Vergleiche mit jenen der neuern Zeit", p. 60

count is perhaps the most reliable because it was done in the wake of a major review of the army's population accounting methods.[36] Still, whatever bias may exist in these data, it is likely a downward bias, i.e. an undercount.

There were, according to the population survey, 66174 boys and 68472 girls aged 5.0–12.0 years in Styria in 1830.[37] Taking the 6.0–12.0 age range, the totals are 56504 and 57610. Put together, the school-age children represented 15.2% of the total Styrian population of about 883000, which is a demographically plausible value (12.9% if we take the narrower age range). These totals are also consistent with birth data, compiled from parish records kept by the local clergy.[38] Styria reported around 207500 births in 1819–1825. If, as the 1830 count indicates, about 135000 of these children were still around in 1830, or roughly 65% of the combined seven birth cohorts, it implies a survival rate that corresponds with what we know about infant and child mortality at this time.[39]

The same edition of TSOM that carried the 1830 age distribution of Styria also reported the number of the duchy's *schulfähige Kinder*, or school-bound children, reported by teachers for the 1830 school year: 50577 boys and 43784 girls.[40] This was an appreciable undercount, especially for girls, which would obviously affect one's assessment of enrolment. The same table cited 38937 boys and 30182 girls as enrolled in 1830, suggesting that 77% of boys and 69% of girls were in school. The reality was between 8 and 25 percentage points lower, depending on which denominator one chooses.

Unfortunately, most authors, both past and present, have calculated historical enrolment ratios from the data based on the teacher reports because the totals for both *schulfähige Kinder* and *schulbesuchende Kinder* were usually published conveniently side by side in every annual addition of TSOM, whereas census-based demographic data on age composition such as the 1830 Styrian case were rare. This issue was not unique to Styria. To use an example from a different province, Melton cites Wangermann, who cites Weiss, who cites Wilfling's data for Bohemia, implying that "by 1790, [...] two-

---

[36] Kárníková. *Vývoj obyvatelstva v českých zemích, 1754–1914*, p. 287–307.

[37] I specify the ages with one decimal place not in a vain pretense to faux precision but as an attempt to undo the confusion wrought by the Austrian legislation's liberal use of "commenced" and "completed" years of age – as I further explain in the text. The one decimal place is hopefully enough to make clear which cohorts are included and which are not: 5.0–12.0 age range starts on a person's fifth birthday and ends on his or her twelfth. Similarly for 6.0–12.0 year olds.

[38] The system for reporting births, deaths and marriages was in place since 1784. See Bolognese-Leuchtenmüller. *Bevölkerungsentwicklung*, p. 69–89.

[39] Müllner, J. N. *Versuch einer statistischen Geographie von Böhmen*, p. 31; Riegger, Joseph Anton von. *Skizze einer statistischen Landeskunde Böhmens. II. Heftchen.* "II. Haupttabelle über Getraute, Geborne und Gestorbene in Böhmen."

[40] TSOM 1830, Table 81–Volksschulen im Jahre 1830.

thirds of all school-age children in the province were attending Bohemian elementary schools" and that "in some places, the aim of universal public education was achieved."[41] At that time, Bohemia boasted 190601 enrolled pupils out of a reported 284874 school-bound children, which indeed suggests a 67% enrolment ratio. But the school-bound numbers are, again, undercounts of the actual size of the school-age cohort. Data on precise age distribution for 1790 Bohemia do not exist, but a simple, crude calculation can provide an order-of-magnitude sense of the margin of error. Bohemia recorded about 100–120 thousand births per year in the 1780s, or about 700–800 thousand births across a seven-year period.[42] As in Styria in 1830, child mortality was high and about 40% of those born would not live to school age.[43] Thus, by a rough approximation, about 420–480 thousand children could be of school age by 1790, as defined by the law. With 190601 enrolled, a more grounded assessment would therefore put the enrolment ratio at 40-45%, as opposed to two thirds.

With all that in mind, let us revisit Table 2.3. It shows the data reported from schools for several provinces, together with an estimated total number of school-age children. These estimates are rounded to thousands because anything more specific would be faux precision. They represent anywhere between 13% and 19% of the total population, depending on the province, which is also how they were calculated.[44] They serve to provide no more than a broad sense of the number of children within the relevant age range in each province. The crudity of these estimates notwithstanding, the table shows clearly how meager the initial results of the reform were. As Joseph II was setting out to bring the new and improved schooling to the masses in 1781,

---

[41] The first quote is from Melton. *Absolutism*, p. 221, who also refers to the second one in Wangermann. *Aufklärung und staatsbürgerliche Erziehung*, p. 59 and to Weiss, Anton. *Geschichte der Theresianischen Schulreform in Böhmen*, p. 187. For (some of) the original data see Wilfling, Ignaz Richard. *Kalender für Aufseher, Katecheten und Lehrer der Nationalschulen in Königreiche Böhmen auf das Jahr 1790*. Many other researchers take these reported numbers uncritically to calculate enrolment ratios, see for example Beales, Derek. *Joseph II: II. Against the World, 1780–1790*, p. 308; Engelbrecht. *Geschichte Des österreichischen Bildungswesens: Erziehung und Unterricht auf dem Boden Österreichs, Vol. 4.*, p. 111.

[42] Palacký, František. "Gradation der Bevölkerung Böhmens seit den letzten 60 Jahren." p. 203–204.

[43] See for example, Riegger, Joseph Anton von. "II. Haupttabelle über Getraute, Geborne und Gestorbene in Böhmen." *Skizze einer statistischen Landeskunde Böhmens. II. Heftchen.*

[44] In determining which percentage to use in which province, I relied on the reported number of boys aged 1.0–13.0 in relation to overall male population. This was one of the demographic statistics collected by the army with a view of estimating future conscription. Thus, in Lower Austria the school-age cohort represented close to 13% of the total population while in Moravia it was 19%. All other provinces fell within this interval. See Kárníková. *Vývoj obyvatelstva v českých zemích, 1754–1914*.

about 90% of the targeted children were not being reached. In 1780, Bohemia and Lower Austria were ahead of other provinces only because they inherited a richer, denser school network from the pre-reform era. The majority of the most active proponents of reform hailed from these two crown lands.[45] Galicia and Bukovina were recently acquired territories, where Austrian administration barely had a chance to take root. But progress in schooling was slow even in the Alpine provinces of Styria, Carinthia and Tyrol, which had belonged to the Habsburgs for centuries.

The table also shows, again, that the reporting conducted through the school system was incapable of accurately measuring "market penetration" or providing a reliable indicator of how much more schooling was necessary to get everyone in school. The fact that the reported numbers on school-bound children underestimated the size of the school-age cohort does not mean, however, that they are worthless. They merely happen to measure something other than what they were intended to. Since the data could only be collected by teachers, who were already in place and teaching, they carry information about how many children had been "brought into orbit" of the new system, even if the children were not currently enrolled. The phrase "school-bound children", while not a precise and literate translation of *schulfähige Kinder*, at least accurately conveys the fact that those children, who made the teacher's list, were tied to a particular school, which they were supposed to attend. In short, the ratio between actually enrolled children and school-bound children tells us how effective the enforcement of the attendance mandate, among children who were already "in the system", was. In contrast, the ratio between school-bound children and the size of the whole school-age cohort measures the extent of coverage of school-age children by the school system, which is the main focus of this chapter.

A good measure of school coverage requires an appropriate estimate of the total number of children of school age, i.e. the size of the school-age cohort. Here, the legislation introduced a certain definitional ambiguity about which children should be counted as school age. Both the *Allgemeine Schulordnung* of 1774 and the *Politische Verfassung* of 1805 stipulated that the age of compulsory attendance began with the onset of the 6th year, i.e. after a child's fifth birthday. The earlier law, in fact, explicitly required children to start attending "as soon as they entered their sixth year" (Article 12) – which *prima facie* seemed to imply the next day after one's fifth birthday. The 1805 law contained similar language but made explicit the more logical, intuitive interpretation, where new children entered school at the commencement of

[45] This would include, for example, Ferdinand Kindermann, the first leader of the Bohemian school commission and later bishop of Litoměřice, or Aleš Vincenc Pařízek, the director of the Bohemian *Normalschule*. See Šustová. "Význam Aleše Vincence Pařízka v přípravě učitelů elementárních škol"

the next semester, preferably the winter semester, which was also the beginning of the school year. As for the exit from school, the two laws differed somewhat. The *Schulordnung* mandated "six or seven years in school" on the grounds that the curriculum can scarcely be mastered before one's twelfth year. Earlier exit could only take place upon passing an examination.[46] The 1805 law, on the other hand, firmly ruled against exit before one's twelfth birthday, that is to say, pupils who turned twelve during school term were expected to complete at least the current semester. But it contained no specific pronouncement on how long one's school career should be.

The regulations were therefore not entirely clear regarding this issue. Some authors have read them as implying a six-year compulsory schooling but one could just as well justify reading the laws as demanding seven years.[47] When the Education Commission was petitioned to clarify this point in 1836, they argued that children should in general attend school for seven years, but if they delayed enrolment by a year for whatever reason, they should still be able to exit at age 12, provided they pass the year-end examinations.[48] These delayed entrants thus would receive no more than six years of education, but the commission reasoned that at age 12 most children start fully working or learning a trade, so they would not attend school anyway. This explanation therefore did not fix minimum school years either but it implied that 12 was the age of exit, regardless of one's age at entry. By 1851, however, the Ministry of Education ruled against this reading of the law, by then adhered to by many parents and teachers, and instead specified that every child must receive "at least six full years of schooling", that if a child starts attending at seven, he or she must stay in school at least until 13, and that no one can certainly exit school before age 12, even if they started attending at age five.[49] The original ambiguity of the 1774 law – "six or seven years in school" – remained until the liberal reform of 1869.

As will become apparent from the tables and figures below, the ambiguity resulted in marked differences in how various provinces enforced the law and therefore how many children were counted as *schulfähig*. To ensure comparability across various provinces and across time, unless specified otherwise, most of the analysis in this chapter uses estimates of school-age cohort sizes that hew to the letter of the law, which implied seven years of schooling, starting with one's fifth birthday and ending with the twelfth. For each year

---

[46] Hölzl, "Studien zum Pflichtschulwesen in Tirol 1774–1806" p. 95 interprets this as meaning that attendance mandate was defined not in terms of years of schooling but in terms of content and the age ranges mentioned in the law were merely suggestive.

[47] Strakosch-Graßmann. *Geschichte des österreichischen Unterrichswesens*, p. 160 and Kuzmin, Michail N. *Vývoj školství a vzdělání v Československu*, p. 54 are examples of the six-year interpretation.

[48] Weiss. *Geschichte der österreichischen Volksschule 1792–1848. II. Band.* p. 141–2.

[49] LGBl Tirol 192/1851.

Table 2.4: Number of children subject to compulsory schooling, 1865

	Estimated size of 5.0-12.0 age group from:		Estimated size of 6.0-12.0 age group from:		Reported number of schoolbound children	
	birth and death records	census	birth and death records	census	SJOM	DC
	(i)	(ii)	(iii)	(iv)	(v)	(vi)
Lower Austria	235.5	255.2	198.0	219.2	187.9	185.2
Upper Austria	87.2	88.6	74.2	75.6	76.4	74.9
Salzburg	17.0	17.5	14.4	15.0	13.8	14.0
Styria	140.4	145.0	118.4	123.0	107.9	106.1
Carinthia	44.7	43.2	37.9	36.6	32.6	31.3
Carniola	63.7	64.2	53.2	53.5	51.7	43.0
Austrian Littoral	81.8	79.7	67.9	66.5	65.3	63.8
Tyrol & Vorarlberg	113.5	114.5	96.2	97.4	102.9	103.7
Bohemia	780.9	749.6	660.5	633.2	643.5	638.4
Moravia	299.3	295.2	252.3	249.1	251.3	252.2
Silesia	73.0	73.8	60.1	61.6	59.5	59.7
Galicia	753.0	789.5	618.8	659.8	548.3	550.6
Bukovina	81.3	85.6	68.6	73.4	63.3	62.8
Dalmatia		68.3		57.3	29.7	29.0

Notes: The numbers are in thousands. SJOM stands for *Statistisches Jahrbuch der Oesterreichischen Monarchie*, DC stands for *Detail-Conscription*; "census" refers to the 1869 census.

Source: SJOM 1865, *Detail-Conscription*, Schimmer, "Mortalität und Vitalität"; K. k. Statistische Central-Commission. *Bevölkerung und Viehstand der im Reichsrathe vertretenen Königreiche und Länder, dann der Militärgrenze nach der Zählung vom 31. Dezember 1869*

and each province, a school-age cohort is therefore defined as consisting of seven birth cohorts (ages 5.0–12.0). In a few instances, however, where a comparison with a more narrowly defined school age (6.0–12.0) is useful, both estimates are provided.

The earlier Styrian and Bohemian examples suggested that the school administration could not be relied upon to capture the whole number of children that should have been going to school accurately, especially during the early years. Table 2.4 shows that for many provinces, this disparity between reports from different sources persisted well into the 1860s. The table also allows us to adjudicate between them. The year 1865 is very convenient for this kind of comparison because of the variety of sources that, by historical coincidence, produced an estimate of the desired statistic. Uniquely, the school administration alone generated two separate counts, listed in columns (v) and (vi). One, from the *Statistisches Jahrbuch* (SJOM), was part of a long-running series, compiled annually and based on reports submitted by teachers at the outset of the 1864-65 school year. It reflected what was in the school rosters in October 1864. The other reported figures came from the *Detail-Conscription*, a comprehensive and much more detailed survey of all elementary schools in Austria, which was conducted with the help of the Austrian Statistical Commission in spring 1865. My estimates of the total number of school-age children, shown in columns (i) to (iv), also come from two separate sources. One was the statistic of births and deaths, recorded by sex, age and province. The other source was the 1869 census, the best Austrian population count to that date and also the first one to record the year-by-year age structure of every single district in every single province.[50]

There are several observations to be made. First, the data in columns (v) and (vi), supplied by the school system, line up very close to each other: with the exception of Carniola and to a lesser extent Carinthia, where some schools failed to return their entries for the *Detail-Conscription*, the difference between them is under 2%. This is not a big surprise, given that the two sets of numbers ultimately came from the same source, the teachers. Secondly, these reported numbers are significantly lower than the estimates in columns (i) and (ii), which span seven years of age. But for several provinces, they are remarkably close to the estimates in columns (iii) and (iv), which are based on the 6.0–12.0 year-olds. Table 2.4 therefore hints, that in the face of the law's ambiguity, six-year schooling had emerged, by the 1860s, as the de-facto norm in many places.[51] A third important observation is that the estimates based on census and on birth and death records also mostly align, with differences below 4%, except in a few conspicuous cases. The census-based estimates merely sum up those age groups from the 1869 census, which would have been 5.0–12.0, resp. 6.0–12.0, years old in 1865. For the births-and-deaths estimate, I modelled the survival of each of the 1853–1859 birth cohorts to 1865, using the reported deaths by age and sex in each year and province. The difference between the two is net migration: the census-based estimate captures migrants at their destination as of 1869, while columns (i) and (iii) count migrants while they are still in their province of birth.

Migration does not lead to much disparity between the estimates, except in Lower Austria and in Bohemia.[52] The latter province was the most prolific source of migrants to the former, and specifically to Vienna. They were predominantly young men and many migrated very soon after they completed their elementary schooling. This is shown in greater detail in Table 2.5, which splits the Lower-Austrian and Viennese school-age children by gender.

---

[50] Some age structure information was also available in the 1857 census but only for certain specific age groups. See K. k. Ministerium des Innern. *Statistische Übersichten über die Bevölkerung und der Viehstand von Österreich. Nach der Zählung vom 31. October 1857*. Vienna. 1859.

[51] In Tyrol and Vorarlberg, on the other hand, the compulsion apparently went beyond six years. See Chapter 5 for a more detailed treatment of the Tyrolean situation.

[52] In the cases of Bukovina and Galicia, a further added issue is likely incomplete record of births in the early 1850s.

Table 2.5: Estimated size of school-age cohort in Lower Austria, 1865 (thousands of children)

		school-bound	ages 6.0–12.0		ages 5.0–12.0	
		from DC	from birth records	from census	from birth records	from census
Vienna	boys	24.8	26.1	36.6	31.2	41.0
	girls	23.1	26.0	28.1	31.1	32.6
Lower Austria	boys	69.1	72.9	77.6	86.2	91.0
(excl. Vienna)	girls	68.2	73.1	76.9	87.1	90.6
Whole province	boys	93.9	98.9	114.2	117.4	132.0
	girls	91.3	99.0	105.0	118.2	123.2

Note: Estimates "from birth records" take the size of each birth cohort between 1852 and 1859 and survive them to 1865 using death totals by age and gender in each year. The birth and death statistics are adjusted for birth tourism: numerous single women came from the Lower Austrian countryside to the Viennese Alservorstadt maternity hospital to give birth to their out-of-wedlock child and shortly thereafter left the city again. These children did not grow up and go to school in Vienna and are therefore subtracted from the total 1852–1859 Viennese births and added to the rest of the province. See Schimmer, "Anzeige von: Die Bewegung der Bevölkerung in Wien im Jahre 1874". Estimates "from census" take the census data for population by age as of 1869 and back out the 1865 school-age cohorts by adding in all deaths in the relevant birth cohorts that died between 1865 and 1869.

Source: Schimmer, "Mortalität und Vitalität"; Humpel *Statistische Tableaus über die Bewegung der Bevölkerung*; K. k. Statistische Central-Commission. *Bevölkerung und Viehstand der im Reichsrathe vertretenen Königreiche und Länder, dann der Militärgrenze nach der Zählung vom 31. Dezember 1869;* SJOM 1865–1870; Gemeinderath der Stadt Wien. *Die Gemeinde-Verwaltung der Reichshaupt- und Residenzstadt Wien in den Jahren 1867–1870*; Vienna. Städtische statistische Bureau. *Die Bewegung der Bevölkerung in Wien im Jahre 1875; Detail-Conscription.*

The table shows that the difference between the census-based estimate and the one based on births and deaths in Lower Austria is mostly accounted for by immigration to Vienna and that this immigration is almost entirely due to young boys arriving in the city between 1865 and 1869: in Spring 1865, Vienna had around 26100 boys who had been born there between 1853 and 1858 and lived to school age. The census-based estimate takes as a starting point 35700 boys of 1853–1858 birth, who were present in Vienna in December 1869, and adds in another 900 who died between 1865 and 1869 to back out the estimate of 36600 school age boys in 1865. It is significantly higher than the births-and-deaths estimate thanks to the 10500 youths who immigrated to Vienna between 1865 and 1869. Another 4700 male migrants arrived elsewhere in Lower Austria. For girls, the corresponding numbers are much lower: a net 2100 came to Vienna and 3800 to other places in the province. A comparison with the number of school-bound boys and girls, taken from the *Detail-Conscription*, indicates that the Viennese and Lower Austrian school authorities probably also settled on providing six years of schooling to

6.0–12.0 year olds, of which they had a relatively comprehensive count, especially of boys. Contrast these numbers with the data provided for Bohemia in Table 2.4: the estimated size of the school-age cohort based on births and deaths is larger than that generated from the census, which is consistent with emigration.

The main purpose of these considerations is to show that the two "demographic" estimates of the number of school age children can be reconciled even though they are based on two different sets of data. They corroborate each other and so furnish a relatively reliable way of estimating the school-age cohort size, which is a crucial component in assessing school coverage. In contrast to this, the teacher-based data fall short of capturing all school-age children in most cases and, as the example of Tyrol and Vorarlberg shows, are probably not always targeting the same age groups across provinces. The 1830 Styrian case also indicated an unequal treatment of boys and girls by the reporting teachers.

Since school-age children, and families with such children, are usually not very mobile (and certainly not as mobile as young men), an estimate based on births and deaths could provide a very accurate picture of the size of the school-age cohort in a particular place. It can pick up changes in fertility and mortality while also being independent of the age structure of the rest of the population. Unfortunately, it is also very demanding in terms of component data and for most of the 19th century, such detailed information is not available for all the Habsburg lands. The reporting methods that would yield fertility and mortality statistics for each province by age and gender in each year, as used in Tables 2.4 and 2.5, were not implemented until 1851 and even then at uneven speed across provinces.[53]

Consequently, the estimates that are used in subsequent analysis combine available data on population totals in various provinces with whatever information can be found regarding the age structure of those populations. The first component – total population figures for men and for women – were published quite frequently and can be reconstructed with reasonable consistency back to 1780s.[54] The second, age structure and its changes, is somewhat trickier to account for but luckily it changes relatively little across decades. The army tracked the data for various age groups of males: number of boys aged 1.0–13.0 between 1780 and 1801, number of boys aged 0–15.0 in 1827 and those aged 0–16.0 in 1830–1848. The school-age cohorts are a subset of these various age ranges and from the age structures supplied by la-

[53] See Bolognese-Leuchtenmüller. *Bevölkerungsentwicklung*, p. 69–89.

[54] See Kárníková. *Vývoj obyvatelstva v českých zemích, 1754–1914* and Helczmanovszki, Heimold. "Die Bevölkerung Österreich-Ungarns." For an example of the older literature see also Goehlert, J. Vincenz. "Die Ergebnisse der in Osterreich im vorigen Jahrhundert ausgefuhrten Volkszahlungen im Vergleiche mit jenen der neuern Zeit."

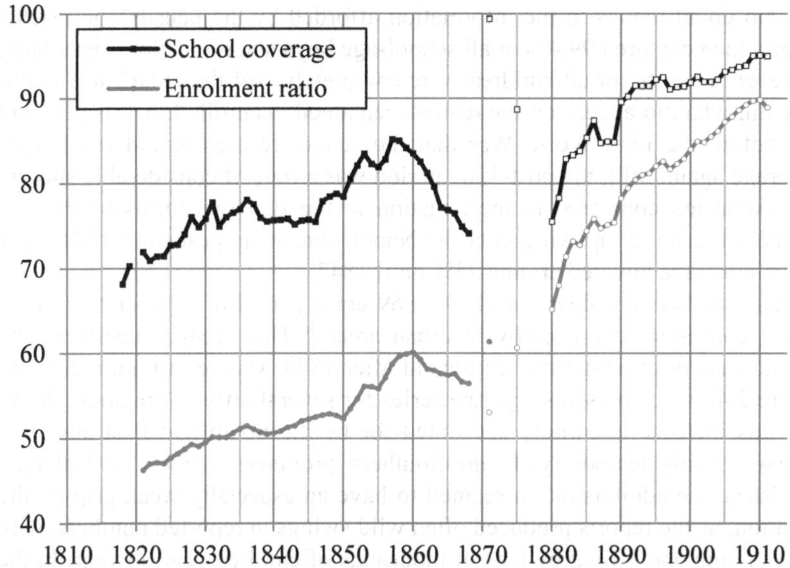

Figure 2.3: School coverage and enrolment ratio in Imperial Austria, 1818–1911
Note: School coverage is the percentage of school-age children who were reported as school-bound by teachers. Enrolment ratio is the percentage of school-age children enrolled in school. The definition of school age changed in 1869 from 5.0–12.0 to 6.0–14.0 years of age: the switch from black to white data markers in the series denotes this change in the definition of the denominator.
Sources: OeStA; TSOM 1830–1865; SJOM 1863–1881; Österreichische Statistik

te 19th century censuses, one can ascertain that they represented a fairly stable proportion of these.[55] I therefore take these ratios and apply them to late 18th and early 19th century data for boys of various age groups supplied by the military, to obtain an estimate of the number of 5.0–12.0 year old boys. To get a similar estimate of girls, I use the gender ratio prevailing in the general population. Estimates for the years between population counts, which were in fact quite frequent in the early 19th century (e.g. every three years between 1827 and 1846), are interpolations.

Figure 2.3 uses these estimates to calculate the percentage of school-age children covered by the school network and the percentage actually enrolled. The stark reality is that the school administration never quite managed to get a complete count of all the school age children. Their records reached peak precision in the 1871 school survey, conducted in the wake of the 1869 cen-

[55] For example, in Bohemia across all the censuses from 1857 to 1910, the 5.0–12.0 boys represented between 56.3% and 57.9% of the 1.0–13.0 age group. Among 0.0–16.0 year-olds, the 5.0–12.0 cohorts constituted between 42.4% and 43.5% over the same period. These are quite narrow ranges, indicating that the age structure did not shift much across time.

sus. No doubt thanks to the information afforded by the census, the teacher reports then captured 99.4% of all school-age boys and girls. Nine years later, however, a quarter of all children were completely "off the radar" and another tenth, who did appear on the rosters, remained unenrolled. It was not until just before the First World War that the school records would reach 95% coverage again. Still, the post-1869 period was a time of considerable success and expansion compared to the situation in the first two thirds of the 19th century. The initial upswing after the Napoleonic Wars peaked in 1831, after which coverage hovered around 75% until 1847.

Many authors consider the 1849–1869 era a period of appreciable school boom, concentrated especially in urban areas.[56] This seems consistent with the increase in coverage and enrolment after 1848, visible in Figure 2.3. But Figure 2.4, which presents separate series for several different regions, shows that this increase is entirely accounted for by the South and East and was, moreover, only temporary. In the Southern provinces, namely in Dalmatia and Istria, the administration seemed to have an especially weak grip on the situation, as the reports produced often wild swings in reported numbers, with tallies rising and falling by tens of thousands of children year on year. In the Czech provinces, corresponding to the modern-day Czech Republic, expansion petered out by 1836. The Alpine provinces, which roughly cover modern-day Austria, even recorded a mild decline of about seven percentage points after 1855.

The main reason for the slow progress was that many provincial supervisory bodies considered the aim of universal schooling effectively achieved and their job done within a decade or two of the Peace of Vienna. For example, already in 1825, the Lower Austrian school commission declared itself satisfied with the state of primary education in its jurisdiction, which sentiment it reaffirmed in 1845.[57] The level that they thereby deemed sufficient was one of six years of elementary schooling: although published statistics of school-bound children do not carry information on precise age distribution, it is conspicuous that the level of coverage in both the Czech and the Alpine provinces stabilized at around 83–85% of all school-age children, which corresponds almost exactly to six out of seven birth cohorts. The six-year norm emerged from lived, practical experience rather than the adherence to the strict letter of the law, which contained several stipulations suggesting longer school time, as discussed earlier. With the exception of Tyrol, the authorities eventually settled on six years and their coverage ended up focusing on 6.0–12.0 year olds. Even those that, for a period of time, aimed for broader coverage

---

[56] Ficker. *Bericht über österreichisches Unterrichtswesen*, p. 42; Engelbrecht. *Geschichte Des österreichischen Bildungswesens Vol. 4.* p. 110–111; Frank. *Die Österreichische Volksschule von 1848–1898.*

[57] Weiss. *Geschichte der österreichischen Volksschule 1792–1848. II. Band.* p. 781, 788.

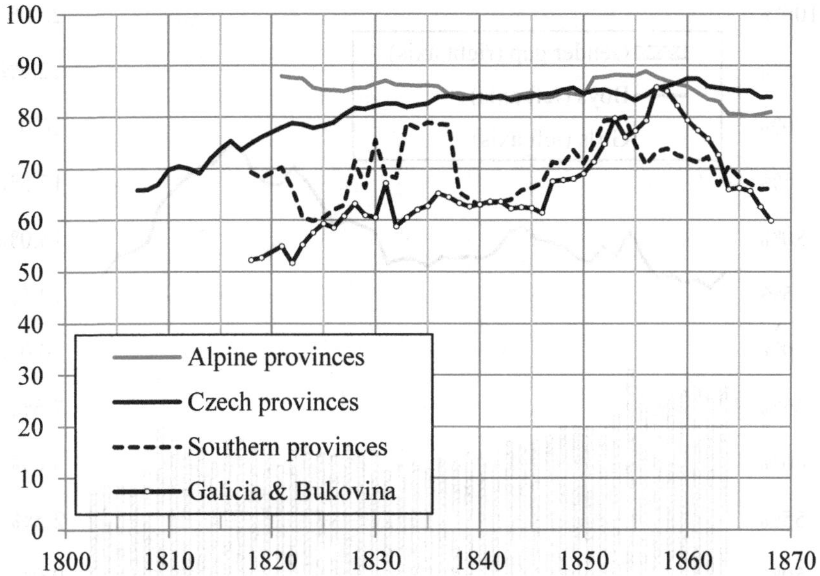

Figure 2.4: School coverage in various parts of Imperial Austria, 1807–1868
Note: School coverage is measured as the percentage of school-age children in an area bound to a particular school and included on official school lists (*Verzeichniss den schulfähigen*). Alpine provinces include Lower and Upper Austria, Salzburg, Styria, Carinthia, Tyrol and Vorarlberg. Czech provinces include Bohemia, Moravia and Austrian Silesia. Southern provinces cover Carniola, the Austrian Littoral and Dalmatia.
Source: OeStA; *Versuch*; *Darstellung*; TSOM 1830–1865, SJOM 1863–1870; for underlying demographic data see text.

(Lower and Upper Austria, even Carinthia) gave up by the 1860s.

Next to geographical differences, school coverage also varied across demographic categories, such as gender and nationality. The law made no significant distinction between boys and girls in defining school age, although it was not expected that girls would advance to the higher classes of the major schools. It allowed for the creation of girl schools (*Mädchenschule*) in larger cities, where pupil numbers were high enough to justify a separate school for each gender. But it was understood that most schools, especially rural ones, would be co-educational, in which case the law merely required that boys and girls sit in separate desks. During the initial phase of school expansion, in the 1780s, Joseph II briefly entertained the idea of charging girls double the tuition fee asked of boys but his Education Commission chairman Gerhart van Swieten persuaded him to abandon the plan.[58] Thus, as far as the blueprint

[58] His clinching argument was that today's girls were tomorrow's mothers and since mothers were also every child's first source of religious instruction, the whole purpose of the school reform to fashion "good Christians" would be undermined, if girls were in any way

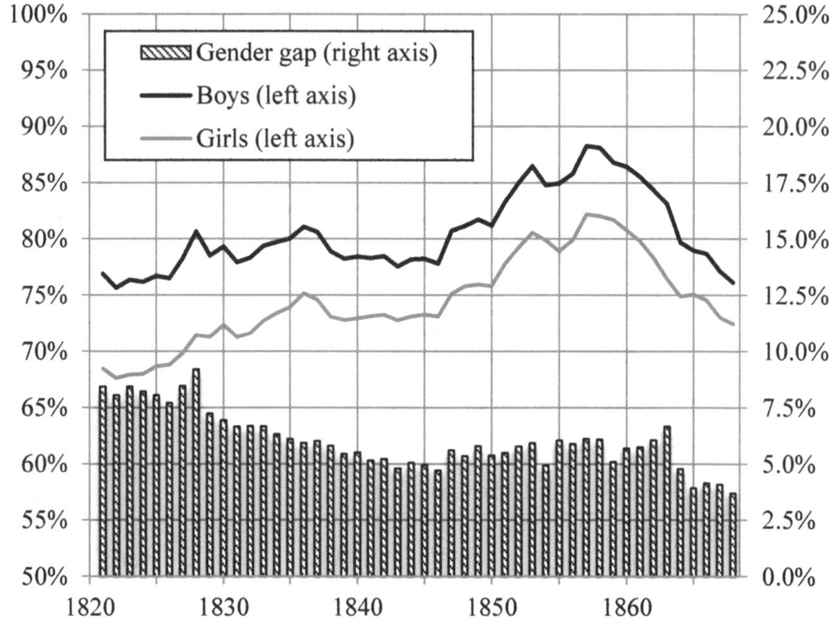

Figure 2.5: Difference in school coverage of girls and boys, 1821–1868
Source: See note on sources under Figure 2.4.

was concerned, the legislation granted boys and girls access to elementary education on equal terms and imposed the same obligations from the start.

This did not always translate to equal treatment on the ground. Disparities between boys and girls, such as are observed in enrolment and attendance, are usually laid at the feet of the parents, who, it is argued, made greater use of girls' labour at home and generally valued women's education less than men's. Yet, the difference in school coverage, as illustrated in Figure 2.5, cannot be so easily blamed on them. The duty to compile the list of school-bound children rested on the shoulders of teachers or local school supervisors and they were expected to both visit each household with school-age children and also consult the parish baptismal records to ensure no one was omitted. The local priest had to sign off on the list as a guarantee of its completeness. Article 307 emphasized that children living in remote areas, such as mountainous pastures, must not be left out of schooling. These checks were written into the law precisely as an antidote to some parents' inclination to deny and hide a child or two and so avoid both paying for tuition and forfeiting the children's potential earnings or labour. The gender gap in coverage observed in Figure 2.5 is therefore something, in which the teachers, as the initial com-

left behind or disadvantaged. See Wangermann. *Aufklärung und staatsbürgerliche Erziehung*, p. 46.

pilers of the lists, must have been at least to some extent complicit: whether from capacity constraints, of his own initiative or to appease parents, they left out some school-age girls in their area from the list. The gender gap reached 9.2% in 1828 and as schools expanded, it (usually) gradually closed. With the overall coverage of girls ranging from 68% to 82%, this was not a huge shortfall but, as will become clear in further chapters, it formed one of many junctures at which girls found themselves at some disadvantage, and their cumulative effect proved quite large. In its early phases, school expansion was accompanied by a considerable gender gap in coverage in all provinces. The earliest data that exist for Bohemia suggest that in 1808, girls had 10.6 percentage points lower coverage than boys. This is similar to the gap in Styria in 1813 (9.2 p.p.) or Dalmatia in 1831 (12.6 p.p.) or in Galicia and Bukovina as late as 1863 (14.1 p.p.). Where full coverage was achieved, the gap was eliminated, but in sparsely schooled provinces pockets of great disparity persisted throughout the 19th century: the Dalmatian school district of Šibenik counted more than twice as many school-bound boys as girls in 1865 and, despite achieving a nearly complete count of both in 1871, it fell back to an almost 3:1 ratio by 1880.[59]

As for the intersection between education and the rising nationalism, so characteristic of the 19th century Austro-Hungarian Empire, the most fraught fault line ran between the German speakers and the rest. By the late 18th century, German had an unambiguous advantage over other, mostly Slavic, languages of the monarchy as an effective *lingua franca* of arts and sciences, as well as public administration and law. So it was, understandably, in schooling. The dominance of German was enforced from the top. At the universities, non-German languages could be taught as subjects of linguistic study but were not used for instruction. Secondary education was entirely Germanized, so that by the end of the 1780s, Czech, for example, disappeared from Austrian *Gymnasia* for almost 70 years.[60] The entrance exam was also in German, so it was practically impossible to get in from a non-German primary school. Among those, the major schools were conceived as potential conduits of German culture and language: in non-German areas, the first grade could be conducted in the local language but second grade would be mixed and higher

[59] K. k. Statistische Central-Commission. *Detail-Conscription der Volksschulen in den im Reichsrathe vertretenen Königreichen und Ländern nach dem Stande vom Ende des Schuljahres 1865.*; –. *Statistik der öffentlichen und Privat-Volksschulen in den im Reichsrathe vertretenen Königreichen und Länder. Nach den von den Bezirks-Schulbehörden für das Schuljahr 1870–1871 vorgelegten Erhebungen bearbeitet.*; –. *Statistisches Jahrbuch für das Jahr 1880 – V. Heft: Volksschulen. Summarische Übersicht sämmtlicher Lehranstalten.*

[60] The decree imposing German as the sole language of instruction on all Austrian secondary schools was issued by Joseph II in 1781. See Šafránek. *Školy české. I. svazek*, p. 155; Kuzmin. *Vývoj školství a vzdělání v Československu*, p. 61.

grades were all in German. Trivial schools, in contrast, could keep teaching in Italian or in Slavic languages, as they were clearly not going to serve as anyone's springboard for further study.[61] Abbot Felbiger, too, wrote his textbooks, lesson plans and the teaching manual in German and the teacher seminaries operated in German. Admittedly, textbooks were translated into other languages remarkably quickly and before long prominent pedagogues and supporters of schooling also arose among the non-German nations.[62] But the head start of the German language nonetheless contributed to a somewhat faster adoption of the new school system and a more extensive school coverage in German-speaking areas. This is clearly visible in Figure 2.4, where the mostly Slav-inhabited Southern and Eastern areas lagged behind the Alpine provinces throughout the period. To an extent, similar dynamic operated within ethnically mixed provinces, such as Bohemia: in 1787, for example, the areas with the lowest coverage were the administrative regions (*Kreise*) centered on Hradec Královė (40.6%), Chrudim (42.7%) and Čáslav (42.9%), all of which had a significant Czech-speaking majority.[63] Still, the overall difference between the German-speaking and Czech-speaking areas was not large – about seven percentage points – and by the late 1820s it disappeared completely, as the whole province moved closer to full coverage.

The ethnic divisions also informed debates about the language of instruction. Here the conditions faced by different nationalities could vary markedly. Figures 2.6–2.8 describe the situation in three broad areas, where the German element coexisted with others: Czechs, South Slavs and Italians. In all three areas, the non-German populations were initially served to a lesser or greater degree by schools that were bilingual, so that many non-German children were exposed to the dominant language.

In Figure 2.6, the Czech provinces of Bohemia, Moravia and Silesia provide a revealing illustration of how the clash over the language of instruction unfolded. German schools, traced out by the plain black curve, increased steadily and continuously. The other two series are quite volatile up until about 1827, moving conspicuously in an almost perfectly opposite direction to each other. It is as if about half of the non-German schools kept switching between Czech and bilingual teaching almost every other year. Without knowing the history of each individual school, it is impossible to definitively determine what exactly happened but the most plausible explanation is that these wild fluctuations reflect a kind of deliberate misreporting, arising from the power play between teachers and the authorities. The fluctuating schools

---

[61] Kuzmin. *Vývoj školství a vzdělání v Československu*, p. 62;

[62] Among the more prominent names one could cite a Chief Supervisor of Austrian schools, Jožef Spendou, who was a Slovenian, or Aleš Vincenc Pařízek, mentioned earlier, who was a Czech.

[63] Calculated using school data cited in Riegger. *Materialien zur alten und neuen Statistik von Böhmen. VII. Heft.* Leipzig and Prague: Kaspar Widtmann, 1788. p. 3–52.

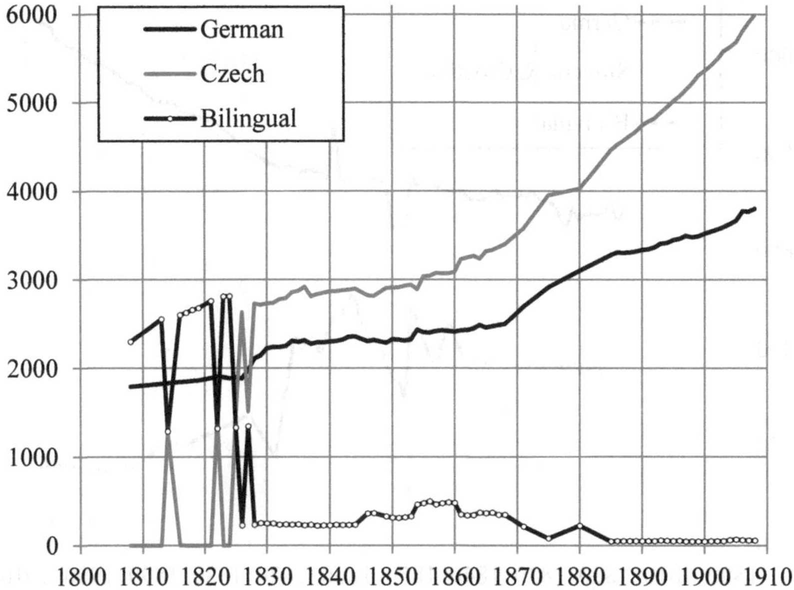

Figure 2.6: Number of schools by language of instruction in the Czech lands, 1808–1908
Source: OeStA; *Versuch*; *Darstellung*; TSOM 1830–1865, SJOM 1863–1870

were almost certainly ones that operated in ethnically Czech areas. From the late 18th century onwards, they continued to be pressured by the government to use German in the classroom, especially in the higher grades.[64] The resistance, put up by the emergent Czech nationalism, was somewhat stronger in Bohemia, which also happens to be where all the switching between Czech and bilingual in Figure 2.6 comes from; all non-German schools in Moravia and Silesia were consistently reported as bilingual. What all this seems to add up to is a situation in which the authorities repeatedly tried to lean on the schools to introduce German in a context where schools operating in the majority Czech areas were ever so strongly trending towards teaching purely in Czech. In some years, the government pushed harder and the Czech teachers either made cosmetic changes to the curriculum or may have just reported their schools bilingual but clearly none of this was permanent because they immediately reverted to Czech whenever the pressure eased. By the late 1820s, the government gave up and accepted the realities: from 1826 onwards, the fluctuations disappeared from the Bohemian record, and in 1828, 98% of Moravian and Silesian schools previously recorded as bilingual switched definitively to the purely Czech column and never looked back. By

[64] See Šafránek, *Školy české I. svazek*, p. 170; Veselá. *Vývoj české školy a učitelského vzdělávání*, p.12; Helfert. *Die österreichische Volksschule I. Band*, p. 472.

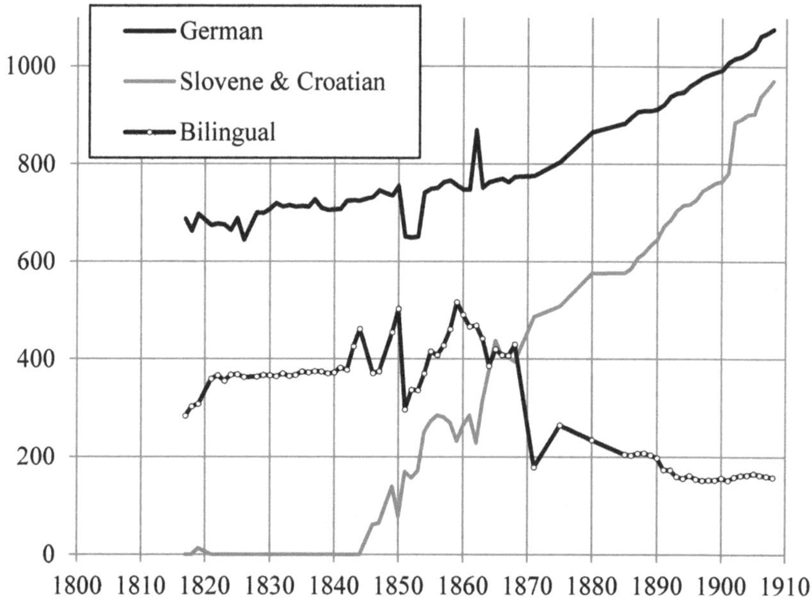

Figure 2.7: Number of schools by language of instruction in Carinthia, Styria, Carniola and the Austrian Littoral, 1817–1908
Source: OeStA; *Versuch*; *Darstellung*; TSOM 1830–1865, SJOM 1863–1870

the 1830s, the exposure of Czech pupils to German in elementary education, especially in the countryside, was relatively limited and bilingual schools never exceeded 10% of the total again. Still, while the Czech schools outnumbered German ones in absolute terms, purely German schools accounted for slightly above 40% of all schools, giving the Germans, who formed 34-36% of the total population,[65] an advantage in access: about 160 school-age children per German school as compared to 210 Czech school-age children per Czech school.[66]

The Czechs certainly fared better than the Slovenes and the Croats in the South (Figure 2.7). Slovenes made up 90% of the population of Carniola and a substantial minority in Styria and Carinthia. Together with Croats and Serbs, South Slavs also formed a majority in the Austrian Littoral. In Carinthia, Slovenian was not even considered a viable language of instruction.[67] Even if it were, the prevailing opinion in high places was that only

[65] Kořalka, Jiří. *Češi v Habsburské říši a v Evropě 1815–1914*, p. 83; TSOM 1851.

[66] *Detail-Conscription* shows that 95% of German pupils and 93% of all Czech pupils attended a school teaching in their mother tongue.

[67] Domej. "Slowenisch als Unterrichtssprache in der Frühzeit des Kärntner Pflichtschulwesens (1774–1848)", p. 334.

German was the proper language of education. Slovenian textbooks were non-existent.[68] This started to change in the early 19th century, when the diocese of Seckau in Styria concluded that bilingual Slovene-German textbooks might improve school attendance in Slovene areas and the Lavantine bishop, Anton Slomšek, himself a Slovene, undertook to write some such textbooks himself.[69] Until 1844, there was, according to the official record, no purely Slovenian or Croatian school in the southern provinces but even mixed German-Slovene schools were signs of progress, compared to the situation before 1800. The strong upward trend in Slavic schools after 1844 shows that the outcome of the language issue was the same as in the Czech case: instruction in one's mother tongue won out over the pro-German intentions of the government. But the material advantage of German schools persisted. While local access varied considerably, on average there were about 195 school-age children per German school but about 380 Slavic school-age children per bilingual or, later, Slovene or Croatian school. In spite of the impressive, practically uninterrupted boom in Slavic schools in the South from 1840s onwards, the gap in access between Germans and Slavs did not disappear even by the First World War.

The Italian situation presents a completely different experience yet again: the Italians were the dominant cultural force in the Austrian Littoral (albeit not the most numerous ethnicity) and a sizeable minority in Tyrol. In Figure 2.8, the big drop in bilingual schools and the corresponding increase in Italian schools in 1825 suggest that the Italians had faced a similar situation as the Czechs and secured for themselves a similar outcome. After 1825, Italian schooling embarked on four decades of mostly robust growth. By the early 1850s, the access to school for Italian and German school children was comparable: about 75 per school. The decline in Italian schooling in the second half of the 19th century is entirely accounted for by developments in Tyrol, which was becoming a scene of heated ethnic strife. The conflict inevitably spilled over into education but by the late 19th century its focus lay primarily in the ongoing and increasingly animated political debate about the establishment of an Italian university.[70] Matters of elementary schooling seemed to have been satisfactorily addressed in 1892 and 1902 through laws granting the Italian minority in Tyrol extensive autonomy over schooling. Yet, as the record shows, the number of Italian schools was in almost continuous decline from 1880 onward.[71]

---

[68] Weiss. *Geschichte der oesterreichische Volksschule, 1792 – 1848. II. Band*, p. 814.

[69] Ibid. p. 829–830.

[70] Engelbrecht. *Geschichte Des österreichischen Bildungswesens Vol. 4.* p. 315–320.

[71] It must be noted that the Tyrolean data were not entirely consistent throughout this period: an example of that is the sudden change in the number of Italian schools between 1871, 1875 and 1880. Even for 1865, different source cite different numbers: for 1865 the *Detail-Conscription* reports 483 Italian schools in Tyrol, while the *Statistisches Jahrbuch* puts the

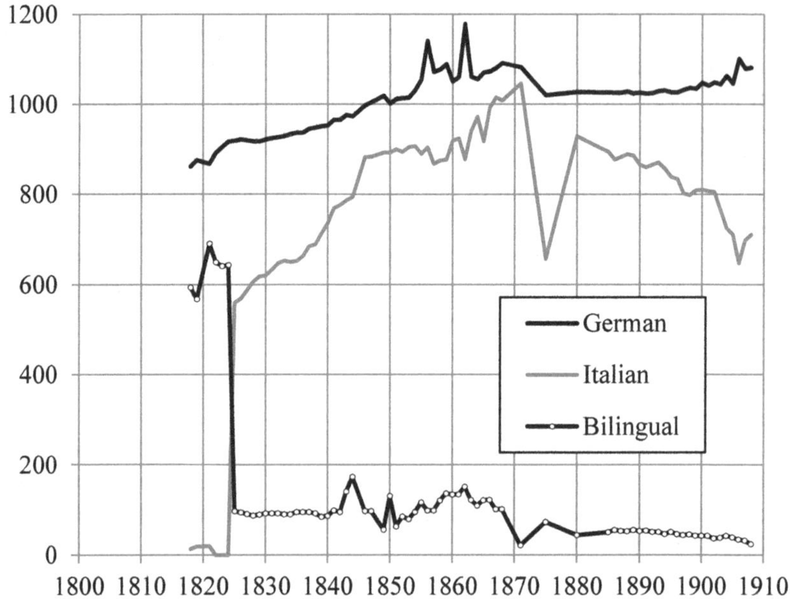

Figure 2.8: Number of schools by language of instruction in Tyrol, Vorarlberg, the Austrian Littoral and Dalmatia, 1818–1908
Source: OeStA; *Versuch*; *Darstellung*; TSOM 1830–1865, SJOM 1863–1870

Was elementary schooling overall a force for Germanization? For the late 18th and early 19th century, the official decrees, promoting or even mandating German as the language of instruction, e.g. at major schools, provide rather unambiguous evidence in the affirmative. Austrian historiography preferred to stress that such efforts were driven by nothing more than an understandable desire for efficiency of administration, a smoother centralization.[72] Such defense probably offered scarce comfort to the Slavic pupils who were on the receiving end of this policy, attending a school that undercut their learning effort by a deliberate instruction in a second language instead of their mother tongue. Equally misplaced, however, were the shrill cries and overwrought accusations that the policy was aimed at the complete elimination of national

total at 868. Similar discrepancy showed up in German schools also. Curiously enough, such discrepancies do not appear in the pupil numbers, so it is possible that the decline in the number of schools was a result of just consolidation. But in Tyrol, the number of Italian schools declined from a peak of 894 in 1868 to just 452 in 1906 – that is rather too much consolidation to take place in the context, no less, of continuous population growth.

[72] Brezinka. "Učitelské vzdělávání mezi státem a církví – rakouský příklad v letech 1774–1869", p. 30; Helfert. *Die österreichische Volksschule*, p. 472.

consciousness and linguistic identity of the non-German nationalities.[73] Clearly, schools with Slavic and other languages of instruction were quite numerous and growing, putting a lie to such claim, even if the figures did offer several indications that the language question continued to be a political battleground. But whatever the government's supposed endgame, the fight proved very quickly unwinnable, as even languages with the weakest of literary traditions (such as Slovenian) were making steady inroads into schools. In terms of ease of access, measured by the cited numbers on pupils per school among Germans and non-Germans, the German language continued to enjoy certain undue privilege, even after the authorities relented in their official promotion of it. As non-German schooling increased, the German-speaking Austrians did not always view this erosion of their cultural primacy with equanimity. In Bohemia, lest the spirit of the Czech national resurgence get out of hand, the obligation of Czech town schools to use German as the language of instruction was restated in 1851.[74] Both the Italian and the Slovene cases show that after a promising upswing in the late 1840s, non-German schooling ran into some headwinds of opposition in the second half of the 1850s, around the time of the Concordat of 1855. It was not until the 1860s that the expansion of non-German education resumed. The gradual erosion of the German advantage continued with the rapid abandonment of bilingual schools and the accompanying explosion particularly of Slavic-language schools after the 1869 liberal reform. Clearly, bilingual instruction, where it had existed as a way to bring the fruits of German culture to the Slavs and not as a purely practical expedient for teaching ethnically mixed populations, had not been the nationalities' first choice and they opted for teaching in their own language wherever and whenever they got the chance.

As a case study, the diocese of České Budějovice in southern Bohemia offers a convenient testing ground to consider the interaction of all these diverse factors – the gender difference, the nationalities question, the deficiency in coverage – in close range. In terms of schooling, České Budějovice was traditionally the least developed diocese in the most developed province. The other three Bohemian dioceses had a denser school network and were more industrialized and more urbanized. It was an ethnically mixed region with the German-speaking quarter of the population living mostly in the mountainous border regions and in larger towns while the remaining three quarters, who were Czech speakers, lived in the rural lowlands.

By the early 1860s, the school coverage of the diocese was complete, geographically speaking. Trajer's comprehensive survey of all the churches, parishes and vicariates of the diocese, published in 1862, has every village

[73] See, for example, Šafránek. *Školy české I. svazek*, p. 159, 267.

[74] Frank, Ferdinand. *Die Österreichische Volksschule von 1848–1898*. p. 30.

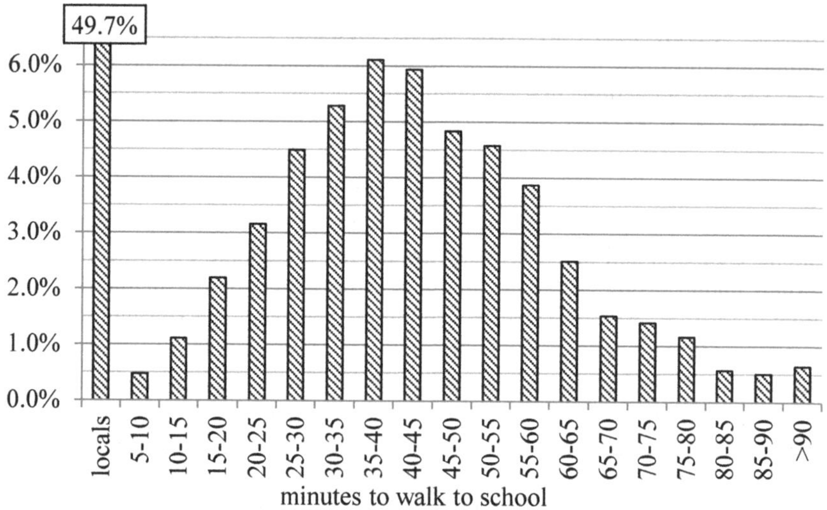

Figure 2.9: Distribution of pupils by time required to walk to school, 1862
Note: Pupils living in a village with a school are coded as "locals". Data pertain to schools in the diocese of České Budějovice.
Source: Trajer, *Historisch-statistische Beschreibung*; www.mapy.cz.

assigned (*eingeschult*) to a particular school.[75] All children, wherever they lived, should at least theoretically have been expected to have appeared on a teacher's list somewhere. In 1865, the total number of school-bound children reported for the diocese represented about 87% of boys and 84% of girls of school age (i.e. 5.0 to 12.0 years). Apparently, the shortfall to full coverage – the missing 13%, resp. 16% – were omitted 5-year-olds: just like many other places in the empire, the diocese of České Budějovice settled on a six-year schooling, starting at age 6.

Figure 2.9 takes the detailed information on catchment areas of all schools to illustrate what that full geographic coverage meant practically. Using the historical maps from the 2nd military survey of the Austrian army, conducted in 1836–1852,[76] it is possible to reconstruct the paths that the south-Bohemian children took to their schools in the 1860s and thus calculate the distances they had to walk and the time it roughly took them. Almost half (49.7%) of all children were bound to a school right in their own village and in Figure 2.9 they are dubbed "locals" and coded as needing under 5 minutes to get there. The rest had longer treks to undertake and about 8% of the children had more than an hour to walk to school. Since Joseph II's 1784 decree, the official regulation demanded that children should not generally walk more

[75] Trajer, Johann. *Historisch-statistische Beschreibung der Diöcese Budweis.*
[76] It is available as one of the map underlays at www.mapy.cz.

than 30 minutes to school but in this south Bohemian bishopric – an area with decent, above-average school coverage – this still was not the case for about 38% of the children eight decades later. In fact, the region counted 15 villages with more than 600 inhabitants, whose children walked 2 km or more to a school in a different village. These places, given their size, clearly had enough school-age children to be obliged to build their own school, in line with the regulation, but for whatever reason they did not. Across the diocese, about one sixth of all communities of 500 inhabitants or more did not have their own school.

Not surprisingly, the distance to school had measurable impact on enrolment. Table 2.6 analyses this impact in the context of a weighted OLS regression. The dependent variable is the enrolment ratio, or the proportion of children aged 5.0–12.0 who were reported to be enrolled in the 1865 school census in each school. To isolate the effect that distance had on enrolment, I control for several potentially influential measures of school quality, such as the tuition fee, the size of school (measured by the number of staff) or whether or not the school was a civic school (*Bürgerschule*). The unit of observation is the school and each is weighted by the number of school-age children living in its precinct in order to avoid a disproportionate influence of a few tiny outlier schools. The surrounding population is split into seven distance bins, of which six enter into the regression, the seventh one (those living farther than 5.5 km from the school) being left out as the default category.

The regression results in columns (i) and (ii) confirm that the enrolment ratio was likely to be higher the closer to school the children lived. Using the coefficients in column (i), if one considered a regular trivial school with an annual tuition fee of 2 fl., then the predicted enrolment ratio would be 0.559 + 0.005×2 + 0.269 = 0.838 for school-age children living within 0.5 km of the school, i.e. about 83.8% of such local children be would be enrolled. In contrast, only 56.9% would be enrolled among those living more than 5.5 km from the school. Between these end points, enrolment declined with distance, other things held equal. Beyond 2.5 km, the impact is already over eight percentage points and beyond 3.5 km it almost did not matter what the distance was exactly, as the enrolment ratio was close to or below 60%.

In column (ii), two more variables are added. The first one is an indicator variable equal to 1 if the language of instruction in a school was German. One can hypothesize that a German school would be more eagerly attended, given that literacy in German granted one access to a wider range of resources – books, manuals, official documents – than would have been the case for Czech at this time. It would also facilitate progress to a secondary school or a university, where German was still the dominant language. At the same time, teaching in German could discourage enrolment among Czech speakers, wherever they happened to be bound to such a school. More generally, enrolment may be lower among children who were bound to a school

Table 2.6: Determinants of enrolment in the diocese of České Budějovice: Results of a weighted OLS regression

	(i)	(ii)	(iii)
1(civic school)	0.123*	0.104*	
	[0.041]	[0.044]	
Number of teachers	0.000	0.001	
	[0.003]	[0.003]	
Tuition fee	0.005	0.003	
	[0.010]	[0.013]	
1(German school)		0.035	
		[0.025]	
1(L2-learner)		-0.068	-0.172*
		[0.053]	[0.086]
Fraction of population living…			
…within 0.5 km from school	0.269*	0.279*	
	[0.103]	[0.101]	
…0.5-1.5 km from school	0.261*	0.261*	
	[0.109]	[0.107]	
…1.5-2.5 km from school	0.230*	0.219*	
	[0.105]	[0.105]	
…2.5-3.5 km from school	0.186	0.189	
	[0.109]	[0.107]	
…3.5-4.5 km from school	-0.033	0.004	
	[0.131]	[0.127]	
…4.5-5.5 km from school	0.068	0.057	
	[0.103]	[0.102]	
Average distance to school			-0.018
			[0.061]
Constant	0.559	0.556	0.838
	[0.108]	[0.108]	[0.066]
N	732	792	2x66
Adjusted R^2	0.181	0.176	0.211
Fixed effects	Vicariate	Vicariate	School

Note: Dependent variable is the proportion enrolled among 5.0–12.0 year-olds. Standard errors are cited in squared brackets. Star (*) denotes statistical significance at 5% level.

that did not teach in their mother tongue and in the diocese of České Budějovice, there were a few cases of both Czechs assigned to a German school and of Germans assigned to a Czech school. For schools that drew pupils both from Czech and German villages, I construct two separate enrolment ratios – one for the German children and one for Czech children.[77] Such schools therefore generate two observations each. Logically, whatever the language of instruction, one of the ethnic groups was not learning in its mo-

[77] The source for my data (Trajer, *Historisch-statistische Beschreibung*) specifies which villages were assigned to which school and whether a village was Czech, German or mixed.

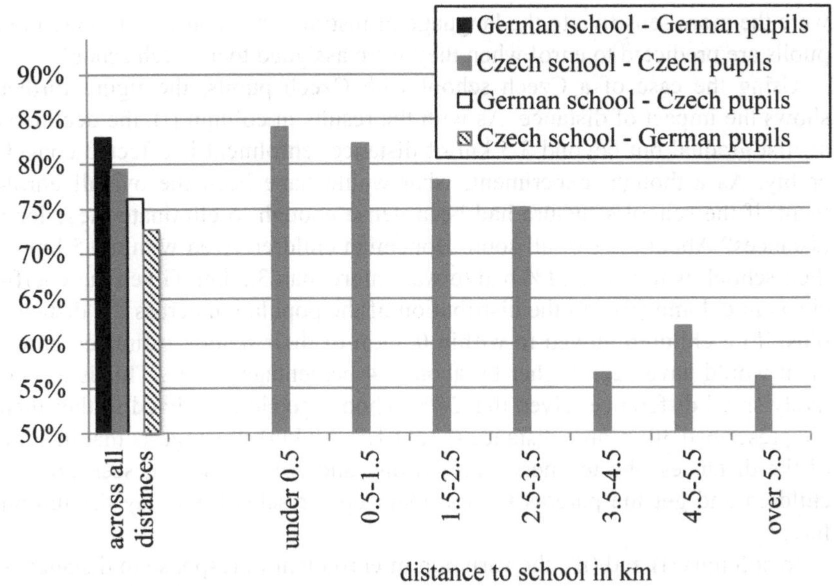

Figure 2.10: Imputed percentage of 5.0–12.0 year-olds enrolled by type of school and distance to school, 1862

Note: The imputation assumes a trivial school with 2 fl of annual tuition (the number of teachers does not make a material difference given the low coefficient).

Source: Table 2.6 for coefficients; Trajer, *Historisch-statistische Beschreibung* for the ethnic and distance distribution of the population.

ther tongue, which could discourage them from enrolling. This is why an indicator variable for L2-learners is included in column (ii). L2 is the standard linguistic notation for a person's second language (L1 being reserved for the mother tongue). L2-learners are therefore pupils who receive instruction in their second language.

The coefficients on distance-related variables in column (ii) are not markedly different from those in column (i). The addition of the ethno-linguistic variables does not substantially change the picture, except for making the decline of enrolment due to distance slightly steeper. The coefficients on German schools and L2-learners are relatively small and not statistically significant. Figure 2.10 uses all these coefficients to illustrate the relative impact of the geographic and the ethnic factors. Assuming a trivial school with 2 fl of annual tuition, Figure 2.10 depicts the predicted enrolment ratio in schools of various types and for children living in various distances from it. The regression predicts the highest overall enrolment of 82.9% for German pupils bound to a German school, followed by Czech pupils assigned to a Czech school. Of the two nationalities, it was apparently the Germans who were the more sensitive to the language of instruction, as only 72.6% German pupils are predicted to enrol when they were assigned to a Czech school.

Using the case of a Czech school with Czech pupils, the figure further shows the impact of distance. As with the results in column (i), the decline is at first gradual but beyond 3.5 km of distance, enrolment is affected considerably. As a thought experiment, what would have been the overall enrolment, if the school structure had been dense enough to eliminate these long distances? About 52% of all south Bohemian children lived within 0.5 km of their school, while only 11% had to walk more than 3.5 km. Given the coefficients in column (ii) and the distribution of the population across the distance bins, if all children moved to within 0.5 km of their school, estimated enrolment would have been higher by about 5.4 percentage points. This is a relatively small difference, given that 38% school-age children lived farther than the prescribed 30-minute distance (about 1.8–2.0 km). It suggests that in spite of the distances, the teachers were willing and able to go out, seek out the children and get the parents to sign them up for school and pay the tuition fees.[78]

In columns (i) and (ii), the variation in enrolment in response to distance is more pronounced than the variation across nationalities. This is partly because 90% of schools were by this time ethnically uniform, with no L2-learners. Most people of either nationality enjoyed (or suffered from) comparable access to schooling. The difference in school coverage between Czechs and Germans was negligible, as it was for enrolment. About 52% of German children and 50% of Czech children went to school locally and those who had to cross the fields, whether Czechs or Germans, faced, on average, a 45-minute walk of 2.6 km. The Germans walked to somewhat better funded and better-staffed schools, as Chapter 6 documents, but they did not live closer to them.

In those places where the two nationalities could not be easily separated into homogenous blocs, each with its own school, such equality of access was harder to achieve. They included both towns with mixed populations as well as remote, sparsely settled areas where numerous small Czech and German hamlets were referred to the same school. In these instances, whatever the language of instruction, children of one or the other nationality would be at a disadvantage as L2-learners. Some 69 out of 732 schools drew pupils both from Czech-speaking and German-speaking villages and for 66 out of those we have sufficiently detailed data to make direct comparisons. As Table 2.7 shows, in these ethnically mixed areas, the schools were usually somewhat closer to the German pupils and, in response, the Germans attained a higher enrolment than the Czechs. Most of these Czech-German differences, howev-

[78] Note that enrolmen is not the same as attendance: as will become apparent in Chapter 5, attendance was somewhat more sensitive to distance.

Table 2.7: Paired t-tests for differences between Czechs and Germans in ethnically mixed schools

	Czechs	Germans	t-statistic	p-value
Distance to school (km)	1.48	1.40	0.52	0.61
Enrolment ratio (%)	71.5	77.8	-0.63	0.53
	L1-learners	L2-learners		
Distance to school (km)	1.22	1.65	-2.81	0.01
Enrolment ratio (%)	83.5	65.8	1.79	0.08

Note: Based on data for 66 mixed schools in the diocese of České Budějovice.
Source: Trajer, *Historisch-statistische Beschreibung*; www.mapy.cz.

er, were not large and systematic enough to be statistically significant. The real dividing line ran between L1-learners and L2-learners, i.e. local majorities and local minorities. The main reason why some children became L2-learners was logistical: the only school within any workable distance happened to teach in the other language.

The two factors reinforced each other in deterring enrolment of these minority pupils: the school was farther for them and on top of that taught in the "wrong" language. Column (iii) in Table 2.6 disentangles the impact of these two forces. The 66 school fixed effects which are included in the regression control for all other aspects of the school quality: the only sources of variation between local majority and minority pupils were the distance they had to walk to school and their L1, resp. L2, status. The coefficients suggest that the "wrong" language of instruction was the bigger source of discouragement. The coefficient on average distance to school indicates a negative effect of distance that is smaller but roughly the same order of magnitude as the impact observed in column (ii): increasing the distance by, say, 3km reduces predicted enrolment by 5.4 percentage points in column (iii) versus 9 percentage points (= |0.279 – 0.189|) in column (ii). But it is not statistically significant for the subset of the 66 ethnically mixed schools. The impact of the L2 status, on the other hand, was sizable: -17.2 percentage points. As such it accounts for almost the whole enrolment gap between L1 and L2 pupils observed in Table 2.7. What the contrast between columns (ii) and (iii) in Table 2.6 suggests is that for the overwhelming majority of south Bohemian children, long distance to school was the more potent disincentive to enrolment. But that was because their assigned school taught in their mother tongue. Wherever the L2 status appeared in the picture, its negative impact uniformly depressed enrolment for all minority pupils near and far, with distance exerting only minor effect on the margin. The school district supervisors who were responsible for ensuring as full a school coverage and as complete an enrolment as possible probably viewed such ethnic misallocations as the lesser of two evils: true, some children were bound to a school with the "wrong" language of instruction but low enrolment was surely better than no enrolment at all. Still, this argument cannot conceal that such practice was a patch, not a solution.

The diocese of České Budějovice was just one among more than thirty bishoprics spanning Imperial Austria. Here, these patches were few and far in between. But in numerous areas across Silesia or in the South Slavic provinces, the same issues played out over much larger areas and populations, where the school network was much thinner than in České Budějovice. The south-Bohemian example serves to show that a shortfall in access to schooling existed even when, by all outward appearances – including the presence of a school, a comprehensive list of school-bound children, a seemingly sufficient total number of teachers – the school coverage looked adequate.

Let us take stock of the available evidence on the expansion of schools in the century that followed Maria Theresa's reform. There were three periods of expansion, corresponding roughly to the 1780s, the 1820s and the 1850s. The impulse for the first of these came from Joseph II and it inspired the formulation of a few policy guidelines that ended up becoming long-standing features of the whole system, namely financing through school patronage. The second was made possible thanks to the end of the Napoleonic Wars and entailed the extension of the recently reformed school system to the many territories recovered by the Habsburgs through the Treaty of Vienna. The last was a consequence of the political changes of 1848 and was driven by the sudden but (as it turned out) somewhat temporary growth in the Eastern provinces. Part of this expansion was also led by mostly urban demand for a more extensive and sophisticated elementary education. In between these bursts of expansion, the school network either stagnated or grew at a leisurely pace. While the French Wars offer a certain alibi to the policy makers for the first lull in school expansion, the slow growth of the 1830s and 1840s occurred at a time of peace and relative political stability – an ideal context for a demanding, large-scale public project, which the expansion of schooling certainly was. Yet, in some respects, such as in the case of the major schools, the Education Commission itself was putting a brake on further expansion, while on several occasions, not least in the late 1820s, it expressed the opinion that the school network was already sufficient. The statistical reconstruction undertaken in this chapter offers an explanation of why the commissioners may have come to this conviction: they consistently underestimated how many more schools and teachers were actually needed and overestimated the share of school-age children actually enrolled. Their channels of data collection were flawed by design and better sources were hard to come by.

Corrected measures reveal that the school network was thinner on the ground and its expansion slower than has hitherto been believed. Taking Imperial Austria (later known as Cisleithania) as a whole, before 1870 the enrolment ratio never exceeded 60% among 5.0–12.0 year-olds and school coverage fluctuated between 75% and 85% from late 1820s until Hasner's liberal reform of 1869. Quite apart from the various omissions and undercounts afflicting the official statistics, even accurate reports on existing schools hid numerous deficiencies in provision, such as when sparse school network required pupils to traverse long distances to school. Until the school census of 1865, the government reports offered no detail on the character of individual schools, so that well-run three-grade parish schools were thrown in with intermittent branch schools, served by an itinerant teaching assistant one day per week, under the same heading of *Trivialschule*. The uniformity of schooling, so strongly emphasized by the 1805 law, was undermined by countless instances of quick fixes, local compromises and corner cutting, so much so that it is often unclear who was in fact getting how much education. Throughout the period, school coverage was lower than the regulation required and lower than the authorities thought it was. The Austrian government could not make good on its own schooling laws and never even realized the full extent of the shortfall.

Chapter 3

The Financing

Austrian public schooling started out as an unfunded mandate. The lack of specifics on the financials of the new system in the 1774 law reflected the reformers' acute awareness that money was a vexatious issue and that almost any solution would be unpopular. Demanding that parents forgo their children's labour for most of the day, most of the year was in itself burdensome to most rural families, especially poor ones. To ask them, on top of that, to pay for the school that was the cause of their loss of income was expected to engender resistance and lead many parents to boycott the system, which threatened to undermine the reform's purpose.[1] As the school reform was being considered, Bohemia, for example, had just come through a famine (1770–1772) and a peasant uprising against crushing feudal dues (1775), which suggested the serfs had little taste for shouldering another burden.[2]

For this reason, the initial steps to implement the new law involved mostly reallocation of existing resources. Many newly established major schools were created by converting former Jesuit or Piarist *Gymnasia* to the new purpose, while retaining, part and parcel, the staff and the income sources. This approach fit nicely with another major trend in education in the 1770s and 1780s, namely the curtailment of secondary education, and the inevitable effect of this move was to reduce the intellectual level of the Austrian schooling system.[3] Nonetheless, in places that were establishing new schools from scratch, the teacher salaries were paid predominantly from tuition fees. The government was anxious to keep the fees low and to waive them altogether for poor parents but the obvious negative consequence was underpaid teachers. Austrian schooling never escaped this quandary until after the liberal reform of 1869, when schools came to be financed through local taxes and tuition fees were gradually abolished.

Once the expansion of the school network got under way during Joseph II's reign, the issue of financing the expansion, that is, how to pay for the construction and maintenance of new school buildings, became more pressing. The most significant consequence to emerge from more than six years of frantic policy discussions between the emperor and the Education Commis-

[1] Ficker. *Bericht über österreichisches Unterrichtswesen*, p. 22.
[2] Vondra. *České země v letech 1705–1792*, p. 175.
[3] Kuzmin. *Vývoj školství a vzdělání v Československu*, p. 59–61.

sion was the establishment of *Schulpatronat*, or school patronage. In a series of decrees issued throughout 1787, the government adopted an already existing institution of parish or church patronage and extended it to schools. Historically, church patrons had often been local feudal lords whose duty was to maintain the local church and whose accompanying "presentation right" meant that they could choose the man for the post of the local priest. *Schulpatronat* added a further obligation to church patrons, namely that they contribute to school construction and maintenance. In many places, the feudal lords thus also became school patrons. Yet even in places where the patronage fell to someone else, such as a local monastery or a factory owner running a school for his child workers, the lords were still obligated to contribute by virtue of being the feudal landowners, who performed certain important judicial and state-administrative duties on their estates. In roping them in through school patronage too, the law turned the landed aristocracy into important stakeholders in the new school system.

Being a school patron usually involved a long-term commitment. While it was possible for patronage to change hands, in most places it fell to longstanding, durable institutions: aristocratic estates, government organizations, religious orders and municipal administrations. When a particular manor or estate changed owners through sale, marriage or inheritance, the identity of the patron may have changed but institutionally the duties were still attached to the same manor. Once assumed, school patronage could not be so easily shed. Of the 420 schools operating in the Styrian diocese of Seckau in 1846 and still operating in 1865, some 389, or about 93%, had exactly the same patron in the early 1860s as in 1846.[4] One could rarely find willing candidates, lining up to assume the responsibility. The opposite was more likely to occur: that no party wished to take on the burden or that the presumed patron shirked his duties and questioned the legitimacy of demands placed on him, which led to protracted disputes, lasting many years and holding up much needed construction work.[5] By the 1860s, the situation slowly began to change, as some towns and local communities decided to take full ownership of their schools and assume patronage instead of having to endlessly negotiate with aristocratic patrons who in the wake of the post-1848 reforms became increasingly disinterested in attending to their duties.[6] But many local communities were reluctant to bear the cost of patronage and in many rural

[4] See *Lehr-Personalstand der deutschen Schulen in der Seckauer- und Leobner-Diözese in Steyermark. Im Schuljahre 1846/47*, *Lehr-Personalstand der deutschen Schulen in der Seckauer Diözese in Steiermark. Im Schuljahre 1861. Abgeschlossen 15. Dezember 1860*, *Lehr-Personalstand der deutschen Schulen des Bisthums Seckau in Steiermark. Im Schuljahre 1864*. There were also 39 schools, predominantly of municipal patronage, that operated in 1846 but did not survive to the 1865 school census.

[5] Adámek, Karel Vácslav. *Paměti o školách v okresu hlineckém*. p. 16, 110, 132.

[6] See, for example, Adámek. *Paměti*, p. 86, 95.

places the abolition of *Schulpatronat* in 1863–1866 caused consternation about the sudden financial shortfall.[7]

Together, the school patron, the feudal lord and the local community formed the three principal pillars on which the system of financing physical infrastructure rested from 1787 until the *Schulpatronat*'s abolition. The three-way split had the school patrons pay for all skilled labor of the craftsmen, the feudal lords contribute the building materials and the local community supply the unskilled labour and transportation (*Hand und Zugrobot*), unless the liable parties freely agreed on a different manner of allocating the costs. The law insisted that the patronage obligations applied to all kinds of patrons, including religious orders or the emperor's own estates. In areas that had been owned by monasteries dissolved by Joseph II, school patronage fell to the *Religionsfond*, which held and administered all the confiscated property of the orders. The obligations were cumulative whenever the school patron and the feudal lord were the same person. In fact, if, say, a free city that did not belong to any feudal estate and that maintained its own church decided to build a school, the city council was responsible for all three parts of the construction costs. The three-way framework applied to school furniture also, while the patron was exclusively responsible for covering all teaching aids. The financing was therefore local – the government or the imperial court did not enter into consideration, except through ownership of crown estates, when they acted as feudal landowners. After 1829, the law allowed two exceptions to this. One comprised the normal schools (*Normalschulen*) in the several provincial capitals, where the full cost was borne by the provincial authorities. The second exception along the same lines was made for major schools in important administrative centres. Smaller places were usually excluded from such subsidy, except in cases where they were liable for more than two thirds of the cost and could prove to the provincial authorities that they were short of funds.

The whole arrangement was incorporated into the *Politische Verfassung* in 1805 with a few further specifications added. The construction plans for a new school had to follow a binding blueprint and had to be approved by civil authorities (Article 397). The regulation specified classroom size, demanding about 38 m^2 for a class of 40–50 pupils (Article 365), with a stove, the teacher's cathedra and two rows of student desks, whose measurements were also regulated (Article 356). Precise rules were laid down for cases where one school catered to a number of villages across several different estates or for a situation where a school operated in rented space. The three-way division also applied to maintenance and repair works (Article 389).

The construction of the trivial school in Bohnice offers an instructive illustration of the interaction between all three interested parties.[8] This village,

[7] See, for example, "Dopisy", *Pěstoun* IV (15), 25. 5. 1865, p. 120.

some 11 km outside Prague, had 269 inhabitants in 1843.[9] Its school dated back to 1738 and served four other similar-sized villages in addition to Bohnice. When the old school building burnt down in July 1827, the first immediate response was to rent a small provisional classroom and to revert to half-day teaching. It took a year, until June 1828, before a commission was sent by civil authorities (*Kreisamt*) to take stock of the situation and start planning for a new construction. Looking to save on the costs, the civil authorities first proposed that Trója, one of the four other villages served by the Bohnice school, go its separate way and build their own school building. Similarly, the village of Sedlec was offered to start sending their children to Roztoky, which meant a longer walk by about 1 km, but at least did not require crossing a river. Both villages rejected these proposals, preferring a construction of a new, larger school building in Bohnice. Their solution was eventually adopted and plans were drawn up to build a brand new two-classroom school. The negotiations about the costs were apparently protracted because the construction did not begin until April 1838. The new school building was completed in November 1839 and was almost immediately full to capacity, since in the meantime the number of students increased from about 125 before the fire to almost 200.

The final account of the whole operation lists 87 detailed line items, which makes it easy to reconstruct the obligations of each party according to law. The resulting sums are cited on the left-hand side of Table 3.1. The right-hand side shows actual payments recorded in the same final account. Bohnice was part of a manor owned by the Bohemian Estates, a kind of corporation of all Bohemian landowning aristocrats, and this institution also acted as the school's patron. It was therefore liable for expenses under either heading. The concurrence of these two roles could make the whole financing negotiations simpler but in Bohnice, the situation was complicated by the fact that the school served villages spread across three different aristocratic estates whose owners were therefore all expected to contribute in line with their feudal obligations. Article 376 of the *Politische Verfassung* suggested that in such cases the costs be split among the different landowners in proportion to the number of peasant houses but this rule was clearly not followed in Bohnice, where the largest manor of the three, Trója, certainly paid far less than its share. An even starker shortfall is apparent in the contribution of the villages. Per Article 368, the local communities were responsible for unskilled labour and transportation and the item descriptions make those dues easy to identify

[8] The following account draws on Kneidl, František. *Paměti školského okresu karlínského*. p. 133–157.

[9] Palacký, František. *Popis kralovství českého čili podrobné poznamenání všech dosavadních krajův, panství, statkův, měst, městeček a vesnic, někdejších hradův a tvrzí, též samot a zpustlých osad mnohých v zemi české, s udáním jejich obyvatelstva dne popisu r. 1843 vykonaného*. Prague: J.G. Kalve, 1848, p. 15.

Table 3.1: Financing school construction in Bohnice, 1838–1839, in fl. C.M.

Obligations		Actual payments	
Local communities	2292	All 5 villages	1713
School patron	2541	Bohemian Estates' Manor	3442
Feudal lord	1658	Trója Manor	789
		Sedlec Manor	319
Ambiguous	61	Payer not specified	289
Total	*6552*	*Total*	*6552*

Note: "Ambiguous" refers to a few line items where either the contributions of the various parties could not be disentangled and/or the description did not allow a conclusive assignment to a particular payer.
Source: Kneidl. *Paměti*, p. 138–145.

in Bohnice accounts. The difference between obligations and payments can partially be accounted for if we add the 289 fl paid by an unspecified party to the village total: the record here cited "extra services, not budgeted in advance" but did not specify whether these were skilled or unskilled work. At any rate, the documentation insists that the transportation and other unskilled work were rendered to the tune of 2292 fl., which is more than the contribution of the villages, so someone else must have paid the balance. Apparently, the villagers, who were able to convince civil authorities to build a two-classroom school in Bohnice against all other proposed alternatives, were also able to bill their feudal lords for the contributions the law expected of the villagers. All in all, the local communities paid between 26% and 30% of the total cost (depending on whom one debits for the "extra services") while more than 52% was covered by the Bohemian Estates. Including the *Kreisamt* as the overseeing civil authority, the building process involved nine different parties, who negotiated over the whole process for more than a decade.

The situation was considerably more straightforward in Šestajovice, a village of comparable size some 25 km to the east of Bohnice.[10] Local children there had been attending a parish school in Jirny, 2 km away, but in 1850 the citizens of Šestajovice decided to build their own school. The civil authorities granted the request in 1855, appointing the village of Šestajovice as the patron of its own school and thereby pre-empting any patron-village conflict. Moreover, since the feudal patrimonial administration had been abolished in 1848, there were no longer any feudal lords to deal with either. The price of not having to interact with other stakeholders was that the community had to shoulder all costs on its own. This included not only all construction costs but also all future repair costs and salary expenses. Still, this must have seemed a good deal to Šestajovice, for the school was completed in 1860.

[10] Kneidl. *Paměti*, p. 473–476.

The case of Šestajovice shows how the framework of school patronage slowly came apart after 1848. With the final abolition of labour dues, *robota*, in September of that year, the last remaining vestiges of feudal administration based on aristocratic estates disappeared. The (now former) feudal lords lost their claims on labour dues but were also relieved of their administrative duties. They expected (quite reasonably) that the obligations connected to school provision would also be moot. This turned out to be only partially true. School patronage remained in place but in June 1849, the Ministry of Education confirmed that school patrons were no longer obligated to contribute to school construction. Other duties, such as sharing in the maintenance and repair costs, remained, however.[11] By the time school patronage was finally abolished in 1863–1866, the financial liabilities decisively shifted to local budgets of towns and villages. Still, the physical infrastructure, as it existed in the mid-1860s, was by and large the fruit of the Josephinian financial framework.

The law's idea of an adequate school building was one with no more than 80 pupils per classroom and teacher. Article 366 advised that schools be built in anticipation of future population growth because wherever the number approached 100 per classroom, an extra classroom had to be built and an extra teacher or assistant hired. Table 3.2 shows how reality squared against this regulation. Across the 11 provinces for which detailed data exist, the average enrolled pupil attended a school with 112.3 children per classroom and 103.5 pupils per member of staff (columns (i) and (ii)). The median school had about 82 pupils per classroom and about 32% of all schools had more than 100 and were therefore in breach of the regulation. Since the compliant schools were the smaller ones, with a relatively low number of enrolled pupils, a majority of pupils attended schools with more than 100 pupils per classroom and about 10% were in schools with more than 170 pupils per classroom.

The variation across provinces was considerable. It may seem counterintuitive at first that those provinces, which had historically been most active in building up their school network, such as Bohemia, Lower Austria and Moravia, would report the most overcrowded schools and therefore score worse than the Southern crown lands, such as Carinthia and the Austrian Littoral. In terms of school construction, the Czech lands were far ahead of the South. The real cause behind this disparity is, of course, the low enrolment in the South, for which even a meager school network was relatively sufficient. The story was somewhat different in Tyrol where the terrain and distances of this Alpine region led to the establishment of numerous small schools, one in almost every valley. They catered to the sparsely settled mountainous areas, which usually had fewer pupils than was typical elsewhere in the empire.

[11] Frank. *Die Österreichische Volksschule von 1848–1898*. p. 22.

Table 3.2: Average level of provision of school, 1865

	Simple ratios			Adjusted for half-day teaching		
	Pupils per classroom	Pupils per teacher	Compliance (%)	Pupils per classroom	Pupils per teacher	Compliance (%)
	(i)	(ii)	(iii)	(iv)	(v)	(vi)
Lower Austria	105.9	94.5	38.2	84.3	75.7	72.8
Upper Austria	104.5	103.8	30.7	77.4	77.3	75.5
Salzburg	80.2	69.3	74.9	78.9	68.0	77.5
Styria	115.9	105.8	38.5	99.9	91.9	54.8
Carinthia	77.0	73.5	74.6	73.7	70.1	80.1
Carniola	118.0	110.3	41.5	100.2	92.8	63.6
Austrian Littoral	78.6	70.2	66.2	72.6	64.3	83.8
Tyrol & Vorarlberg	54.1	51.2	92.3	53.4	50.5	94.7
Bohemia	122.6	114.4	29.0	116.2	108.9	34.7
Moravia	125.7	112.0	31.7	118.3	105.7	39.4
Silesia	116.3	106.5	32.5	106.1	97.3	47.7
Overall	112.3	103.5	38.2	102.5	94.7	51.0

Note: Compliance (%) measures the percentage of pupils enrolled in a fully compliant school. Data describe the situation as of Spring 1865.
Source: Detail-Conscription.

The pupil-teacher ratios were somewhat better than the pupil-classroom ratios because hiring a teaching assistant was cheaper and easier than building a new classroom when a school crossed the regulation threshold. But even so, slightly less than half of all pupils attended a school with more than 100 pupils per teacher.

Given the dire physical constraints faced by many schools – the 1865 school survey found about 200 of them with more than 250 pupils per classroom – local communities frequently resorted to the easy way out offered by Article 350 of the *Politische Verfassung* and split their pupils into two groups for half-day instruction. This meant the children got less than the full complement of schooling but it made the resources go farther and the injunction to build extra space and hire extra staff now kicked in at double the usual thresholds. Columns (iv) and (v) in the table show that this adjustment did not help all that much. The impact was largest in Lower and Upper Austria and in Styria but in most other provinces with insufficient infrastructure, most pupils were still enrolled in overcrowded schools.

Columns (iii) and (vi) summarize all of this information by showing the proportion of all enrolled pupils attending schools that were in line with the regulation, both in terms of classroom space and teaching staff. The first of these, column (iii), offers a more stringent definition of compliance, namely whether a school had enough resources to teach everybody all day without invoking Article 350, as was the clear preference of the policy makers. In column (vi), compliance allows for half-day teaching. The overall compliance of 38.2% indicates that, as of 1865, the school infrastructure fell far short of the target set for it by the government and even with all the half-day adjustments counted in, about a half of all pupils were in non-compliant schools. In the upper tail of the distribution, with 150 or more enrolled pupils per classroom even *after* the half-day adjustment, the schools must have not just expected but outright relied on the assumption that most of the enrolled pupils would not actually attend most of the time. Such a model of "fractional reserve schooling" obviously made proper enforcement of compulsory attendance not just difficult but even, potentially, undesirable.

The availability or lack of appropriate educational infrastructure was a function of the system of financing, which was relatively decentralized, as the example of Bohnice illustrated. School patrons came in all shapes and sizes and approached their duties facing a variety of incentives. Available records from several bishoprics allow us to identify the patrons and link them to about 40% of all the schools covered in the 1865 school survey. This "Patronage sample", as I call it, of 4841 patron-school matches is not perfectly representative of all Austrian schools but it is broad enough to provide a good sense of the range of experiences that the financing system engendered.

Table 3.3 groups the patrons into several categories. The biggest of them were the feudal, or manorial, lords who served as patrons for about 43.8% of the linked schools and were the most frequent type of patron in every diocese with the exception of the Styrian Seckau. Since their patronage duties usually arose in consequence of their feudal landownership, it generally holds that the bigger the landowner, the greater the overall involvement in school financing. The most prominent aristocratic families thus ended up saddled with substantial school-related outlays. The princely family of the Schwarzenbergs was listed as patrons for 147 schools in the subsample, the Liechtensteins for 107, the Clam-Gallases for 69. The top ten most frequently listed aristocratic surnames account for about a third of all the schools with feudal patrons.

Strictly speaking, one might count the emperor among feudal landowners but in Table 3.3 the Crown is included under central government patronage. The emperor, too, assumed this role in most cases by virtue of being the local landowner. But as the ruler and therefore ultimate author of the policy, his incentives were different. While the realm's aristocrats could be anything from active to lukewarm to outright derelict in their duties, the monarch had an interest in implementing his own policy. After all, the Court had a history going back at least to the 18th century of using Crown estates as the laboratories and leading examples for policies that were later extended to the whole monarchy. Moreover, the category does not include just the ruler but also government bodies and institutions of various kinds, for instance, archbishops and provincial governors, other members of the imperial family as well as administrators of important state-owned enterprises. The Court had some form of authority or leverage over all of these, which meant that their attenti-

Table 3.3: School patrons by type in selected dioceses in the early 1860s

Diocese	Type of patron (%) Central government	*Religionsfond & Studienfond*	Monasteries	Manorial lords	Towns & villages	Private owners	Other patrons	Total number of schools
Vienna	22.5	13.4	24.5	28.7	12.3	1.1	0.5	644
Sankt Pölten	28.6	2.8	26.0	40.3	8.9	0.4	0.9	461
Seckau	16.7	27.3	16.0	11.3	28.4	0.2	0.0	450
České Budějovice	3.1	10.4	5.6	48.8	32.4	0.4	0.0	732
Hradec Králové	7.8	8.2	3.8	52.0	28.2	0.5	0.0	960
Litoměřice	3.7	4.6	1.9	66.2	23.8	0.1	0.1	842
Brno	3.6	18.5	5.7	38.2	33.2	0.0	1.3	752
Overall	10.5	11.5	10.0	43.8	24.9	0.4	0.4	4841

Note: Some schools had more than one patron, which is why the percentages add up to more than 100% in a line. Horizontal lines separate dioceses in different provinces: Vienna and Sankt Pölten in Lower Austria, Seckau in Styria, Brno in Moravia and the remaining three in Bohemia. The publications listed here are the sources for school patron identification, on the basis of which the Patronage sample was created.
Source: Trajer, *Historisch-statistische Beschreibung der Diöcese Budweis*; Kaiser, *Lehrer-Schema oder Ausweis*, Huber, *Lehrer-Schema oder übersichtliche Zusammenstellung*; Šrůtek, "Soupis veškerého učitelstva národních škol v diecési Kralohradecké"; Pátek, Johann. "Katalog des gesammten Lehr-Personales an den Volksschulen der Brünner bischöflichen Diözese"; Maresch, "Verzeichniss des gesammten an den Volksschulen der Leitmeritzer Diözese"; *Lehr-Personalstand der deutschen Schulen des Bisthums Seckau*

on to the school patronage was informed not only by the law but also a direct line of subordination.[12] Not surprisingly, schools with patrons of this type were most often found around Vienna and in Lower Austria.

The government exercised further more or less direct control through the patronage by the *Religionsfond* and the *Studienfond*. These two endowment funds accounted for another 11.5% of all schools. The *Religionsfond* was the more important of the two, accounting for almost nine tenths of all schools in this column. This was because the *Studienfond* was mostly reserved for just a few of the most crucial schools, primarily those in provincial capitals and those that served as training grounds for new teachers. In contrast, the *Religionsfond* patronized numerous schools operating on the domains of abolished monasteries.

Many of those monasteries and religious orders that had not been abolished ended up serving as patrons anyway. They account for about 10% of the subsample and some prominent abbeys carried financial responsibility for several schools at once. In the bishoprics covered by the table, the most represented religious order were the Benedictines: the Abbey of Göttweig cared for 33 schools, Melk for 29. But Augustinians, Cistercians and Premonstratensians were also frequent patrons. In some of the schools under their patronage the orders supplied the teaching, too. For example, of the 29 schools patronized by the famous Benedictine "Scottish" Abbey (*Schottenstift*) in Vienna, 15 were in the city and the monastery provided not only financial support but also supervision and religious instruction. But there were also some very long-distance patronage relationships. The Augustinian Abbey in Reichersberg on the Inn river, a stone's throw from the Austrian border with Bavaria, patronized 17 Lower Austrian schools southeast of Vienna, some of them as far as 300 km away.

Municipal patronage accounts for about a quarter of all schools in Table 3.3. While the vast majority of these cases are small village schools supported by the local community, municipal patronage was disproportionately more likely to be found in cities and towns. Among schools in communities of 2000 or more inhabitants, about 33% had the town for a patron, compared to 24% in the smaller places.

The last two columns in the table refer to the rare cases that did not fall in any other category. Private patronage usually applied to factory schools where an entrepreneur who employed children was obligated to ensure that they would also receive some schooling, if the children could not get it elsewhere. But as the table shows, it was not a widespread practice.

---

[12] See Šafránek's account of the lead that the imperial estates took in implementing the new schooling policy so as to serve as a "template and encouragement to other landowners." Another example of imperial estates leading the way was the gradual phase-out of serfdom. See Šafránek. *Školy české I. svazek*, p. 160–164; Vondra. *České země*, p. 109–110.

Among the patron types, the aristocratic landowners have historically been judged least favourably by historians and researchers of education. They get blamed for the slow spread of schooling, documented in the previous chapter, as many observers note that support for the school was an obligation without any immediate return to the feudal lords.[13] Conversely, one could adduce in favour of the central government that it was implementing its own policy, that monastic orders had both a long history of involvement in education and preaching and also a stake in buttressing Catholic religiosity, of which the Austrian school was a clear conduit, and that municipalities, when serving as patrons, were spending money on the education of the children of their own citizens. The boom in municipal schooling after 1848 and again after the abolition of the school patronage in the early 1860s seemed to prove that, when liberated from the fetters of the anachronistic institutional framework of feudal patronage, local communities could make great strides in school provision.[14] But truth be told, this judgment infers conclusions from no more than a few vivid anecdotes and from the various patrons' real or presumed incentives. None of the contemporary writers had the means to systematically assess the impact on schools of the various kinds of patronage and grim stories of aristocratic obstruction find ample counterpart in numerous local histories that describe the active involvement of feudal lords in schooling.[15] Aristocrats were, in fact, often among the main proponents of making the schooling more practical and rigorous, as recounted in the case of the *Realschulen* in Chapter 1.

The low opinion of the landed interests in relation to popular education is not confined to the case of Austrian schooling either. In many national histories, the political economy of mass schooling features opposition from the landed aristocracy who, even when they do not have to pay for it, consider broadly available education a threat to their economic interests – and with some justification. In the succinct formulation by Oded Galor:[16]

"Unlike the agrarian economy, which was characterized by a conflict of interest between the landed aristocracy and the masses, the process of industrialization has brought about an

[13] Ficker. *Bericht über österreichisches Unterrichtswesen*, p. 35; Frank, Ferdinand. "Kurzer Überblick über die geschichtliche Entwicklung des österreichischen Volksschulwesens", p. 62.

[14] Frank. *Die Österreichische Volksschule von 1848–1898*. p. 23.

[15] Hoffmann, Anton. *Geschichte der Haupt- und Mädchenschule in Reichenberg*. p. 23–30; Kneidl. *Paměti*; Adámek. *Paměti*; Šafránek. *Školy české. I. svazek*, p. 202. Weiss reprints all the Bohemian reports from 1775 to 1791 and in every one of them, prominent aristocrats are listed among the most illustrious "Wohltäter gegen die Schulen" – benefactors of schools. To be sure, the local histories also describe many instances of conflict – but even in those it is not always the case that the obstruction to school expansion is coming from the aristocratic patrons. See Weiss, *Geschichte der Theresianischen Schulreform in Böhmen. II. Band.*

[16] Galor, Oded. *Unified growth theory*. p. 144.

additional conflict between the entrenched landed elite and the emerging capitalist elite. The capitalists who were striving for an educated labor force supported policies that promoted the education of the masses, whereas landowners, whose interest lay in the reduction of the mobility of the rural labor force, favored policies that deprived the masses from education.“

The “Tory opposition theory”[17], as it has been called, recognizes that, in an industrializing economy, the skills taught in school are usually more useful and therefore better rewarded in the dynamic manufacturing sector than in the traditional agricultural sector.[18] As a result, skilled workers have an incentive to migrate from the countryside to the city, making agricultural labour scarcer and therefore more expensive. If the landowners are also financially liable to support rural schools, they are doubly hit: on top of lower profits due to higher labour costs they also bear the direct cost of skill creation, while the industrial sector then reaps the fruits.

The presence of these political fault lines has been observed and documented for many European countries. In Prussia, large landowners were most effective in holding back the spread of schooling in those areas where the distribution of land ownership was most unequal.[19] As serfdom gradually withered and peasants became more footloose, the *junkers*' power to stand in the way of education waned and school enrolment responded to rising popular demand. Spain followed this pattern also[20] and the same relationship between highly concentrated land ownership and low provision of schooling reappears in British data well into the late 19th century. In places where peers retained their influence by holding on to various local offices, the school boards raised less tax revenue and hired fewer teachers, relative to areas where this was not the case.[21] Even in the USA, high concentration of landownership went hand in hand with less schooling. Here landowners did not enjoy the same kind of centuries-long entrenched aristocratic privilege more typical of Europe, but they were often able to leverage their economic power into effective political organization in local elections.[22]

This view of the political dynamic also implies that, apart from the capital owners, the main support for mass schooling is likely to come from the general population who are the “target audience” of such schooling policy. The positive correlation between the extension of suffrage and public spending on

---

[17] Lindert Peter. *Growing Public: Social Spending and Economic Growth since the Eighteenth Century*. p. 100.

[18] Goñi, Marc. “Landed Elites and Education Provision in England” p. 2.

[19] Cinnirella, Francesco and Hornung, Eric. “Landownership concentration and the expansion of education.”

[20] Beltrán-Tapia, F., Martinez-Galarraga, J. “Inequality and education in pre-industrial economies: Evidence from Spain.”

[21] Goñi, Marc. “Landed Elites and Education Provision in England” p. 4.

[22] Vollrath, Dietrich. “Inequality and school funding in the rural United States, 1890.”

schooling is well established for countries across Europe and America.[23] Even in places with very little room for the popular vote, like Russia, greater representation of the masses in the local and regional government led to increases in spending on public goods such as schooling.[24] Given how expensive mass schooling inevitably is, it is scarcely a surprise that rich elites and poor masses stood at opposing political sides of this "the greatest shift of resources from upper income groups to the poor".[25]

How well does the "Tory opposition theory" fit the Austrian situation? In most of the cited cases of other countries, the political analysis relied either on voting data or on various proxy measures of landowners' clout, such as the degree of land ownership inequality. In the case of Austria, elected representation did not become a permanent part of the country's constitutional framework until 1861 and even then the suffrage applied to less than a quarter of all adult males,[26] which makes an analysis of voting patterns unfeasible for most of the period under consideration. But the institute of the school patron, where landowners and common citizenry of towns and villages frequently negotiated over school-related claims and liabilities presents a convenient alternative, as it offers a more direct insight into the relative power of various constituencies than proxy measures of inequality. Using the 1865 *Detail Conscription*, which reported a wide range of different measures of each school, the impact of patrons can be analysed from three separate angles: qualitative, quantitative and compliance-related.

Table 3.4 shows how the patrons compared in terms of school quality in 1865. The majority of the schools were regular trivial schools with two grades. Municipal patrons showed the greatest eagerness for an enhanced curriculum, with 5.2% of their schools being major schools, followed by central government. Since the government wished to retain control over teacher training, central authorities served as patrons for schools that were attached to teacher training courses, usually in provincial and regional centres, which account for the 4.1% of major schools under their patronage. For municipal patrons, this was not a consideration, which is why their willingness to invest in a three-grade or four-grade school can be more readily interpreted as a measure of genuine demand for a broader curriculum. The table, however, highlights that there was a big difference between town and village, so much so that the readings for the two categories frequently form the end

[23] Mariscal, Elisa and Sokoloff, Kenneth L. "Schooling, Suffrage and the Persistence of Inequality in the Americas, 1800–1945"; Go, Sun and Lindert, Peter. "The uneven rise of American public schools to 1850."

[24] Nafziger, Stephen. "Did Ivan's vote matter? The political economy of local democracy in Tsarist Russia."

[25] Lindert Peter. *Growing Public.* p. 87.

[26] Cvrček, Tomáš and Zajíček, Miroslav. "The making of a liberal education: Political economy of the Austrian school reform, 1865–1880." Table 2.

Table 3.4: School quality by type of patron, 1865

Type of patron	Type of school (%)			Grades	All-day teaching
	Major	Trivial	Provisional		
Central government	4.1	92.2	3.7	2.34	69.3
Religionsfond & Studienfond	2.5	93.0	4.5	2.29	83.1
Monasteries	3.0	92.7	4.3	2.35	63.0
Manorial lords	0.9	93.5	5.6	2.12	80.2
Towns & villages	5.2	62.3	32.5	2.10	88.8
Towns	33.2	62.0	4.8	3.42	94.1
Villages	0.1	62.3	37.6	1.85	87.9
All other patrons	5.4	56.8	37.8	2.14	75.7
Overall	2.5	85.3	12.2	2.17	80.0

Note: Towns are defined as settlements with more than 2000 inhabitants. For definitions of different kinds of schools, see discussion regarding Table 2.1 in Chapter 2.
Source: Detail-Conscription; Patronage sample.

points for the range of reported values. As school patrons, a third of the towns – here defined as settlements with more than 2000 inhabitants in the 1869 census – operated a major school. In contrast, more than a third of the villages settled for a much watered-down and cheap education: provisional schools were usually either staffed by a teaching assistant, who had not yet been fully certified, or relied on an itinerant teacher, who only showed up to teach on specific days of the week. The state of these schools gives an indication of what kind of education rural dwellers desired, when they were in a position, as patrons, to actually make the decisions. More than that, they can perhaps fairly be considered representative of the mass of the population in general, since the vast majority of Habsburg subjects was rural and, in line with this fact, about six out of seven municipal patrons were villages (the rest were towns). The average number of grades offered in schools under village versus urban patronage shows that, occasionally, rural schools did not even bother to deliver on the second grade of the legally prescribed education.

In light of their less than stellar reputation, the record of the aristocratic landowners is rather unremarkable, one way or other: the schools in their care do not substantially differ from those patronized by the monasteries, the *Religionsfond* or the central government, except that they are less likely to support a major school or a school that offers more than two grades. Over 90% of the aristocratic patronage applied to schools in the countryside, which naturally invites a comparison with village patronage, and the conclusion is clear: with a manorial lord as patron, a rural school was, on average, of somewhat higher quality, even if it was slightly less likely to offer all-day teaching.

The contrast is less clear-cut in Table 3.5, which captures the material side of things. Recall that the main task of a school patron was to coordinate, and

Table 3.5: Physical infrastructure of schools by type of patron, 1865

Type of patron	Average per school: Enrolled pupils	Class-rooms	Teachers	Own school building (%)	School building in disrepair (%)
Central government	186.4	1.86	2.14	90.6	25.8
Religionsfond & Studienfond	167.5	1.72	1.92	89.2	30.6
Monasteries	157.5	1.71	1.95	88.1	25.1
Manorial lords	169.0	1.53	1.64	93.2	35.6
Towns & villages	137.5	1.59	1.76	89.0	30.9
Towns	391.3	4.13	5.09	79.1	12.3
Villages	90.9	1.13	1.15	90.8	34.3
All other patrons	134.1	1.51	1.73	62.2	21.6
Overall	161.0	1.61	1.77	90.6	32.0

Source: Detail-Conscription; Patronage sample.

contribute to, necessary construction and maintenance work, so as to ensure that the school had the requisite physical infrastructure, in which to function. On this score the landowners did not acquit themselves well. Admittedly, the schools in their care were most likely to operate in their own buildings, which was an important consideration: it was usually a sure sign of inadequate provision, when schools had to rent (mostly unsuitable and ill-fitting) space around town.[27] But with 90.6% of all schools owning their buildings, aristocratic patronage did not stand out as exceptional. Moreover, their schools were the most likely to require some repair or reconstruction (35.6% of school buildings under their patronage were in disrepair) and had a below average number of classrooms (1.53), which was especially inadequate with a view to the average number of pupils enrolled (169.0). In absolute numbers, the landowners paid for more classrooms and more school buildings than village patrons but not in proportion to the number of pupils. And while, on this score, the manorial lords cared for schools that were above average in size, it is also true that other patrons with even bigger schools apparently did comparably better.

Finally, Table 3.6 presents the provision ratios and an overall measure of compliance. Here the landowners have unambiguously the worst record of all patrons. Their schools crammed the most pupils into a classroom and were most likely to be understaffed. Hence, they also had the lowest compliance rate: under aristocratic patronage, only 24.1% of pupils were enrolled in a school that met all the basic regulations set out in the *Politische Verfassung*. In fairness, other patrons did not fare that much better. Even the central government displayed lower compliance (30.7%) than the overall average (32.6%) and the schools under village patronage often met the regulation by

[27] See Adámek. *Paměti*, for numerous examples.

Table 3.6: Compliance with regulation by type of patron, 1865

Type of patron	Pupils per classroom	Pupils per teacher	Compliance (%)
Central government	117.2	105.8	30.7
Religionsfond & *Studienfond*	112.8	106.0	38.7
Monasteries	107.1	95.2	39.7
Manorial lords	127.8	119.2	24.1
Towns & villages	103.7	93.5	46.1
Towns	107.7	88.0	43.7
Villages	100.5	97.9	48.0
All other patrons	110.9	106.6	33.3
Overall	117.9	108.7	32.6

Note: A school is considered compliant when it had fewer than 100 pupils per classroom and per teacher and also offered an all-day instruction. This definition is informed by Articles 346 and 349 of the *Politische Verfassung*.
*Source: Detail-Conscrip*tion; Patronage sample.

virtue of being too small to ever run the risk of having more than 100 pupils in the whole school, let alone a single classroom. The most impressive, from the point of view of compliance, was the record of towns: urban schools were large and required proportionately more physical capital, so a 43.7% compliance rate indicates that urban dwellers took their patron duties much more seriously than anybody else. They, however, bore responsibility for only 187 schools out of the 4841 in the subsample, so their better care was a drop in the bucket of the whole system.

Overall, the assessment of landowners as school patrons yields mixed results. On the one hand, it is difficult to brand them obstructionists of mass schooling when they, as a group, shouldered the plurality of all school patronages, provided 93% of their schools with own premises and by and large avoided the slapdash inadequacy of provisional status, characteristic of so many village schools. On the other hand, the infrastructure they built fell mostly short of the regulation and lagged behind what other patrons were able to supply. But as the following analysis will show, the landowners' deep pockets were useful in two respects: in supporting schools with many pupils and in responding to changes in the schools' needs through time.

Tables 3.4–3.6 report overall averages, which furnish a useful overall picture of the situation, but fail to account for potential confounding factors that might operate in the background. For example, aristocratic patronage was far more prevalent in Bohemia than elsewhere, while the government, including the *Religionsfond*, was the most prominent actor in Styria. Similarly, municipal patronage was insignificant in the diocese of Sankt Pölten but played a great role in Brno. Could it be that such inter-provincial and inter-diocesan differences affect the comparison? Perhaps the government-sponsored schools in Styria look more adequately supplied than the Bohemian schools of aristocratic patronage partly because mountainous Styria's lower population density made for smaller schools with fewer pupils, which were therefore cheaper to build and easier to bring to compliance, than was the case in the densely inhabited Bohemian plains. An ideal comparison would thus involve observing various types of patrons in similar circumstances, as if next to each other, so as to control for such confounding factors.

The probit models shown in Table 3.7 move closer to such ideal comparison by including not only some of the basic relevant demographic variables (an indicator variable for urban status, natural log of town population, size of enrolment) but also fixed effect variables for 324 civil districts. These were small administrative units, generally with less than 20000 inhabitants, which means that many of the potential confounding factors varied very little within them. Consequently, the coefficients on the indicator variables for each patron type capture by and large the differential impact of patronage on compliance, controlling for other aspects specific for each district through the fixed effects.[28]

The first model, reported in columns (i) and (ii), includes all schools, regardless of the enrolment numbers. The average marginal effects capture the impact of explanatory variables on the probability of compliance. The patrons that stand out as most conducive to successful compliance are the municipal ones: towns and villages. A school with a town for a patron had about 20.4% higher probability of being compliant than that with an aristocratic patron, all else equal. For village patronage, the effect is 12.9%, which is a statistically significant difference.[29] Given that the overall fraction of compliant schools was 32.6%, this is a sizeable impact. The likelihood of compliance was further significantly affected by the size of the place in which the school stood. The first demographic variable in the table is an indicator equal to 1, if a municipality had at least 2000 inhabitants, 0 otherwise. Next is the natural log of urban population (coded as 0 for villages). Compared to a village, a school in a town of exactly 2000 inhabitants was roughly 15.1% more likely to be compliant. The positive effect then increased further with town size. Adding 10% to a city's population increased the probability by about 2.1%.

This strong impact of the urban status and population highlights the chasm between town and country that had been baked into the schooling law from the beginning and which the subsequent economic developments made even

[28] Note that since some schools had more than one patron (a few had even three different ones), the patron categories are not mutually exclusive and can therefore all enter into the specification.

[29] The probability differences are calculated as differences in the average marginal effects of the respective school patron types in Table 3.7: $0.250 - 0.046 = 0.204$ and $0.175 - 0.46 = 0.129$. The same applies to the reported impact of population size: $-1.491 + 0.216 \times ln(2000) = 0.151$.

Table 3.7: Determinants of compliance – a probit model

Variable	All schools Coefficients (i)	Avg MFX (ii)	Big schools Coefficients (iii)	Avg MFX (iv)
School patron types:				
Central government	0.212	0.057	0.523*	0.137*
	[0.185]	[0.050]	[0.238]	[0.062]
Religionsfond & Studienfond	0.097	0.026	0.407	0.106
	[0.191]	[0.052]	[0.246]	[0.064]
Monasteries	0.077	0.021	0.290	0.076
	[0.195]	[0.053]	[0.255]	[0.067]
Manorial lords	0.169	0.046	0.459*	0.120*
	[0.179]	[0.048]	[0.231]	[0.060]
Towns	0.929*	0.250*	1.149*	0.300*
	[0.240]	[0.064]	[0.277]	[0.072]
Villages	0.650*	0.175*	-0.018	-0.005
	[0.183]	[0.049]	[0.248]	[0.065]
All other patrons	0.557	0.150	0.614	0.160
	[0.309]	[0.083]	[0.453]	[0.118]
Demographic variables:				
1(town population ≥ 2000)	-5.535*	-1.491*	-0.596	-0.156
	[1.328]	[0.356]	[1.314]	[0.343]
ln(town population)	0.803*	0.216*	0.121	0.032
	[0.165]	[0.044]	[0.163]	[0.043]
Enrolment (in 100s)	-0.654*	-0.176*	-0.143*	-0.037*
	[0.031]	[0.007]	[0.036]	[0.009]
N	4562		2349	
Pseudo-R^2	0.315		0.216	

Note: Dependent variable is equal to 1, if a school was compliant with existing regulation, zero otherwise. See note under Table 3.6 for definition of compliance. "Avg MFX" stands for average marginal effects. Standard errors are reported in square brackets and asterisk (*) denotes statistical significance at 5%. Big schools are schools with over 100 enrolled pupils. Fixed effects for 324 civil districts were included. Note that some observations are perfectly predicted by the fixed effects and therefore drop out from the estimation.

starker. This divide generated more variation in how different areas and populations experienced elementary schooling than most of the patronage. Note that the first four patron types – from central government to manorial lords – recorded wildly divergent rates of overall compliance in Table 3.6: from the low of 24.1% for aristocrats to a high of 39.7% for monasteries. Yet, in columns (i) and (ii) of Table 3.7, these same four patron types are practically indistinguishable, with no more than 3.6 percentage points between them, once the demographic variables are included. Whether due to higher standard of living in cities or due to more diverse and sophisticated urban labour markets, compliance was easier to achieve for urban schools, no matter whom they had for patron. This was one reason why patrons disproportionately more involved with urban schools – such as the *Religionsfond* – appeared more successful in reaching compliance in Table 3.6. Conversely, patrons saddled with mostly rural schools – such as the landowners whose custodies were 92% rural – appeared neglectful of their duties. But why could the aristocrats not achieve compliance at least as well as the villages? After all, the gap between them was almost 24% in Table 3.6! The difference between rural schools of aristocratic patronage and of village patronage was in size: as Table 3.5 illustrated, the former had on average almost 80 pupils more than the latter. The marginal effect of enrolment in column (ii) of Table 3.7 suggests that this could dampen the likelihood of compliance by 14%, *ceteris paribus*.[30] This accounts for a good part of the overall compliance gap (though not all of it).

To zero in on the difference that patrons could make when the burdens of patronage were somewhat more involved, the focus shifts in columns (iii) and (iv) to schools which had at least 100 enrolled pupils, meaning that compliance required at least a little bit of effort. When a school was established for a small number of pupils (i.e. less than a 100), then even if it started with just one teacher in one classroom (as it usually would), it was automatically compliant. Conversely, a school with more than 100 pupils faced a real chance that the physical infrastructure could plausibly fall short of what was required, if one of the teachers resigned or a classroom became temporarily unusable.

In this second specification, the demographic variables lose much of their explanatory power: the difference in compliance probability between a town of 2000 and a small village is only 0.087, or 8.7%, and is not statistically significant. The impact of enrolment is also negligible: adding an extra 10 pupils to a school would depress the imputed probability by mere 0.4%. But, the specification also confirms that when a school increased beyond a certain size, small villages were no longer willing and able to cope as patrons. As in column (ii), so in column (iv) the first four types of patrons are relatively similar to each other – the biggest difference between their marginal effects is rather small – only 0.061, or 6.1%. And, as in column (ii), here too, the impact of a town patronage is the largest. The most pronounced difference between the two specifications is how low the impact of village patronage sinks relative to all the others, when only big schools are considered.

It is instructive to think of the dynamic playing out in the background. The total population and the school-age population of a community are strongly correlated. Hence, a small village could expect a small number of enrolled pupils, if it opened a school for them. Under what circumstances could a small village ever end up with a big school of more than 100 pupils? Usually, this happened when the school catered to several close-by villages at once, as

---

[30] The calculation, using average marginal effects, as above, is: $-0.176\times0.8 = -0.141$.

in Bohnice. This was a frequent arrangement in the countryside, where the average school served around four villages. What column (iv) of Table 3.7 shows, then, is that when such a situation arose and a school grew in size, the landowning patrons were far more able to rise to the occasion than when the villagers were patrons themselves: the difference between them in likelihood of compliance was 12.5%. Rather then being the brake on the education of the countryside, the aristocrats supported the bigger and financially more burdensome rural schools.

They were also more flexible in responding to changing needs resulting from population growth and immigration. Schools obviously had to adjust to the shifting demographics of the villages and towns they served. New schools were being established in places that had been sending their children to another village in order to cut their walking distance and improve attendance. Such a move also alleviated overcrowding pressures on pre-existing schools. These new schools were often founded under the patronage of their village. This was, for example, the case for 12 out of 23 new schools that appeared in the Styrian diocese of Seckau between 1846 and 1861.[31] So villages were more eager than other patrons to start a new school. But in contrast to other types of patrons, whose founding acts usually established stable and robust schools which lasted, villages were taking on a kind of entrepreneurial gamble. They set up a modest provisional or itinerant school, assumed patronage over it, operated it for a few years and hoped that later, pleading financial difficulties, they could rope in a more deep-pocketed patron – a feudal lord or the *Religionsfond*, perhaps – who could then bear the requisite share of maintenance costs. Tellingly, of the 31 Styrian schools that changed patrons between 1846 and 1861, 20 made precisely such a move, while only one changed patrons in the opposite direction.[32] But the 1846 record also listed 44 Styrian schools which did not survive to 1865 and all but 4 of those had the village as a patron in 1846. Clearly, such start-up gambles could fail.[33]

Even in areas where the school network was already quite dense and new schools did not need to be established, the race between existing physical resources and population growth never stopped. The province of Lower Austria offers a good opportunity to look at how effectively the system faced this issue because the province regularly published relatively detailed directories of extant schools. The Lower Austrian school and teacher directory published in 1852, in particular, contains almost as detailed information for each school

---

[31] *Lehr-Personalstand der deutschen Schulen in der Seckauer- und Leobner-Diözese in Steyermark. Im Schuljahre 1846/47*; *Lehr-Personalstand der deutschen Schulen in der Seckauer Diözese in Steiermark. Im Schuljahre 1861. Abgeschlossen 15. Dezember 1860*

[32] The school in Eggersdorf had the Seckau bishop for a patron in 1846 but became a village school by 1861. The remaining ten changes involved swaps between various government agencies or from one feudal lord to another.

[33] There were also 73 schools with an unbroken village patronage from 1846 to 1861.

as the 1865 school census, which makes such analysis possible.[34] The province had 1143 schools in 1865, with 91 of them in Vienna, up from 1128 (83 in Vienna) in 1851. The imperial capital was easily the liveliest education market in the country and the only one where private schools and private educators could seize a non-negligible market share.[35] The city also introduced many innovations during this period of rapid growth, such as the 3-grade "enhanced parish school" or physical education as part of the curriculum (1862).[36] The Viennese city hall sought to take over all of the city's elementary schools as early as May 1848 but had to retreat after the defeat of the 1848 revolution. Until April 1864, when school patronage was abolished in Lower Austria, many Viennese schools in the city still relied on the patronage of the central government (such as the empire-wide prototype school, the *k.k. Normal-Hauptschule*, dating back to 1771), of religious bodies (such as the Scottish Benedictines in the Inner City) and, of course, of the city of Vienna. No school in Vienna had a feudal landowner for a patron.

To size up schools of feudal patronage, one has to focus on the Lower Austrian countryside. The total number of schools did not change much over the period 1851–1865, suggesting that the school network was already considered sufficient. The average school counted about 130–135 enrolled pupils and this value stayed about constant. Most of the investment in physical infrastructure consisted of improving and updating existing capital stock, such as building bigger and more classrooms. On this score, some modest progress was made. Even as the number of enrolled pupils increased by about 6% over those fourteen years, classrooms became somewhat less crowded and teachers more available. Whereas in 1851 there were on average 106 pupils per classroom, by 1865 this number fell to 95. The ratio of pupils-per-teacher fell from 90 to 86 during the same time. About 11.2% of all schools outside Vienna built an extra classroom and 14.2% hired an extra teacher.[37]

In the Lower Austrian countryside, more than a third of the schools had a landowner for patron, another third the central government (including the *Religionsfond*) and yet another quarter a religious order, such as the Benedictines of Melk. The remaining tenth of all schools were patronized by the local communities. The patrons' attitude to the costly business of school expansion

---

[34] Kaiser, Joseph. *Lehrer-Schema.*

[35] The data in Kaiser, *Lehrer-Schema* suggest that various private institutions accounted for about 10% of all enrolled pupils, although it is not clear whether all of them were in primary school age. Some of the private schools in Vienna were, for example, finishing schools for young ladies, which catered to an age range that overlapped to some extent with that of the elementary school. But Vienna was unique in this respect – other large cities, such as Graz, had no private primary schools.

[36] Frank. *Die Österreichische Volksschule von 1848–1898*. p. 12–23.

[37] Cvrček and Zajíček. "The rise of public schooling in nineteenth-century Imperial Austria: Who gained and who paid?" Table 6.

Table 3.8: Probit model of classroom expansion, 1851–1865

Variable	Coeff.	Avg. MFX	Coeff.	Avg. MFX
Patron type: 1(religious order)	-0.471	-0.061		
	[0.249]	[0.032]		
Patron type: 1(manorial lord)	-0.144	-0.019		
	[0.202]	[0.026]		
Patron type: 1(municipality)	-0.502	-0.065		
	[0.412]	[0.053]		
1(non-compliant in 1851)	0.152	0.031		
	[0.280]	[0.035]		
1(non-compliant in 1851) × 1(urban)	1.357*	0.168*		
	[0.369]	[0.050]		
1(urban)	0.595		1.068*	0.140*
	[0.544]		[0.260]	[0.033]
Pupils per classroom in 1851	0.017*	0.002*	0.018**	0.002**
	[0.003]	[0.000]	[0.002]	[0.000]
Growth in pupil population, 1851–65	2.111*	0.274*	2.038*	0.268*
	[0.375]	[0.046]	[0.358]	[0.045]
Change in steam engine HP, 1851–63	0.005	0.001	0.004	0.001
	[0.006]	[0.001]	[0.006]	[0.001]
School district fixed effects	Yes		Yes	
Civil district fixed effects	Yes		Yes	
N	721		730	
Pseudo-R^2	0.454		0.445	

Note: The sample includes Lower Austrian schools outside Vienna that existed in both years and reported all variables. "Avg. MFX" stands for average marginal effects. The variable 1(urban) takes on 1 for communities of 2000 inhabitants or more, 0 otherwise; 1(non-compliant in 1851) is equal to 1 for schools that reported more than 100 pupils per classroom in 1851. Star (*) denotes statistical significance at 1%. Standard errors are in square brackets.
Source: Cvrček and Zajíček. "The rise of public schooling in nineteenth-century Imperial Austria: Who gained and who paid?" Table 8.

obviously varied with local circumstances: the enrolment numbers, the wealth of the community, the strength of enforcement of the regulations by the state and church authorities. The probit model used in Table 3.8 controls for these forces explicitly in order to isolate the net impact of various types of patron, other things held equal.[38] The dependent variable is equal to 1 if a school built an extra classroom between 1851 and 1865, and 0 otherwise.

Most of the coefficients and marginal effects in the table have expected signs and sizes. A classroom was more likely to be built when the number of pupils was large and when it was increasing. For instances, the variable "Growth in pupil population" is a ratio between 1865 pupils and 1851 pupils,

[38] For example, the change in steam power controls for how well and how much a village was plugged into the ongoing industrialization and the attendant economic development; the urban dummy variable the difference between urban and rural schools embedded in the law.

so a value of, say, 1.05 implies a 5% increase over the 14-year period. The average marginal effect on this variable (+0.274) implies that compared to a school that recorded no growth in pupils, the one with a 5% growth is estimated to have been 1.4% more likely to build an extra classroom. The impact of pupils per classroom is also positive: an increase by 10 pupils per classroom raises the likelihood of classroom expansion by about 2%. On the other hand, the pace of industrialization, proxied for by the steam power, did not make much difference.[39]

Then there is the contribution of the different patrons. As discussed earlier, both past and current research recognizes the diverse incentives that shaped the decisions of various stakeholders in relation to the school. The point of this analysis is to see if they were divergent and strong enough to produce visible differences, as some authors argued they did. It should be possible in principle to draw a line from those hypothesized incentives to specific outcomes. For one, the central government, as the author and instigator of the whole school policy, had a direct stake in enforcing its own regulations, so one should expect that schools under its patronage would expand when overcrowded but not otherwise. The landowners should have been the most reluctant supporters of school expansion, given that they did not draw any direct benefit from it – unlike manufacturing, agriculture was not a very human capital-intensive sector so to the landowners school patronage was an expense that did not yield much of a return. The schools in their patronage should have expanded rarely. In contrast, if elementary education opened the door to better paid manufacturing jobs, municipal patrons should have build extra classrooms eagerly, perhaps even ahead of the regulation requirements – after all, the town and village elders realized perhaps more immediately than all other patrons that the schools served their own children whose opportunities in life could potentially be enhanced through education. Moreover, since any school construction involved negotiations between the local community and the patron, villages that assumed patronage of their own schools did not run the risk of getting bogged down in endless talks with a potentially obstructionist landowner. The incentives of the monasteries are not clear cut one way or other: on the one hand, the church was a pillar of the school policy and therefore faced similar incentives as the government; on the other, abbeys were, and acted as, large landowners and could expect corresponding economic payoff from patronage (i.e. none). So, in terms of their readiness to pay for an extra classroom, towns and villages should rank above central government, which in turn should rank above landowners, with religious orders somewhere between the last two. For the purposes of comparison, the patronage by the government institutions, including the *Religionsfond*, is left out of the estimation in Table 3.8, which implicitly sets its net contribution to

[39] In Chapter 6, I discuss the likely reasons why this was the case (see pp. 224–231).

zero and turns it into a benchmark against which other types of patron can be compared.[40] Hence, given the ranking derived here, the impact of municipal patronage should be positive and that of manorial lords negative.

The patron dummy variables have all negative coefficients and marginal effects, which means that their impact was weaker than that of government patronage. Specifically, schools of monastic and municipal patronage were 6.1%, resp. 6.5%, less likely to build an extra classroom than schools of governmental patronage, while feudal lords as patrons expanded schools with 1.9% lower probability. None of these effects are statistically significant, which suggests that these differences were not very pronounced or systematic. In other words, what Table 3.7 showed in cross-section, Table 3.8 documents across time: feudal lords do not stand out as a brake on the expansion of the school system, as being systematically laxer patrons than the others. They were, in fact, slightly more likely to finance classroom expansion than the other two types of patron in the table but the difference is not systematic enough to be statistically significant.

What turns out to be very significant, however, is the interaction between non-compliance and urban location. The coefficients imply that, generally, urban schools were somewhat more likely to expand than countryside schools, and non-compliant schools than compliant schools, but the expansion was especially likely in schools that were both urban and non-compliant in 1851. Figure 3.1, which uses the results from Table 3.8 to impute probability of classroom expansion, gives an indication of how that interaction played out in various contexts. The variations between patrons were dwarfed by the difference between the country and the city. But not only were towns more likely to expand generally, they were especially more likely to expand upon crossing the regulation threshold. The impact of the 101st pupil in the classroom lifted the likelihood of classroom expansion to anywhere from 30% to 50%, depending on the type of patron.[41] In the countryside, however, having 100 enrolled pupils per classroom did not produce much beyond a blip in the probability of expansion because two thirds of rural schools instead took the easier and cheaper route and switched to half-day teaching. This, again, was true across the sample regardless of patron.

The reason why this is important is also the reason why Table 3.8 contains the two rightmost columns. There, the probit model is estimated without the compliance and patron variables. For those variables that are kept on, the co-

---

[40] Similarly, the "private/other" category of patrons also drops out because it covered only a small number of schools, none of which built an extra classroom over this period. Lacking any variation in the dependent variable, the coefficient of this type of patrons could not be estimated.

[41] It should be noted that the location of that break – at the 101st pupil – is not a outcome of estimation but is imposed by the specification: the variable 1(non-compliant in 1851) switches from 0 to 1 at that value.

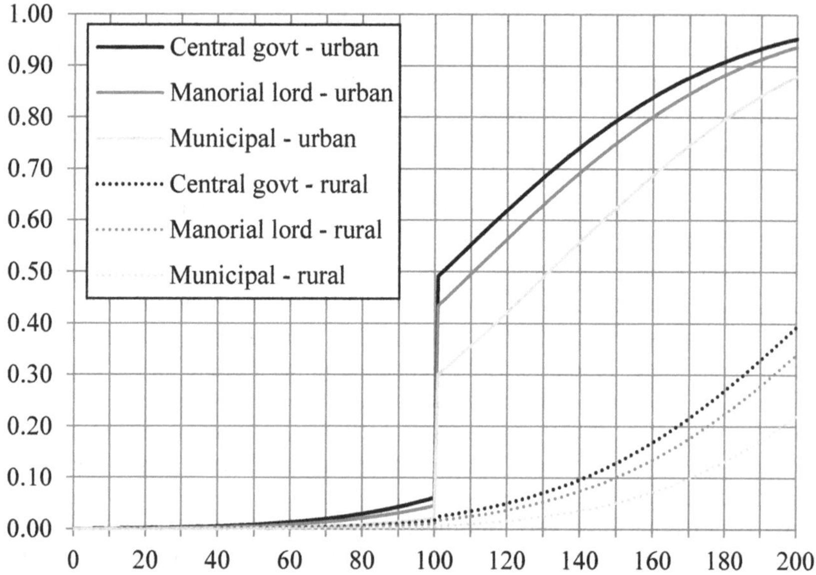

Figure 3.1: Imputed probability of classroom expansion in Lower Austria, 1851–1865
Source: Cvrček, Tomáš and Zajíček, Miroslav. "The rise of public schooling in nineteenth-century Imperial Austria: Who gained and who paid?" Figure 1.

efficients and average marginal effects are largely unchanged. The stark contrast between the urban schools and rural schools remains: the urban ones were 14% more likely to build an extra classroom, other things held equal. Seeing only this second specification, one could easily conclude that such a large lag in the countryside was the work of the large landowners who were the politically dominant class outside cities. In other words, it is easy to blame the landowners for a shortfall in schooling infrastructure when the inference comes from proxy estimation instead of the direct observation of different patrons' decisions furnished by the more extended model.

Physical infrastructure was just a portion of the overall cost of elementary schooling and in an average year, it was the less prominent one. The bulk of the day-to-day expense was paying for the teaching staff. Here the law envisioned substantial financial participation on the part of the pupils' families. Section 10 of the *Politische Verfassung* was wholly devoted to dealing with teacher salaries and therefore also regulated tuition fees. By a decree from 1785, which the 1805 law incorporated, teachers were entitled to at least 130 fl per year, teaching assistants 70 fl per year. It was understood that in the countryside, teachers were likely to also serve in the local church, which would enhance their income. By Article 176, the rates charged of students were to be determined on the assumptions that school would be in session for

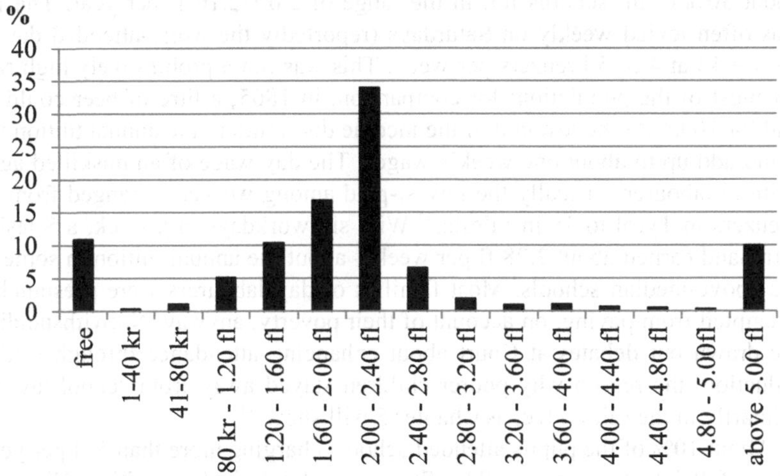

Figure 3.2: Distribution of pupils by annual tuition fee, 1865
Note: Not included are pupils from 8.8% of schools that failed to report tuition fee data. Also excluded are pupils from Galicia, Bukovina and Dalmatia, which did not levy tuition.
Source: Detail-Conscription.

47 of the year's 52 weeks and factoring in an expected 90% collection rate (the remaining 10% accounting for absences due to ill health and truancy). Every year, upon compiling a list of all local school-bound children, the teacher, in cooperation with local authorities, was supposed to determine, which families counted as too poor to pay tuition, and their children were entitled to enrol for free. If more than three children from one family were enrolled concurrently, the fourth and subsequent children also attended for free (Art. 182), although this provision only applied in the countryside. The government left the village and town elders to set the rates, unless a province-wide regulation abolished tuition fees across the land.

No detailed survey of tuition rates was conducted until 1865. The school census, conducted in that year, recorded the tuition fee for about 90% of all schools and tuition revenue for almost all of them. Some schools charged different rates to different age groups. In 1861 in Bohnice, for example, 6–8 year-olds paid 2 kreuzers per week, 8–10 year-olds 2.5 kreuzers and older pupils 3 kreuzers.[42] That nuance is unfortunately lost in the 1865 school data, which only record one rate. Figure 3.2 presents the distribution of enrolled pupils by tuition fee. Across the provinces where tuition fees were levied, over 1700 schools (or 17% of all) reported that their pupils attended free of charge. Among those that levied the fee, the median rate was 2 fl per year and

[42] Kneidl, *Paměti.* p. 151.

about 30% of all schools fell in the range of 2.00–2.10 fl per year. The fee was often levied weekly on Saturdays (reportedly the worst-attended day of the week) at 4 or 5 kreuzers per week. This was not a prohibitively high rate for most of the population: for comparison, in 1865, a litre of beer could be had for 10 kr. At the low end of the income distribution, the annual tuition fee could add up to about one week's wages. The day wage of an unskilled agricultural labourer – usually the lowest-paid among workers – ranged from 88 kreuzers in Tyrol to 38 in Silesia.[43] With six workdays in a week, a Silesian farmhand earned about 2.28 fl per week – about the annual tuition in some of the above-median schools. Most families of day labourers were presumably exempted from paying, on account of their poverty, anyway. Notwithstanding the drawn out debates at Court about enhancing attendance through tuition reduction, the reason why poorer children stayed away from school lay not primarily in the tuition fee, as Chapter 5 will show.[44]

About 10% of the pupils attended schools charging more than 5 fl per year. These fell into two groups. The first was schools in large cities. Viennese pupils paid 5.50 fl per year, Prague children generally 5.70 fl. The second group comprised schools of religious minorities. For example, the Jewish schools in Mělník and Pardubice asked for 26 fl per year, or 0.50 fl per week, as did the Protestant school in Brno. Among the 23 schools that charged over 8 fl per year, 18 were either Protestant or Jewish schools. It is not clear why their demands were this extreme but the decision came from within the communities.

Higher tuition fees were also charged in schools that had broader curriculum. In the median two-grade school, the fee was 1.91 fl compared to 2.50 fl in a four-grade school and 3.33 fl in a seven-grade civic school (*Bürgerschule*). Major schools across the land asked for a gulden more than branch schools, and schools in the city were more expensive than in the countryside. Co-educational schools had lower tuition fees than single-sex schools, which is a reflection of the fact that single-sex schools were almost invariably an urban phenomenon – the countryside could not afford separate institutions for boys and girls.

On top of all that, the attitude towards tuition varied considerably across provinces. Galicia, Bukovina and Dalmatia consistently levied no tuition, their funding relying on the *Religionsfond* before 1848 and on public budget of the province or of local communities. The situation in the remaining crown lands is summarized in Table 3.9. The South and South-West of the empire stands out as offering tuition-free schooling to most (though not all) of their students. Tyrolean schools were the "cheapest" chiefly because 85% of them

---

[43] TSOM 1865 II. Theil: Tafel 2.

[44] For an account of policy discussions regarding tuition fees, see Weiss, *Geschichte der österreichischen Volksschule 1792–1848. II. Band.* p. 621–636.

Table 3.9: Tuition fees across provinces, 1865

Province	annual tuition fee (fl) median	annual tuition fee (fl) 90th percentile	% pupils exempted	tuition revenue (fl per school)	base salary expense (fl per school)
Lower Austria	2.35	5.50	22.7	291.65	441.93
Upper Austria	1.68	2.27	14.3	212.32	291.79
Salzburg	1.75	2.00	9.3	146.85	240.77
Styria	1.60	2.10	21.5	154.48	194.14
Carinthia	2.00	2.57	36.9	99.40	189.29
Carniola	0.00	1.75	87.0	30.11	294.67
Austrian Littoral	0.00	2.20	78.2	26.89	372.64
Tyrol & Vorarlberg	0.00	1.05	73.2	17.25	136.31
Bohemia	2.06	2.52	13.7	291.94	399.71
Moravia	1.70	2.52	13.4	224.88	316.47
Silesia	1.29	2.16	12.3	156.48	275.84
Overall	2.00	2.70	22.5	205.77	321.19

Note: Galicia, Bukovina and Dalmatia are not included because they did not levy tuition fees.
Source: Detail-Conscription.

offered only half-year schooling. Strictly speaking, even Carinthia should count as part of this low-tuition region, since the data for this province likely overestimate the extent of tuition collection: about 31% of schools there did not report any tuition-related data, possibly because they were not levying any.[45] At the other end of the range, Lower Austria and Bohemia, the two most densely schooled provinces, were also the most expensive.

Once the rates were set and the exemptions determined, the teachers and the communities were rather effective in collecting the requisite sums. More than three quarters of the schools collected more than 90% of the expected tuition revenues and some even overshot their target thanks to fines.[46] On a per-paying student basis, the largest shortfall was recorded in Lower Austria but even there it did not exceed 4 kreuzers per child over the whole year.

The table also shows how successful the various provinces were in covering their salary expenses by way of tuition: on average, the tuition revenues fell short. In the 1865 school census, only about 13% of all schools collected more in tuition than was their base salary expenditure. The shortfall had to be made up from other sources. Some villages set aside plots of lands, the return on which subsidized the teacher, or tapped various charitable trusts that had been established by some local benefactor but many communities simply paid the balance out of the public budget. School patrons were also available to

45 The table is constructed only from schools that reported their tuition fees.

46 According to Article 177 of *Politische Verfassung*, truants had to pay a fine equal to double the tuition fee.

Table 3.10: Regression analysis of tuition fees

Dependent variable	Fraction exempted	Annual tuition fee	Salary coverage
mean	0.133	2.104	0.809
s.d.	0.138	1.239	0.324
Type of school (Major school = 0; Co-educational school = 0)			
Trivial school	0.034*	-0.132	0.005
	[0.017]	[0.152]	[0.044]
Provisional school	0.017	-0.296	-0.003
	[0.018]	[0.163]	[0.047]
Girl school	0.097*	-0.635*	-0.202*
	[0.018]	[0.158]	[0.044]
Boy school	0.107*	0.834*	-0.215*
	[0.018]	[0.161]	[0.046]
Amount of Instruction (Year-round all-day = 0)			
Year-round half-day	0.004	0.146*	0.024
	[0.005]	[0.041]	[0.013]
Half-year all-day	0.014	-0.420	0.078
	[0.038]	[0.326]	[0.100]
Half-year half-day	0.008	0.019	0.043
	[0.072]	[0.621]	[0.182]
1(town>2000)	-0.357*	-4.553*	0.158
	[0.032]	[0.287]	[0.083]
ln(town population)	0.048*	0.599*	-0.012
	[0.004]	[0.033]	[0.010]
Extent of curriculum (1-grade school = 0)			
2-grade school	0.019*	-0.082	0.001
	[0.006]	[0.050]	[0.014]
3-grade school	0.032*	-0.080	-0.007
	[0.007]	[0.060]	[0.017]
4-grade school	0.052*	-0.585*	-0.209*
	[0.015]	[0.134]	[0.038]
5-grade school	-0.063	-0.634	-0.265*
	[0.048]	[0.571]	[0.128]
6-grade school	0.018	0.048	-0.178*
	[0.034]	[0.302]	[0.089]
7-grade school	-0.011	-1.091*	-0.218*
	[0.031]	[0.288]	[0.079]
School patron type			
Central government	0.056*	-0.046	0.012
	[0.013]	[0.119]	[0.035]
Religionsfond & Studienfond	0.049*	-0.137	0.014
	[0.014]	[0.127]	[0.037]
Monasteries	0.032*	0.023	0.063
	[0.014]	[0.125]	[0.037]
Manorial lords	0.035*	-0.022	0.037
	[0.013]	[0.118]	[0.035]
Towns	0.042*	1.695*	-0.010
	[0.017]	[0.155]	[0.045]

Villages	0.032*	-0.038	0.022
	[0.014]	[0.123]	[0.036]
All other patrons	0.050*	-0.291	-0.059
	[0.024]	[0.209]	[0.062]
Constant	0.029	2.185	0.785
	[0.022]	[0.200]	[0.058]
N	4767	4555	4480
Adjusted R^2	0.194	0.246	0.059

Note: Standard errors are in square brackets. Asterisk (*) denotes statistical significance at 5%. "Fraction exempted" is the fraction of enrolled pupils who were exempted from paying tuition and it takes on values between 0 and 1. "Salary coverage" is the ratio of tuition fee revenues and salary costs at each school. All explanatory variables except the natural log of urban population, *ln*(town population), are indicator variables. The left-out default categories are noted next to subheadings in the table, except for school patron types, which are not mutually exclusive.

contribute, although they were not under a legal obligation to do so, strictly speaking.

In short, tuition fees were affected by numerous different considerations, which sometimes pushed in opposite directions. The broad averages cannot say anything about their relative strength, but the regression analysis conveyed in Table 3.10 can. It covers three interconnected aspects: exemption from tuition, the annual tuition fee and the extent to which tuition revenues covered a school's salary expenses. The main pattern that emerges from the pile of coefficients is again the stark contrast between country and city. Schools in towns of more than 2000 inhabitants charged a higher tuition, other things held equal, but they also exempted more pupils from paying it. Compared to a village, a town of 5000 inhabitants exempted about 5.1% more pupils while charging 55 kreuzers per year more on average. Apparently, these two effects largely cancelled each other out in revenue terms, which is why in the third column, town schools do not stand out against country schools in terms of their salary coverage. The large and significant impact of having a single-sex school is in fact part of the same pattern – as mentioned above, these were very rare in the countryside whereas they comprised 27% of all schools in towns and cities. The urban influence even "explains away" to a great extent the difference between various types of schools (major vs trivial vs provisional schools) and between schools with different amounts of instruction. The three regressions combine into a picture where the urban schools were generally more expensive: they were bigger, required more staff and had to pay the teachers more, given that cities had a somewhat higher cost of living. They also had to pay for the urban poor who could not pay themselves but were under the same obligation to enrol. This was plausibly a larger problem in the city than in the countryside. All this added up to urban schools charging higher fees to a somewhat lower proportion of their students: the fact that major schools and 4-grade, 5-grade or higher-grade schools were generally the more expensive schools turned on the fact that such schools predominantly operated in cities. Once the urban environment is controlled for, these gradients either disappear or go the opposite way. With regards to the school patrons, Table 3.10 shows that they did not, by and large, make much of a difference in this area. It is true that, in schools patronized by the central government and the *Religionsfond*, a somewhat higher percentage of students was exempted from paying than, say, in schools of village patronage. That difference, however, was only 2.4 percentage points. This is not a very surprising result given that exemption depended primarily on the local social situation and the guidelines for exemption were outlined in the law – there was not much room for discretion.

The patrons did not have much impact on salary coverage either. Here one might actually expect differences. If, for example, one kind of patron – say, the central government – supported schools systematically more than others, even in the form of contributing not only to the physical infrastructure but also to teacher salaries, then schools under such patronage could charge less of their students. In such cases the percentage of salary expenses covered by tuition would be lower and the coefficient on such patrons would be significant and negative. But the estimates do not reveal any such pattern – the coefficients are small and, outside the catch-all category of "All other patrons" which covers only 37 observations, not statistically different from each other ($F(5, 4457) = 2.05$; p-value = 0.069). Patrons apparently did not go out of their way to support schools, or if they did, they did so in equal measure.

The only disparity between the patrons that stands out is in the middle regression. When a school had the town for a patron, the tuition fees were significantly higher: a coefficient of +1.69 stands out against the small and mostly negative net impact of the other six types, which are not statistically different from each other ($F(5,4532) = 1.69$; p-value = 0.133). The fact that city-based schools charged more on average is already captured by the urbanization variables whereas this result implies that, if an urban school also had the town hall for a patron, it charged another 1.69 fl per year on top of that. In addition, this higher tuition did not seem to translate into a higher coverage of salary expenses. Put together, these results imply that towns as patrons ran more expensive schools and passed most of that extra cost on to the pupils. Recall from Table 3.4 that these schools were most often all-day schools, most likely to be major schools and had the highest number of grades on average. The average school with a town patron had a salary bill of 1768 fl, paid to about 5.3 teachers, while town schools with other patrons had only 1247 fl and 4.3 teachers. Country schools spent an average 366 fl. on 1.6 teachers. The town really was different from the countryside.

Seeing that the system drew in resources from, and made stakeholders of, a diverse set of individuals, institutions and constituencies, what could one say

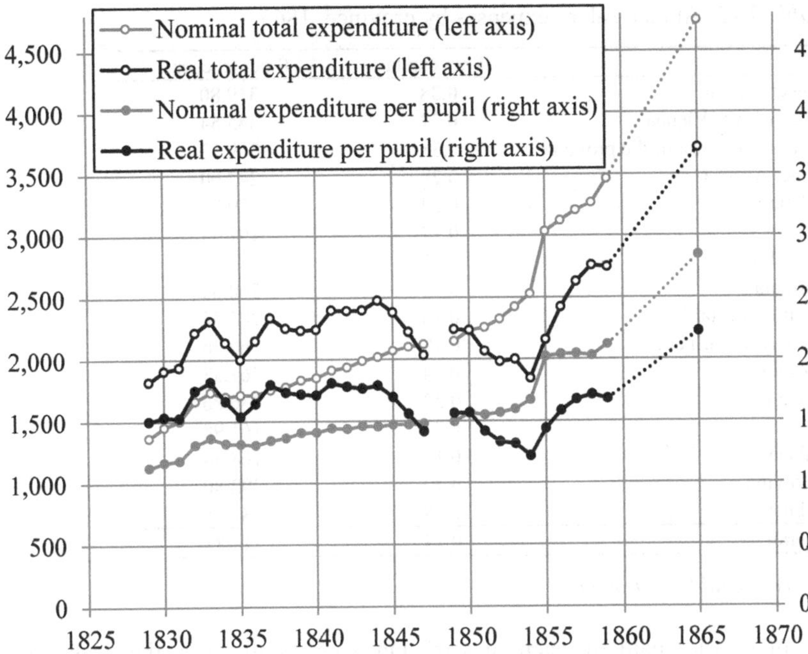

Figure 3.3: Expenditure on teacher salaries, 1828–1865 (thousands of fl)
Source: Versuch; *Darstellung*; TSOM 1830–1865.

about the overall educational spending in relation to the rest of the economy? The aggregate data on this point are not available in great abundance and what is available is not entirely reliable. From 1829 onwards, government statistical reports on schooling, published in the *Tafeln zur Statistik* (TSOM), cited a figure labeled "Expenditure" and from the 1840s occasionally even of primary schools' sources of revenue. The revenue numbers usually dovetailed with expenditure figures, although sometimes they diverged by a wide margin. The spending figure was not clearly defined. From its usual placement next to teaching staff totals, one can surmise it pertained to salary expenditures. The only year, in which the interpretation of the expenditure figure is certain, is 1865, when the document specified that it referred to teacher salaries. For what it is worth, Figure 3.3 tracks the reported expenditure data.

In nominal terms, the spending was growing. For the three decades before 1855, it expanded at the rate of 1.9% per year. Thereafter, the growth even accelerated. But from 1840 on, the salary fund was losing the battle against inflation and the growth in pupil numbers. Real total expenditure peaked in 1844 at 2.47 million gulden (in 1850 prices). The subsequent rapid rise in price level, which was also one of the contributing factors to social unrest that spawned the revolution of 1848, gradually but relentlessly eroded the va-

Table 3.11: Annual salary expenses by province, 1865

	fl per capita	fl per teacher
Lower Austria	0.38	319.80
of which: Vienna	0.37	345.54
of which: rest of the province	0.38	309.73
Upper Austria	0.29	247.00
Salzburg	0.37	229.71
Styria	0.19	191.35
Carinthia	0.17	133.95
Carniola	0.15	200.84
Austrian Littoral	0.30	283.57
Tyrol & Vorarlberg	0.18	60.46
Bohemia	0.34	261.53
Moravia	0.32	236.26
Silesia	0.21	161.98
Galicia	0.10	168.38
Bukovina	0.10	292.80
Dalmatia	0.08	82.08
Overall	0.23	214.88

Source: Detail-Conscription.

lue of salaries paid to teaching staff. On a per-pupil basis, the peak came already in 1841, at 1.81 fl and by the trough of 1854 the spending declined by a third to 1.22 fl per pupil. The turn-around in 1855 started in the Slav-populated provinces, especially in Galicia and Bohemia and to a lesser degree in Moravia and Silesia. In these Czech provinces, which were the main contributors to the upswing in spending, the money came primarily from an aggressive increase in tuition fees: in Bohemia, for example, tuition revenues jumped from less than 300000 fl in 1854 to 791000 fl by 1865. In Silesia, the haul almost doubled between 1859 and 1865. The increase in per-pupil spending was thus mostly paid for by the pupils' parents. Even in other provinces, where tuition was not a prominent source, the extra money came from schools' "own resources" as the official statistics called it – local endowments, payment for the teacher's church service, voluntary gifts – but not from central government funds. In Tyrol, these "own resources" grew from 39000 fl to 67000 between 1851 and 1859, while another 37000 fl were raised by towns, villages and landowners over the same period.

For the society as a whole, covering these operational costs was not particularly burdensome. One measure of this burden is expressing the cost in per-capita terms. Table 3.11 shows that the whole salary bill came to about 23 kreuzers per person per year in 1865. Even in provinces with the most developed and most expensive school network, such as Bohemia and Lower Austria, teachers were hired at negligible cost to society. For comparison, recall that a day's wage of an unskilled labourer ranged from 38 to 88 kreuzers.

Moreover, the 1860s were the most generous decade to date: between 1830 and 1860, the per-person real annual cost (at 1850 prices) fluctuated between 10 and 15 kreuzers. To put it in a different perspective, one may compare the elementary teachers' salary bill with the expense dedicated to other sections of the educational system: the secondary schools and various institutions of higher learning (mostly universities and polytechnics). In 1865, there were 12177 students in tertiary education and 45243 at secondary schools in Imperial Austria – minuscule numbers compared to the 1.67 million pupils enrolled in elementary schools. Still, the country spent 3.89 million fl on these educational institutions, of which about 58.1%, or 2.26 million fl, went to salaries and remuneration of 3601 teaching staff.[47] In contrast, the 22100 primary school teachers ran up a salary bill of 4.75 million fl. Compared to their secondary and higher-level counterparts, elementary school teachers were getting a raw deal.[48]

As a final exercise, let us assess the size of the whole elementary school sector against the rest of the economy by expressing the overall spending on primary education as a share of GDP. Estimating this will require a few heroic assumptions but since the purpose of the exercise is merely to construct a plausible range, rather than a precise point estimate, the main concern is to avoid an error by an order of magnitude. That should be possible even with heroic assumptions. Choosing the year 1865 as the best documented, the starting point and the only relatively precise item in the tally is the 4.75 million fl of salary expense. The grand total of elementary school expenditure needs to include not only this amount but also the costs of building and operating the physical infrastructure. Firewood for heating was the most important item in day-to-day operation, so much so that the law devoted a separate article to it, requiring 6 fathoms, or about 18 m^3, of wood per classroom per year (Article 391). There were about 21800 classrooms in the 14000 schools in Imperial Austria in 1865 and combining the regulation amount with the firewood prices prevailing in that year puts the overall cost of heating all the schools at 1.29 million fl. per year.[49]

Then there is the construction of new school buildings. Almost every school had a building, so seeing that 242 new schools were opened in 1865, one can assume that roughly similar number of new school buildings were built for them. In addition, a fraction of existing schools were rebuilding or replacing their old premises with new and improved structures. Systematic,

[47] TSOM 1860–65 II. Theil, Tafel 14. "Lehranstalten in den Jahre 1860 bis 1865", pp. 148–162.

[48] TSOM 1860–65 II. Theil, Tafel 14. "Lehranstalten in den Jahre 1860 bis 1865", pp. 104–147.

[49] TSOM 1860–1865 II. Theil, Tafel. 2 "Markt-Durchschnitsspreise in den Jahren 1860 bis 1865" Of the two types of wood cited by this publication, I am using the more expensive hard wood which also yielded more heat.

aggregate data on this process are hard to come by but one can make reasonable inferences from local histories, such as one written by Karel Adámek about the schools around the Bohemian town of Hlinsko.[50] Across the 44 school locations, which operated before the 1869 school reform and for which he gives construction dates, the median school building served for 50 years before being replaced.[51] If this estimate were applied to the whole monarchy, it would imply that about 2% of existing school buildings would be replaced with new ones every year. In 1865, that would mean about 280 new constructions among the existing 14000 schools. Adding this to the buildings for newly opened schools yields a total construction effort of about 520 schools in 1865. The costs obviously varied, depending on size. At one end of the spectrum, a new boys school in Karlín, then a suburb of Prague, built in 1864 for 611 pupils cost almost 60000 fl.[52] At the other end, the village school in Dědová for 91 pupils was purchased for 1500 fl in 1852.[53] Small villages, even with the contributions from the school patrons, obviously had smaller budgets (recall they had to contribute about a third of the cost) and also needed smaller schools, given their lower number of pupils. From the (mere) 11 instances of schools built between 1850 and 1880 for which a total construction bill is available, it seems that the median cost was 7000 fl, which was enough to erect a building for roughly 100 pupils. Using this figure would bring the total expenditure on school construction in 1865 to 3.64 million fl.

Adding up the three amounts – salaries, firewood and construction and maintenance – that formed the bulk of all school-related expenditures puts the total spending at 9.7 million fl. Varying the assumptions provides a sense of the range of plausible values: granting the average school 8 fathoms of firewood per classroom and assuming that not 2% but 3% of existing school buildings were replaced at a cost of 10000 fl instead of 7000 fl brings the expenditure up to 13.1 million. Conversely, assuming a 1% renewal rate at 4000 fl per building and only 4 fathoms of firewood reduces the estimate to 7.1 million fl. The conclusion is clear: the overall expenditure in 1865 was somewhere around 10 million gulden.

The nearest date for which an estimate of Imperial Austria's GDP exists is the year 1870. It was constructed by Max-Stephan Schulze on the basis of the employment structure recorded in the 1869 census and is equal to 4349 mil-

---

[50] Adámek. *Paměti.*

[51] This calculation excludes all school buildings constructed after the 1869 school reform, which introduced a new system of financing. The age of school buildings still standing as of 1891 is obviously censored, which biases the estimated duration downwards, implying faster building replacement than was actually the case.

[52] Kneidl. *Paměti*. p. 122.

[53] Adámek. *Paměti.* p. 81.

lion fl in 1913 prices.[54] The 1865 GDP was likely somewhat lower than in 1870, given the boom of the late 1860s, but not too much lower, as the economic development was disrupted by the Austro-Prussian war of 1866 and its fallout: subtracting four years of, say, 2% annual growth to account for all that would bring the GDP to 4 billion gulden, flat, still in constant 1913 prices. Further, to express the figure in 1865 prices requires subtracting the intervening inflation, which accumulated to 40% over the almost fifty-year period.[55] That yields a nominal 1865 GDP of 2882 million fl.

Bringing the numbers together, the 10 million gulden of overall expenditure on elementary schooling amounted to 0.34% of GDP in 1865 – a third of one percent. The high (13 mill.) and low (7 mill.) estimates of spending would put the fraction at 0.45% and 0.25%, respectively. If the post-primary education spending is added, the whole education sector adds up to almost 0.5% of GDP. It is unlikely that the share was higher at any time before 1865. The status quo in 1865 was a product of the expansion of the 1850s and early 1860s, documented in the previous chapter and in Figure 3.3, so spending in 1865 probably stood at an all-time high: note that the per-capita expenditure on teachers, which made up a half of the total, was also significantly higher in 1865 than at any time before.

Analogous statistics for other countries at the time (so as to put the 0.34% share in perspective) are hard to come by. Perhaps the closest in terms of definitions are Alain Carry's data for France.[56] His figure for the mid-1860s is also about a third of a percent of GDP, although his total does not include the expenditure on private elementary schools, which played a much bigger role in the French education market than they did Austria. For another comparison, the Swiss canton of Zurich was spending about 0.65% of its GDP on all science and education (not just elementary) in 1860.[57] Another possibility is to make comparisons across time for the same countries instead of across space in the same year. By 2016, the Republic of Austria spent 0.9%, the Czech Republic 0.8% and Slovenia 1.5% of their GDP on primary education – this, of course, out of a much larger GDP and in a situation where elemen-

[54] Schulze, Max-Stephan. "Patterns of growth and stagnation in the late nineteenth century Habsburg economy." Schulze quotes the figure in Austrian crowns (at 8697.3), a currency introduced in the reform of 1892–1900, when Austria-Hungary joined the gold standard. The conversion rate was 1 fl = 2 K, hence the amount cited in the text.

[55] Cvrček, Tomáš. "Wages, Prices and Living Standards in the Habsburg Empire, 1827–1910"; Mühlpeck, Sandgruber and Woitek. "Index der Verbraucherpreise 1800–1914"

[56] See Carry. *Le compte satellite rétrospectif de l'éducation en France.* I cite the estimate from Lindert. *Growing Public Vol. 1*, Figure 5.5.

[57] I thank Ulrich Woitek for sharing this data point with me through personal communication. For a discussion of regional GDP in Switzerland, see Stohr, Christian. "Multiple Core Regions: Regional Inequality in Switzerland, 1860–2008". For data on education spending, see *Historische Statistik der Schweiz HSSO*, 2012, Tab. U.3a. at hsso.ch/2012/u/3a.

tary schooling has long ceased to be the frontier of mass education. For the whole educational sector (excluding R&D), the shares reached 4.4%, 3.3% and 4.1%, respectively.[58] Compared to these values and to available contemporary values of other countries, the 0.34% of 1865 was low.

One point of difference is that today the vast majority of primary education spending is public, which cannot be said so unequivocally of the 19th century system. It is hard to separate public and private precisely, partly because the distinction is not clear definitionally: when an aristocratic landowner, who by the early 1860s was just as much a private citizen as the farmers who were once his serfs, paid for a third of a school's construction cost or donated firewood due to an anachronistic obligation lingering from the pre-1848 era and still on the books fifteen years later, was this expenditure public or private? At least what is clear is that a non-negligible proportion was definitely not tax-financed public spending: the tuition fees, which in most provinces covered teacher salaries, were roughly a fifth of the overall amount. About 7% of buildings used for teaching were let by their private owners free of charge – an in-kind private contribution. Local governments sometimes raised funds for schools by appealing to the public for voluntary donations.[59]

The Austrian schools were rarely private in terms of their management and control: in that respect, the church and state were very much on top of things. In regards to costs, however, the government did not want to be involved all that much. The 1865 government budget lists the State Ministry's total expenditure on education at 3.1 million fl., and that mostly went to secondary and higher schools, not elementary ones. In contrast, in that same budget, army and navy received 104 million fl. while servicing the public debt required another 116 million fl.[60] Those were the real government priorities. The costs of maintaining schools and paying teachers were passed on to others and it perhaps bespeaks the government's acute awareness of this burden's scant popularity that it was kept relatively low and the schooling consequently underfinanced. In the countryside, costly regulations went unenforced because the rural population did not want to pay for it all either. It cannot be said that the shortfall was a result of any particular constituency's active resistance: even landowners and abbots paid their dues as patrons. A more accurate diagnosis lay in a certain popular indifference resting on the realization that, outside the towns with their fancy four-grade *Hauptschulen* and convenient subsidies from the *Studienfond*, the kind of school that the government designed and alone tolerated was not worth the investment. The hardest hit by this outcome were precisely the people on whom the success of any educational enterprise hinges the most: the teachers.

---

[58] OECD. *Education at a Glance 2018*. Table C2.1.

[59] Adámek. *Paměti*. p. 35.

[60] SJOM 1865, p. 411, 416, 420.

Chapter 4

The Teachers

The fundamental schooling law of the monarchy, the *Politische Verfassung*, had many things to say about teachers, their duties and their rights. Thanks to this plethora of rules and regulations, teachers across the empire shared in a common professional experience, which marked them out as a distinct group. Becoming a teacher typically meant accepting the whole package: the likely salary range, the promotion prospects, the degree of social prestige, the clearly defined pedagogical mission and so on. Who were the men and (some) women who found this package appealing enough to join the teaching corps? As in previous chapters, available historical data offer a way to gauge the extent to which the reality of teachers' life matched the law's blueprint, to identify what caused the discrepancy between them and consider the alternatives (e.g. in the private education market) that existed on the sidelines.

In regards to the government's expectations of their teaching methods and skills, section 4 of the law outlined the basic tenets of the desired pedagogy: that the subject matter – primarily the religious curriculum – pass through the pupils' memory (cognition) to their "heart" (moral sentiment, i.e. internalization) so as to eventually inform their will (compliance) (Articles 39–41). Then, in reference to all further specifics, Article 42 continued:

> "Since, however, most trivial school teachers cannot be expected to possess the outstanding abilities necessary for a reasonably conducted, sophisticated instruction, they must further strictly adhere to all those expositions precisely delineated in the *Methodenbuch* and at all times strive that designated subject matter be memorized and illustrated through individual examples."

The regulation was clearly not a vote of confidence in the teachers' abilities. The bar of expectations was low and deliberately so: pedagogical creativity and talent for teaching were absolutely not sought after but rather actively discouraged. From 1775 until 1849, the training of teachers consisted of a simple three-month course for trivial school teachers and a six-month course for major school teachers.[1] They were open to applicants (overwhelmingly

[1] There existed a few rare exceptions. The teacher training program in Salzburg apparently offered a 12-month course, the one in Linz a 10-month one. Lower Austrian teacher training centres obtained an exemption in 1832 whereby they could double the trivial school teachers' training to six months. See Engelbrecht. *Geschichte des österreichischen Bildungswesens*

men) who had completed elementary schooling and were of upstanding personal conduct. The training focused exclusively on the teaching candidates' proper and full absorption of the principles of the *Methodenbuch*. While school overseers repeatedly called for an extension and deepening of teacher training, they invariably ran into a most potent obstacle to their efforts: the government itself. The Education Commission was convinced that the teaching of the *trivium* in the countryside – the predominant destination of young teachers – did not require more than the existing three months of preparation. In fact, extending it could even be detrimental to the success of the school's mission because any over-education might alienate the teacher from the simplicity of rural life and undermine his ability to connect with his pupils in the classroom.[2] Plus, what if they then also asked for higher pay? The potential link between better training and increased salary demands further counted against such proposals: as long as teachers were paid primarily by way of tuition fees, making them more expensive because of higher qualifications was not the way to endear them to rural parents. One could even find occasional arguments in favour of a *reduction* of teacher training. A Tyrolean schoolman put forward one such proposal, holding that the preparation for teaching at a rural school was more akin to an apprenticeship and that it was better to place a teacher trainee by the side of an experienced older colleague and let him watch and learn (and, incidentally, supply unpaid assistance in the name of "gaining experience").[3]

One advantage of a short training course was that the three-month programs, *Präparanden*, could produce new teachers in large numbers. Already at the end of the Napoleonic Wars, the teacher training courses in Bohemia alone, a province with about 2700 elementary schools, produced over 300 fresh graduates per year, and by mid-1820s more than 2000 lay teachers and 600 future catechists (from the ranks of the clergy) earned their certificates annually across all Imperial Austria.[4] Even though the pace slowed down somewhat in the 1830s and 1840s to about 1500 yearly lay trainees and 500 clerical ones, the training courses must have instructed a total of almost 50000 new lay teachers and about 15000 clergy between 1815 and 1845.[5]

Vol. 3, p. 233; Scheipl and Seel. *Die Entwicklung des österreichischen Schulwesens, 1750–1938*, p. 29–30.

[2] Engelbrecht. *Geschichte des österreichischen Bildungswesens Vol. 3*, p. 232–234.

[3] Jellouschek. "Das Reichsvolksschulgesetz", p. 294. Admittedly, the question of whether teaching is an art, a trade or a science has been around as long as teaching itself, so the Tyrolean schoolman was not necessarily standing outside the mainstream of the mid-19th century. See Binder, Ulrich "State Official – Public Official – Pedagogic Official: Development of Teaching Profession in Austria, France and Germany in the 18th century".

[4] OeStA, karton 1968/4, 12.

[5] Unfortunately, a complete time series of annual graduates are not available. These statistics also omit the Italian provinces of Venetia and Lombardy, which operated under a some-

Yet, Austria's 1846 statistical yearbook reported only 19250 lay staff and not quite 9000 religion teachers in active employment and some of those (perhaps up to 20%) were aging old-timers who had acquired their training during or even before the Napoleonic wars.[6] The gap between supply and demand was quite large.[7]

Where did the thousands of surplus certified teaching candidates go? It is easier to explain away the catechists: Article 110 of the *Politische Verfassung* demanded that no candidate for priesthood be admitted without the requisite certificate in catechism and pedagogy but many among the clergy, who duly obtained it, subsequently ended up in such types of spiritual service as did not require them to teach. The fate of the laymen is less clear. Obviously, some would not show up in the 1846 totals because they retired or died in the intervening period. Some of the rest served as tutors of aristocratic children – such appointment required official certification no less than public school teaching. Some tried their luck in the small private education market in large cities. The rest probably gave up on the profession for lack of available appointment. At any rate, the data indicate a persistent oversupply of potential applicants, which must have worked towards keeping teachers cheap.

Still, the active teaching corps numbered in the tens of thousands. Piecing together their "collective portrait" is made easier by the wide availability of teacher directories, which started appearing in the first half of the 19th century. These were usually published by diocesan authorities and aspired to encompass all the school-related staff within the bishopric – teachers, assistants and catechists. Even school patrons were listed sometimes. The earliest ones only noted the school location and the name of the teacher. Later editions also added year and place of birth and sometimes the year and place of training. Even as the range of data reported increased over time, somehow no single directory covered all the information that one might wish to know.[8] The following depiction therefore has to draw on sources from different prov-

---

what different legislation (see Chapter 1). Hungary is also not included in the totals.

[6] TSOM 1845–46, Zweiter Teil, Tafel 11: Lehranstalten im Jahre 1846, p. 22.

[7] The implication of these numbers is quite the opposite to the claims by some researchers that the training courses were incapable of supplying certified teachers in sufficient numbers. See for example, Veselá. "Příspěvek k historii učitelského vzdělávání", p. 18. As will become clear, there are other signs, which point in the direction of oversupply of available staff rather than shortage (although local situation may have varied considerably). A shortage of staff may have been a problem in the very early years of the system, say, before 1790, but by the 19th century, the stream of teacher graduates clearly outnumbered the demand.

[8] For example, the Viennese diocese did not list salaries, the one in České Budějovice omitted personal data of teachers, the Lviv Catholic directory did not cover the data on teacher training and so on. Some of the information can be supplemented from publications in neighbouring years, for the directories were updated regularly, but most cannot because each diocese usually kept its format mostly unchanged year to year, including or omitting the same data.

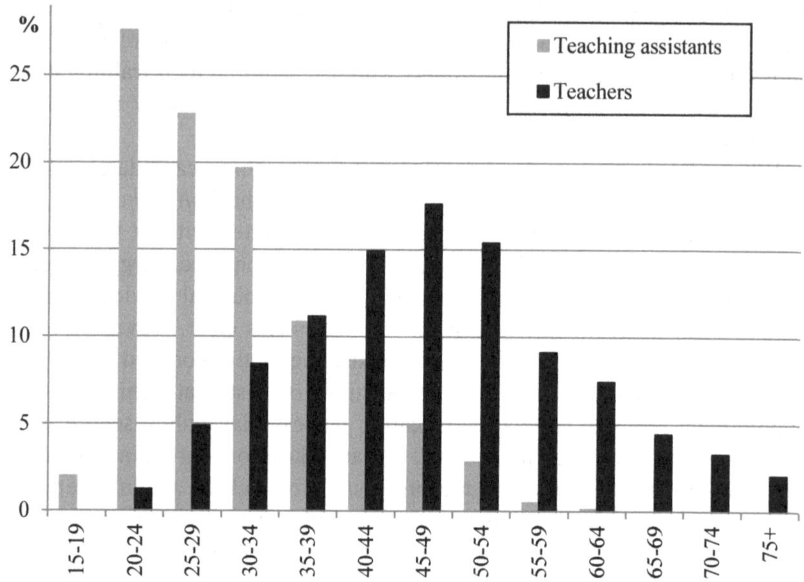

Figure 4.1: Age distribution of male lay teaching staff, Lower Austria, 1852
Source: Kaiser. *Lehrer-Schema.*

inces for different aspects. Inevitably, all claims of empire-wide representativeness must rest on the observation that the legislation regulating teaching was uniform across the whole country.

The Austrian teachers were predominantly men, as women had a hard time breaking into the teaching profession at public schools, even at the lowest levels of trivial schools. Apart from the barriers posed by the prevailing gender norms, they also faced the very practical obstacle that until 1840 there were no training courses for women.[9] The 1865 *Detail Conscription* reported that only 9.4% of all teachers at public schools were women. In the European context, this put Austria close to the bottom of the rankings: Belgium could boast 40% female teaching corps already in 1840 while in England and Wales some 60% of teachers were women in 1877. The Austrian record was comparable to that of Germany where women made up less than 20% of teachers until shortly before the First World War.[10]

The profession fell into two ranks: teachers and teaching assistants (*Gehilfen*).[11] Figure 4.1 shows a typical age distribution of each rank, drawing on the teacher directory published in Lower Austria in 1852. Upon gradu-

[9] Engelbrecht, *Geschichte des österreichischen Bildungswesens Vol. 3*, 234.
[10] Albisetti. "The feminization of teaching in the nineteenth century", p. 255.
[11] At the major schools in cities, the assistants could use a somewhat more respectable title – "subordinate teacher" (*Unterlehrer*).

Table 4.1: Career progression among teachers in Lower Austria, 1852

	Men		Women
	Vienna	Lower Austrian countryside	Whole province
Teachers			
Age in 1852	47.2	47.9	36.7
Age at training	19.1	17.3	22.4
Age at start of career	22.6	18.9	25.7
Job tenure (years)	9.3	17.2	8.0
Teaching assistants			
Age in 1852	35.1	28.2	29.4
Age at training	17.7	17.3	18.4
Age at start of career	20.2	18.7	21.4
Job tenure (years)	8.6	5.3	5.6

Note: Reported are averages for each statistic.
Source: Kaiser. *Lehrer-Schema.*

ating from the training course, which the majority of applicants completed between ages 16 and 19, the first appointment (if any) would be assistantship. Per Article 119, a promotion to a full teacher status could follow after a year of assistantship.[12] In Lower Austria at this time, assistants made up a little over a quarter of all male lay teaching staff. Success in progressing to the full teacher status depended not just on meeting age and experience criteria but also on obtaining a corresponding appointment: one reason why some lingered in their assistant status well into their forties and fifties was because they failed to "get a school", i.e. secure a job as a full teacher. The median teaching assistant was about 29 years old and the figure makes clear that their numbers dropped off significantly after about age 35. Combined with the median age at training of 17, the data suggest that a freshly minted graduate could expect about 10–15 years of assistantship before either securing a full teaching position or dropping out of the profession.

Based on the same data, Table 4.1 gives a broad idea of how a teacher's career might have been expected to progress. While the available information does not allow for much nuance, it is at least possible to compare men to women and Vienna to the countryside across the two basic professional ranks. In the countryside, fresh graduates usually moved into an assistantship within a year or two. In Vienna, the gap between training and first appointment was somewhat longer – almost three years for both men and women – which is likely related to the fact that the Viennese schools were more likely to be major schools (*Hauptschulen*), which required of their staff a little extra training on top of the basic three months. Major schools were also the reason why the Viennese assistants were significantly older on average then their

[12] The person in question also had to be at least 20 years old.

rural counterparts: most major schools were led either by a director or a head teacher (*Oberlehrer*) who was the sole staff member of teacher status; all his subordinates were usually *Unterlehrer*, which are coded in the table as teaching assistants. Unlike in the countryside, where every school either had one teacher or at most one teacher and one assistant, the ratio between teaching assistants to teachers was higher in Vienna because the schools were bigger and their teaching staff greater. Consequently, the pipeline to promotion from assistant to teacher was slower in Vienna but, at the same time, teaching assistantship at a good major school in the imperial capital carried more prestige than the same post in the country, to say nothing of the lifestyle amenities available in the metropolis. Consequently, both by necessity and by preference, the Viennese *Unterlehrern* accepted somewhat longer stints in assistant positions. This fact also shows up on the last line of the table: the average rural assistant was reported to have been in his current post only since 1846, reaching a job tenure of only 5.3 years, whereas in Vienna the average current appointment dated to 1843, the same as for teachers. In terms of stability of employment, the gap between teachers and assistants was certainly bigger in the countryside where the average teacher apparently held the same job since 1834 – more than 17 years as of the end of 1851. What this all implies is that in the countryside, a typical young man starting out in teaching could expect to go through about one or two assistantships before finding by his mid-thirties a teaching post which he would then hold on to for the rest of his career. In Vienna, in contrast, the job market for either rank was both a little more stable than rural assistantships and also somewhat more flexible than the rural teacher market.

The urban-rural divide, so pronounced in all other aspects of public schooling, could not but affect the teachers also. It was naturally at its starkest in the very region that included the imperial capital. Vienna accounted for about 30% of all elementary school personnel in all of Lower Austria – roughly proportional to her 28% share of the province's overall population. As a place of employment, it had plenty to recommend itself. The schools were better funded and equipped. The dense urban school network allowed for multiple appointments. About 10% of Viennese teachers worked at more than one school (although most kept it down to two). Viennese schools generally offered a more extensive curriculum, as town schools usually did, which encouraged specialization among teachers. About a sixth of all teachers in Vienna listed a specialization – drawing teacher, music teacher, writing teacher – compared to almost none in the countryside. Numerous private outfits specialized in teaching daughters from well-to-do families, offering a package of elementary education supplemented by a finishing school. They had staff for instruction in piano, dance, French conversation and needlework. Thus, adjacent to the public school network were a host of teachers of foreign languages and of various social skills who mostly worked for private institutions but who occasionally supplied their expertise to public ones also. These were the ones most likely to cumulate appointments: one, Eduard Dupuis, a Vienna native, taught French at no fewer than six private schools at once. The specialists most likely to combine private and public appointments were the drawing teachers, whereas language instructors overwhelmingly kept to the private sector. A unique, and wholly separate, category of specialists were the catechists, who, too, often served several different schools. Undoubtedly, the job market for teachers was quite lively in Vienna. A similar situation but on a smaller scale existed in other large cities of the empire. The Catholic diocese in Lviv had more than a third of all its Catholic teachers operating in Lviv itself and more than a half of those worked for private institutions. The Lviv teacher directory (unlike the Viennese one) even sheds light on the city-country pay difference: whereas the average Lviv teacher received 285 fl annually, outside the city the average was 225 fl and in places of less than 5000 inhabitants it rarely exceeded 200 fl.[13]

In contrast to the variety of experiences in Vienna, the rural arrangements were rather uniform. The vast majority of teaching staff held a single post. Multiple appointments, where they appeared, attached predominantly to catechists and, given the distances in the countryside, they were a bane and not a boon. Consider the case of Plazidus Leidl, who taught religion at four separate schools, each in a different village. Stationed in the parish of Maria-Dreieichen in the northeastern part of the Lower Austria, he also served branch schools in Rosenburg-Mold (1.7 km away), Zaingrub (4.4 km) and Mörtersdorf (5.2 km). This likely added up to an almost 25 km-long trek every week. At least Leidl did not have other priestly duties to attend to, unlike approximately half of rural catechists who worked concurrently as local parish priests. In the rare cases where lay teachers had to travel to teach, the job was given to teaching assistants who were at the bottom of the professional pecking order.

Table 4.2 brings together all these observations in summarizing the various roles that the Lower-Austrian school workforce played. It also highlights the differences between men and women. For women teachers, the private education market was an even more important factor than for men. Over 80% of all Lower-Austrian female educators were in Vienna and almost half of them worked in the private sector. The private-public distinction correlated with a significant difference in their status. In the public sector, they usually worked as teachers of housework either in all-girl schools or in all-girl classes of coeducational schools. Their status was low, pay meager and some of them were in teaching as an extension of their husband's career – by virtue of be-

[13] The data pertain to the year 1844. See *Katalog des an den Volksschulen der Lemberger lat. Erzdiözese angestellten Lehrpersonals, für das Jahr 1844.* Lemberg: Peter Piller, 1844.

Table 4.2: Composition of school staff by role, Lower Austria, 1852 (%)

	Men (N = 3157)	Women (N = 361)
Catechist	29.3	
serving also as local priest	13.4	
School management	3.1	16.3
Teacher	42.8	69.3
among them: specialists	4.4	11.6
among them: teachers of housework	0.0	41.8
Teaching assistant	25.9	16.6
Other	1.3	0.0

Note: The percentages add up to more than 100% within a column because some individuals served in more than one capacity (e.g. "Principal and teacher"). "Specialists" refers to teachers with a specified subject, e.g. French, Dance, Music or Drawing. "School management" includes directors, head teachers and owners of private schools. "Housework", or *weibliche Arbeiten*, was a subject taught by women teachers to female pupils.

Source: Kaiser. *Lehrer-Schema.*

ing married to a school's head teacher or director. In the private sector, women's roles were more varied. They were every bit as specialized as their male counterparts, teaching French and Italian, dancing, singing, and how to play musical instruments – in addition to all the skills then considered the domain of woman's work (e.g. embroidery and housework). That last specialization applied to a plurality of all women teachers – almost 42% – across both private and public education. Most importantly, many of the women working privately were founders, owners and managers of their own educational enterprise. This was the reason why in Table 4.1 the average female teacher was more than a decade younger than the average male counterpart: when women started their own private schools, they did not appoint themselves as assistants, especially since they were directly involved in running the business. Table 4.2 shows that 16.3% of them had some role in the management of a school. About half of female-led schools were modest, one-person outfits. But some were quite large. The largest of them, a private school for girls founded in March 1851 by Belgian-born Delphine Lefevre, had 16 people in its employ, ten men and six women, which made it larger than most Viennese schools. Going against the grain of prevailing social mores, in more than a few cases, the woman principals were employing their own husbands.

Overall, the contrast was quite stark: the public sector was 95% male, the private one almost had a gender parity. Public schooling was mostly unwelcoming to women. The private education market, on the other hand, especially in a large city like Vienna, was every female educator's best friend. This observation illustrates a broader point emerging from the teacher data as a whole: the private sector (to the extent that it was tolerated) was a refuge for everything that was in any way off the beaten path – not just for women's en-

Table 4.3: Places of birth and of work of Lower-Austrian teachers, 1852 (%)

School location:	Vienna	Lower Austrian countryside	Total
Birthplace		Male lay teachers (N = 2173)	
Vienna	6.2	1.5	7.6
Lower Austrian countryside	11.2	55.2	66.4
Other Habsburg provinces	7.9	11.2	19.1
Abroad	1.2	0.1	1.3
Unknown/uncertain	1.9	3.6	5.5
Total	*28.4*	*71.6*	*100.0*
		Catechists (N = 933)	
Vienna	2.9	7.6	10.5
Lower Austrian countryside	3.2	35.9	39.1
Other Habsburg provinces	4.9	33.3	38.3
Abroad	0.0	1.0	1.0
Unknown/uncertain	0.4	10.7	11.1
Total	*11.5*	*88.5*	*100.0*
		Female teachers (N = 310)	
Vienna	49.4	5.8	55.2
Lower Austrian countryside	7.4	4.5	11.9
Other Habsburg provinces	8.4	5.2	13.5
Abroad	5.2	0.3	5.5
Unknown/uncertain	10.3	3.5	13.9
Total	*80.6*	*19.4*	*100.0*

Note: The city-country division follows Vienna's 1850 city limits.
Source: Kaiser. *Lehrer-Schema*, 1852.

trepreneurship but also for foreign languages, schooling for religious minorities, instruction in special skills and so on. Still, except for some teaching staff overlap, institutionally, most of the private education was deliberately kept at arm's length from the public sector with only limited intermingling and integration of the two.

One might surmise that teachers were somewhat more mobile than the general population, especially in their youth. First, they usually had to move to enrol in a training course, which operated not only in provincial capitals but also in other, smaller, mid-sized towns, such as Sankt Pölten or Wiener Neustadt in Lower Austria. Second, their initial assistantships were likely to be of short duration, especially if the newly certified educator was on the lookout for a teaching position somewhere, ensuring further need to move. There is no obvious *a priori* intuitive answer as to which way the teacher migration could be expected to go – city or country. On the one hand, the training courses were located in towns and urban citizenry was also generally more enthusiastic about schooling, so it is plausible that the cities would serve as the breeding ground for teachers who would then move to the countryside in search of employment. On the other hand, the same factor – the strong presence of, and support for, schooling – also made the cities potential magnets for aspiring candidates from the countryside. The urban market promised the most interesting opportunities, of which Vienna was a shining example. The presence of the capital and its sheer domination over the rest of the province makes Lower Austria the most convenient case study for determining how strong the lure of the city was, if at all. Did the city teach the countryside or vice versa?

As Table 4.3 shows, the city relied on outsiders to staff its schools, both public and private, to a tremendous extent. With 431000 inhabitants in 1851, Vienna made up about 28% of the population of Lower Austria, then standing at 1.54 million. As it happened, the capital also employed an almost perfectly proportional 28.4% of the province's male lay teachers. Yet, less than a quarter of those Viennese teachers were also born-and-bred Viennese. It drew in not just people from its immediate provincial hinterland but from all over the empire.[14] There was even a smattering of a foreign presence – mostly in the private sector, teaching foreign languages. In comparison, there was almost no migration in the opposite direction to speak of, at least within Lower Austria: Vienna-born teachers were reluctant to teach in the countryside. Yet, even the rural areas received a sizeable inflow of teachers from elsewhere, primarily from other Habsburg provinces such as Bohemia, Moravia and Upper Austria.

As for those who ended up in the capital, Table 4.4 offers a further detail on the men's migration patterns, using the information on each teacher's place of training. Outside the 17% of Viennese teachers who were also born and trained there, a good number moved to Vienna long before their teaching appointment, coming to one of the training programs there. The evidence suggests (but cannot prove, for that would require a complete continuous list of appointments for each person) that a frequent way of getting a job at a Viennese school was to come to study there first.

The migration patterns were different among the catechists: more of the Vienna-born were placed in the countryside than in Vienna (even as about the same number migrated from elsewhere to Vienna). The presence of catechists from other provinces was also much more prominent there. This pattern can almost entirely be put down to the fact that in the countryside the duty to teach religion was frequently one of the duties of the parish priest. Only one

[14] Most of the 1.9% teachers with "unknown/uncertain" place of birth probably also fell into the category: in most of these cases, the uncertainty stemmed from the fact that the teacher's birth place was a village of a common name (e.g. "Neudorf"), of which there were many across all Habsburg provinces. Cases where a teacher's birthplace was not recorded at all were rare.

Table 4.4: Male teachers' paths to Vienna, 1852

Birthplace	Place of training	%
Lower Austrian countryside	Vienna	19.1
Vienna	Vienna	17.0
Lower Austrian countryside	Outskirts of Vienna	11.5
Other Habsburg provinces	Other Habsburg provinces	10.2
Other Habsburg provinces	Vienna	8.8
Lower Austrian countryside	Lower Austrian countryside	5.8
Other paths		27.6

Note: The percentages apply to the 617 male lay teachers operating in Vienna in 1852. "Outskirts of Vienna" refer to the teacher training programs in Klosterneuburg and in Korneuburg outside Vienna.
Source: Kaiser. *Lehrer-Schema.*

of the 107 catechists teaching religion in Vienna also served as a parish priest. In the countryside, more than a half did. All men of the cloth had to have made their vows of service and so they went where the Church sent them, which, as the table indicates, was often to rural parishes. They could not operate as "free agents" the way lay teachers did, deciding at any point in their career whether they wanted to look for a new appointment. The contrast between the two groups is revealing: the lay teachers, who had a choice, left the countryside for the city; the priests, who could be ordered around, were sent to serve in the sleepy backwaters.

Women's placement was another story. The reasons behind their overwhelming concentration in Vienna have already been discussed. Outside Vienna, women mostly operated right in the Viennese suburbs in Fünfhaus, Hernals and Ottakring or in other towns, such as Krems and Sankt Pölten. More so than men, lay or clerical, the female educators were locals: five out of eight Viennese women teachers were also born in the city, as were most of the suburban ones also. This contrast with men shows how far the opportunities of a large city could go in breaking down gender barriers: the educational market in Vienna could serve as a vehicle for a certain amount of social mobility for women but apparently not much geographical mobility.

Having mined the Lower Austrian teacher directory for all that it can reveal about the province's school staff, Table 4.5 provides a useful corrective as to how much those findings are generalizable to other provinces. The most comprehensive source for the whole of Imperial Austria's schools, the *Detail-Conscription*, provides a snapshot of the situation (in 1865) in sufficient detail to separate out the provincial capitals from the countryside in most of the Habsburg provinces. Somewhat reassuringly, the rural situation was broadly similar across the board (with a few conspicuous exceptions). Few major schools (*Hauptschulen*) operated in the countryside; thus the proportion of major school teachers there was low and anywhere from a fifth to a third of

Table 4.5: Selected characteristics of school staff in Imperial Austria, 1865

	% lay school staff who…				
	…taught in major schools	…were teaching assistants	…were female	…taught half-year school	…taught at a German school
Lower Austria	26.1	42.6	7.0	0.2	99.9
of which: Vienna	*71.5*	*61.8*	*14.1*	*0.0*	*100.0*
of which: countryside	*7.6*	*34.8*	*4.1*	*0.3*	*99.9*
Upper Austria	7.2	36.0	5.4	0.1	100.0
of which: Linz	*59.4*	*59.4*	*28.1*	*0.0*	*100.0*
of which: countryside	*5.1*	*35.1*	*4.5*	*0.1*	*100.0*
Salzburg (province)	5.8	24.8	19.8	0.0	100.0
of which: Salzburg (city)	*19.6*	*35.3*	*70.6*	*0.0*	*100.0*
of which: countryside	*2.1*	*22.0*	*6.3*	*0.0*	*100.0*
Styria	10.1	33.1	7.1	2.4	72.7
of which: Graz	*29.9*	*31.0*	*33.3*	*0.0*	*100.0*
of which: countryside	*8.4*	*33.3*	*4.8*	*2.6*	*70.4*
Carinthia	8.3	20.0	11.5	4.1	75.4
of which: Klagenfurt	*31.0*	*20.7*	*69.0*	*0.0*	*100.0*
of which: countryside	*6.6*	*19.9*	*7.1*	*4.4*	*73.6*
Carniola	19.8	16.0	12.7	12.9	17.3
of which: Ljubljana	*45.9*	*10.8*	*48.6*	*0.0*	*97.3*
of which: countryside	*16.4*	*16.7*	*8.0*	*14.5*	*7.6*
Austrian Littoral	26.8	28.3	35.2	2.6	1.6
of which: Trieste & Gorica	*48.9*	*24.2*	*44.5*	*0.0*	*4.9*
of which: countryside	*11.9*	*31.1*	*28.9*	*3.8*	*0.2*
Tyrol	4.7	27.6	30.3	77.0	58.2
of which: Innsbruck	*25.0*	*4.2*	*54.2*	*0.0*	*100.0*
of which: countryside	*4.5*	*27.8*	*30.1*	*77.7*	*57.8*
Vorarlberg	7.9	48.5	8.5	69.4	100.0
Bohemia	14.8	39.9	3.0	0.2	41.9
of which: Prague	*21.6*	*34.1*	*26.4*	*0.0*	*25.0*
of which: countryside	*14.6*	*40.1*	*2.3*	*0.2*	*42.5*
Moravia	12.5	35.9	4.1	0.1	26.4
of which: Brno	*73.7*	*64.2*	*17.9*	*0.0*	*56.8*
of which: countryside	*10.3*	*34.9*	*3.6*	*0.1*	*25.3*
Silesia	10.0	32.0	7.6	0.0	53.7
of which: Opava/Troppau	*31.8*	*18.2*	*36.4*	*0.0*	*100.0*
of which: countryside	*9.3*	*32.5*	*6.6*	*0.0*	*52.2*
Galicia	11.9	36.6	9.0		
Bukovina	14.4	4.4	5.0		
Dalmatia	19.0	25.4	14.6		
Overall	14.8	36.1	9.4		

Note: Galicia, Bukovina and Dalmatia did not report certain aspects in sufficient detail, which is why the construction of some of the statistics was not possible for these provinces.
Source: Detail-Conscription.

rural teachers were assistants. The proportion of women in the countryside overwhelmingly stayed in single percentages, while they made up a significant proportion of urban school staff. In some provincial capitals, such as Salzburg, Klagenfurt and Innsbruck, they even made up the majority of teachers. The two exceptions to this pattern are Tyrol and the Austrian Littoral where women had a strong presence even in rural schools. It is not clear from the record why that was except to note that in both cases the women were concentrated in schools with Italian pupils and language of instruction. In the Tyrolean case, that means the bishopric of Trient and in the case of the Austrian Littoral the areas in the west of the province, around Trieste and Gorica, as well as in some of the Italianised bigger cities in Istria.

In terms of the manner of employment, the table shows that most teachers could expect to be employed throughout the whole year. In the cities, this was a universal practice: no self-respecting city could get away with running just a half-year school. In the countryside, the situation was somewhat different but half-year schooling was by and large the domain of poor provinces with an underdeveloped school network. The big exception here again was Tyrol and Vorarlberg where more than three quarters of all teachers were teaching during winters only. These Alpine provinces were exceptional in their arrangements, which were a function of particular local economic circumstances.[15] The pressure for half-year schooling did not originate with the teachers but rather with the parents and local employers.

Moving the analysis out of Lower Austria brings up the monarchy's nationalities question, in which the teachers played an important part. In Chapter 2, I discussed this issue with regards to the general availability of schools by language of instruction and argued that the German language started the 19th century with a certain advantage but that it gradually weakened with time as Slavic and Italian schooling grew. Table 4.5, approaching the matter from the point of view of teachers, is broadly consistent with that conclusion. In ethnically mixed provinces, the proportions of staff serving at schools with a German language of instruction is generally slightly higher than, but roughly proportional to, the proportions of German-speaking pupils. In Styria, for example, 69% of pupils were German and 72.7% teachers taught in German. In Silesia, the respective numbers were 53.8% and 53.7%. The starkest disparity existed in Carniola, where only 6.1% of the pupils were Germans but 17.3% of the teachers worked at German schools – a consequence of the relative under-provision of schools in the Slavic parts of the province. From Table 4.5 alone, then, it would seem that, excepting Carniola, the concerns of the nationalities were being adequately and proportionately addressed at least by 1865.

---

[15] Chapter 5 discusses this issue in greater detail.

Table 4.6: Characteristics of school staff across nationalities

Czech provinces	German schools (N = 2405)	Czech schools (N = 3608)	t-test
% teaching assistants	37.40	29.43	-8.09
% female teachers	1.36	1.16	-0.91
Staff per 100 pupils	1.64	1.16	-20.42
Staff-related expenditure per pupil	3.21	2.47	-15.72
Average income from teaching (fl)	214.82	231.81	7.61
Normalized avg income from teaching[a]	256.83	192.02	-15.55
Average number of grades	2.15	2.05	-4.40
Classrooms per 100 pupils	1.57	1.13	-17.27
Tyrol	German schools (N = 780)	Italian schools (N = 485)	t-test
% teaching assistants	22.24	16.98	-2.79
% female teachers	12.77	40.98	16.53
Staff per 100 pupils	3.72	2.62	-7.09
Staff-related expenditure per pupil	2.11	1.65	-4.65
Average income from teaching (fl)	66.99	69.19	0.74
Normalized avg income from teaching[a]	172.68	95.70	-9.06
Average number of grades	1.52	2.07	10.05
Classrooms per 100 pupils	3.54	2.46	-7.08
Provinces with South-Slav population	German schools (N = 730)	South-Slav schools (N = 528)	t-test
% teaching assistants	23.31	14.40	-4.72
% female teachers	3.82	2.69	-1.42
Staff per 100 pupils	1.90	2.05	1.49
Staff-related expenditure per pupil	2.47	2.41	-0.22
Average income from teaching (fl)	142.80	149.58	1.12
Normalized avg income from teaching[a]	199.20	198.99	-0.01
Average number of grades	2.43	2.11	-7.11
Classrooms per 100 pupils	1.78	1.96	2.01

Note: [a]"Normalized avg income from teaching" measures the average income of a teacher after controlling for the size of the school in terms of the number of pupils: it is calculated as the 100×(total salary expenditure per teacher per pupil) and can be interpreted as what a teacher would earn on average, given the schools financial realities, if the school had exactly 100 pupils. "German schools" are schools with a German language of instruction. Analogous definitions apply for Czech schools, Italian schools and South-Slav schools. Czech provinces include Bohemia, Moravia and Silesia. Provinces with South-Slav population include Styria, Carinthia, Carniola and the Austrian Littoral, where the South-Slav population consisted mostly of Slovenes and some Croats. The comparisons do not include bilingual schools. The South-Slav comparisons also ignore Italian schools operating in the Austrian Littoral.
Source: Detail-Conscription.

But those percentages of German teachers speak only to the extensive margin of the issue – the question of how many. The other part was the intensive margin, i.e. how well supplied and provided for the teachers and their schools were. This aspect opened up ample room for substantial differences between German and non-German schools, which gave ground for plausibly legitimate complaints of pro-German bias and were thus no less politically salient than the question of staff totals and their ethnic composition. The statistics reported in Table 4.6 more or less indicate that the German schools were, on average, better than their non-German counterparts along many dimensions. The t-statistics are quite large in most cases outside the South, indicating clear systematic differences. Compared to both Czech schools in the Czech lands and to Italian schools in Tyrol, the German schools had more staff per 100 pupils – mostly on account of employing more teaching assistants. They therefore also spent more on staff on a per-pupil basis. Note that in terms of simple averages, the German teachers in the Czech provinces (but not in Tyrol or in the South) actually ended up earning less from teaching than their counterparts at Czech and Italian schools. This is partly due to the higher number of assistants in German schools but the bigger part is the difference in the size of school: German teachers were teaching in smaller schools with fewer fee-paying pupils. Once the size is controlled for, through normalization of average income, it emerges that the German teachers were actually getting better remuneration in comparable appointments. For example, in the Czech provinces, a German teacher in a school of 100 pupils could expect, given the financial realities of German schools, about 256.83 fl of annual income from his school duties whereas a teacher in a Czech school of the same size would have been paid 192.02 fl. In Tyrol, the differences were probably also affected by the remarkable prominence of women in Italian schools – female teachers were certainly cheaper than men and if they formed over 40% of the teacher corps, as they did in the Italian part of Tyrol, it surely affected the average. Curiously, the smallest differences between German and non-German schools were observable in the regions with South Slav populations, although even here the German schools employed more assistants and spent more on their teaching staff. The differences, however, were not as strong and were more likely to be statistically insignificant.[16]

[16] The predicament of the South-Slav population was of a somewhat different nature: Table 4.6 reports statistics for the 528 schools that actually taught fully in Slovene or Croatian. But there were in fact another roughly 220 schools where Slavic pupils were the majority but the language of instruction was either German or the school was bilingual. So even if the South-Slav schools in Table 4.6 look comparable to the German ones, the table construction understates the degree to which the South-Slav population was underserved by the existing school infrastructure. In short, once a Slovene school was established, it was relatively similar to a nearby German school, as Table 4.6 shows. However, the network of Slovene schools was much thinner than that of German ones.

What appears consistently across the three areas of inter-ethnic friction is that German schools spent more on their staff per pupil and that German teachers were better remunerated, controlling for school size. Note that the differences did not just stop with the teaching staff. German schools also taught a more extensive curriculum in the Czech and South-Slav provinces and usually also had more classrooms available. The higher number of grades offered by German schools was partly a result of the fact that major schools were predominantly teaching in German still in 1865 (even though this predominance was waning).

These differences do not by themselves constitute evidence of bias or deliberate discrimination. If more money went into German schools, which overwhelmingly taught in German-majority areas, then one natural explanation could be that the German areas were richer and more developed to begin with, which would account not only for the more generous spending on teachers but also explain why these schools also offered a somewhat more sophisticated curriculum (more grades). The t-tests simply establish the fact of difference but do not offer any grounds to pin the differences on this or that cause. To make a plausible case for official bias in favour of German schools would require ruling out the economy as the reason behind their higher spending and staffing values. For that, the comparison would have to be more "apples-to-apples", ideally holding all else, including economic development, equal and allowing only the language of instruction to vary.

One opportunity to that end is to exploit a temporary quirk in the Austrian public administration: the schools, supervised until 1868 by the Catholic Church, were organized by vicariates; the economy (e.g. taxes, courts, business licensing etc.) was from 1849 administered along the lines of new civil districts. The borders of vicariates and districts did not overlap because each responded to the specific administrative needs of their respective hierarchies: one clerical, the other civil. The new civil administration, introduced in the wake of the 1848 revolution as a replacement of the old feudal framework, reflected the most recent economic realities arising from the gradual spread of industry: old royal towns lost their ancient privileges whereas new, emerging industrial cities acquired some limited rights of self-government. Important public offices moved from traditional feudal seats to growing urban centres so as to be closer to the hubs of economic activity. Most importantly, the civil reform of 1849 cut up the empire's territory very finely, so that the hundreds of newly created districts ended up very small and consequently quite homogenous within, both economically and socially. They were somewhat smaller than even the vicariates.[17]

[17] According to the 1857 census, median civil district had fewer than 20000 inhabitants. See K. k. Ministerium des Innern. *Statistische Übersichten über die Bevölkerung und der Viehstand von Österreich. Nach der Zählung vom 31. October 1857.*

The opportunity that this peculiar administrative situation offers is this: if school supervision operated along church lines, through vicariates, I can compare how German-majority vicariates' treatment of German and non-German schools differed from those with a Slavic or Italian majority in terms of school staffing and spending – all the while also controlling for the economic environment by focusing the comparison on schools that resided in the same civil district. The analysis must focus on those civil districts and vicariates that straddled ethnic boundaries or that encompassed ethnically mixed cities, so that both German and non-German observations are present. For each school, I therefore constructed three indicator variables: one for whether a school operated in a German-majority vicariate, one for whether it was a school catering to the vicariate's ethnic minority (e.g. a Czech school in a German-majority vicariate or a German school in an Italian-majority vicariate) and one for a combination of German language of instruction and a minority status. If German enjoyed a systematic preferential treatment from the authorities, it should show up in the following ways: even after controlling for their economic situation through district fixed effects (i) German-majority vicariates should report higher values of spending and staff per pupil, (ii) minority (e.g. Slavic or Italian) schools in German-majority vicariates should report lower values than German schools in the same vicariates, and (iii) German schools catering to German minorities in Slavic and Italian-majority vicariates should report higher values than the Slavic or Italian schools in those vicariates.

Such analysis lends itself straightforwardly to a simple OLS estimation with district fixed effects, the results of which are reported in Table 4.7. Across Imperial Austria, there were about 2840 schools, operating in ethnically mixed areas and spanning 273 civil districts, which can be used for this analysis. This is perhaps the closest I can get to comparing like with like using these data: thanks to the civil district fixed effects, the estimates come from putting side by side schools that were literally within a day's walk of each other and therefore operated within a similar economic and social environment (the same civil district). Controlling for city/village population size also ensures that the estimates do not conflate the German/non-German difference with an urban-rural difference.

With the exception of column (iii), the pattern is always the same: controlling for all else, the German-majority vicariates reported on average 0.74 more teachers per 100 pupils, 1.73 fl more staff-related expenditure per pupil and 110.53 fl higher normalized income from teaching than vicariates without German majority. So, German-majority vicariates were doing better overall on all these aspects, other things held equal: the only (negative) coefficient breaking this pattern – in column (iii) – is both statistically and practically insignificant. Next, the impact of minority status is consistently negative across all specifications, as expected. Here, too, the effect is statistically

Table 4.7: Determinants of staff and expenditure at German and non-German schools

Dependent variable:	(i) Staff per 100 pupils	(ii) Staff expenditure per pupil	(iii) Avg income from teaching	(iv) Normalized avg income
Sample mean	1.48	3.00	220.39	227.74
Sample st. dev.	1.08	3.83	102.00	207.26
1(German-majority vicariate)	0.74*	1.73*	-0.74	110.53*
	[0.08]	[0.30]	[7.54]	[15.63]
1(minority school)	-0.37*	-0.87*	-0.22	-67.12*
	[0.08]	[0.29]	[7.40]	[15.33]
1(German minority school)	0.64*	1.77*	14.23	111.69*
	[0.11]	[0.39]	[9.85]	[20.40]
Fixed effects for population size:				
1(from 3K to 5K)	-0.15	0.83	51.67*	-118.84*
	[0.11]	[0.41]	[10.32]	[21.37]
1(from 5K to 10K)	0.08	1.48*	111.11*	-104.86*
	[0.14]	[0.50]	[12.72]	[26.34]
1(from 10K to 20K)	-0.38	1.01	108.14*	-135.32*
	[0.22]	[0.77]	[19.53]	[40.45]
1(from 20K to 50K)	0.16	2.47	198.12*	-66.54
	[0.46]	[1.64]	[41.26]	[85.45]
1(above 50K)	1.74	8.80	147.20	-19.64
	[1.00]	[3.56]	[89.69]	[185.73]
Constant	1.16	2.06	209.87	190.62
	[0.04]	[0.15]	[3.80]	[7.88]
N	2847	2847	2840	2838
Adjusted R^2	0.19	0.17	0.26	0.23

Note: In all regressions, 273 district fixed effects are included. Standard errors for these OLS coefficients are reported in square brackets. Asterisks (*) denote statistical significance at 1%. *Source: Detail-Conscription.*

significant and empirically meaningful in three out of four specifications: minority schools did worse than schools for local majorities, *ceteris paribus*. Finally, there is the fixed effect for German minority schools, i.e. those that were catering to German pupils in non-German vicariates: here, the coefficients are positive across the board and also quite sizeable, again with the exception of column (iii). Note that in absolute value, these coefficients are bigger than those on a simple minority school fixed effect. The combined impact was therefore positive!

What this means can be illustrated with a simple numerical example: take, for instance, a Czech school in a Czech-majority vicariate with completely average overall values, such as are reported right under the column headings in Table 4.7. Such a school would have 1.48 teachers per 100 pupils. An average German school in a neighbouring German-majority vicariate would have, according to regression results in column (i), 1.48 + 0.74 = 2.22 teachers per 100 pupils, all other things held equal. If each of these two vicariates then also had some minority schools – the Czech one a German school and the German one a Czech school – then the results imply that the Czech school in the German vicariate would have 1.48 + 0.74 – 0.37 = 1.85 teachers per 100 pupils whereas the German school in the Czech vicariate would have 1.48 – 0.37 + 0.64 = 1.75 teachers per 100 pupils. Within either of the two vicariates, the German schools were better staffed than the Czech ones.

Now consider staff expenditure per pupil (column (ii)): starting again from the assumption of a perfectly average Czech school in a Czech-majority vicariate with 3.00 fl of per-pupil spending, a similar calculation for staff-related spending per pupil will yield 4.73 fl of spending in German schools in the German-majority vicariate, 3.86 fl of spending in minority Czech schools in that same German-majority vicariate and 3.90 fl of salary expenditure per pupil in a minority German school in the Czech vicariate. Here, the German schools end up at higher absolute value than the non-German ones regardless of a majority or minority status. The same result would follow using coefficients from column (iv). Only the estimation for average teacher income (column (iii)) fails to yield sizeable and statistically significant coefficients although even here, with the exception of the first coefficient, the pattern is the same as in the other specification.

Across three of the four analyzed metrics, German schools fared better than Czech schools, and majority schools fared better than minority schools – unless the minority was German in which case it also fared better than the non-German majority. The combined evidence of tables 4.5–4.7 thus adds up to a subtle but definite pattern: on the surface, the numbers and shares of non-German teachers and schools looked broadly adequate, proportional and fair (Table 4.5). Peeking under the lid, however, revealed a number of systematic advantages favouring German schools (Table 4.6). Finally, the regressions in Table 4.7 showed that these differences persist even when comparing schools in the same civil district and the same vicariate (and thus, presumably, operating in the same economic and social milieu), just with different languages of instruction. By this analysis, then, German schools – and by extension German teachers – fared better just by virtue of being German. What was the mechanism through which the preferential treatment worked? We cannot presume some special subsidy for German schools – after all, the vicariates did not have a separate slush fund to spend on them. Rather, the authorities encouraged and pressured the best-appointed local schools to "go German" or at least to introduce the language in higher grades in the interest of spreading the "higher culture." Such pressures were documented more often in the first half of the century but their effects clearly lingered on still in 1865.

Speaking of teacher incomes, they were by no means high, whether in German schools or elsewhere. Figure 4.2 shows the distribution of annual in-

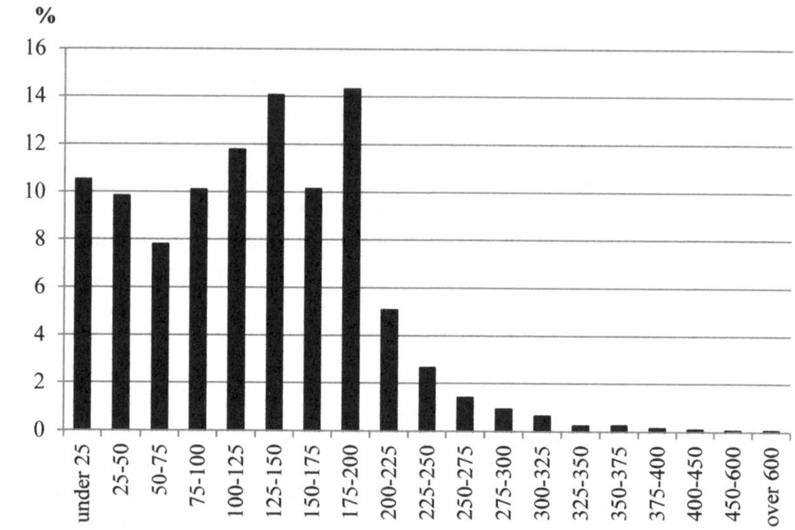

Figure 4.2: Distribution of annual earnings of rural teachers relative to unskilled labourers, 1865

Note: Unskilled day labourer's annual earnings = 100. They were calculated using day wages and annualized by assuming 300 workdays in a year.

Source: Detail-Conscription for teacher wages; Cvrček. "Wages, prices and living standards" for the unskilled wages.

come for rural teaching staff (i.e. both teachers and assistants). For each province, annual earnings of an unskilled labourer serve as a benchmark with a base value of 100. Thus, in the figure, a value above 100 implies that a teacher earned more from his teaching duties over the year than a local unskilled labourer and values below 100 that he earned less. The underlying data are limited to rural teachers since the benchmark also applies to agricultural, i.e. rural, unskilled labour. The median teacher could expect to draw about as much from his teaching duties as would equal an unskilled labourer's annual earnings. Less than a tenth of all rural teachers could boast of earnings that were double that and a non-negligible proportion of them did significantly worse. The rather fat lower tail of the distribution mostly consists of half-year teachers from Tyrol and a few other places, who were obviously only paid during the time when they were active. But even if they were removed from the sample or their earnings pro-rated to their full-year equivalent, the bulk of the distribution would still fall somewhere between 75 and 175, which is where about half of all teachers can be found in Figure 4.2. The data make abundantly clear that for large swathes of the teaching profession, the income drawn from teaching was not enough to sustain them at any decent standard of living. Note that the *Detail-Conscription* cited not only monetary payments but also all of the in-kind ones, evaluated at local prices as the law required, as well as income streams from school-affiliated fields and other real estate.

To supplement their income, teachers drew part of their livelihood from church service. Fully incorporated into the *Politische Verfassung*, this institutional arrangement dated back to Joseph II. Back in the 1780s, when these financial matters were being decided, the underlying rationale was to make teachers as small a burden on the public purse as possible.[18] The combination of teaching and church duties actually seemed to go rather well with the teacher's overall subordination to priestly supervision anyway. As part of the formalization of the teaching profession, the law required that each teaching position be based on a decree, issued by provincial authorities, specifying all income sources, and that teachers account annually for all of their sources of income in accordance with the decree, so that individual liable parties could be solicited for their contributions.

Many of these accounts – *Fassions* or *Fasse*, as they were called – have survived in the archives. As an illustration, Table 4.8 reproduces one pertaining to the teacher and teaching assistant in Třeboratice (near Prague) in 1861. As can be seen, a *Fassion* was supposed to be a comprehensive document from which anyone sufficiently versed in school administration could accurately reconstruct the full picture of a school's operation.[19] The sources of income for the teacher were numerous, falling into three broad categories: teaching, organ service and altar service. Each of these in turn split into several smaller items. As for teaching-related income, the two staff members in Třeboratice were doing relatively well. Their school served six villages and had almost two hundred pupils to draw on for tuition fees. Since only ten enrolees were freed from it, the school raised over 400 fl per year in revenue, split between the teacher and his assistant. The school was also endowed with almost a hectare of agricultural land, from which the Třeboratice teachers drew about 2% of their income. Somewhat atypical for a rural school, Třeboratice received a small subsidy from the *Schulfond*, although the bigger boost was the philanthropic attention of a certain Alexander Ritter von Schöller, a prominent Austrian industrialist in the sugar-refining business, who in 1849 bought an estate in Velké Čakovice and Myškovice (two of Třeboratice's six school-bound villages) and who supported both staff members by appreciable amounts even though he was not the school patron.[20] The income from organ service is evidence that the average village teacher had to be a competent mu-

[18] See Chapter 1 for further discussion.

[19] While the (very brief) methodological introduction to *Detail-Conscription* of 1865 does not say so explicitly, it is likely, given the range of statistics and the organization of the report, that the data assembled in it were collected from these *Fassions*.

[20] Würzbach. *Biographisches Lexikon*, Vol. 31, p. 89–92.

Table 4.8: An example of a *Fassion*, 1861

Diocese: Prague	Region: Prague
Vicariate: Prosek	Civil district: Karlín

Fassion
of all incomes and outlays in relation to the school, organ and altar service in Třeboratice

Type of school:	2-grade parish school	
Villages covered:	Třeboratice, Velké Čakovice, Letňany, Myškovice (all in distict Karlín), Mirovice, Veleň (district Brandýs nad Labem)	
School patron:	Count Černín z Chudenic	
Schoolbound children:	103 boys 92 girls = 191 in total (enrolled: 186)	
By village:		
Třeboratice	11 boys	12 girls
Velké Čakovice	36 boys	36 girls
Letňany	21 boys	14 girls
Myškovice	10 boys	15 girls
Mirovice	10 boys	6 girls
Veleň	15 boys	9 girls
School building:	own	
Premises:	2 classrooms, teacher apartment of 6 rooms, assistant teacher quarters with 1 room – all in very good condition, quite new	
Instruction:	year-round, all-day with 10 hours per day	
Teacher:	five hours daily	
Assistant teacher:	five hours daily in Czech language	

Religious instruction is delivered by the parish priest.

Income from teaching	
a) Income from land:	
Net income from school fields of 1 yoke & 600 fathoms (≈ 7913 m²)	6.36 fl
Garden by the old school building of 70 fathoms (≈ 252 m²)	0.52½fl
Garden by the new school building of 200 fathoms (≈ 719 m²)	1.57⅓fl
b) Contribution from the *Schulfond*, annually	11.11½fl
c) Other contributions: Alexander Ritter von Schöller from Velké Čakovice	52.50 fl
d) Tuition from 175 paying pupils	345.58 fl
	417.65 fl
Income from organ service	
a) From the village – New-Year Collect	6.30 fl
b) From the church treasury in Třeboratice	12.60 fl
of which: for Easter Passion singing	1.68 fl
in Čakovice	13.09 fl
c) *Taxa stola* for funeral music, annually	13.40 fl
Income from altar service	
Net income from church field of 1 yoke, 700 fathoms for daily bell-ringing	4.54 fl
	467.68½fl
Income of teaching assistant	

a) From the church treasury in Čakovice	73.50 fl
b) From the church treasury in Třeboratice	10.50 fl
c) From the village, a share of tuition revenue	73.50 fl
d) Contribution of Ritter von Schöller from Velké Čakovice, annually	52.50 fl
	210.00 fl
Outlays	
Cleaning of two classrooms	25.20 fl

Note: Numerical errors (e.g. wrong sum-total of school-bound children) appear in the original. Conversions of area units into m² are not in the original but are added.
Source: Kneidl. *Paměti školského okresu karlínského.* p. 493–494.

sician, playing at events both regular, such as the Sunday mass, and incidental (funerals).[21] Finally, the teacher's church duties included bell ringing as well as assistance at the altar during service and in Třeboratice this was a source of about 1% of the teacher's overall income.

The main import of this example of a *Fassion* is to show how many diverse and multifarious streams of income the teachers drew on. Indeed, the range of sources tapped in the countryside testified both to the adhockery practiced by the authors of the legislation and the creativity of the rural population, saddled with finding the money wherever. Throughout the land, they included cash payments, usufruct from school-owned land, in-kind payments of grains, meat, salt, wood, butter, eggs, beer and other goods drawn from a plethora of sources including parents, village treasuries, school patrons, private foundations, church property, bequests, central funds such as the *Religionsfond* and *Studienfond* and irregular gifts of all kinds.[22] And, while income diversification is generally a sound way to hedge against uncertainty and risk, the practical considerations of operating such a disparate system often outweighed those benefits. In many instances, the teachers were responsible for collecting the money themselves. Such was the case of the tuition until 1848, and of, for example, the New-Years Collect where the teacher drew income from the annual caroling among the households of the children that he taught. Such a scattered manner of financing must have also affected their loyalties and work priorities: the teaching assistant in Třeboratice was actually more financially dependent on money from local churches than on

[21] A teacher could not play at events of popular entertainment, such as weddings and dances, which were strictly *verboten* to him as per Article 252, their potential for side income notwithstanding. The same article also barred him from running a pub concurrently with a school, which seemed even more counterintuitive to the country folks: the pub was usually the biggest room in the village and thus a perfectly serviceable classroom. It was also empty during the day, making it available for teaching. Best of all, it turned a sure profit, which could be another source of income for the teacher. Alas, the Education Commission showed no appreciation for the beauty of economies of scope. See Pietsch. *Die Theresianische Schulreform in der Steiermark*, p. 146.

[22] See Kneidl. *Paměti* for a range of examples of rural *Fassions*.

his share of the tuition revenue, which surely focused his mind as to whom he most needed to keep happy – whether the pupils' parents or the parish priests.

Needless to say, the situation was a recipe for frequent and intractable conflict regarding financial claims and demands. Being one's own debt collector and enforcer (in the first instance) put many a teacher in a difficult position in the local community, especially if the party in arrears was his social superior, such as the aristocratic patron, or even just the village's richest farmer. The *Politische Verfassung* devoted several articles to specifying procedures for dispute resolution but resolution of such conflicts could take years.[23]

Of course, underneath the heterogeneity of financial sources and the complexity of salary arrangements, there also existed considerable variation in pay that depended on the individual characteristics of the teachers. One of the motivations for young assistants aspiring to a full teacher status and rural staff applying for appointments in cities was that higher rank came with higher income. Teachers also hoped, as most career workers do, that their income would increase with years served and with the amount of work rendered. Accounting precisely for all the determinants of the teachers' income requires data of considerable detail, which most teacher directories failed to supply. In most of them, the very statistic of interest – income – is missing. Conversely, where the pay is listed, as in the *Detail-Conscription* or in the parish survey of České Budějovice, the teacher characteristics are left out.

The best available source for this kind of exercise is the *Katalog* of teachers in the Roman Catholic diocese of Lviv (Lemberg) in Galicia in 1844. It contains not only all the personal data, such as the date and place of birth and career duration (specified, helpfully, by years and months), but also itemized accounts of school-related income, including the distinction between cash payments and in-kind payments.[24] This diocese stretched across most of the eastern part of Galicia, which is today part of the Ukraine, but also covered Catholics (such as there were) in Bukovina. The Orthodox schools of this area, which easily outnumbered the Catholic ones, reported to the Orthodox bishops in Lviv, who compiled their own teacher directory, so their data are not included in the Catholic *Katalog*. The same applies to Jewish and Protestant schools but their numbers were relatively small. The Lviv Catholic data are therefore meager in terms of number of observations (351 individuals in all) and selected along religious lines but at least contain the necessary minimum information to make income analysis possible.

That information is shown in Table 4.9. Before delving any deeper, it is worthwhile to compare the Lviv teachers with the Lower Austrian ones at least in those areas where the content in the two directories overlapped. It

[23] See for example Kneidl. *Paměti*, p. 149, 201–203.

[24] The in-kind income, or *Naturalien*, is specified in quantities (e.g. 5 fathoms of hardwood) but they can be evaluated using Galician prices from *TSOM* for 1844.

Table 4.9: Teachers of Lviv Catholic diocese – descriptive statistics, 1844

	Men	Women	t-statistic	p-value
Observations	294	57		
Personal characteristics				
Age	41.2	34.2	4.47	0
Age at career start	24.8	22.6	2.25	0.025
Experience (years)	16.8	10.4	3.19	0.002
Job tenure (years)	9.3	7.5	1.13	0.259
Birthplace: % born in…				
...Lviv	6.1	29.8		
...other Galician cities	6.8	12.3		
...Galician countryside	55.8	28.1		
...other Habsburg provinces	21.8	19.3		
...abroad	3.1	5.3		
Employment & school characteristics				
% catechists	9.9	0.0		
% school management	7.1	22.8		
% teachers	74.8	70.2		
of which: specialists	13.6	10.5		
of which: teachers of housework	0.0	14.0		
% teaching assistants	9.2	19.3		
% employed in a major school	39.1	0.0		
% employed in a trivial school	39.5	0.0		
% employed in a girl school	2.0	61.4		
% employed in private sector	18.4	38.6	-3.44	0.001
% employed in Lviv	31.0	73.7	-6.42	0
# pupils	181.8	196.5	-0.56	0.577
Income from teaching				
Total income (fl)	235.05	185.72	1.64	0.103
Cash income (fl)	191.51	167.73	0.76	0.449
% receiving accommodation	63.01	40.91	2.04	0.043
In-kind income (fl)	18.29	0.72	2.16	0.032

Note: Not all statistics are available for all observations. "Other Galician cities" refers to cities of more than 10000 inhabitants in 1869. "fl" refers to Austrian gulden of Conventional currency (C.M.) but is decimalized in this table.
Source: Katalog des an den Volksschulen der Lemberger lat. Erzdiözese angestellten Lehrpersonals, für das Jahr 1844

provides a gauge as to how much (or little) the Galician data can be trusted to support conclusions that could be generalized to Austrian teachers more broadly: if a certain pattern prevails both in the vicinity of the imperial capital as well as in rural eastern Galicia, there is a good chance that it reflects firm structural features institutionally embedded in the profession, such that would vary relatively little with local conditions. The data overlap applies to, in particular, age, migration and position within the teaching profession. The Galician and Lower Austrian teachers were of comparable age and both groups started their careers in their early twenties (cf. Table 4.1). In terms of job tenure, Lower Austria – especially the countryside – reported somewhat more durable appointments: recall that in Lower Austria, the rural appointments lasted a long time. The average teacher was found to have held his current job for over 17 years. In the Lviv diocese, the average tenure stood at 9.3 years for men and 7.5 years for women. Even though Lviv dominated its surroundings to a much smaller degree than Vienna, the patterns of teacher migration in the two provinces are nonetheless similar. The teaching corps drew heavily on the rural-born and comparable proportions came from other Habsburg crown lands (21.8% in the Lviv diocese and 19.1% in Lower Austria – see Table 4.3). In both provinces, women were more likely to be employed in the big city (73.7% in Lviv vs 80% in Vienna) and were also much more likely to be native to it. In Lviv, just like in Vienna, women teachers thrived in the private sector where they often served as the owners and managers of their educational business but given the greater prevalence of public girls' schools in Lviv, the private share there (38.6%) did not reach the 50% that it did in Vienna. The public girls' schools were also responsible for the lower proportion of housework teachers among Galician women, compared to Lower Austria, because they were more likely to employ women at all teaching positions, not just as housework teachers. A comparison with Table 4.5 also shows that the Lviv diocese teachers were atypical in that a disproportionate number of them were employed in urban major schools – almost 40%, well above both the Galician and Lower Austrian rates in 1865.

Let us now consider the information that is particular to the Lviv teacher directory: income data. They are, unfortunately, available only for those teachers who were employed in the public schools, because private ones were not obligated to report the financials. Among those, for whom income data are available, about 61% received some portion of their remuneration in in-kind payments and in almost all of those cases, accommodation was involved.[25] In addition to that, teachers received usually foodstuff and various other agricultural products (e.g. hay). For about one out of ten teachers, these *Naturalien* amounted to more than 30% of all school income. The overall average, however, was less than 10%. Paying the teacher in produce was more likely in the countryside; cities offered mostly just accommodation.

[25] Some teachers received a rent allowance in cash instead of an actual room or apartment to live in. I use these cases to assess the value of "free apartment" in those cases where the rental value was not specified: I put it at 40 fl C.M. Hoszowski puts the rental price in Lviv in 1841-45 at 57 fl C.M. but the rental data in the Lviv *Katalog* are consistently lower (when they are specified) and, for comparison, the vast majority of teachers in Chernivtsi (Czernowitz) in Bukovina were receiving 40 fl C.M. of rent allowance. See Hoszowski. *Ceny we Lwowie w latach, 1701–1914.*

Table 4.10: Determinants of teacher income in Lviv Catholic diocese (OLS)

Dependent variable:	ln(total income)			ln(cash income)
	(i)	(ii)	(iii)	(iv)
Experience	0.055*	0.060*	0.032*	0.037*
	[0.007]	[0.007]	[0.007]	[0.007]
Job tenure	-0.025*	-0.031*	-0.021*	-0.022*
	[0.008]	[0.009]	[0.007]	[0.008]
1(ordained)	-0.314	-0.294	-1.077*	-0.975*
	[0.333]	[0.337]	[0.255]	[0.280]
1(woman)	-0.152	-0.776*	0.191	0.215
	[0.194]	[0.391]	[0.379]	[0.416]
Type of school				
1(major school)		-0.229	-0.280*	0.077
		[0.127]	[0.126]	[0.139]
1(girls' school)		0.552	0.013	0.283
		[0.360]	[0.376]	[0.412]
Occupational rank				
1(catechist)			-0.183	-0.049
			[0.442]	[0.485]
1(school management)			-0.419	-0.335
			[0.414]	[0.455]
1(teacher)			-0.950*	-0.843
			[0.428]	[0.470]
also: 1(specialist)			0.643*	0.631*
			[0.250]	[0.274]
also: 1(teacher of housework)			-1.179	-1.362
			[0.630]	[0.691]
1(teaching assistant)			-2.475*	-2.260*
			[0.451]	[0.495]
1(other)			-1.265*	-1.126
			[0.612]	[0.672]
ln(local population)			0.090*	0.176*
			[0.039]	[0.042]
Constant	4.482	4.530	5.224	3.772
	[0.108]	[0.117]	[0.542]	[0.595]
N	238	238	238	238
Adjusted R^2	0.253	0.267	0.616	0.595
H_0: $\beta_{experience} + \beta_{job\ tenure} = 0$				
F-test	22.060	21.910	4.950	7.600
p-value	0.000	0.000	0.027	0.006

Note: Standard errors are in the square brackets. An asterisk (*) denotes significance at 5%.

To see how the remuneration reflected the teachers' characteristics, both personal and professional, I estimate a standard Mincerian earnings function where the natural log of income is regressed on a person's years of experience, professional rank, job tenure, gender and some other job-related variables.[26] The results are summarized in Table 4.10. To see how robust the estimated coefficients are, I formulated three specifications, which vary by the extent of explanatory variables included.

The coefficients, which are most stable and robust across columns (i) to (iii) are experience and job tenure. In all specifications, the pattern is the same: a small positive and significant coefficient on experience and an even smaller but also significant negative coefficient on job tenure. Given the log-linear nature of the Mincer equation, the coefficients capture the percentage change in income in response to a change in an explanatory variable. To use an example from column (i), an extra year of experience would increase a teacher's total income by 5.5% while an extra year at the same job would decrease his salary by 2.5%. At first glance, the contrast of the positive effect of experience and a negative one of tenure seems contradictory: after all, both are measures of time spent at work – for persons in their first job, they are in fact the same number. How could they have opposing effects? What would it actually mean to say that the labour market rewarded overall experience but punished commitment to a specific job? The key lies, in fact, precisely in the observation that for a continuing jobholder, both experience and tenure increase at the same pace whereas for a person changing jobs, experience continues to accumulate whereas job tenure resets to zero. This presents a specific (and, ultimately, intuitive) picture about how the average teacher would achieve a salary increase. Consider a teacher who has 9 years of experience, with 4 years at a given appointment. Moving into his tenth year of teaching and fifth in his current job, his income would increase by about (5.5%–2.5%=) 3% according to column (i), 3.1% according to column (ii) and 1.1% according to column (iii). These are relatively small increments, even though they were real and systematic: the hypothesis that the two effects cancelled out is rejected in every specification, as the bottom of the table shows. Now what if, after 5 years at his job, the teacher found a new position elsewhere? His overall experience would increase to 11 years while his tenure, at the end of his first year at the new post, would be 1. The net overall effect would be $0.055\times1 - 0.025\times(-4) = 0.155$ or 15.5%, which is a noticeable jump. In the other two specifications, the analogous result would be 18.4% and 11.6%. In other words, what the combination of the two opposing effects reveals is how the teachers of Lviv diocese could navigate the market to achieve a higher salary: by applying for, and switching to, a new job. Such a move always required a negotiation, which was an opportunity for the applicants and for

[26] The usual Mincer equation also includes a measure of education but since the teacher education was so rigidly standardized, not to mention its brevity (3 months only on top of basic elementary education), its omission from the regression does not impact the estimation. There was no substantial variation in education among the teachers. See Mincer. "Investment in Human Capital and Personal Income Distribution."

their potential employers to revisit the *Fassion* and see what could be changed so that the parties might come to a mutually acceptable solution. However, once the deal was sealed, the regression results suggest, the terms were largely set in stone and adjusted only marginally thereafter. Note that the recorded and reported cash payments were all nominal, so working under a *Fassion* that remained unchanged through the years exposed the teacher incomes to erosion through inflation.[27] The silver lining of relative employment security thus came with the cloud of considerable income rigidity.

This conclusion receives further corroboration from another part of the dataset, not used in the regressions. Whenever a teaching post was created or the salary amended, it required a stamp of approval from the provincial authorities. Along with the job tenure of each teacher, the Lviv directory helpfully listed, in a separate entry, the date of issue of the relevant official decree for that post. For about half of all male teachers in the sample, the decree was issued concurrently with the date of appointment (where "concurrent" is defined as within ±6 months of the appointment, allowing for the work pace of the Austrian bureaucracy). Another one sixth of teachers worked under a decree that predated their appointment by more than half a year and sometimes by decades. That leaves about a third of the teachers whose decree was updated (hopefully with a pay raise) during their current appointment.[28] In other words, the odds of getting a raise once an appointment was accepted were less than even.

The regression results reveal that teachers who belonged to religious orders were very low paid and often received nothing. (This category does not include parish priests who were the usual catechists.) The record is somewhat inconsistent here because some of these teachers have no recorded income while for others, the *Katalog* explicitly states that they were teaching "unentgeltlich", or *gratis*. Monks and nuns relied on their orders' houses for room and board, which the schooling system took as an opportunity to employ them at a deep discount. In fact, coefficients on *1(ordained)* underesti-

[27] As it happened, up to 1844, the teachers of Galicia did not need to be too worried about inflation because the provincial price level fluctuated around a remarkably stable long-term average. But then, within a decade after 1845, prices doubled. See Cvrček. "Wages, Prices and Living Standards in the Habsburg Empire, 1827–1910".

[28] A rudimentary probit analysis of the likelihood of a decree update at any point after initial appointment revealed a dynamic exactly opposite to that observed with income: for every year of job tenure, likelihood of a new decree increased by about 2.6% but every year of experience reduced it by 2.1%. Overall, then, for every year on the job, the likelihood grew by 0.5%, which is next to nothing. Here, in contrast to the case of income, the two effects apparently did cancel out; H_0: $\beta_{\text{experience}} + \beta_{\text{job tenure}} = 0$ cannot be rejected at any reasonable level of significance. Still, the result is consistent with the posited interpretation that the hiring of a new teacher was the usual occasion for revisiting the terms of employment, without which it would take decades before a decree was sufficiently out of date to make a serious revision likely.

mate the effect of being ordained: those who worked free of charge are not even included in the regressions. The coefficient is estimated from the few clerical teachers who received at least some compensation and it is clear, from the regression, that it was only very partial.

With regard to which type of school paid what salary, the estimation presents a bit of a surprise in the form of a negative coefficient on *1(major school)*. These were the most sophisticated institutions among schools and they usually drew the most experienced staff because their curriculum was more extensive than at trivial schools. They could be, therefore, expected to pay better than the trivial schools. This indeed obtains for simple averages: the mean salary in a major school was 289 fl, whereas in a trivial school it reached 189 fl, a significant difference ($t = -5.63$). Yet, once other characteristics are controlled for in the context of regression, the major schools apparently paid less.[29] The implication is that major schools paid overall higher salaries not because of their status as major schools but because of other characteristics that correlated with it. One such characteristic was their urban location: note that the coefficient on *1(major school)* becomes even more negative in column (iii), once the natural log of the population of the school's location is included. The size of the city mattered: the coefficient of 0.090 means that moving from a city to another that was twice as large would increase one's salary by about 6.5%, all else constant. Another reason for the negative coefficient on *1(major school)* was that major school teachers had on average somewhat more experience than trivial teachers (22.0 years vs 16.6 years) but actually shorter job tenures (8.4 years vs 11.4 years). The average age at appointment was 37.6 at major schools and the appointee would arrive with an average 13.5 years of experience under his belt, compared with only 5.2 years of experience of appointees at trivial schools who were only 30.2 years old at the moment of appointment. What the negative coefficient on *1(major school)* means, then, is that the move to a major school was apparently associated with a smaller jump in income than would have been expected purely on the basis of the estimated effects of experience and tenure. Coming to work at a major school thus must have been motivated by other, non-monetary amenities such as the urban location, greater prestige of the job or more pleasant working conditions. For the teaching assistants, the pattern was somewhat different. At major schools, the teaching assistants were less experienced (3.2 years vs 7.2 years) and also less likely to stay for long (2.6 years vs 6.6 years) than assistants at trivial schools. Assistantships at major schools were apparently brief stints compared to trivial schools. Here the obvious non-monetary amenity seems to have been that the major school was a good springboard for a good first teacher appointment of these

[29] Being the omitted category in the regressions, trivial schools serve as the benchmark against which other types are compared.

assistants. In short, the contradiction between the observed higher salaries in major schools and negative coefficients in Table 4.10 must be accounted for in terms of selection and confounding factors, such as the urban location etc.

The set of variables that is introduced in column (iii) captures the stratification of the teaching profession. Since the categories are not all mutually exclusive, they can all enter into the regression concurrently. In terms of results, there are no major surprises here, as the coefficients roughly reflect the pecking order one would expect to have prevailed in Austrian schools of the time. Catechists fared best, followed by school directors. The coefficient on *1(teacher)* is lower still and also statistically different from that on school managers. The exception were the specialists, such as language, drawing and music teachers, who apparently earned significantly better than just plain teachers. At the bottom of the heap were the teaching assistants, some of whom apparently worked for nothing.

If one should adopt a teacher at a trivial school as the benchmark, then the regression results imply that, *ceteris paribus*, a catechist earned more than double the teacher's salary, while a school director received about 70% more and a specialist about 90% more. Teaching assistants, on the other hand, earned 80% less. Most of these were teacher candidates – little more than students at the Lviv training course – and working in the schools as part of their overall training for what amounted to a student stipend (their teacher income averages less than 50 fl per year). These results put the impact of experience and tenure into perspective. Clearly, playing the teaching job market, if one were skilled and able to do that, was an effective way to increase one's income. But at the outset of one's career, the crucial issue was to make the jump from assistant status to a full teaching status. Moving on further to a directorship was even better but most teachers never reached that far.

The knottiest of interpretations in Table 4.10 concerns women. Of the 57 women teachers in the Lviv dataset, only 22 could be included in the regression analysis because the other 35 worked in the private sector and thus their income data are unavailable. The remaining 22 all worked in girls' schools, some as teachers, some as teaching assistants and some as housework teachers. With all these strongly correlated factors at play, the coefficient on *1(woman)* alone will not be enough to account for how women fared relative to men. In column (i) this coefficient is negative but not statistically significant. In column (ii) it is significantly negative but once combined with the girls' school coefficient, which applied to all women, the resulting value (-0.224) becomes again insignificant. In column (iii), the coefficient on *1(woman)* even turns positive (albeit insignificant) and that on *1(girls' school)* becomes effectively zero. So where did the gender gap in earnings, equalling almost 50 fl in Table 4.9, come from? The regression needs to account for that somehow. The most obvious answer lies in the dummy variable

1(teacher of housework), which was an exclusively female teaching position. The coefficient on this dummy (-1.179) is not statistically significant (most likely on account of the scarcity of observations on women) but it is sizeable and implies that housework teachers earned about 70% less than teachers generally and were comparable, in salary terms, to teaching assistants.[30] So women's lower average salary, observable in Table 4.9, came primarily from their occupational composition. The regression results suggest (and with merely 22 observations it should not count as more than as a suggestion) that women were not necessarily getting a lower salaries for the same work but rather that the system reserved for them only the lowest paid occupations, among which the most visible one was as a teacher of domestic work.

The right-most column in Table 4.10 applies the broadest specification to the cash component of teacher income. Given that the coefficient sizes and significance levels are very similar in columns (iii) and (iv), it is safe to conclude that most of the determinants of the total income operated through cash income. The most noteworthy difference is that the cash income was much more responsive to local population size: the elasticity was +0.176 in column (iv) as opposed to +0.090 in column (iii). This result reinforces the earlier observation that villages were more likely to pay teachers in kind.

The limited sample size in the Lviv data means that the results in Table 4.10 must be interpreted with caution. They can be pushed only so far to support general claims applicable to all of Austria. If any could be considered robust, it would be the observation that teacher incomes tended to increase mostly at the moment of appointment but not much during tenure and that a teacher was likely to enjoy an especially notable income boost, if an appointment also coincided with a promotion to a higher status, e.g. from assistant to a full teacher. Then it could increase by tens of percent at once.

The problem was how to get there. In the first two decades of the system, (before the end of the 18th century) certified teachers were still relatively scarce and the expansion of the school network generated new employment opportunities at a rate that must have made it relatively easy to find an appointment. Where the network was already somewhat denser and new positions were not opening up fast enough, fresh graduates migrated to the less covered places, as did, for example, Bohemian teachers to Styria in the 1790s or Moravian and Silesian teachers to Galicia as late as the 1840s.[31]

As the school network approached full coverage or if its extension stalled, the competition for posts became more intense. This may come as a surprise,

---

[30] The specification takes teachers of housework as a subcategory of teachers, so both coefficients (on *1(teachers)* and on *1(teacher of housework)*) apply. In column (iii), they add up to -2.129 which is not statistically different from -2.475, the coefficient on *1(teaching assistant)*.

[31] Pietsch. *Die Theresianische Schulreform in der Steiermark*, p. 149; *Katalog des an den Volksschulen der Lemberger lat. Erzdiözese angestellten Lehrpersonals.*

seeing that teachers were getting paid at the level of unskilled day labourers. The answer is that in certain social strata – more likely those close to the bottom of the social hierarchy – the teaching profession seemed like a viable path to some social advance and material improvement. At its best, the advance could be appreciable. If a teacher patiently climbed the professional ladder all the way to a directorship of an urban major school, which would be about as far as a successful career could go in this line of work, he would be a prominent, well-known person in his town, a boss of more than ten other staff members and earning over 500 fl annually – not a bad run for, say, an ambitious peasant boy.[32] But even in the less exceptional circumstances of a typical trivial school teacher, the job offered various minor perks. It offered a secure employment thanks to the law's protection against arbitrary dismissal. Teachers were freed from military service. Legally, they shared in the status of public servants, such as when it came to old-age pensions and care for their widows. Already in the 1770s and again in an 1811 decree, they were declared local dignitaries (*Honoratioren*), which denotation admittedly carried prestige rather than material benefits but in the class-conscious Austrian society that still counted for something – after all, only about one quarter of one percent of the population fell in this group.[33] With the gradual introduction of municipal self-government after 1848, local dignitaries acquired the right to vote in municipal elections, a fairly rare privilege in Austria throughout the 19th century. None of this could, however, conceal the generally low pay and so it is not surprising that the teaching profession attracted applicants from the poorer strata of the population, men who were often "raw and unsophisticated" upon enrolment in the training course.[34]

Overall, the teacher training courses did not complain of lack of applicants. In Lower Austria, Bohemia and Moravia, interest was so strong that in 1822 the authorities could afford to raise the admission bar.[35] Since fresh graduates outnumbered available posts, getting a good placement was growing increasingly difficult. Many clearly gave up. To give an example, the training courses of Lower Austria certified 182 new lay teacher candidates in 1846.[36] Yet according to the teacher directory, only 35 members of the class of 1846 taught at a public school in 1851. Migration to other provinces and

[32] Such was the life story, for example, of Franz Moysel, the director of the major school in Liberec in 1850-1855, who indeed came from peasant parents. The director of the major school in Lviv earned 600 fl in 1844. See Hoffmann. *Geschichte der Haupt- und Mädchenschule in Reichenberg*. p. 93, 109; *Katalog des an den Volksschulen der Lemberger lat. Erzdiözese angestellten Lehrpersonals*, p. 7.

[33] Becher. *Statistische Übersicht der Bevölkerung der österreichischen Monarchie*, p. 361.

[34] Pietsch. *Die Theresianische Schulreform in der Steiermark*, 145.

[35] See Article 117 and its accompanying footnote in the *Politische Verfassung*.

[36] TSOM 1845-46 Zweiter Teil, Tafel 11 – Lehranstalten, p. 31.

private tutoring in aristocratic households can go only so far in explaining the discrepancy. On balance, migration streamed into Lower Austria, not out of it, indicating that the incentives for those already in Lower Austria were strong to stay. Families sufficiently rich to pay for their own teacher were a minuscule fraction of the population, not to mention that any appointment to tutoring a noble child one-on-one was unlikely to be a long-term position because children tend to grow up: unlike a village of several hundred people, an aristocratic family does not keep supplying fresh cohorts of six-year olds year after year. This segment of the market thus could not absorb the balance of the class of 1846.

One way to secure a position was to "inherit" a post through a family connection. Some teachers absolutely turned their school into a family business.[37] Teacher dynasties can be detected, for example, in the Lower Austrian teacher directory. Although the father-son links are not explicitly acknowledged, just by relying on surnames, places of birth and plausible distance in years of birth, one can identify at least 41 different families where at least two members were in the teaching profession and often the father and the son worked as a teacher-assistant duo in the same school.[38]

As the 19th century wore on, those who did not have their father's job lined up faced slowly deteriorating prospects of a quick advance. The evidence of that emerges from the changes in the relative number of teachers and assistants across time. Consider Figure 4.3, which captures the situation in Bohemia, Moravia and Silesia. The middle series, teaching staff per 100 school-age children, shows a robust growth before 1840 that even outpaced population growth, which was the fastest these provinces have seen in recorded history.[39] The school network was still in expansion mode, getting denser. New schools were springing up and existing ones were expanding their staff. This is evident in the top series which shows that the average number of staff members per school increased from 1.28 in 1808 to 1.65 in 1836. And yet, the percentage of assistants among all teaching staff (the bottom time series, linked to the right-hand axis) was increasing from 18.8% in 1808 to 43.4% in 1847. The absolute number of teachers grew by 600 in 1813–1846 to reach 5200, whereas the number of assistants grew from 1239 to 3931 over the same period. In other words, despite the robust growth of the school network

[37] Pietsch. *Die Theresianische Schulreform in der Steiermark*, 145.

[38] For example, Franz Niedermeyer, born in 1797 in Witzelsdorf, was appointed teacher in Probstdorf in 1816. Franz Niedermeyer Jr. was born there in 1822 and, having taken the teacher course in 1840, joined his father as an assistant in Probstdorf in 1844. The son then succeeded his father at the main teacher post in Probstdorf in 1863. See Kaiser. *Lehrer-Schema*, p. 228; Huber. *Lehrer-Schema*, p. 160. A similar story could be told for the Pollands in Hollenstein, the Schmidls in St Christophen, the Arnbergers in Niederkreuzstetten, the Bartsches in Arbesbach, the Hofers in Pillichsdorf, the Lers in Altenwörth and many others.

[39] Karníková, *Vývoj obyvatelstva v českých zemích, 1754–1914*, p. 65–66.

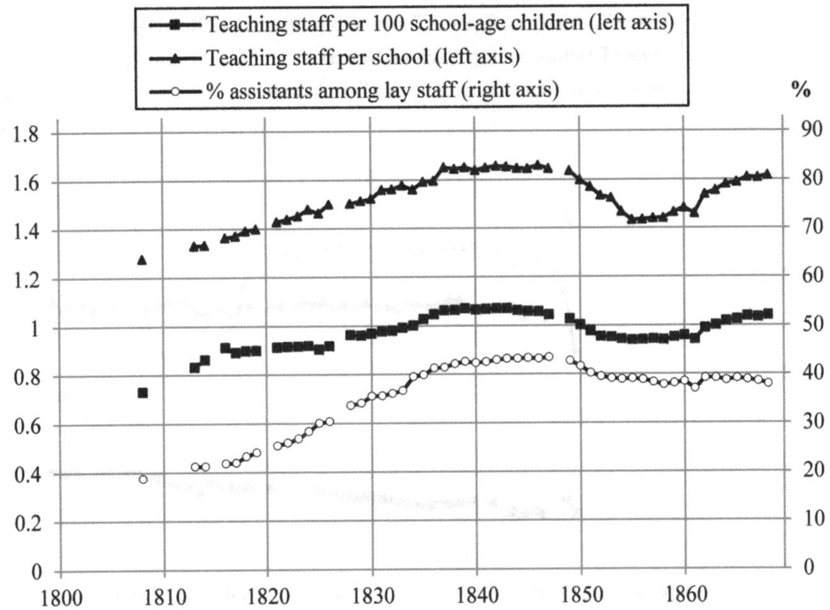

Figure 4.3: Teachers in the Czech provinces, 1807–1868
Note: Czech provinces comprise Bohemia, Moravia and Silesia.
Source: TSOM, SJOM, OeStA

in the Czech lands, the inflow of new job seekers was bigger than the network could absorb: if the average teacher retired after, say, 25 years in his post (and choosing any realistic number will not change the basic calculation), about 4% of the posts could be expected to become vacant every year: that adds up to about 200 out of the roughly 5000 in total. But the teacher training centres in the Czech lands produced over 700 new graduates every year in the late 1820s and early 1830s. No wonder the competition became more intense and the odds of success grew long. This graph does not show how many graduates failed to find even an assistantship position but we can tell that those who did become assistants and who hoped to progress to full teachers faced ever longer wait times, i.e. ever longer stints in the (meagerly paid) assistantship positions.

Then in 1849, the trend broke and the percentage of assistants started falling again down to 37% in 1861. If this fall in percentage had coincided with the continuing expansion of the school system, it would have been a sign that the up and coming young pedagogues were breaking through and finally getting into the teacher positions in greater numbers and faster. Instead, as the figure shows, schools were actually cutting staff and the axe fell mostly on the assistant posts. It was not until the second half of the 1850s and the 1860s that the expansion resumed. Still, it remains a fair assessment that throughout

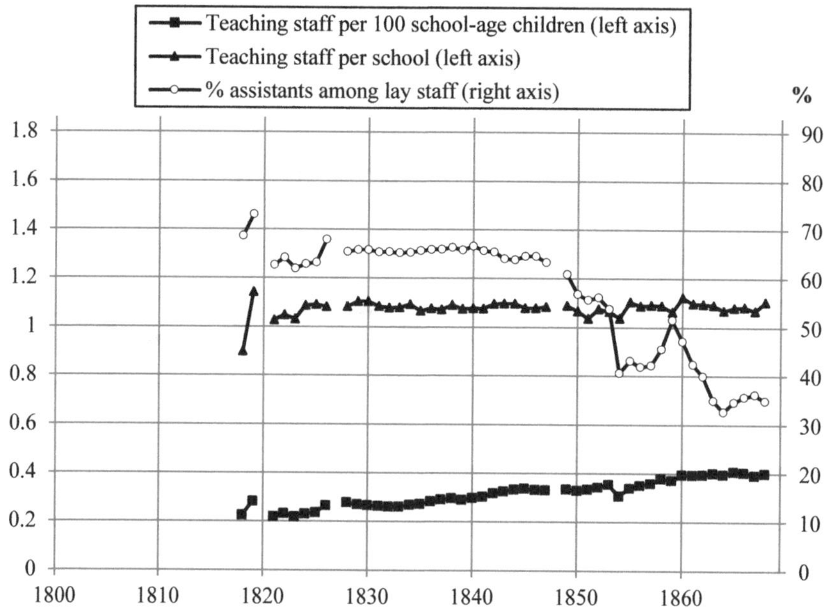

Figure 4.4: Teachers in Galicia and Bukovina, 1818–1868
Source: TSOM, SJOM, OeStA

the first half of the 19th century an increasing proportion of assistants were discovering that the assistantship was less and less a stopover on the way to better things and increasingly a dead end.

The situation was not as bad in the Alpine provinces but the overall trends worked in a similar direction. The proportion of assistants among all staff increased from 28.5% in 1822 to 37.1% in 1844, then declined to 31% by 1859 and then increased again. The southern parts of the empire, i.e. Carniola, Dalmatia and the area around Trieste, had the lowest proportion of teaching assistants – around 15%. A robust extensive growth of the school network came in the 1840s and by 1853 the share of assistants fell to 11%. These provinces offered a clear illustration of the fact that the best chances of quick professional progress (although it would be progress from a very low starting point) was possible in places, which were still building up their school network.

Such was also the case of Galicia and Bukovina, as Figure 4.4 shows. This graph reproduces the same series as Figure 4.3 did for the Czech lands and the picture is clearly different. Right after the Napoleonic Wars, assistants made up more than two thirds of all teaching staff. Most existing schools had exactly one staff member and it was usually a teaching assistant, i.e. most villages were either not willing or not able to pay for a full teacher. As the network slowly spread to the countryside – note the ongoing increase in the number of teaching staff per 100 school-age children – and as more resources were poured into it, the share of assistants eventually (from about 1840) started declining, at first gradually, but after 1848 much more sharply. The schools, run on the cheap with only assistants for staff, started converting the positions into proper teacher posts and by late 1860s, the share of assistants in Galicia and Bukovina was similar to that observed in the Czech lands.

These provincial variations notwithstanding, the record of the Czech and Alpine provinces was paramount for the profession as a whole because the bulk of the country's teachers worked and lived there. The most vocal spokesmen for their trade also came from these crown lands.[40] What they said when they spoke inevitably reflected their experience: that the Austrian teaching profession's social position was never very high to begin with and that, in the first half of the 19th century, it mostly further deteriorated. Across all the analysis in this chapter, this basic observation must surely emerge as the key facet of teachers' functioning within the system. The state dangled in front of their eyes the promise of a certain degree of social advance where sons of simple peasants could become respectable *Honoratioren*, with a stable job and income. At first, the trick worked and admissions into training courses were ample. But getting an appointment after graduation was where the trouble started and, as decades went on, the hopes of converting an assistantship into a full teaching position were only getting dimmer. This changed the equation because so much of that promised social advance usually coincided with changing jobs, progressing to a higher-level appointment. Moreover, when it came to bolstering the profession's prestige, what the government gave with one hand it took away with the other: the state's distrust of the teacher, his constant subordination to the priestly oversight, the deliberate pressure to keep him "cheap" so as not to burden rural communities, the intransigent refusal to upgrade his training – all these dented the respect for the educator in the eyes of his fellow citizens. Naturally, the teachers and teaching candidates gravitated to where the chances of advance were the greatest: the cities, with their good schools and a job market in education as well as other skilled jobs. It was the private sector, marginal though it was in the great scheme of things, where the teaching profession could enjoy somewhat more breathing space and where the rigidities of the official regulation did not press down as strongly. But it was not enough to counter the trends.

Their frustrations transmuted into organized political activity at the first auspicious moment.[41] In 1848, a Pedagogical Union was formed and profes-

---

[40] Prominent among them, to name at least one such spokesman, was an official of the Viennese Consistory Joseph Kaiser, who was incidentally also the compiler of the Lower Austrian teacher directories.

[41] See Engelbrecht. *Geschichte des österreichischen Bildungswesens Vol. 3*, p. 242.

sional periodicals started proliferating.[42] Overturning sixty years of deliberate policy to prevent them from uniting in collective action, teachers started meeting at district conferences to voice their concerns – so much so that, in 1853, the Ministry of Education felt obliged to forcibly restrict their agenda to issues pertaining only to individual schools but not the system in general.[43] The gag order did not last long. By the early 1860s, Austrian representatives started attending German teacher congresses, breaking the country's long-standing intellectual isolation in educational matters.[44] Within Austria, teacher conferences became a regular, legally mandated fixture of the educational landscape and before long, having found their platform, teachers started petitioning the government for a wholesale reform. Indeed, many of the ideas that the liberal legislation of 1868–69 ended up enacting first appeared in some teacher petition.[45] The move to professional self-organization and the active participation in the reform debates of the 1860s ensured that teachers were among the main winners of the liberalization, as I argue in Chapter 7. It was high time, too, and no surprise that they stood to gain because, to put it bluntly, their situation was so low that the only way was up.

---

[42] Frank. "Kurzer Überblick über die geschichtliche Entwicklung des österreichischen Volksschulwesens in den letzten fünfzig Jahren", p. 69. The aforementioned Joseph Kaiser commenced publishing his *Oesterreichisches pädagogisches Wochenblatt* already in 1842 but the real take-off in professional periodicals came after 1848. See Winckler. *Die periodische Presse Oesterreichs*, pp. 206–209. The journal *Oesterrichische Schulbote*, which started appearing in 1851 as a prominent press organ of the teaching profession, exists to this date under the title *Erziehung und Unterricht*.

[43] Frank. *Die Österreichische Volksschule von 1848–1898*, p. 12.

[44] Ibid. p. 15.

[45] Veselá mentions, for example, that an 1848 petition of 500 Czech teachers proposed the extension of compulsory schooling to age 14 for boys and age 13 for girls. See Veselá. *Vývoj české školy a učitelského vzdělání*, p. 28; Jellouschek. "Das Reichsvolksschulgesetz", p. 295.

Chapter 5

The Pupils

In 1770, as plans for school reform were slowly taking shape, a government report estimated that in Vienna the proportion of 5 to 13 year-olds, enrolled in public schools, stood at 24%.[1] Another 41%, or about 8000 children, were receiving no education whatsoever. The remaining third of the Viennese youths, it was surmised, were either home-schooled or taught at the unapproved, unregulated and unsupervised *Winkelschulen*, the reformers' anathema.[2] At least the imperial capital was ahead of the rest of Lower Austria, where enrolment reached 16%. Lower still, the duchy of Silesia found only 4% of children in schools in 1772.[3] Other provinces supplied, at best, piecemeal information, usually just from the provincial capital, but they all struck the same note: schooling was in a disappointing state. The Moravian metropolis of Brno not only reported a lively undergrowth of *Winkelschulen* but, to add insult to injury in the eyes of the reporter, many of them were led by women.[4]

These reports show that the question of enrolment, its extent and growth, was of eminent interest to policy makers. Sincerity of religious conviction, internalization of work ethic or acceptance of traditional authority – the ultimate aims of school reform – could not be easily measured but the leading experts were confident that the tried and tested method of abbot Felbiger would surely produce results once applied to a school's captive audience. The task of the day was bringing the audience in. This made the enrolment ratio, arguably, the most crucial indicator of whether the Theresian school reform was succeeding. No wonder the law so carefully specified and standardized the reporting duties now imposed on teachers, including form specimens and deadlines.

Later historians largely adopted the same standard, though too often without an appropriate (or often any) critical evaluation of the component data.[5]

---

[1] Helfert. *Die österreichische Volksschule,* p. 66.

[2] The report put their number at 59, with 317 pupils. See Melton. *Absolutism*, p. 12. One contemporary also estimated that there were about 2000 private family tutors (*Hauslehrer*) in the city. Gruber, Johann Leonhard. *Freymüthige Beurtheilung*. p. 73.

[3] Helfert. *Die österreichische Volksschule,* p. 55.

[4] Helfert. *Die österreichische Volksschule,* p. 52.

[5] See Weiss. *Geschichte der österreichischen Volksschule 1792–1848. II. Band*, p. 763–969; Lenderová et al. *Z dějin české každodennosti*, p. 199; Kuzmin. *Vývoj školství a vzdělání*

The systematic deficiencies in accounting for the school-age cohorts, documented in Chapter 2, made enrolment ratios look higher than they actually were. The authorities were somewhat aware of the problem but lacking an effective remedy, they mostly just let it slide. In one revealing episode, the government inquired of Tyrolean school administrators how it was possible that the number of school-age children went from 61000 in the 1781 report to 34241 in 1782. Tyrol responded by simply furnishing a third number: 42538 school-age children for 1784.[6] It is unlikely that any one of these three figures was within 10000 of the real total.[7] For another example, Dalmatia, a province of about 300000 inhabitants, kept reporting fewer than 20000 school-age children for several decades, yet these laughably low numbers continued to be published without comment.[8] As Chapter 2 showed, proper accounting for all the children of school age casts the success of the reform in a much dimmer light than an uncritical reading of the statistics would suggest: school coverage was lower than the authorities thought it was and which age cohorts were to be covered by compulsory schooling varied from province to province and decade to decade.[9]

This matters because the first step in assessing the enforcement of compulsory schooling is getting the denominator right, that is, identifying the right target age range and accurately counting the children falling within it. Figure 5.1 shows the age profile of enrolment for selected provinces in 1865 – the only year for which the age composition of pupils is known.[10] The variation across provinces was substantial. At one end, there is the Austrian Littoral, where enrolment did not exceed 45% in any one of the birth cohorts. Children were eased into schooling rather gradually, with only 33% enrolled at age 6. The Littoral is broadly representative of the South-Slav provinces, like Dalmatia and Carniola, where school density was low and enrolment meager. Carinthia, an Alpine province, did somewhat better with two-thirds of 7-year-olds enrolled and staying for about four years before enrolment started eroding. At the other end were Upper Austria and Tyrol. Of all the provinces, the

---

v Československu, p. 63.

[6] Hölzl. "Studien zum Pflichtschulwesen in Tirol 1774–1806", p. 137.

[7] Tyrol had about 600000 inhabitants in the 1780s. Assuming any realistic age structure, which usually implies about 12% of the population being 6.0–12.0 year olds and 14% 5.0–12.0 year olds, the size of the school-age cohort varied between 72000 and 84000 pupils, depending on one's choice of age range. See Goehlert. "Die Entwicklung der Bevölkerung von Tirol und Vorarlberg", and Liechtenstern. *Handbuch der neuesten Geographie des Österreichischen Kaiserstaates. I. Theil*, p. 573.

[8] See *TSOM* 1830–1865.

[9] Needless to say, statistical analysis pertaining to enrolment in this and other chapters of this book rely on the corrected numbers.

[10] The source is *Detail-Conscription*. Unfortunately, the age distribution was not cross-tabulated with gender.

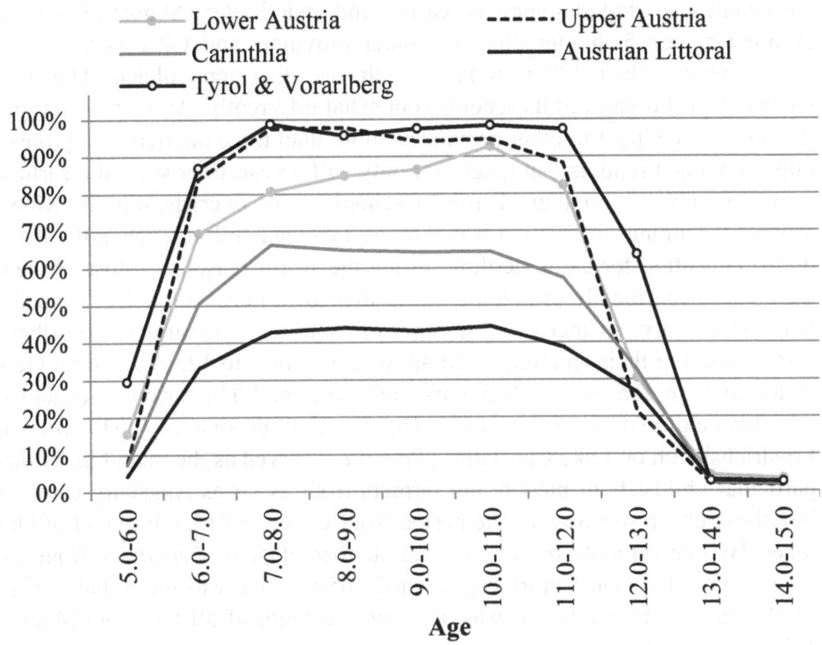

Figure 5.1: Age profile of enrolment in selected provinces, 1865
Source: Detail-Conscription.

Upper Austrian record most looks like a result of the conscientious enforcement of strict regulation guidelines: almost no-one was in school before age 6, but upon reaching it, 84% were on the rosters and 97% were by age 7. Upper Austrian teachers were able to keep the children in school firmly into their 11th year but come age 12, enrolment dropped off from 88% to 21%. Compared to the gradual and low arc of the Littoral, a tell-tale sign of lax enforcement, Upper Austria's "box-shaped" record suggests a province that was successful in consistently hewing to a six-year compulsory schooling between the ages 6.0 and 12.0. Few pupils ever stayed in school beyond the law's requirements.

Tyrol presents a special case.[11] The schools there had an even firmer grip on pupils, especially those between ages 7 and 12, than in Upper Austria but

[11] In most statistics, Tyrol and Vorarlberg are reported together, since Vorarlberg was a rather small province of 102000 inhabitants (compared to 776000 in Tyrol) in 1869 and the Austrian K.K. Statistische Central-Commission did not consider it worth a separate entry in most of its publications. Thus, while most of the discussion around Tyrol refers to Tyrol specifically and not to Vorarlberg, it often rests on statistical data that conflates both of these. But given the disproportionate size of Tyrol relative to Vorarlberg, it is a safe bet that the aggregate numbers by and large reflect the Tyrolean experience. Moreover, in what follows in the present discussion, the two were in fact subject to very similar trends and practices.

enrolment also started somewhat earlier and ended later. Almost 30% were enrolled at age 5, higher than any other province, and 64% were still in school beyond their 12th birthday, which was also unparalleled. This was because Tyrol organized its schools somewhat differently. As shown in Table 2.2, in stark contrast to other provinces, more than three quarters of Tyrolean pupils attended schools that taught for only half a year. Ever since the earliest years of public schooling, Tyrolean schools were overwhelmingly winter schools.[12] Summer instruction was rare, as Tyrolean children generally abandoned education for cattle herding during the warm seasons.[13] Most of them were employed locally or helping out in their own households. But from the late 18th century, an increasing number of families in Tyrol and Vorarlberg started sending their children, aged anywhere from 7 to 17, to southern Germany to earn money as shepherds and herders.[14] They were nicknamed "Swabian children", or *Schwabenkinder,* after their destination.[15] The town of Friedrichshafen on Lake Constance (*Bodensee*) served as the main hub of this particular child-labour market and farmers from as far as Augsburg came to hire these cheap workers for the period from the end of March to end of October. By one estimate from 1839, the number of *Schwabenkinder* from the Upper Inn valley and Vorarlberg reached 2650, which was more than a fifth of all seasonal migrants.[16] It was also about a tenth of all the school-bound children in these two regions.[17]

Report after report from Innsbruck informed the Education Commission in Vienna that this pattern was so entrenched and so vital for the local economy that it was futile to expect a successful enforcement of year-round schooling as was usual in other provinces. Efforts to expand schools had been running into opposition at least since the late 1780s precisely due to this issue.[18] Parents were not convinced school had much value to offer and complained that the six years long compulsory schooling kept their children away from useful and productive work.[19] It is not surprising that the force of law was only weakly applied. One provincial report from 1798 noted that only three of the appointed local school supervisors made any inspection visits and that none

[12] Hölzl. "Studien zum Pflichtschulwesen in Tirol 1774–1806", p. 105.

[13] Weiss. *Geschichte der österreichischen Volksschule 1792–1848. II. Band*, p. 922, 929.

[14] Rohrer, Joseph. *Uiber der Tiroler: Ein Beytrag zur Oesterreichischen Völkerkunde*. p. 49.

[15] The most authoritative account of this phenomenon is Uhlig, Otto. *Die Schwabenkinder aus Tirol und Vorarlberg*.

[16] Adults sought work in Swabia also. Staffler. *Tirol und Vorarlberg, statistisch und topographisch*, p. 370.

[17] TSOM 1839: Tafel 55.

[18] Weiss. *Geschichte der österreichischen Volksschule 1792–1848. II. Band*, p. 921–922.

[19] Ibid., p. 922.

ever fined any parents for their children's truancy, as the regulation required, because they did not want to fall out with their neighbours.[20]

In the face of such realities, the school authorities forswore changing what they could not and instead tried to make the best of the situation. An 1833 provincial decree required that a child submit a certified proof of good school attendance in winter before being issued a passport to Swabia in the spring.[21] By sacrificing summer attendance, this regulation strengthened the incentives for the winter one. In 1867, provincial authorities stopped issuing passports to children under 10 altogether and tightened the rules by requiring a proof of poverty in addition to the attendance certificate. Moreover, *Schwabenkinder* became obligated to attend school for two more winters in addition to the regular school age.[22] This idea was not new. Already in 1822, the provincial governor requested that the school age be altered for Tyrol from 6–12 to 8–14 or 7–13 but it was rejected by Vienna.[23] The proposal grew out of the recognition that winter schools had their own problems: high in the Alps, they were usually snowed in during winters, so children, especially small ones, could not attend, even when they were currently home. While the adjustment in school age was not formally implemented in Tyrol until the 1867 ordinance (and even then only for the itinerant children) it seems that in the meantime the realities forced this kind of outcome nonetheless. This is why, in Figure 5.1, Tyrol and Vorarlberg report 64% enrolment among 12-year-olds – more than any other province by a large margin. Both parents and school authorities by and large accepted a trade-off where the school year was cut down to a half in most schools but pupils attended them over a longer span of years. The reason why Tyrol consistently reported more enrolled pupils than school-bound children was because it *de facto* adopted a seven-year school attendance, even when *de iure* the law was ambiguous and was usually interpreted as implying six-year schooling.[24]

Perhaps no other province was as starkly peculiar as Tyrol and Vorarlberg but even smaller variation matters to how one interprets enrolment data. Figure 5.1 is useful for showing the age at which children went to school and in what numbers but it cannot reliably say how much schooling the pupils signed up for. For reasons outlined above, there was much less actual classroom time behind the high Tyrolean enrolment numbers compared to, say, Silesia, a province with a lower enrolment ratio but widespread year-round teaching. This is nicely illustrated by Table 5.1. In column (i), pupils aged 6.0–12.0 are divided by all children aged 6.0–12.0 to yield the percentage en-

[20] Hölzl. "Studien zum Pflichtschulwesen in Tirol 1774–1806", p. 108.

[21] Uhlig. *Die Schwabenkinder aus Tirol und Vorarlberg*, p. 101.

[22] Verordnung der k.k. Statthalterei vom 30. November 1867, Nr. 14800, ALEX.

[23] Weiss. *Geschichte der österreichischen Volksschule 1792–1848. II. Band*, p. 931.

[24] This is also the reason why in the rest of this chapter, attendance in Tyrol and Vorarlberg is calculated using seven birth cohorts in contrast to just six used for all other provinces.

Table 5.1: Enrolment and expected years of schooling, 1865

	Percent enrolled among…		Expected years of schooling	
	6.0–12.0 year-olds	5.0–13.0 year-olds	enrolled pupils	all school-age children
	(i)	(ii)	(iii)	(iv)
Lower Austria	82.2	66.5	5.34	4.80
Upper Austria	92.6	72.4	5.14	4.99
Salzburg	85.4	69.8	5.95	5.50
Styria	69.8	56.9	5.38	4.09
Carinthia	61.3	50.7	5.66	3.83
Carniola	44.3	36.9	5.57	2.75
Austrian Littoral	40.9	34.4	5.83	2.65
Tyrol & Vorarlberg	95.6	83.4	4.28	4.08
Bohemia	90.5	73.6	5.83	5.72
Moravia	91.8	74.0	5.80	5.73
Silesia	84.7	68.3	5.74	5.30

Note: Column (iii) is calculated for enrolled 6.0–12.0 year-olds, i.e. it measures expected years of schooling conditional on enrolment by adding the six age cohorts between ages 6.0 and 12.0 – when this measure falls short of 6.00, it is because some pupils are enrolled in half-year or half-day schools. For Tyrol & Vorarlberg, a seven-year schooling period is assumed. Column (iv) is calculated across all 5.0–13.0 year-olds, enrolled or not, because as a measure of unconditional expected years of schooling, it must properly include also the time spent in school before age 6.0 or beyond 12.0 by some of the children. When this measure falls short of 6.00, it is because some children were completely unenrolled, contributing zero years of school to the average.
Source: Detail-Conscription.

rolled within this age cohort. It gives a sense of how successful the authorities were in getting to schools those who were the primary target of compulsory attendance. Several provinces score above 90% with Tyrol highest among them and Upper Austria a close second. The second column includes the edges of the school age range: the precocious 5-year olds and the overstayers above 12. The percentage falls off significantly compared to column (i) because in most provinces the enrolment among these cohorts was close to zero. (Consistently with Figure 5.1, this was not the case in Tyrol.)

Then in column (iii), the age-specific enrolment ratios are weighted by type of school to yield expected years of schooling, thereby incorporating the obvious observation that pupils attending a half-year school over a course of six years end up getting only three complete years (six half-years) of education. To give an example: imagine a province where 80% of all enrolled pupils attend a year-round school and 20% a half-year school. Then the average pupil goes to school 90%, or nine-tenths, of the whole school year (0.8×1 + 0.2×0.5 = 0.9). If the same pattern persists over the six years of her school career, this will add up to 6×0.9 = 5.4 expected years of schooling. If, on the other hand, 80% of pupils are in half-year schools and 20% in year-round schools, the expected years of schooling will be 6×(0.8×0.5 + 0.2×1) = 6×0.6 = 3.6 years. Column (iii) performs this kind of calculation for every single province, using actual data on type of school, accounting also for the fact that some schools were half-day schools (weighted at 0.7 – see discussion in Chapter 6 and Table 6.3) and some were even half-year half-day schools and therefore offered only a third (0.7×0.5 = 0.35) of the classroom time supplied by the year-round all-day schools. The results in column (iii) are telling: the high achievers in enrolment come last in expected years of schooling. The Tyrolean situation has been discussed above.[25] The reason behind the low reading for Upper Austria is the high proportion of half-day schools (see Table 2.2). The leading province was Salzburg where practically any child that enrolled in 1865 could expect six full years of morning and afternoon school.

Finally, column (iv) adds in the unenrolled to calculate the expected years of schooling for the average child. This amounts to adding up all the school-type-weighted age-specific enrolment ratios across the 5.0–13.0 age range.[26] This rearranges the ranking once more. Now the best performers are Bohemia and Moravia, provinces, which were not only able to enrol over 90% of school-age children but also to supply them, by and large, with "full-time" schools. In some provinces, the difference between columns (iii) and (iv) is quite large in consequence of the high share of unenrolled children. One can interpret the difference as a measure of inequality in education: in Tyrol and Vorarlberg, almost everyone enrolled and almost everyone got the same roughly four years worth of schooling, which is why columns (iii) and (iv) for the province have similar values. In the Littoral, conversely, 40% of children were enrolled and received close to six years while the remaining 60% had none, leading to an overall 2.62 expected years of schooling for the average child.

The 1865 data thus furnish a reality check for what became of the ambitious goal of Maria Theresa's ministers to give every child in the empire six years of education. After nine decades of effort and four years before the whole system was dismantled, only Bohemia and Moravia can be said to have achieved at least 90% of that vision. The south was not even halfway there and the Alpine provinces, too, were well below target.[27] This was true even for Lower Austria whose average was pulled up by the booming school infra-

[25] Note that, for the sake of consistency with the earlier exposition, the Tyrolean expected years of schooling assume enrolment for seven years.

[26] A similar concept, lifetime months of school attended, is used by Robert Margo for American population before 1940. See Margo. "Race, Educational Attainment and the 1940 census", p. 192.

[27] The values for Galicia, Bukovina and Dalmatia were not sufficiently detailed and reliable to be cited in the table but their results were almost certainly worse than even those of the Austrian Littoral.

structure of Vienna. Outside the capital, which accounted for almost a third of the province's population at the time, the schooling situation resembled more that of Styria and Upper Austria than that of the city. In their reports, the provincial school commissions frequently invoked the mountainous Alpine environment as the insurmountable obstacle to the noble mission of elementary schooling[28] but the commendable record of Salzburg puts the lie to such claims. An area as mountainous as any, this archbishopric came under Habsburg rule after 1815 with much of the groundwork for its schools already in place. It fulfilled the requirements of the Austrian law, as Table 5.1 indicates, without letting the Alps get in the way. Within Tyrol, too, the area with the worst school provision was Trentino, south of the Alps, rather than the mountainous north, which again shows that mountains were more an excuse than a real obstacle.[29]

The geographic pattern of strong enrolment in the Czech provinces, mediocre record in the Alps and a poor showing in the south was very persistent across time. This is clearly visible in Figures 5.2–5.4. Bohemia, Moravia and Silesia started from rather low enrolment ratios in the 1770s but enjoyed two major spurts, one in the decade before the French Wars and another from 1805 to about 1830. By 1835, all three Czech provinces reached a level where more than 90% of all 6.0–12.0 year-olds were enrolled. In the context of the Austrian schooling policy, these crown lands were the success stories and it is a testimony to the overall pace of diffusion of elementary education that they took "only" sixty years to get close to full enrolment. Once the infrastructure was in place, it was sufficiently robust to later be able to respond to new policy alterations. The break in the series in 1869 marks a legal change in the compulsory school age: the 1869 liberal reform extended it from 6.0–12.0 to 6.0–14.0. The record of the Czech provinces shows that local schools were able to absorb the roughly 33% increase in pupils within a decade and a half (even though Silesia, the smallest and poorest of the three, was somewhat slower). The new curriculum, introduced in 1869 and more oriented towards practical subjects, as opposed to religion, was readily taken up as the economy of the Czech provinces successfully progressed, by the late 19th century, into the more human capital-intensive sectors usually associated with the Second Industrial Revolution, such as chemicals, food processing and sophisticated machine-making.[30]

The Alpine provinces in Figure 5.3 offer a more mixed record. There are the high-enrolment provinces like Lower and Upper Austria and Tyrol. But in each of these, as I have argued above, the high enrolment values obscure the presence of some kind of local peculiarity that makes the record actually less

---

[28] Weiss. *Geschichte der österreichischen Volksschule 1792–1848. II. Band*, p. 930.
[29] Weiss. *Geschichte der österreichischen Volksschule 1792–1848. II. Band*, p.930–1.
[30] Good, David. *The Economic Rise of the Habsburg Empire*, p. 129–134.

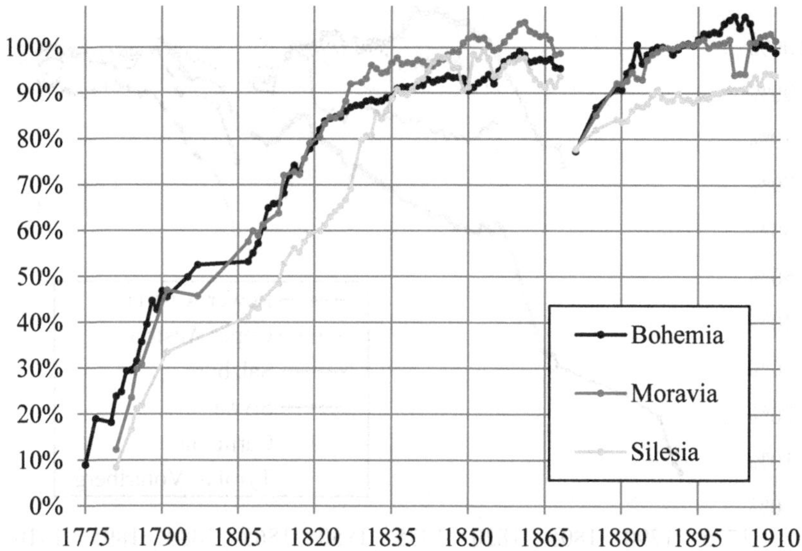

Figure 5.2: Enrolment ratio in the Czech provinces, 1775–1910
Note: The denominator for the enrolment ratio consists of 6.0–12.0 year-olds in 1775–1868 and of 6.0–14.0 year-olds in 1870–1910. The reason why the enrolment ratio crosses 100% in a few instances is that the student body occasionally included students who were outside the legal age range (repeat students and precocious pupils).
Source: For data on enrolled pupils TSOM, SJOM, OeStA, Weiss. *Geschichte der österreichischen Volksschule 1792–1848. II. Band*; for the denominator (number of school age children) see discussion in Chapter 2.

impressive than meets the eye. The Lower Austrian record in fact suggests a decline in enrolment from 1835 onwards and the likely reason behind the enrolment values above 100% in the 1830s was the high school enrolment among 13-year-olds especially in Vienna. With the growth of secondary schools in the capital, most of the 13-year-olds who wished to continue with their studies enrolled in a *Gymnasium* and later *Realschule* and therefore gradually ceased to appear in the data of elementary school enrollees. As in the case of the Czech provinces, the data for Styria and Lower Austria show a surge in school provision right after the adoption of the 1805 *Politische Verfassung* but here it largely petered out by the early 1820s. It then resumed, at a slower pace, in Styria and Carinthia in the late 1820s. It is unfortunate that comparable data for the pre-1820 years are not available for the other Alpine provinces but that is largely a consequence of the chaos and territorial changes wrought by the Napoleonic Wars. Tyrol and Vorarlberg were ceded to Bavaria for a decade in 1805; Salzburg first became Austrian at the Peace of Pressburg in 1805 but was lost at the disastrous Treaty of Schönbrunn in 1809, which also cost the Habsburgs parts of Carinthia and Upper Austria.

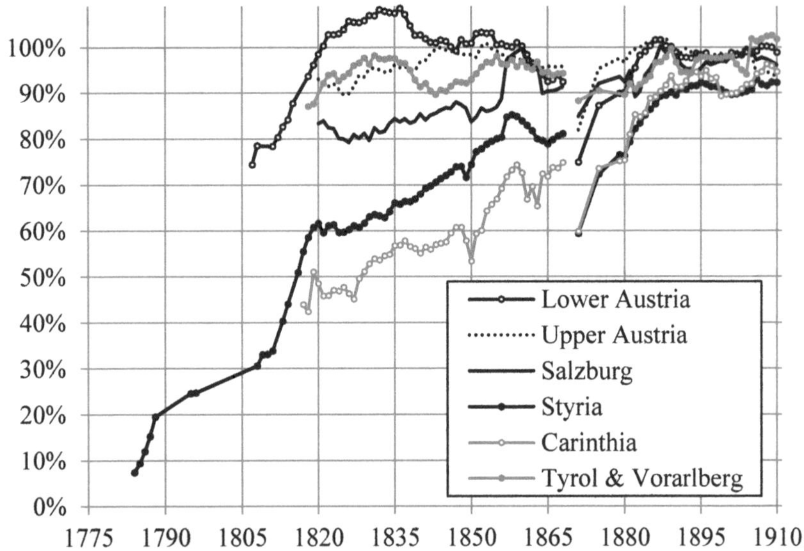

Figure 5.3: Enrolment ratio in the Alpine provinces, 1775–1910
Source: See note under Figure 5.2.

Upon returning to the Habsburg fold after 1815, Carinthia and Salzburg recorded some gradual progress but there was a considerable disparity between the provinces still in the late 1860s. Figure 5.3 shows that the territory that today makes up the Austrian republic (minus Burgenland) did not achieve broad uniformity of schooling provision until about 1890. The extension of school age enacted in 1869 took almost two decades to adjust to in places like Carinthia and Styria.

Enrolment was lowest in the southern and eastern provinces, covered in Figure 5.4. Data for the years before 1818 are generally unavailable, except for a few, not entirely reliable, one-time snapshots (such as the one conveyed in Table 2.3) but seeing the dynamic in the figure, it is clear that late 18th and early 19th century enrolment ratios were low and most likely below 10% across the board. The vast majority of children in these places did not go to school in 1820 and outside the Littoral and Carniola, which made some progress in the 1840s and 1850s, they were still staying out in droves in 1860. Different provinces had different take-off moments even though they were all subject to the same laws and regulations: the Littoral, with its major urban centres such as Trieste, Gorica and Gradisca, took off in late 1830s and early 1840s,[31] Carniola in the 1850s, Galicia in the 1870s, Bukovina in the 1880s

[31] Istria, also part of the Austrian Littoral, did not share in this rise – its situation was much more similar to that of neighboring Dalmatia.

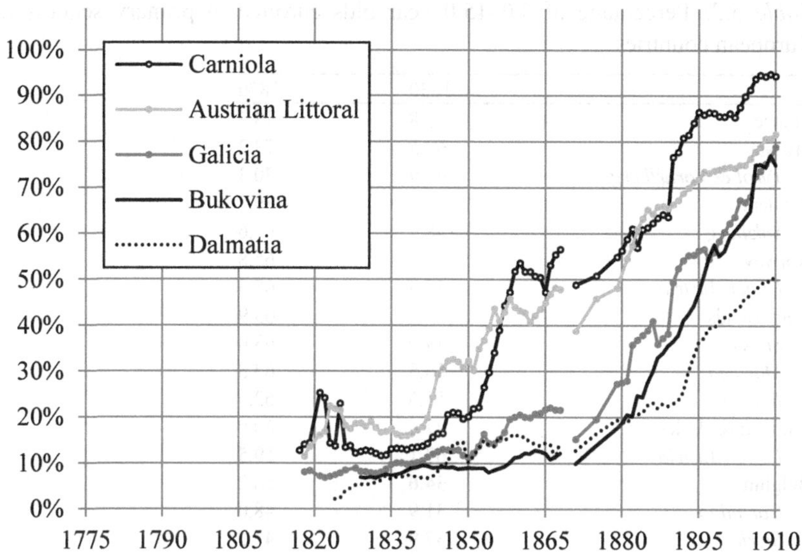

Figure 5.4: Enrolment ratio in the Southern and Eastern provinces, 1775–1910
Source: See note under Figure 5.2.

and Dalmatia in the 1890s. For almost all of these provinces, the golden age of school expansion did not really come until after the 1869 liberal reform.

The inescapable inference from the combined evidence in these three figures is that the regulations and directives pushing for full enrolment were ignored in most places most of the time. The poor record of 1865 was not a one-off – a bad year or a momentary lapse – on the contrary, it was more likely close to the best result that the then-existing Austrian schooling system produced up to that time. Clearly, local conditions were the most important driving force behind the spread of schooling, not the policy fiat of central authorities. The range of experiences within Imperial Austria was so wide that its provinces spanned as broad an interval of values as the rest of the European continent combined. The states and territories in Table 5.2 are ranked in terms of their enrolment as of 1870, which is calculated as a proportion of 5.0–15.0 year olds in elementary schools in order to ensure comparability across countries. By this time, Austria had already passed the 1869 school reform but since the implementation legislation was still being discussed in provincial assemblies, one can view the 1870 results as a product of the pre-reform system. The value for Imperial Austria, as a whole, was 42.6% but its component parts, highlighted in italics, ran the gamut from Tyrol to Bukovina and scarcely any convergence took place between 1830 and 1870. Of course, internal variation is bound to exist within any country but not ne-

Table 5.2: Percentage of 5.0–15.0 year olds enrolled in primary schools in European countries

	1830	1870
France	38.8	73.7
Prussia	69.5	73.2
Tyrol & Vorarlberg	67.9	70.3
Scotland		69.7
Salzburg	48.1	67.6
Norway		65.8
Upper Austria	57.3	65.3
Netherlands		63.9
Silesia	49.0	63.0
Moravia	56.5	62.8
Bohemia	53.6	62.6
England & Wales	27.4	60.9
Lower Austria	67.1	59.5
Belgium	34.6	58.2
Carinthia	31.9	48.0
Styria	37.9	47.2
Imperial Austria	35.5	42.6
Spain		40.1
Carniola	7.8	39.3
Ireland		38.4
Austrian Littoral	10.9	31.4
Kingdom of Hungary		33.4
Italy	2.8	28.6
Greece		25.3
Galicia	5.0	12.3
Dalmatia	3.2	10.3
Russia (1890 figure)		9.9
Bukovina	4.1	7.9

Note: The listed countries and provinces are ranked by enrolment in 1870.
Source: Lindert. *Growing Public*, Table 5.1.; TSOM, SJOM.

cessarily to the same extreme extent: for example, going from Scotland through England to Ireland, Great Britain showed a much more uniform record than Imperial Austria.

Enrolment varied not only by geography and age but also by gender. Figure 2.4 in Chapter 2 showed that a gender gap existed with respect to school coverage, which in the early years of the 19th century reached as high as 9%. A similar pattern appeared with enrolment. Figure 5.5 shows the century's record on this score. Among 6.0–12.0 year-olds, the gap started at 11% in 1820 when fewer than 50% of school-age girls were enrolled. It fell to 7.3% by 1841 but stagnated thereafter and in 1868 still stood at about the same value. Further progress in closing the gap and bringing all girls into schools

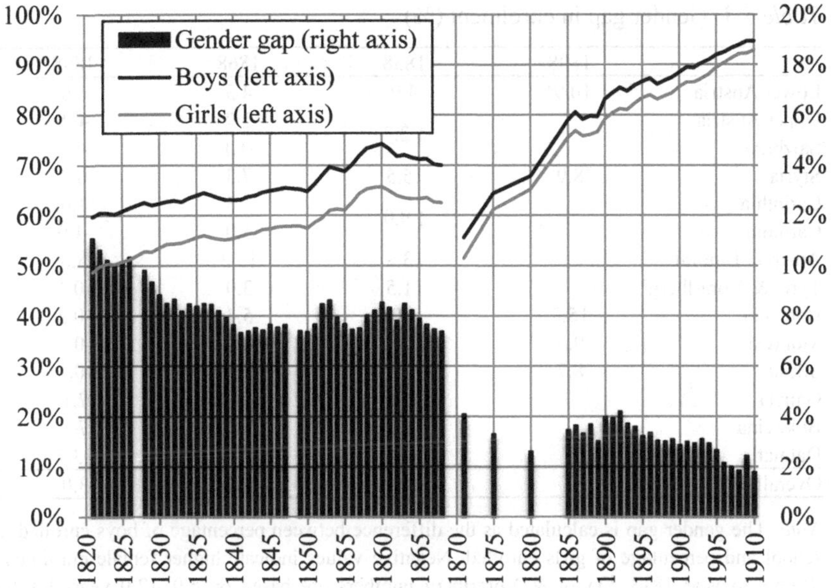

Figure 5.5: Enrolment of boys and girls, 1820–1910
Source: See note under Figure 5.2.

was not made until the 1890s. It declined to 1.7% just before the First World War. A good part of that decline in 1890–1910 occurred thanks to the spread of private schools, which catered strongly to girls. They taught about 4.2% of all enrolled girls in 1910 (compared to 2.2% of boys), so without them the gap would have been about twice as large.

Not surprisingly, the gender gap was very uneven across provinces because its size was a function of the local school system's overall stage of development.[32] In a pattern that reoccurred in province after province, as school network grew, the enrolment first increased through greater uptake of boys and the gender gap increased. Then, as growth continued, the enrolment of boys became close to full while the ongoing increase in the enrolment of girls gradually closed the gap again. In Table 5.3, the clearest example of this pattern is in Styria. With overall enrolment at 30.5% in 1808, the gender gap reached 8.9%. Thirty years later, almost two third of Styrian children were in school: 74% of boys and 58.5% of girls. The gap was at its widest. By the end of the century, it vanished, with 92% of all school-age children of either gender enrolled. In some areas, like Dalmatia and the Littoral, the disparity reached considerable proportions at its peak and given the late take-off in

[32] As Peter Lindert points out, "a sure sign of a country with a backward educational system was a wide gap between male and female enrolments." Lindert. *Growing Public*, p. 94.

Table 5.3: Gender gap in enrolment (%)

	1808	1838	1868	1898
Lower Austria	10.9[a]	4.9	4.3	0.0
Upper Austria		} 2.7	2.7	-0.5
Salzburg			-1.1	-1.6
Styria	8.9	15.5	7.3	0.4
Carinthia		} 9.0	7.5	1.0
Carniola			5.0	-1.0
Austrian Littoral		13.8	13.2	5.6
Tyrol & Vorarlberg[b]		11.5	3.0	-0.4
Bohemia	15.7	7.0	5.4	-0.2
Moravia	9.3	} 7.6	4.7	-0.5
Silesia	8.7		5.7	-0.1
Galicia		} 8.8	11.7	7.1
Bukovina			9.2	7.8
Dalmatia		9.8	19.6	13.7
Overall		8.2	7.4	3.0

Note: The gender gap is calculated as the difference between percentage of boys enrolled in school and percentage of girls enrolled. Negative values indicate higher female enrolment. [a]Refers to year 1813. [b]Tyrol & Vorarlberg numbers are based on 5.0–12.0 year-olds for readings in 1838 and 1868. All other values are based on an enrolment ratio for 6.0–12.0 year-olds.

school development observed in Figure 2.5 it was narrowing only very slowly in the last third of the century.

The format of enrolment reporting in Austria offers a clue as to where the shortfall in girls' enrolment primarily came from. As Chapter 2 explained, teachers were required to keep as comprehensive a list as possible of all school-age children in their school precinct but since the school network was not always sufficiently dense to cover the whole population, the number of school-bound (or covered) children usually fell short of the total size of the school-age cohort. A child could therefore be unenrolled due to one of two underlying causes: either she did not appear on any teacher's list of school-bound children and was therefore not even assigned to any particular school (lack of coverage), or she was listed and thus required to enrol but for various reasons did not (lack of enforcement).[33] Parents were frequently cast as the

[33] Strictly speaking, the teachers lists did occasionally include children who were not currently covered by the school network. For example, when a school was too small to cater to all the villages in a parish, only some of those villages were considered covered (*eingeschult*). A local teacher compiling a comprehensive list of all children required to go to school (*schulfähige Kinder*) in the parish would then also include those from villages currently not covered (*nicht eingeschult*). The *Detail-Conscription* of 1865, the only source with appropriately detailed data on this, indicates that only about 2.4% of all *schulfähige* children lived in *nicht eingeschult* places. Thus, the vast majority of those who made the teachers' lists were also living in places unambiguously tied to a particular school. There was, however, certain

main culprits behind widespread truancy, not only by the educational authorities but also by researchers, both past and present, the usual reproach being that they did not have proper appreciation for the wholesome worth that education brought.[34] Yet, they cannot be blamed for the shortfall resulting from a lack of coverage: obviously, no school implies no enrolment. Once a village was integrated into the school network (*eingeschult*), assigning the blame became more complicated. The teachers usually had a financial incentive to enrol as many pupils as possible because the tuition revenue represented a non-negligible proportion of their income. At the same time, they were constrained by the physical resources at their disposal, which were sometimes quite limited, as Chapter 3 showed. It would have been counterproductive to try to persuade parents to enrol their children in a school that did not have the capacity to seat them. Parents, for their part, had their own, primarily economic, reasons for shirking their duties. Enrolment meant to them both a direct cost of tuition fee and sometimes of textbook purchases as well as the indirect cost of forgone child wages or child labour. It is therefore conceivable that the less than perfect enforcement of compulsory schooling rested on a tacit agreement between the parents, who were less than fully cooperative, and the local school notables – the teacher, the priest and the school overseer – who looked the other way.

Table 5.4 shows whether the backsliding of either kind had a gender slant. It takes all the unenrolled children as a percentage of the whole school-age cohort and splits them into two groups: the portion that stayed out of school due to lack of coverage and the rest, who were covered and therefore school-bound but remained unenrolled due to weak enforcement. In 1825, about 40% boys and 50% girls were not enrolled in Imperial Austria. Of these, comparable numbers of boys and girls, about 28–29%, were staying away from school out of weak enforcement. The bigger gender imbalance was in coverage, where twice as many girls were missing from the rosters as boys. By 1865, the situation improved along both dimensions but unequally: while the gender difference in coverage narrowed, the gap in enforcement grew. Overall, lack of enforcement was the main cause for less than full enrolment, as about two thirds of all unschooled children were actually covered. As for the gender gap in enrolment, however, a disparity in school coverage was still the more important cause, as it had been in 1825: 5.7% fewer girls were covered, or about two thirds of the 7.9% boy-girl difference in enrolment. Here, the responsibility falls primarily on the teachers (and their superiors) who compiled the lists

amount of variation across provinces in this respect: from 0.4% in Silesia to 16% in Austrian Littoral.

[34] Lenderová et al. *Z dějin české každodennosti*, p. 199; Hölzl. "Studien zum Pflichtschulwesen in Tirol 1774–1806", p. 132–138; Weiss. *Geschichte der österreichischen Volksschule 1792–1848. II. Band*, p. 779–780, 941; Kuzmin. *Vývoj školství a vzdělání v Československu*, p. 55, 57.

Table 5.4: Causes of enrolment shortfall in selected provinces

		1825		1865	
		Lack of coverage	Lack of enforcement	Lack of coverage	Lack of enforcement
Overall	Boys	11.6	28.3	7.4	21.4
	Girls	21.1	28.9	12.6	24.1
Styria	Boys	9.1	22.8	9.3	7.8
	Girls	22.2	26.5	14.2	10.8
Austrian Littoral	Boys	7.9	66.1	5.5	42.3
	Girls	10.7	79.5	5.6	57.1
Dalmatia[a]	Boys	87.8	4.6	44.7	32.0
	Girls	94.4	4.4	48.2	46.9

Note: "Lack of coverage" denotes the percentage of school-age children who were not enrolled in school because they were not covered, i.e. not living within the precinct of any school. "Lack of enforcement" denotes the percentage of school age children who were school-bound but nonetheless unenrolled. School age is defined as 6.0–12.0 years of age, except in Tyrol, which applied a 7-year compulsory school attendance. [a]The first set of Dalmatian data refer to year 1827, not 1825.

from parish birth and baptismal records and from personal visits with individual families.

The situation varied from province to province and Table 5.4 offers three distinct examples of how it could play out. Styria is an example of a province where school coverage did not improve much over time, especially for boys. Enforcement, however, gradually grew tighter for both boys and girls at about equal rate. The Austrian Littoral is almost Styria's perfect opposite. The reported school-bound numbers accounted for 90% of all school-age children already in 1825 and comparable numbers of boys and girls were covered (although somewhat more girls were left out). The large disparity in enrolment of boys and girls was due to very different degree of enforcement, which was significantly weaker in the case of girls. By 1865, the overall enrolment was better and, as in Styria, this was largely due to stricter enforcement since coverage had been almost full throughout, but the lack of enforcement still had the same gender gradient as it did forty years earlier. The Littoral is therefore a case of mostly gender-neutral coverage and highly unequal, if tightening, enforcement. Finally, there is the Dalmatian situation, which was characterized by mostly inadequate school infrastructure for most of the 19th century. Progress was being made – after all, the number of schools operating in Dalmatia went from 12 to 223 over the four decades covered by the table – but the province still remained largely underserved. Its inclusion in Table 5.4 is motivated by what is perhaps the starkest example of an almost wholly toothless enforcement in the Austrian context: even though coverage improved appreciably through the increase in schools, enrolment of girls registered negligible change. The 98.9% of girls not enrolled in 1827 became 95.1% of girls still not enrolled in 1865, except by then almost half of them were actually covered. Not that the boys' record was outstanding, but by 1865 the boys' enrolment ratio was almost five times that of girls (23.3% versus 4.9%). In terms of coverage, or lack thereof, both genders faced comparable situations: 55.3% of boys and 51.8% of girls had access to a school. The large shortfall in girls' enrolment was down, almost entirely, to a lack of enforcement, which, in the case of girls, was practically total. It would be, perhaps, unfair to lay the blame here on the, roughly, 260 teachers who were active in Dalmatia at that time and who doubtless knew that the law prescribed compulsory schooling to both girls and boys equally. The near universal absence of girls from school indicates a broader, society-wide attitude, which the parents inevitably shared and which affected their decisions regarding their daughters' schooling.

Most modern-day analysis of the reach and extent of historical schooling across the world is based on enrolment numbers, as Table 5.2 illustrates. Enrolment ratio is certainly a useful indicator, as far as it goes, but, as a measure of actual exposure to instruction, it has its shortcomings. The statistical record may show a particular village as fully covered and all local children as enrolled but that will still say little about whether the children were actually attending on any given day. Historical attendance rates are much harder to reconstruct than enrolment ratios because the surviving records are sparser and more difficult to process, as will become clear.

In Austria, attendance was, of course, compulsory by law and from the 1780s onwards, the authorities invested non-negligible effort and resources into coming up with ways to enforce it as fully as possible. In 1782, priests were obliged to exhort their parishioners from the pulpit to send their children to school and to read to them verbatim the 1781 decree specifying the penalties for truancy. In 1788, teachers were made to report parents of truants to the authorities on a weekly basis.[35] In 1805, this system was formalized in the *Politische Verfassung*, which also reiterated when and how fines should be administered (Articles 177–178). Inspection reports drawn up by district school supervisors frequently commented on the state of attendance and sometimes offered remedies.[36]

Austrian official sources rarely, if ever, made a conceptual distinction between enrolment and attendance. The word *Schulbesuch*, used in all statistical publications, does literally translate as "school attendance" and those articles of the law that dealt with penalties for truancy clearly used it in this meaning. But in a statistical context, it always implied enrolment. Attendance itself – the actual presence of pupils in the classroom – was never systematically reported, except for one relatively crude count of missed-out school days for

---

[35] Adámek. *Paměti*, p. 8.

[36] See Kneidl. *Paměti*, p. 364 for an example.

the school year 1870/71. That does not mean that this information was not collected. Section 15 of the *Politische Verfassung* carried several detailed provisions on this matter, instructing teachers to maintain an attendance log and the total number of days missed by a pupil had to be entered into the examination protocol at the end of each school year. On a school-leaver's certificate, attendance was marked on a grading scale, as if it were a regular school subject: very diligent, diligent and rare (Article 106). District supervisors, who presided over the final exam in every school of their district, had to check and sign off on the complete examination report but the attendance numbers were not passed on to the central school administration. Consequently, most remarks about attendance in the existing literature consist of imprecise guesses without much context.[37]

The attendance logs were documents of ephemeral importance (beyond their function as a source for the examination protocols) and most of them have been long discarded. Those that do survive in the archives carry only partial information on the children. The exam protocols are not very useful on their own either because they do not usually note the total number of school days in a year, so as to allow the calculation of the percentage of days missed. Schools varied in the length of school year and especially in their exam date, given that a district supervisor could not be in more than one place on any given day.[38] A full slate of at least the most basic data on both the pupils, such as their date of birth, address and parental occupation as well as their attendance, and on the schools, specifically the total number of school days over the school year, can only be reconstructed, if several documents for the same school and the same year survive in their completeness. First, the roster of local school-age children (*Verzeichniss der schulfähigen*) carried the children's date of birth, address and father's occupation. Second, the attendance logs usually had their age next to marks of attendance. Third, the teaching log recorded the lessons delivered each day, yielding the total number of school days in a year. Having reviewed the records of 52 schools in four different archives, I have pieced together the necessary data for 17 of them and they are listed in Table 5.5. They comprise what I denote the "Attendance sample" on which all of the following analysis of attendance is based.

The sample contains data for one school year, 1864/65, the choice of which was motivated by the opportunity to supplement as well as to confront these archival data with information conveyed in the *Detail-Conscription* of 1865. In Table 5.5, the confrontation takes place in the two columns containing enrolment numbers (columns (ii) and (iii)), each from a different source.

---

[37] See for example Engelbrecht. *Geschichte Des österreichischen Bildungswesens, Vol. 3*, p. 236; Hölzl. "Studien zum Pflichtschulwesen in Tirol 1774–1806", p. 133.

[38] The start and end dates could even vary year to year for the same school. Kneidl. *Paměti*, p. 339.

Table 5.5: Schools in the "Attendance sample"

School	*Detail-Conscription* Class-rooms	Archival sources Enrolled pupils		Attend-ance (%)	Enrollees per classroom	Attendees per classroom
	(i)	(ii)	(iii)	(iv)	(v)	(vi)
Brázdím	1	84	82	78.2	84.0	64.2
Bystrá nad Jizerou	1	99	101	83.2	99.0	84.0
Čelákovice	3	283	95	57.2	94.3	54.4
Dřevčice	1	117	116	59.6	117.0	69.1
Horní Počernice	2	150	146	86.0	75.0	62.8
Jesenný	1	143	186	63.4	143.0	117.9
Kamenice u Jílového	1	100	104	53.1	100.0	55.2
Koloděje	1	161	177	41.7	161.0	73.8
Kostelec u Křížků	2	251	258	62.0	125.5	80.0
Loukov-Háje nad Jizerou	1	104	168	45.5	104.0	76.4
Mukařov	2	239	196	30.6	119.5	30.0
Panenské Břežany	1	113	113	76.0	113.0	85.8
Říčany	2	309	117	65.8	154.5	77.0
Sluštice	2	353	111	41.5	176.5	46.1
Úbislavice	3	246	133	78.2	82.0	104.0
Vidochov	1	119	116	79.0	119.0	91.7
Zvánovice	1	124	125	65.8	124.0	82.2

Note: "Attendance" is the percentage of school days attended, on average, by the pupils enrolled in the school. "Enrolees per classroom" are calculated from the *Detail-Conscription* data in the first two columns. "Attendees per classroom" are calculated from the archival sources. Note that the archival data for schools in Čelákovice, Říčany, Sluštice and Úbislavice yielded attendance for only one class. The ratio of attendees per classroom adjusts for this fact.
Source: Detail Conscription and archival sources.

For most of the schools, the two numbers are close, deviating by no more than a few percent, which is consistent with ordinary population change.[39] Then there are schools (e.g. Čelákovice, Říčany, Sluštice and Úbislavice) in which the archival search yielded significantly lower enrolment totals than contained in the *Detail-Conscription*. This discrepancy is easily explained by the incompleteness of the surviving archival record: either the requisite information has not survived for some of the classes or particular sheets are missing. Cases where a discrepancy is real and worrisome are those where the *Detail-Conscription* reported considerably lower enrolment than indicated by the archives today (namely Jesenný, Koloděje and Loukov-Háje nad Jizerou). A difference of forty or more pupils cannot be explained by migration, especially since the archival record actually shows that most of the recorded pu-

[39] Note that while the archival data are constructed to reflect the situation at the start of the school year, in the autumn of 1864, the *Detail-Conscription* data were collected in the spring of 1865.

pils were in the classroom at least a few days every month. In the case of Loukov-Háje nad Jizerou, one could partly harmonize the numbers by assuming that the teacher reported only 6.0–12.0 year old enrolees to the *Detail-Conscription* and excluded all pupils under age 6 (of which there were 55 – Loukov is an outlier in this respect) but other schools' data check out without assuming such idiosyncratic behaviour, making this at best an ad-hoc explanation. But some discrepancy is to be expected in such historical datasets and it is reassuring that, for a majority of the schools, the enrolment records corroborate each other or at least are not contradictory.

Nevertheless, the Attendance sample cannot be taken as representative of the whole Austrian experience. It is clearly a convenience sample, subject to all the idiosyncrasies of selective reporting, document preservation and archival availability. All the sampled schools come from only four school districts within a single province, Bohemia, and pertain to only one school year. They were all country schools and all operated year-round, offering full-day schooling. On these grounds, it is perhaps defensible to argue that these 17 schools are typical for the Bohemian countryside, where most schools were of this kind, but one needs to be careful in generalizing to the whole of Imperial Austria, especially the least developed provinces where the reality of village education was likely bleaker than in Bohemia. In short, the evidentiary value of this small dataset is that it contains such a range of variables as to allow a new and somewhat more data-based look at those broad patterns that had been previously asserted by others, on the basis of even more impressionistic evidence: patterns, such as that girls had generally lower attendance than boys, that the highest attendance could be expected in the middle of the school age range (8–10 years), that throughout the year, attendance responded to the rhythm of agricultural labours as well as to weather, and that there was a strong social gradient in attendance.

Starting from the most aggregate statistics, consider the attendance rates cited in Table 5.5, column (iv). They convey the percentage of all school days attended by the average pupil. The numbers span a broad range, from a mere 30.6% in Mukařov to an impressive 86% in Horní Počernice, with an enrolee-weighted average of 61% across the whole sample. Bohemia had fairly strong, consistent and almost full enforcement of enrolment by 1865 but, on the attendance front, the shortfall was still appreciable. The gaps in attendance affected the use of the physical school space. In reviewing the relation between classrooms and enrolees, I speculated in Chapter 3, that some schools were so short of space and so far beyond the prescribed pupils-per-classroom regulation that they must have *relied* on less than full attendance. Shedding light on this, the last two columns of Table 5.5 calculate the pupil-per classroom ratios first using the enrolment totals from the *Detail-Conscription*, as in Chapter 3, and then again using attendance data. It turns out that almost all the sampled schools overstepped the decreed threshold of a

Table 5.6: Descriptive statistics of the "Attendance sample"

	Mean	Std. Dev.
Age of pupil	8.69	1.90
% girls	50.9	50.0
Number of school days	196.9	13.1
Attendance (% days present)	60.9	27.7
School size (# pupils)	137.9	45.4
Distance to school (km)	1.164	1.299
Tuition fee	1.98	0.29
Village population	533.2	376.5
Number of schools	17	
Number of villages covered	77	

Note: The Attendance sample contains 2344 observations of individual pupils although not all carry the full record of all the variables.
Source: Attendance sample.

maximum of 80 children per classroom (per Article 345 of the *Politische Verfassung)*, if one uses the number of enrolees (col. (v)). A majority even crossed the limit of 100 pupils per classroom, which should have triggered a physical expansion of the schools (Article 346). But, the schools fell mostly within the regulation if one estimates the average number of pupils in attendance per classroom using the information on attendance (col. (vi)). The village elders in Zvánovice, for instance, may have reasonably concluded that no costly classroom expansion was necessary, even with 124 pupils on the roster of their single-classroom school, since on any random day there would not be more than 80 pupils around, given the 65.8% attendance.

The Attendance sample contains information on 2344 pupils. The descriptive statistics are presented in Table 5.6. Each pupil's age is calculated as of 1st October 1864 and the distance is calculated using historical maps.[40] The sample is clearly drawn from the countryside – the largest among all the sampled villages was Říčany with 1571 inhabitants in 1869.[41] Except for its exclusively rural provenance, the sample does not seem to be "demographically slanted" in any other particular direction: half of the children are girls and the average age is close to the middle of the school age range but slightly below it as one would expect, in the context of an ongoing population growth. Eighty percent of the pupils commenced the school year sometime between 11th September and 3rd October 1864. The exam dates were more

[40] About three quarters of the records include precise date of birth, as for the rest that has only the year of birth, a middle of the year birth date was assigned (1st July). This introduces a certain amount of measurement error into the estimation but excluding these imprecise records from the sample does not material change the results. As for the distance calculation, see the discussion in Chapter 2 in relation to the dataset from the diocese of České Budějovice.

[41] K. k. Böhmische Statthalterei. *Orts-Repertorum des Königreiches Böhmen.*

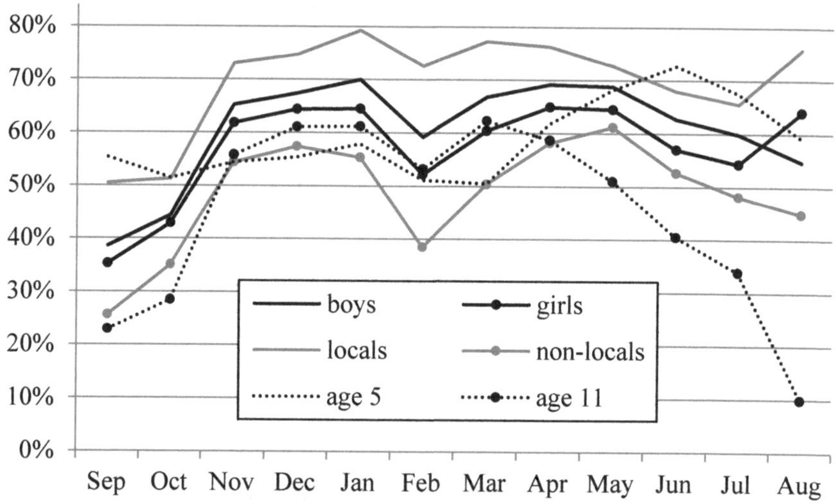

Figure 5.6: Attendance profile by month and type of pupil
Note: "Locals" are pupils who live in the village where the school is located.
Source: Attendance sample

spread out: the earliest fell on 17th May, the latest 31st August but, generally, early starters also had earlier exam dates. The total number of sampled school days ranged from 166 to 222, with some minor variation also coming from school-level differences in the length of religious holidays.

Figure 5.6 shows how attendance varied through the year. Even though October was a school month for most of the pupils, the school year was clearly off to a slow start. The first month when the school can be said to have truly been fully in session, with attendance above the annual average, was November. The children then kept attending somewhat consistently until about May, except for the dip in February caused by heavy snow.[42] The uptick in attendance in August, in some series, is a product of a paucity of data in that month.

The figure reports monthly attendance for several different demographic groups so as to highlight some of the regularities observed in the data. The most obvious one is that the attendance was significantly lower among non-locals and that these non-local children were especially sensitive to the vagaries of weather. Whereas the locals' attendance dropped a mere 6.7 percentage points between January and February, the non-locals' attendance went from 55.4% to 38.5%. The figure also illustrates that distance to school was a stronger influence on attendance than gender. Girls were consistently less diligent school-goers than boys. There is no obvious difference in seasonal

[42] One of the schools even completely shut down in February on account of snow.

Table 5.7: Mean comparisons by gender and by location

	boys	girls	t-test	p-value
Age	8.70	8.69	0.153	0.879
Complete birth record (%)	76.1	73.4	1.493	0.136
Tuition fee (fl per year)	1.99	1.98	0.430	0.667
Distance to school (km)	1.155	1.173	-0.345	0.730
Attendance (%)	63.5	58.4	4.430	0.000
Village population	540.3	526.4	0.890	0.373
	locals	non-locals	t-test	p-value
Age	8.62	8.77	-1.715	0.086
Complete birth record (%)	80.9	68.7	6.862	0.000
Tuition fee (fl per year)	2.10	1.87	20.970	0.000
Attendance (%)	71.2	50.6	19.300	0.000
Village population	781.1	287.7	41.979	0.000

Note: "Complete birth record" lists the percentage of pupils for which the school roster recorded the full day, month and year of birth, as opposed to a partial record (only year of birth or age in years) or the data missing altogether.
Source: "Attendance sample". Tuition fee was taken from *Detail-Conscription*. Village population is taken from K.k. Böhmische Statthalterei, 1872. Distance to school is based on the historical maps on www.mapy.cz.

patterns between boys and girls – the gender gap does get slightly bigger in January-March but only by about three percentage points. Not surprisingly, five-year olds[43] had a lower than average attendance, especially in the autumn months (except in September which is caused by a few outliers), but they started showing up in greater numbers in the Spring. Some reached their sixth birthday over the winter and so their higher attendance reflects the fact that they started school in earnest with the arrival of the Spring semester. The opposite applied to 11-year olds. Once they started turning 12 during the year, they also gradually stopped coming to school, which is why their attendance rate took such a dive from March onwards. But even before that, very few of them attended during the harvest months (September and October) and their overall record was below average.

Table 5.7 corroborates the basic observation from Figure 5.6 – namely that gender made less of a difference in attendance than distance – and adds a few more dimensions to the issue. Most of the variables do not exhibit any marked difference between boys and girls. The overall gender gap in attendance was 5.1 percentage points, the only statistically significant difference among the gender-based comparisons. Boys were slightly more likely to have a complete birth record. It would be a tangible indicator of a lower social status of girls, if the parents and parish clerks could be shown to have paid

[43] Note that this category refers to children aged 5.0–6.0 on 1st October 1864.

less attention to the girls' precise birth date but the difference is not statistically significant at any reasonable level.

Such a gap in birth recording is, however, strongly in evidence for locals versus non-locals. The non-locals came, on average, from smaller villages, some of which did not have their own church. This could have affected how conscientiously the baptismal records were kept. But, it is also plausible that the blame for incompleteness falls on the teachers: the difference between locals and non-locals could arise if, for example, the teacher neglected to trek to those neighbouring villages to compile his rosters from official baptismal books and instead decided to supplement the information by enquiring with the pupils themselves. It is also possible that non-local pupils were children of non-local parents who themselves had lower school attendance (and enrolment) in their childhood and were therefore less likely to be literate and numerate, relative to local parents. The shortfall in non-locals' attendance was quite large – over 20 percentage points. The fact that non-locals paid somewhat less in tuition fees is more a statistical artifact of how villages were assigned to schools: larger villages which were able to fill their schools from local children and therefore did not have any non-locals also happened to be the more expensive schools. In contrast, schools with a larger catchment area sought to keep the tuition fee lower so as not to compound the discouraging effect of distance.

The numerous factors that affected attendance can be split, for analytical purposes, into four categories: the environmental (such as distance to school), school-related (such as tuition fee and size of the school), family-related (the parents' occupation or social status) and individual (gender, age). I assess their relative importance in the context of a simple OLS regression with fixed effects. The unit of observation is the individual child whose overall proportion of days attended in the 1864/65 school year is the dependent variable. While the attendance rate is by definition constrained to fall between 0 and 1, there were very few pupils with these extreme values, so the impact of truncation on the estimation results is likely negligible.

A short explanatory note is in order regarding the pupils' fathers' occupations. Most of the occupations are agricultural but they span the whole social spectrum of a 19th century village. About 6.4% of the pupils came from families of large farm owners (*statkář* or *Grundbesitzer*), who stood close to the top of the village social hierarchy, followed by 10.6% with peasant fathers (*rolník*, *Bauer*), 31.4% were children of cottagers (*chalupník*, *Häusler*) and 16.1% of agricultural labourers (*nádeník*, *Taglohner*).[44] These four employ-

[44] The main index of stratification across these four groups consists in how much land they had. There is inevitably going to be some overlap between them but one may perhaps say, without much oversimplification, that a farm owner differed from a peasant in that the former produced primarily for the market while the latter primarily for their own consump-

ment categories cover almost two thirds of the sample. In addition, 16.1% reported a father with a craft, from shoemaker through carpenter to blacksmith, while 4.7% were fatherless – the record either showed the mother's occupation or described the pupil as orphan. For about 10.2% of pupils, no parental occupation was recorded. This could mean that the pupils came from the village poor, who had no particular occupation to report, but it could also be just an innocuous omission. Not quite 2% each remained for traders and for white-collar workers. The latter category included teachers and members of the local public administration. There were a few cases where a parent held two jobs, which is why these categories are not entirely mutually exclusive. When a mother's occupation was reported, I coded that child as being fatherless but I also placed the mother into one of the occupational categories, based on her reported job (e.g. a seamstress is coded as a craftswoman).

Table 5.8 shows the regression results. The model in column (i) includes only school-level characteristics, together with school district, or vicariate, fixed effects. The results indicate that attendance was higher the better staffed a school was, with 4.8% more days attended by an average child in a school with three teachers compared to a school with only one. It also helped if a school was close: every kilometre of distance lowered attendance by 6.6%, or about thirteen days. The positive coefficient on the tuition fee is not as surprising as may seem at first. Parents were obligated to pay it once a child was enrolled but failure to send a child to school could result in a penalty equal to double the tuition fee. The coefficient thus measures the strength of this deterrent and it was not all that strong. An extra gulden of annual tuition (implying a 2 fl penalty in case of complete absence) would increase attendance by 6%. It is a robust, statistically significant coefficient but it is rather small. The most counterintuitive are the coefficients on the number of grades. Three-grade schools apparently had lower attendance than two-grade and even than one-grade schools. These effects are large and significant. The result does not imply that the third grade specifically was poorly attended but that schools, which had a curriculum extending into the third grade had lower attendance, *ceteris paribus*. The reason why this result is counterintuitive is because the third grade was where the curriculum finally moved beyond the rote learning of religion and basic letters and into some more useful subjects, including more advanced arithmetic (see next chapter). In towns, certainly, extending the curriculum was generally the aim throughout the 1850s and 1860s.[45] Apparently, in the countryside, if the data are to be believed, the attraction of that third grade was not enough to boost attendance and instead

tion. Cottagers, then, were akin to subsistence farmers or farmers who work their own land but also occasionally hire themselves out to large farm owners. Agricultural labourers, of course, owned no land and worked for someone else.

[45] Frank. *Die Österreichische Volksschule von 1848–1898*, p. 15–22.

Table 5.8: Determinants of attendance – Regression results

	(i)	(ii)	(iii)	(iv)
School quality fixed effects				
Two-grade school	-0.054*	-0.002		
	[0.014]	[0.016]		
Three-grade school	-0.202*	-0.160*		
	[0.005]	[0.005]		
Two teachers	0.018	-0.008		
	[0.009]	[0.009]		
Three teachers	0.048*	0.076*		
	[0.014]	[0.017]		
Tuition fee (fl per year)	0.060*	0.101*		
	[0.016]	[0.019]		
1(Girl)		-0.050*	-0.050*	-0.041*
		[0.003]	[0.003]	[0.013]
Age		0.230*	0.250*	0.252*
		[0.007]	[0.007]	[0.029]
Age^2		-0.014*	-0.015*	-0.014*
		[0.001]	[0.001]	[0.002]
Distance to school (km)	-0.066*	-0.065*	-0.060*	
	[0.001]	[0.002]	[0.002]	
Village population (in thousands)		-0.027*	0.011	
		[0.007]	[0.007]	
Father's occupation fixed effects				
White collar		0.086*	0.112*	
		[0.015]	[0.015]	
Farm owner		0.078*	0.093*	
		[0.012]	[0.011]	
Peasant		0.061*	0.089*	
		[0.011]	[0.011]	
Craftsman		-0.010	0.015	
		[0.011]	[0.011]	
Trader		-0.025	-0.009	
		[0.015]	[0.015]	
Cottager		-0.028*	-0.012	
		[0.011]	[0.01]	
Agricultural labourer		-0.069*	-0.052*	
		[0.011]	[0.011]	
No father		-0.075*	-0.058*	
		[0.011]	[0.011]	
Unknown		-0.109*	-0.037*	
		[0.012]	[0.013]	
Constant	0.492*	-0.463*	-0.256*	-0.358*
	[0.035]	[0.051]	[0.032]	[0.120]
Fixed effects	Vicariate	Vicariate	School	Family
N	2296	2087	2087	958
Adjusted R^2	0.369	0.429	0.456	0.643

Note: Standard errors are in brackets. Asterisk (*) denotes significance at 5%. The dependent variable is the share of school days attended over the school year 1864/65.

correlated with lower levels. In a small sample such as this one, it is entirely possible that the negative coefficient is due to some specifically local, entirely idiosyncratic factor, yet the large negative coefficient persists even in column (ii) where all the individual-level explanatory variables are also included. In the context of this small sample, this negative effect of the third grade cannot be quite satisfactorily accounted for or explained away.

The coefficients in column (ii) confirm some of the observations made so far. Girls did have a systematically lower attendance than boys by about 5%, other things controlled for. Age enters in a quadratic form and the coefficients imply that the peak attendance came between the ages of 8 and 9. This is consistent across all three specifications in Table 5.8. The gradient is not too steep: the imputed difference between attendance at age 6 and at age 8 is 6.8%, although from 8 to 12, it declines by 20%. To tie this result up with earlier discussion, all the analysis regarding age shows the same pattern, whether it is for enrolment or attendance: the most auspicious years for schooling were when the child was between 8 and 10 years of age.[46] Figure 5.1 showed that enrolment reached its peak among 7.0–8.0 year olds, after which it plateaued, and started falling after age 10. The age coefficients in column (ii) of Table 5.8 basically lead to the same conclusion regarding attendance. The explanation behind this pattern is not difficult to guess: this was the age range at which the children were old enough to be able to go to school on their own but still young enough to be relatively dispensable in the rural home economy. Next, the impact of village population is practically negligible and changes sign from column to column, so this was not a major factor.[47]

Finally, there is the impact of the social status of a pupil's family, as proxied by the father's occupation. The occupations are listed in descending order by size of coefficient in column (ii) and it is remarkable how closely the ranking correlates with the social hierarchy of a 19th century village. Children of white-collar fathers were the most diligent attendees, followed by farm owners and peasants, whereas orphans and children of agricultural labourers had the most scattered attendance record. The differences are also quite large in absolute terms: there was a 19.5% difference between the white-collar families and families of unknown social status in their average attendance, *ceteris paribus*. To put this in perspective: going from the top to bottom of

[46] Peak enrolment and attendance at ages 8–10 already appears in the first school reports for Styria in 1779. It was a broadly observed pattern. See Pietsch. *Die Theresianische Schulreform in der Steiermark*, p. 45.

[47] One could hypothesize that a large village may have meant a bigger and potentially somewhat more diverse local labour market, which could have acted as an incentive for more diligent school attendance but the analysis does not bear this out.

Table 5.9: Estimated total days of school attendance

	Schooldays attended
Local son of a white collar father	993
Local daughter of a farm owner	912
Local son of a cottager	847
Farm owner's daughter living 1.5 km away from school	806
Peasant's son living 2.4 km from school	796
Orphaned girl living 2 km from school	592

Note: The table uses coefficients from column (ii) of Table 5.8 to estimate the total number of school days attended over the course of six years.

that social hierarchy has comparable negative impact on attendance to moving 3 km farther away from the school. The results are also quite robust: in column (iii), I mostly replicate the specification from column (ii) except that I replace the fixed effects for four vicariates, in which the schools were located, with fixed effects for the 17 schools. This washes out all the school-specific variables but the remaining individual-level variables by and large stay unchanged, including the social gradient of attendance.

In order to better illustrate, in concrete terms, what the coefficients in column (ii) imply, Table 5.9 shows how large a variation in outcomes one could observe even within the limited area covered by the Attendance sample, when some fairly commonplace values are plugged in. Using the linear and quadratic coefficients on age, I calculate the expected total number of school days attended over one's whole six-year school career for the six hypothetical children listed in the table. Not surprisingly, a local boy from a white-collar family is predicted to have attended almost a thousand days of school from age 6 to 12. Moving down the social ladder to a cottager's son erases almost 150 school days off the total – or about three quarters of a school year. The real obstacle to attendance was distance: coming from a well-situated farm-owning family is barely enough to outweigh the negative impact of a 1.5 km trek to school – a mostly manageable distance, shorter than for 80% of non-locals – but the added 5% gender penalty means that a non-local farm-owner's daughter would end up missing more school days than the cottager's son. The hypothetical pupil on the last line of the table was hit with a trifecta of negative influences: a large distance to school (2.4 km is, in fact, the median distance among non-locals in the sample), low social status and a female gender. Compared to the white-collar local boy, the orphaned girl is predicted to have missed cumulatively more than two full years of school, attending, in total, only about three years' worth.

Certain degree of social stratification in access to schooling was explicitly written into the law in various forms, such as the distinction between the cur-

Table 5.10: Annual earnings in selected occupations in Bohemia, 1852

	man	woman	child
Occupations where literacy was likely to be useful			
Printers and bookbinders	260.60	90.00	37.50
Clockmaker	167.15		
Blacksmith	123.95		
Median occupation	*157.65*	*82.50*	
Occupations with ambiguous use for literacy			
Glass hardware factory	167.50	101.85	78.75
Corn miller	136.20		
Milliner	124.30	66.65	
Median occupation	*133.05*	*75.00*	
Occupations unlikely to use literacy			
Cotton spinnery worker	193.40	91.50	63.50
Paper mill worker	135.80	76.25	47.50
Sugar refinery worker	105.00	76.55	57.00
Agricultural laborer	101.12	77.30	
Median occupation	*130.80*	*77.50*	

Note: Annual earnings are reported in fl C.M. but have been decimalized.
Source: Handels- und Gewerbekammer Reichenberg, *Bericht über die materielle Lage der Arbeiter*; Mitch. *The Rise of popular literacy*, p. 213–214.

riculum offered to urban dwellers and to peasants or the effective exclusion of the countryside from secondary education. In terms of attendance, however, the law treated all pupils identically. Yet, even in the context of the one component of the school system that was designed to operate according to uniform rules, strictly enforced against everybody, towards the same educational end for all, there persisted considerable inequality.

The close correlation between a father's socio-economic status and attendance would have been no surprise to contemporaries who understood how such social gradient arose.[48] The usual economic forces were at work. The most obvious and explicit cost of schooling was the tuition fee, which practically operated as a regressive tax. It was not large in absolute terms but it still affected families living close to subsistence and counting every kreuzer they had to spend. Yet, this direct cost of schooling was not the largest. The largest was the opportunity cost of forgone earnings or labour of the child. How large was it?

Table 5.10 lists expected annual earnings for a few selected occupations. They come from an 1852 report by the Reichenberg Chamber of Trade and Commerce on the economic status of workers in North-East Bohemia. While a mid-1860s source on wages would be preferable (so as to align with the

[48] An inspection report cited in Kneidl. *Paměti*, p. 364 notes: "Better-situated parents send their children to school diligently, poorer ones need their children either to house-sit or send them to work."

time frame of the Attendance sample), this report is still useful both because it refers to a geographic area overlapping with that covered by the Attendance sample and also because it provided wage data on a large number of occupations: 113 distinct job titles for men, 36 for women and 21 for children. My table lists a handful of them in two nested rankings. I split the occupations into three groups, depending on the degree to which they made use of literacy. This classification is taken from David Mitch's analysis of job advertisements in England, approximately in the middle of the 19th century.[49] Within each group, the occupations are then ranked in terms of men's annual earnings. I also report the annual earnings for the median occupation in each literacy rank.

The Chamber's report primarily focused on industrial workers and craftsmen but included information about domestics, day labourers and farm workers. Male agricultural labourers could command about 23 kreuzers per day in the summer and 18 in winter, while female ones received 17 kr in the summer and 14 in winter. The authors of the report calculated the expected annual earnings of both on the assumption that they worked 150 days per year at each of the two rates, reaching a total of 101.12 fl for a man and 77.30 fl for a woman, as reported in the table.[50] Unfortunately, the report cited no direct evidence on children's day rates in agriculture but it is reasonable to assume that they would have been somewhat lower than in the industry, as was the case with adult wages. Across the 21 child occupations listed, the annual earnings ranged from 23 fl to 87 fl but over two thirds of all jobs offered between 34 and 60 fl, with an overall median of 52 fl. So, a plausible first guess could put the annual earnings of a child agricultural worker at 45 fl. This would imply a day wage of 10 kr in the summer and 8 kr in winter, if the child worked the same 300 days as adults.

If one considers a hypothetical family of agricultural labourers, with both father and mother working, their overall annual income would add up 178.42 fl. Sending their school-age child to work instead of school all year would bring in another 45 fl, an increase of 25%. Of course, the parents faced a trade-off between these child earnings and potential fines and other repercussions for truancy, so full-time work and 100% school absence may not have been the optimal allocation. In the Attendance sample, children of agricultural labourers recorded an average 55% attendance rate, or 108 out of 197 school days. If those school days were clustered mostly in winter, when the daily wage rate was lower, the child's attendance would entail about $108 \times 8 = 864$ kr = 14.4 fl of forgone income out of the potential 223 fl that the house-

[49] Mitch. *The Rise of Popular Literacy*, p. 213–214.

[50] See Handels- und Gewerbekammer Reichenberg. *Bericht über die materielle Lage der Arbeiter*, p. 76, 88–89. Note that before the 1858 currency reform, there were 60 kreuzers to a gulden.

hold could have if the child never went to school. That would have been about 6.5% of potential annual family income – roughly equal to the family's annual spending on firewood.[51] Clearly, the same loss of child income would hurt less in the family of a farm owner or a self-supporting peasant or some village craftsman (say a miller) who were all richer than mere labourers. On the other hand, the lure of extra earnings would be much stronger in places with factory employment. The data from Table 5.10 show that a similar family working in a cotton spinnery could earn almost 350 fl and each day in school could cost it up to 16 kr of income.[52] A hundred days of school attendance would cost them 7.6% of annual income. In a family working ina glassworks, the same arrangement would mean forgoing 9.4 % of potential income.

However crude, these calculations show that in all the above cases the forgone income was indeed a much higher cost of schooling than the tuition fee of 2 fl per year.[53] Having mentioned the regressive impact of the fee, it is worth noting that given the low variance of child wage in the countryside, the opportunity cost of school attendance was also by and large regressive, with the poorest families hit the hardest. It is therefore somewhat disingenuous to chastise poor 19th century parents, as some authors do, for failing to see the value in education: in the countryside, other things were arguably of greater immediate value.[54] The parents were quite literally right on the money.

The argument about child labour, however, makes no distinction between boys and girls – and, in fact, even the 1852 report quoted a single wage rate for all children, regardless of sex. If boys and girls generated comparable income, why did the girls systematically attend less school than boys? So far, the discussion of this gender gap was mostly framed in terms of the differential treatment of boys and girls by the school administration – whether they were equally covered, whether the enforcement was equally strong and so on. But coming back to Table 5.8, column (iv) turns the focus on the contribution by parents. This last specification makes use of the fact that many pupils in the Attendance sample were siblings: they can be identified not only by a common surname (which in a village could attach even to individuals who

---

[51] Cvrček. "Wages, Prices and Living Standards", Table 1.

[52] The 1852 report put the number of workdays in industry at 240 per year.

[53] A similar observation in the context of Great Britain was made by Horace Mann already in 1851: "It is not for the sake of saving a penny per week, but for the sake of gaining a shilling or eighteen pence per week that a child is transferred from the school to the factory or the fields." Apparently, at 18:1 or even 20:1, the British ratio of forgone earnings to out-of-pocket costs of school was even higher than in the case of Austria. Cited in Mitch. *The Rise of Popular Literacy in Victorian England*, p. 151.

[54] See, for example, Kuzmin. *Vývoj školství a vzdělání v Československu*, p. 57; Lenderová et al. *Z dějin české každodennosti*.

were only distant relatives) but also by same address (house number and village of residence) and father's occupation.

The Attendance sample includes 958 siblings from 449 different families. In column (iv) of Table 5.8, the attendance rate is estimated through a fixed-effects model with a dummy variable for each family, which absorbs all the variation between them. The estimated coefficients on age and gender reflect only factors that operated within families, namely the parents' differential treatment of their children on the basis of these characteristics. The fact that the coefficients are practically identical across columns (ii)–(iv) implies that both the gender gap and the age profile of attendance originated predominantly with the parents. How so? Consider the alternative explanation: one could plausibly imagine a world where parents strive to treat all their children equally and always send them to school together, except that for whatever reason families with only daughters send them on fewer days than those with only sons, while families with a mix of both land somewhere in between. Such a record would still generate a negative coefficient for girls' attendance in columns (ii) and (iii) but it would yield a zero in column (iv). Instead, the gender gap of -0.041 is close in value to the -0.050 reported in columns (ii) and (iii) and strongly significant, indicating that the gap originated deep inside families as a gap between brothers and sisters, not as a gap between families with daughters versus families with sons. Parents, by and large, did not treat all of their children equally when it came to school attendance.

The wage data in Table 5.10 suggest an obvious explanation for the gap: literacy and numeracy brought greater labour market returns to men than to women. Entering an occupation where literacy was likely to be useful promised a man a potential earnings boost of 20% over those jobs, which did not have much use for it. There was obviously considerable overlap between the three groupings but the big boon to a literate worker was that none of the literate jobs were wretchedly paid (e.g. below 120 fl per year) and some paid quite high above average (e.g. printing and typesetting). For women, literacy did not offer much of an upside and it did not necessarily protect from the downside – print shops would have paid her about the same as cotton spinneries. Parents who pondered the costs and benefits of sending their children to school therefore faced strong economic reasons – even in the countryside – for treating their sons and daughters differently: the income they could earn as children was an equally strong incentive for keeping them out of school but the higher future earnings that men could command, if literate, weighed in favour of sending the son to school more often than the daughter.

An attentive reader will have noticed a recurring theme in the discussion of the differences between boys and girls: Table 5.4 reported a gender gap in school coverage disadvantaging girls, but fortunately (one could say) it was small: around 5%. The gender gap in enrolment of covered children also worked against girls, yet it, too, was reassuringly small – on the order of 3%.

The attendance analysis showed once more a negative effect for girls and once again it barely crossed 5%. At any one of these nodes, if studied in isolation, one might conclude that the Austrian schooling was by and large tolerably close to equal treatment. In reality, the cumulative impact of all the slights was probably substantial. Instead of a single large and visible barrier, a school-age girl faced pushback (or neglect) at every turn and from every decision-maker, whether it was her father, teacher or local school supervisor.

Given the non-representativeness of the Attendance sample, the question remains, to what extent the patterns it uncovers are generalizable to the rest of the Austrian Empire. In the absence of a similarly "micro" dataset for other provinces, the analysis needs to make do with the only empire-wide survey where questions of enrolment and attendance were treated jointly – however cursorily and superficially – and that is the 1870–71 school census. This source has several drawbacks. It was the first survey to take place under the new 1869 schooling law, organized in haste and therefore open to underreporting, as the statistical commission readily admitted.[55] The unit of observation was the school district rather than a school, meaning that local detail was lost. In Galicia, the new administrative infrastructure was not even in place, making the Galician data unusable. But there are also a few pluses. One, as mentioned, is that in addition to all the usual questions about enrolment it included four questions about pupil absences (except for private schools), which did not appear in any other survey before or after. Another is that it took place right on the heels of the 1869 population census, which can be linked to it, district to district. The 1870–71 school census had the most reliable information on school-age children of all the surveys conducted at any time from 1774 to 1914 because teachers and school inspectors could cross-check their own tallies against those from the population census. The third advantage is that it took place so soon after the liberal reform that the data substantially describe (however incompletely) the pre-reform school system that is the subject of this book. In most provinces, the implementation legislation was just barely passed or still being debated and most schools still operated under the old rules.

All that the school census had to say about attendance and absenteeism was combined into four simple entries, reporting for each school district the number of enrolled pupils who missed (i) up to two weeks (ii) up to 4 weeks (iii) up to 8 weeks and (iv) more than 8 weeks of school in the 1870–71 academic year. Cross-tabulation either by age or gender was not given. Table 5.11 presents the evidence by province. The first four numerical columns

[55] K. k. Statistische Central-Commission. *Statistik der öffentlichen und Privat-Volksschulen in den im Reichsrathe vertretenen Königreichen und Länder. Nach den von den Bezirks-Schulbehörden für das Schuljahr 1870–1871 vorgelegten Erhebungen bearbeitet*, p. III–IV.

Table 5.11: School absences and under-enrolment in the 1870–71 school year

	% of enrolled pupils who missed				average % schooldays missed	% school-age children not enrolled
	up to 2	2 to 4	4 to 8	over 8		
	weeks of school					
Lower Austria	26.8	17.0	16.6	22.7	18.1	24.0
Upper Austria	30.2	18.5	17.0	17.3	15.1	17.7
Salzburg	25.2	15.5	15.5	13.9	12.5	14.6
Styria	26.0	20.7	21.0	23.4	19.4	40.3
Carinthia	21.7	17.2	18.6	27.3	21.0	40.1
Carniola	21.7	15.1	14.8	17.6	14.4	51.2
Triest	24.8	11.5	8.5	8.8	8.0	40.7
Gorica and Gradisca	23.5	22.5	18.8	24.8	20.0	58.7
Istria	14.4	11.0	10.7	11.7	9.8	71.7
Tyrol	24.6	12.9	8.1	5.3	6.0	11.2
Vorarlberg	41.5	11.4	4.6	2.3	3.9	3.7
Bohemia	17.6	14.6	16.9	34.1	24.5	22.2
Moravia	20.0	15.6	18.0	34.2	24.9	21.5
Silesia	19.7	15.2	16.0	28.8	21.3	22.0
Bukovina	15.7	14.2	16.3	31.3	22.7	90.1
Dalmatia	19.6	11.7	9.6	14.1	11.3	87.3
Overall	21.3	15.6	16.4	27.8	20.8	30.6

Note: "Average % schooldays missed" is a weighted average of the first four columns, taking the mid-point of each absence interval and assuming 40 weeks of school overall. The percentage of school-age children not enrolled is calculated out of the base of all 6.0–14.0 year olds, which was the school age introduced by the 1869 liberal school reform.
Source: K. k. Statistische Central-Commission. *Statistik der öffentlichen und Privat-Volksschulen in den im Reichsrathe vertretenen Königreichen und Länder. Nach den von den Bezirks-Schulbehörden für das Schuljahr 1870–1871 vorgelegten Erhebungen bearbeitet.*

show the percentages of enrolled pupils falling into each of the absence intervals. They do not add up to 100% because some proportion of pupils (about 18.9% in the whole country) had apparently flawless attendance. In about a third of the provinces, the largest percentage falls in the highest category, the chronic truants who missed more than 8 out of the 40 weeks comprising the school year. Using the midpoints of the four intervals, I calculate the percentage of schooldays missed by the average pupil. For the whole of Imperial Austria, this average percentage of schooldays missed was 20.8%, or about 8.3 weeks. Of course, this average only applies to children who were actually enrolled in school. Those, who were not, missed the whole year and their share is recorded in the rightmost column of Table 5.11. Clearly, across the empire, the majority of pupil-schooldays missed were a result of under-enrolment as opposed to truancy and absenteeism but, in places such as Bohemia and Moravia, the two sources were of comparable size. The pattern that emerged from the analysis of the Attendance sample was that parents pa-

Table 5.12: OLS results for school absences and under-enrolment

Variable	% school-age children not enrolled	average % schooldays missed	% chronic truants	% pupil-schooldays missed
Share of jobs requiring literacy	-1.067*	-0.343	-0.551	-1.230*
	[0.245]	[0.182]	[0.296]	[0.239]
Share of jobs not requiring literacy	-0.067	-0.034	-0.086	-0.096
	[0.085]	[0.063]	[0.103]	[0.083]
Share of agricultural employment	0.092*	0.070*	0.119*	0.131*
	[0.046]	[0.034]	[0.055]	[0.045]
Urbanization rate	0.144*	-0.049*	-0.071	0.091*
	[0.033]	[0.025]	[0.040]	[0.032]
N	272	272	272	272
Adjusted R^2	0.842	0.539	0.520	0.811

Note: All regressions include province-level fixed effects. Standard errors are in square brackets. An asterisk (*) indicates statistical significance at 5% level. "% chronic truants" is the share of enrolled pupils who missed more than 8 weeks of school. "Urbanization rate" is the proportion of the district population living in towns of 3000 or more inhabitants. For other variables, see explanation in text.

Source: K. k. Statistische Central-Commission. *Statistik der öffentlichen und Privat-Volksschulen in den im Reichsrathe vertretenen Königreichen und Länder. Nach den von den Bezirks-Schulbehörden für das Schuljahr 1870–1871 vorgelegten Erhebungen bearbeitet.*

id attention to the pros and cons of sending children to school. There was both the immediate opportunity cost of forgoing a child's labour, when sending them to school, and also the long-run benefit of a potentially higher wage. If these considerations applied more broadly across the empire, it should be possible to account for the variation in enrolment and attendance through variation in local labour market conditions – whether locally there were many jobs that required literacy versus those that did not and whether agriculture was a major sector or not.

The 1869 population census split the working population into 50 different occupations, which can be assigned a "literacy score" using Mitch's methodology, as was the case in Table 5.10. This yields for each district a percentage of the local labour force employed in jobs requiring literacy (lawyers, priests, teachers, public officials) as well as a percentage of jobs where literacy was useless (day labourers, certain types of factory workers etc.).[56] The census is also the source for estimating agricultural employment as a percentage of overall employment. I use these percentages, together with the urbanization rate, in a regression where various measures of under-enrolment and absenteeism are the dependent variables. The results are reported in Table 5.12.

[56] Note that Mitch's classification also includes two more categories of jobs where the use of literacy was ambiguous.

In broad contours, the OLS regressions offer results consistent with those yielded by the analysis of the Attendance sample. The consistently negative coefficients on the share of literate jobs imply that the more sophisticated the local labour market, the lower the absences and the higher the enrolment. For 90% of all districts, the share of literate jobs fell somewhere between 1.1% and 11.1%. Moving from the low to the high end of this interval, that is, increasing this share by ten percentage points, cut under-enrolment by 10.7%, i.e. more pupils were signed up for school. For absences, the effect is weaker but not negligible: a reduction in the average percentage of schooldays missed by 3.4%. This means the average pupil would attend for an extra seven days. (Per Table 5.11, the average child missed about 41 days in 1870–71). It also reduced the percentage of chronic truants by 5.5% and cut the share of pupil-schooldays missed – the combined effect of under-enrolment and absenteeism – by 12.3%. So, better prospects of a more sophisticated job went hand in hand with greater involvement with the school, primarily through higher enrolment but also a somewhat higher attendance, too. The share of literacy-free jobs did not seem to have any impact: the coefficients are all tiny and statistically indistinguishable from zero.

High agricultural employment had the opposite effect. In an average district, about 57% of all workers were in agriculture but across the country the share spanned the whole range, from 0.5% in large urban districts to 97% in Dalmatian Imoski. The regression results suggest that higher agricultural employment meant more children staying away from school: an increase by one standard deviation (0.23 or 23%) implies 2.1% more unenrolled children, 1.6% more missed schooldays on average and a 3% increase in missed pupil-schooldays overall. Controlling for the urbanization rate in the regression is a way to ensure that the coefficient on agricultural employment captures the economic ramifications of agriculture, rather than proxying for other correlates such as rural culture or low population density.

To what extent do the conclusions from the Attendance sample and from the 1870–71 school census complement each other, given that one dataset is quite detailed but very local and the other spans the whole empire but offers only a few crude measures? The Attendance sample showed that the gender and age pattern of school attendance had a plausible economic logic to it, consistent with the parents viewing schooling in terms of costs and benefits. The seasonal variation in schooling reflected the rhythm of the agricultural cycle. The 1870–71 survey data indicated that similar mechanisms were at work not just in a few pockets in Bohemia but more generally across the empire. Enrolment and attendance responded to the potential payoff of literacy on the local labour market while agricultural employment kept children out of school. Both sources thus furnish evidence that parents had a rather unsentimental view of the school (paying for a service tends to have that effect). The shortfall in enrolment and attendance also suggests that the school did not have all that much to offer to many people. If the local economy did not reward literacy and numeracy or if the school was not too efficient in teaching those useful skills, then the optimal course of action was to ignore it or to attend only just enough to avoid incurring punishment.

On a more abstract level, the Austrian record lays bare the motivation, the effectiveness and the limitations of making schooling compulsory. As mentioned in Chapter 1, the German cultural sphere, of which Austria was a part, relied on state force in education from the start whereas other West-European countries made schooling compulsory by and large only at later stages, to mop up the last holdouts still staying away from the classroom. By then, however, the bulk of their school-age cohorts were already receiving some kind of elementary instruction, because the school had proved its usefulness to a broad segment of the population. The Austrian school could not make that claim and the compulsory nature of the school system was a not-so-tacit admission that voluntary participation would have been limited. Actual participation – an end result of the tug-of-war between the cost-benefit considerations of parents and the government's uneven enforcement of compulsory attendance – was in fact well below the mandated levels and the range of outcomes observed across Austria was so varied one has to wonder whether the force of law made much of a difference at all. In some provinces, its stipulations remained ignored for almost the whole century that it was in force. Even where the bulk of school-age children were enrolled, they were not always getting the six years of schooling the law envisaged. Moreover, when the force of law did make a difference and successfully coerced reluctant parents into sending children to school, it made life worse especially for the poorest strata of the countryside. The steeply regressive nature of the costs associated with school attendance, of which the direct cost of tuition was the less important part, meant that poor parents had the strongest reasons to try to limit their exposure to the school system.

Chapter 6

The Learning

One of the short poems that Abbot Felbiger included in his textbook for the new elementary schools was titled "Zufriedenheit mit seinem Zustande", or "Contentment with one's station."[1] In a fatherly tone, it discouraged pupils from all futile social striving and instead impressed upon them the duty to conscientiously attend to the tasks associated with their social status. It was a practical expression of the school reformers' main aim to use the school as a tool of social control.[2] Learning to read was merely a vehicle to this end and the Felbigerian method would have had to have been judged a failure, if, against the injunctions presented in the poem and elsewhere in the curriculum, the pupils took their newly acquired mastery of letters as a stepping-stone for something bigger, such as further education geared towards real social advance. Felbiger wrote as much himself: "By instilling this profound truth in pupils [to be content with one's station in life] we hope to stifle any inclination to pursue further studies."[3]

This important aspect of the Theresian school reform deserves more emphasis than it usually gets: even as the *Allgemeine Schulordnung* laid the groundwork for a substantial extension of elementary schooling to practically everybody, other parts of the broader educational reform – those focused on secondary and tertiary education – pursued a very deliberate reduction in both the availability and the sophistication of higher-level education. In order to get the desired network of major and trivial schools up and running, the newly created educational authorities cannibalized pre-existing school infrastructure, including many well established secondary schools that had been around for centuries.[4] Such a move, inevitably, entailed a certain waste of expertise, as instructors in advanced subjects were now reduced to teaching basics. Other institutions were abolished outright so that in Bohemia, for example, only 14 out of 27 *Gymnasia* were left standing after the reorganisation. They were being abolished precisely on the grounds that having many of them could lead to wide-

---

[1] ABC oder Namenbüchlein, p. 40.

[2] Melton. *Absolutism*, p. 204.

[3] Felbiger, Ignaz. *Nachrichten von dem für die K.K. Staaten vorgeschriebenen Katechismus*. Vienna, 1977, p. 26 cited in Melton. *Absolutism*, p. 216.

[4] For example, the Jesuit *Gymnasium* in the Bohemian town Bohosudov (then known as Mariaschein) had existed since 1679 but was converted into a major school in 1779. Many Piarist secondary and lower-secondary schools underwent the same change.

spread education.[5] The court elites, who designed the school reform, continued to focus on stifling popular access to education as their animating impulse. As late as the 1750s, the official opinion still viewed the whole notion of popular education – part and parcel – as a potentially dangerous and, at any rate, a "Lutheran" thing to do. The changing cultural landscape, described in Chapter 1, called for a reconsideration but by 1770s, when the Theresian reform was introduced, the only shift was to move the "choke point" one level up from zero schooling to rudimentary schooling.[6] Even that concession was made on the strict condition of complete control over what the peasants were going to learn.

The *Allgemeine Schulordnung* of 1774 was very specific on the point of content. The curriculum was fully spelled out for each type of school, together with a detailed weekly timetable, summarized in Table 6.1. The law assumed that teaching would take place six days a week, except that rural schools would have either Wednesday or Thursday afternoon off. Starting at 8am, the instruction was scheduled to go on until 4pm everyday, with at least a two-hour break for lunch. Trivial schools had only two grades, one for younger and one for older pupils, although they would have to be all taught concurrently, where only one classroom was available. In the countryside, the majority of the week was allocated to learning to read and write: literacy-related subjects took up 17.5 hours for the younger and 19.5 hours for the older pupils, with more attention, understandably, devoted to basic spelling and letter recognition in the lower grade. Still, rural trivial schools did not teach much in terms of active application of literacy, such as written composition, and even the oldest children were subjected to 4.5 hours of spelling every week, whereas the fourth-graders in major schools could, by then, move on to other things.[7] The hours allocated to religion may seem low in light of the reformers' insistence that this was the most important and difficult subject, but given how much religion intruded into general reading lessons, the allocations underestimate the extent of religious instruction that the pupils were actually exposed to. Numeracy was certainly the least important of the three Rs, with only one hour per day. There was apparently no room in the rural timetable for any *realia*, such as natural science or geography.

The allocation in a major school could take advantage, pedagogically, of the finer division of the curriculum into four grades, instead of just two. The first grade offered a gradual start for the smallest of children, with at most three dai-

---

[5] Kuzmin cites the official formulation that such closures were necessary "so that urban and rural youth, not very capable and lacking in talent, would not be encouraged in education and that their strong and often uncontrollable desire for learning could be suppressed." See Kuzmin. *Vývoj školství a vzdělání v Československu*, p. 59.

[6] Melton. *Absolutism*, p. 89.

[7] The range of subjects taught was even broader in a *Normalschule*, which was each province's prototypical (norm-setting, hence *Normal*) school and which was a cut above a major school.

Table 6.1: Allocation of teaching time to various subjects according to *Allgemeine Schulordnung* of 1774 (hours per week)

	Trivial school		Four-grade major school			
	Younger	Older	First	Second	Third	Fourth
	children		grade			
Arithmetic	6	6	0	0	6	6
Home Economics	0	0	0	0	0	6[c]
Numeracy total	*6*	*6*	*0*	*0*	*6*	*12*
Spelling	9.5[a]	4.5	12	6	0	0
Reading	3	8[a]	0	12	7	0
Writing	5	5	0	6	12	6[b]
Writing to dictation	0	2	0	0	0	0
Written composition	0	0	0	0	0	6
Literacy total	*17.5*	*19.5*	*12*	*24*	*18*	*12*
Religion	1	1	2	2	7	6
Bible reading/history	5	5	0	0	1	1
Religion total	*6*	*6*	*2*	*2*	*9*	*7*
Geography	0	0	0	0	0	1
History	0	0	0	0	0	1
Natural science	0	0	0	0	0	6[c]
Other total	*0*	*0*	*0*	*0*	*0*	*8*
Weekly total	*29.5*	*31.5*	*14*	*26*	*33*	*33*

Note: For better comparability across different types of school, the table reports the number of weekly hours per subject, not the number of lessons (which were of varying duration). [a]The values of 9.5 hours of spelling for younger pupils and 8 hours of reading for older pupils rest on my interpretation of the daily one-hour afternoon joint class of "Spelling and Reading" as implying spelling for the younger pupils and reading for the older ones. If reinterpreted to mean that both age groups did both activities, then the values would be 7 hours of spelling and 5.5 hours of reading in both columns. [b]Pupils intending to continue to a *Gymnasium* could choose Latin instead. [c]Home economics was to be taught in the summer semester, natural science in the autumn semester.
Source: Allgemeine Schulordnung. Anhang Lit. B and Lit. D.

ly hours of school and home by 2pm. Instruction in reading and writing progressed appropriately from spelling in the first grade all the way to written composition in the fourth grade. Able pupils could even opt for Latin in place of their 4th grade writing class, which would prepare them for the entrance exam at the *Gymnasium*. Arithmetic, however, received as meager attention here as it did in the countryside. In fact, it received no attention at all in the first two grades. On the other hand, in the final year for one semester, pupils were exposed to some of the practical side of numeracy in the form of home economics. At least the fourth-graders had the opportunity to learn basic biology, history and geography, the latter two focused on the lands under Habsburg rule.

The teaching method that had won abbot Felbiger not only fame but also the prestigious position of chief architect of the Austrian school reform rested on several main principles. One was group learning, such as when several pupils or even the whole class would read the same text out loud together.[8] Felbiger argued that, in a class of 80 or more, this was the most effective way to keep most pupils focused on the lesson. Another principle was memorization through tabulation.[9] The "output" of learning, in Felbiger's view, was knowledge committed to memory and thereby internalized. The teacher would summarize the content of a lesson, such as a Biblical passage, into a succinct statement and write out the first letter of each word in the statement on the board. The letters would serve as cues for pupils who would repeat the statement until it was memorized and the letters could be erased. To check on the success of each lesson, the teacher was to employ another component of the method, questioning (*Katechisieren*), where he would ask pupils leading questions, to which the lesson statement was the right answer.[10] In structuring the content, Felbiger advised to start from definitions, progress to general rules and conclude with examples of application.[11] Together, the precepts combined into an integrated whole, reinforced each other and also carried implications for the whole school system. Group reading required identical textbooks for all as well as a teacher's consistent adherence to them. The textbooks were published and approved for the whole empire, thereby assuring uniformity of curriculum everywhere. The tabulation method of memorization relied on successful mastery of letters, which in Felbiger's view strengthened the pupils' incentives to learn them. It also required that teachers be trained in using the method appropriately, which called for a unified and standardized system of teacher training. The pedagogical and the institutional thus formed an organic unity.

The contrast between the ample time allocated for literacy and rather meager attention to numeracy was something the timetables for all the types of school had in common.[12] At least reading and writing were instrumental in facilitating religious and moral instruction, but arithmetic had little to offer in that regard. The curriculum contained in *Anleitung zur Rechenkunst*, an arithmetic textbook, covered the common Arabic numerals and the four basic numerical oper-

[8] Felbiger. *Methodenbuch*, p. 12.

[9] Felbiger. *Methodenbuch*, p. 32–59.

[10] Felbiger. *Methodenbuch*, p. 58.

[11] Pacher. "Der elementare Rechenunterricht", p. 62.

[12] The secondary importance of numeracy was a widely held view among the policy-making elites. Emperor Joseph II himself believed that the purpose of schooling was that "all serfs learn to read and write according to their ability and then a bit of counting" – numeracy was an afterthought. See Engelbrecht. *Geschichte Des österreichischen Bildungswesens Vol. 3*, p. 101.

ations, as well as the rule of three. Pupils were also introduced to the practical art of conversion between various currency and measurement units.[13] Major schools progressed one step further to fractions in the fourth grade.

While Felbiger's *Lehrart* was a success with court officials, the same cannot be said of the general public. Parents complained, for example, that "children are taught too much stuff and the teaching method is Lutheran and bad."[14] Outside the Court, enlightened circles in Vienna dubbed the Austrian version of it "a bad copy of a mediocre original."[15] Soon, the method came in for criticism also from the leading pedagogues of the day, even those, such as Joseph Anton Gall, who had started their career helping Felbiger introduce it. In a memorandum written in 1786, Gall had something critical to say about each and every one of Felbiger's principles.[16] The group reading and declamation of memorized statements, while perhaps effective in the hands of an experienced and committed pedagogue, often devolved into rote learning with rather uneven results, when used by the graduates of a three-month teaching course. Slower or lazy pupils could easily hide in the crowd while diligent ones spent most of their mental energy memorizing formal definitions. The tabulation method was more of a source of confusion than a learning aid because the same initial letter could associate different words for different pupils, which then wreaked havoc in the group recitation. Moreover, a sentence memorized, it turned out, was not the same as a sentence understood and absorbed. Felbiger had been aware of this problem and his main remedy was to have the teachers vary the leading questions during *Katechisierung* as much as possible.[17] This, again, was easy enough for a skilled teacher but the more commonplace outcome, in Gall's view, was that the process of questioning did not push pupils towards understanding, because it was structured so as to confine them to merely repeating rather than reformulating the acquired information. Gall further argued that the learning process should not start from defining abstract concepts since a child's mind is better attuned to the concrete and specific. This applied not only to class time but also to textbooks, which in Gall's opinion were too abstract and detached to inspire a child's interest.

Of all these objections, the one that impressed Rottenhan's revision commission the most, as it started its work in 1795, was that there was too much content in the curriculum. Since the commission cared that pupils properly internalize the lessons of religion and morality, it was also receptive to the charges that the memorization approach did not yield quite the results it had promised.

---

[13] Felbiger. *Anleitung zur Rechenkunst*, p. 41–59.

[14] See Pietsch. *Die Theresianische Schulreform in der Steiermark*, p. 143. The "Lutheran" accusation was a reference to the fact that Felbiger found the inspiration for his method in the Berlin *Realschule* of the Protestant pedagogue Hecker in the 1750s.

[15] Engelbrecht. *Geschichte Des österreichischen Bildungswesens Vol. 3*, p. 101.

[16] Weiss. *Geschichte der österreichischen Volksschule 1792–1848. II. Band.* p. 771–773.

[17] Felbiger. *Methodenbuch*, p. 64–67.

Table 6.2: Allocation of teaching time to various subjects according to *Politische Verfassung* of 1805 (hours per week)

	Trivial school		Four-grade major school				
	Younger children	Older	First	Second	Third	Fourth Year 1	Year 2
Arithmetic	4	4	4	5	3	3	3
Geometry/Stereometry	0	0	0	0	0	3	3
Construction basics	0	0	0	0	0	2	1
Home Economics	0	0	0	0	0	0	0
Numeracy total	*4*	*4*	*4*	*5*	*3*	*8*	*7*
Spelling	0	0	1	0	0	0	0
Reading	7	4	6	4	1.5	0	0
Writing	4	2	4	3	3	3	2
Grammar	0	1	2	2	3	1.5	1
Writing to dictation	0	2	0	3	3	1.5	1
Written composition	0	1	0	0	2	3	3
Literacy total	*11*	*10*	*13*	*12*	*12.5*	*9*	*7*
Religion	3	3	3	3	2.5	2	1
Bible reading	2	3	2	2	3	2	2
Religion total	*5*	*6*	*5*	*5*	*5.5*	*4*	*3*
Latin script	0	0	0	0	1	0	0
Natural science	0	0	0	0	0	0	4
History	0	0	0	0	0	0	0
Drawing	0	0	0	0	0	10	10
Geography	0	0	0	0	0	2	2
Other total	*0*	*0*	*0*	*0*	*1*	*12*	*16*
Weekly total	20	20	22	22	22	33	33

Note: Rural school refers to "*Trivialschule auf dem Lande*", teaching all day.
Source: Politische Verfassung.

As Table 6.2 shows, the *Politische Verfassung*, the result of their deliberations, which in 1805 replaced the 1774 law, reduced the total weekly hours in (the mostly rural) trivial schools. Pupils now received one weekly lesson in grammar and one in written composition but the law clarified that the latter should not venture beyond simple letter writing. Major schools retained the applied subjects in the fourth grade, which was now split into two years. Home economics was gone from the curriculum and replaced by subjects both formal, such as geometry, and practical, such as an introduction to the basics of construction (*Baukunst*). Spelling (*Buchstabenkennen*), a separate subject in the 1774 timetable, was now subsumed under general reading instruction, not least because it had been so closely tied to the tabulation method, which was now abandoned.[18] The emphasis on memorization remained, however, except that it was now supposed to be accompanied by "understanding" and "heart", i.e. full internalization.

For the next six decades, the curriculum remained narrow and static. A pupil opening her textbook in 1830 would find the same stories on the same pages as her mother had read in school twenty years earlier and as her daughter would twenty years later. Two thirds of the approved reader-book for trivial schools was devoted to recounting Biblical history, so a reading lesson was mostly just another catechism. Other sections instructed pupils about the duties of simple peasants towards their superiors or included general moral advice.[19] Country and city schools had different textbooks – one of the many points of deliberate distinction between them. It was not until after the upheavals of 1848 that the Viennese authorities gradually came around to updating the materials. A new reader appeared by the mid-1850s, first for major schools and urban schools, with sections on the empire's history and geography and even on children's everyday experiences. By the early 1860s, it was translated from German into the empire's other languages and became available also in the countryside.

Table 6.2 illustrates the stark contrast in content between the two basic types of school, trivial and major, but it does not cover the whole range of eventualities and arrangements that the law provided for. Aware of the often dire and precarious situation of the rural schools, policy makers came prepared with timetables and lesson allocations for schools that might have to resort to half-day teaching (younger children in the morning, older ones in the afternoon) or schools where all pupils, regardless of age and grade, might have to be taught in the same classroom. Such arrangements inevitably implied further watering down of the curriculum and reductions in learning time for pupils.[20] Over the six years of a child's school career, such adjustments could accumulate into substantial differences in classroom hours. Table 6.3 estimates these differences by taking the law's timetables and adding up those classroom hours, assuming 40 weeks of school per year.[21] The numbers imply that even a well-endowed and well-staffed trivial school, which taught pupils all day and each

---

[18] Ficker. *Bericht über österreichisches Unterrichtswesen*, p. 25.

[19] For an example, see e.g. *Lesebuch für die zweyte Klasse der Land-Schulen in den k.k. österreichischen Staaten*, published in 1832, where the retelling of Old Testament stories takes up 150 of the book's 230 pages.

[20] For the teacher, half-day instruction actually meant a higher teaching load because he had to teach three hours in the morning and two in the afternoon, whereas all-day teaching consisted of four hours for everybody – two before lunch and two after.

[21] The *Politische Verfassung* allowed for no more than 5 weeks of school holidays across the year (Art. 88) but once Christmas, Shrovetide, Easter, Pentecost and other religious holy days (and the accompanying school holidays) were added in, the combined effect was to cut another six or seven weeks off the school year. The schools in the Attendance sample in

Table 6.3: Allocated total classroom hours over the course of six years of schooling (based on *Politische Verfassung*, 1805)

	Subjects related to…				Total
	Numeracy	Literacy	Religion	Other	
Normal school or 4-grade major school	1240	2660	1100	1160	6160
3-grade major school	960	3000	1240	80	5280
All-day trivial school (separate classrooms)	960	2480	1360	0	4800
All-day trivial school (single classroom)	960	1480	1080	0	3520
Half-day trivial school	560	1680	1280	0	3520

Note: Assuming 40 weeks per school year. In Normal and 4-grade major schools, pupils attended the first grade for two years. I also assume they attended each grade for two years in the 3-grade school. "(separate classrooms)" refers to all-day rural schools which had separate classrooms for younger classes and older classes and therefore could teach different content to each group. "(single classroom)" refers to schools where both grades were taught concurrently.
Source: Politische Verfassung.

class in a separate classroom, delivered to their pupils 20% fewer school hours overall than a *Normalschule* or a four-grade major school. Single-classroom schools were down to almost a half.[22] Half-day schools in turn taught only about 70% of the hours of all-day schools. Not surprisingly, the lessons they had to forgo, compared to normal and major schools, appear in the "Other" column: those were the geography, natural science and drawing lessons that were restricted to the major-school curriculum. But another big part of the overall difference came at the cost of numeracy-related subjects. It was the first thing to sacrifice, whenever class time was cut. Religious instruction, on the other hand, received its due of teaching hours regardless of the circumstances. The provision of literacy-related teaching also varied across the school types and this, of course, reflected the large variation in the sophistication of writing classes at major schools versus trivial schools.

The lessons in trivial schools were not only fewer in numbers but also tediously repetitive with only two grades' worth of content spread across six years of expected school attendance. It was inevitable that conscientious pupils would hear some lessons again and again, year after year. The younger class in such a school consisted of 6–8 year olds, who attended first grade for two years

Chapter 5 reported an average of 197 school days over the year and they all operated a 5-day school week, which would imply not quite 40 weeks of schooling in a year.

[22] Practically, there was not much differences between a half-day school and a single-classroom school. While the half-day school split its pupils into a morning group and an afternoon group, the all-day single-classroom school had to make basically the same split but within each lesson: the teacher would first read for half an hour with the younger pupils, then half an hour with the older ones etc. At any point, half the class would be idle – the law offered no advice on what they should be doing during such time.

and covered its content twice. The older class were aged 8 to 12, so the second grade was repeated four times. Consequently, quite apart from the benign and useful kind of repetition where exercise classes are scheduled to review newly introduced material, pupils of trivial schools literally revisited the same lessons, from the same textbook, using the same practice problems, year after year. Given the tight content control, inherent in the law, teachers had little leeway to mix it up to keep the pupils' attention. For example, an 1860 reader-book for the second grade of trivial schools contained about 200 items (poems and short articles) split into five roughly equal thematic sections, so that each week one item from each section could be read in class (as the attendant instruction helpfully explained) – the clear implication being that the book should be covered in a year, every year.[23] This did not mean that each school year was exactly identical with the next but the overlap between them was substantial. To give an illustration, the teaching log of the trivial school in Mříčná in Bohemia shows that the same story about the doodlebug was read in class on 26th September 1862, 28th October 1863 and 18th November 1864.[24] This applied to other subjects, too. The parish priest of Mříčná, who taught catechism, started each school year with the attributes of God, spent most of October explaining the notion of repentance so as to prepare the pupils for their first confession on All Souls Day, covered the twelve articles of faith before Christmas, the Ten Commandments by Easter and concluded with a late Spring exposition of the Catholic sacraments. The precise timing of this or that lesson may have varied from year to year but, by and large, the pupils in the older class, if they kept up their attendance, received instruction in their faith four times over.

Thus, not only did the rural trivial school offer less classroom time, it also covered significantly less material even within those subjects that it had in common with the major school. The contrast is visible in Table 6.4, which shows the total *unique* lessons – lessons that broke new ground – delivered to pupils over their six years in school. In other words, I take the values from Table 6.3 and filter out all the repeated years. Here, the quality differences between schools come out most starkly. A four-grade major school had something new to offer its pupils almost every year of their enrolment, hence the fivefold advantage over its rural counterparts. As in Table 6.3, the biggest gap opened up in numeracy-related subjects, where the ratio between highest and lowest value was almost 7:1 and, in those outside the *trivium,* more than 5:1 (adding Religion and Other together). But even in literacy-related subjects, the major schools delivered much more. The third and fourth grades moved from simple mastery of letters into learning more elegant scripts, some finer points

[23] *Druhá čítanka a mluvnice pro katolické školy v císařství rakouském*. Vienna: c. k. školní knihosklad. 1860, p. 333.

[24] Státní okresní archiv Semily, *Fond "Národní škola Mříčná"*, "Denník přednešených učbozástojů", 1861–1872, inv # 18.

Table 6.4: Estimated number of hours of unique lessons over the course of six years of schooling

	Subjects related to…				Total
	Numeracy	Literacy	Religion	Other	
Normal school or 4-grade major school	1080	2140	900	1160	5280
3-grade major school	480	1500	620	40	2640
All-day trivial school (separate classrooms)	320	840	440	0	1600
All-day trivial school (single classroom)	260	420	360	0	1040
Half-day trivial school	160	480	400	0	1040

Note: Assuming pupils attend the first grade in Normal school for two years.
Source: Politische Verfassung.

of grammar, the use of different writing styles and penmanship. The lessons in geography covered the Austrian Empire in the penultimate year and the rest of the world in the final one. The geometry classes were specifically geared towards practical use in crafts. The stereometry classes also included basic mechanics. In shorts, the major school could potentially be useful and practical, whereas the trivial school was mostly repetitive.

These observations support the conclusions regarding attendance, presented in the previous chapter. In Table 5.9, I estimated the total number of school days attended by children in various hypothetical life situations in order to show the steep social gradient in attendance. Children from poorer backgrounds missed more school, I argued, because their labour was needed elsewhere and this may have put them at a disadvantage in terms of access to education. Since the lessons were mostly the same, year after year, the loss of education due to absence was probably quite low. It made good sense to cut down on attendance and do something more useful once a child turned, say, ten because by that time, the average pupil would have been exposed to everything the trivial school had to offer at least twice. One could practically skip half the school year and still not miss anything important – it had all been covered before. If the hypothetical orphan girl of Table 5.9 missed different lessons in different years or if she even concluded (with some justification) that attendance in her final year of school was, in fact, rather superfluous, the difference in educational attainment between her and the son of a white-collar father would still not be all that great. Thus, within the student body of a rural trivial school, variation in total schooling received was much lower than the variation in attendance. At the same time, comparable attendance records in a major and a trivial school corresponded to very different amounts of acquired education.

With the teaching and curriculum structured this way, what outcome could one expect from a school system such as Austria's? How religiously informed, literate and numerate were the children by age 12? This raises the question of the effectiveness of the whole learning process. It is certain that the school system had a good chance of making a big impact because the pre-1774 level of literacy was low. According to one Jesuit report from 1760, in the Carinthian village of Zell only 4 out of 650 inhabitants could read. Census takers, sent out in 1787 to collect population data, discovered that the village elders in most places were not even able to co-sign the worksheets.[25] But these are mostly impressionistic anecdotes, which may not even be all that representative: perhaps the reason why they were noted down was precisely because they were not i.e. because they were unusual even to contemporaries.

By some indications, the effectiveness of the teaching methods was not very high. Sometimes, even the physical circumstances of the school conspired against learning. School buildings that were constructed in the first rush of the 1780s often left no leeway for subsequent population growth and soon became inadequate. Classrooms were too crowded, with up to six pupils per desk, meaning that none of them had enough elbowroom to actually practice writing.[26] Lacking sufficient practice with the hand-written word, pupils often completed their six years being only able to read printed text but not, say, a hand-written note.[27] Once they left the school, their exposure to written and printed word grew even sparser than it had been in school and many forgot even the little that they had learnt. Miroslav Riedl, an historian of schooling in south Moravia, quotes a revealing testimony of one 19th century author:

"Every time my mother, who had very diligently attended school for six years in her youth, was invited to be someone's godmother, she asked me to write down her name for her, so that she could practice it a couple of times and later be ready when asked to sign her name in the parish book."[28]

It is revealing in two respects: first, as a rare first-hand admission that diligent school attendance did not, necessarily, lead to literacy, and secondly, as a commentary on the reliability of one's signature as an indicator of literacy.

One might, at least, still argue that the *lack* of a signature is a sign of illiteracy. Starting from this premise, Riedl investigated south-Moravian land appraisal registers, which required each property owner in each village to mark his agreement with an official appraisal of his land.[29] His sample dates back to 1843 and consists of property-owning peasants, all men, who must have been of school age sometime in the early decades of the 19th century. They all resided in villages of fewer than 500 inhabitants. Of the 3908 individuals that he collected records for, 49.4% did not sign their names. The rate of illiteracy, if it may be so interpreted, varied widely across the 24 villages for which he cites signature rates – in some the signatures were missing for more than 90% of the

---

[25] Melton. *Absolutism*, p. 10. Also, Allen estimates that some 21% of Austrian/Hungarian adults could sign their name in 1800. See Allen. *The British Industrial Revolution*, Table 2.6.

[26] Pietsch. *Die Theresianische Schulreform in der Steiermark (1775 – 1805)*, p. 123.

[27] Riedl. *Zavádění povinné školní docházky*, p. 50.

[28] Riedl. *Zavádění povinné školní docházky*, p. 91.

[29] Riedl. *Zavádění povinné školní docházky*, p. 92.

peasants; in others, all signed their name. Most importantly, they all lived in places that were served by a school already in the late 1780s – in other words, excepting some unusually long-lived individuals among them, these peasants must have been already the second generation to live under the system created by the Theresian school reform.

An analysis like Riedl's offers an interesting peek at the educational status of the common population in a particular place at a specific moment but does not form a good basis for a general conclusion. A more reliable measure of popular literacy would require more systematically collected data, which are not so easy to come by. In the absence of a decent-sized dataset of individual records linking a person's school career with some acceptable gauge of literacy, any quantification of literacy will have to rely on aggregates. Here, the starting point is to say that no systematic data on literacy were collected until the census of 1880 and numeracy was not measured at all. Published data from the 1880 census only cite literacy for the whole population in each province without any distinction of age.[30] Literacy was self-reported with all the attendant issues of possible upward bias, of which the contemporaries were well aware.[31] From 1890 onwards, the census data on literacy began to be tabulated not only by province and gender but also – crudely – by age: the statistical commission split the population into decadal birth cohorts, e.g. all those born in 1870–79, in 1860–69 and so on. Thankfully, these age groups remained unchanged in all subsequent censuses, allowing for some useful comparisons across time.

The literacy that is of interest here is the literacy of generations who went to school before 1869 and if it should bear on the issue of the school's effectiveness in teaching then one would ideally want to know about the youths' literacy right out of school. But that is tricky. Even the last generation to have gone to school under the 1805 law, i.e. those born in 1850–59, were already in their thirties in the 1890 census, the earliest point at which the cohort's literacy can be ascertained. It is tempting to take the reported adult literacy rates at face value as indicators of literacy actually acquired in school, as some authors do. Michail N. Kuzmin, for example, argues that the "efficiency of the public schools in the Czech lands increased from 66.4% literacy in the cohort born

[30] Respondents had the choice of declaring themselves fully literate (capable of both reading and writing), semiliterate (able to read but not to write) or illiterate. This continued to be the practice in all censuses until the First World War.

[31] See Schimmer. "Gedanken über die Durchführung der nächsten Volkszählung in Österreich." p. 170. According to one member of the central statistical commission, the reason why a literacy question had not been included already in the 1869 census was because the Austrian statistical commission could not agree on a workable criterion for determining that a person is literate. As more and more countries (including the Kingdom of Hungary) put the question of literacy on the census, apparently content with relying on self-report, Austria, too, jumped on the bandwagon and introduced the question in 1880. See Ficker. "Ein weiterer Beitrag zur Organisierung der nächsten Volkszählung in Oesterreich." p. 257–258.

1800–1809 [...] to 85.1% in the 1830–39 birth cohorts."[32] The numbers he cites are simply percentages of literate citizens among the surviving members of the respective cohorts in 1890. But of the roughly two million who were born in the Czech provinces in the 19th century's opening decade, 1.1 million of which were still alive by school age, a mere 28000 survived to 1890, so Kuzmin's assessment of the "efficiency of the public schools" rests on less than 3% of this generation's school-goers.[33] Unless one is willing to assume that mortality and migration affected literates and illiterates identically throughout the century, the 28000 octogenarians in 1890 will not be representative of what their cohort looked like when they had just left school.

In fact, tracking a particular age group through time will almost inevitably show the proportion of literates among them to be increasing, even if they are well past their schooling years, a phenomenon one may call education creep. There are several reasons why this happens. One, of course, is later-life learning. There is no reason why a person could not acquire literacy in adulthood, especially if, say, changing labour market conditions offer strong incentives for it. Another is misreporting. In the context of a generally rising educational attainment among the young, older cohorts are more likely to invent qualifications that they do not have than to deny those that they do.[34] So, illiterates are more likely to report themselves literate than vice versa.[35] Yet another potential factor is the difference in mortality. There is some evidence that death visited illiterate households sooner than literate ones, although literacy explains relatively little of overall mortality variation.[36] One could hypothesize that if literates held better-paid jobs throughout their lives and had higher income, they could also enjoy higher consumption of better quality and have easier access to medical services. In such cases, they would be more likely to survive for longer than illiterates. This argument presumes that literacy correlated with higher social status and that there existed a strong social gradient in mortality, which is not a settled question.[37] Yet, for the present purpose, the existence of a causal

---

[32] Kuzmin. *Vývoj školství a vzdělání v Československu*, p. 70.

[33] The rough cohort estimates are based on Kárníková's population totals and Fialová et al.'s birth and death rates. See Kárníková. *Vývoj obyvatelstva v českých zemích* and Fialová et al. "Fertility decline in Czechoslovakia during the last two centuries".

[34] See Steckel, "The Quality of Census Data for Historical Inquiry." p. 591 for an example of how individuals may change their responses to census question about literacy from one census to the next in a linked sample.

[35] This bias continues to appear in modern censuses across all levels of education. See, for example, Black et al. "Measurement of Higher Education in the Census and Current Population Survey".

[36] Smith. "Differential Mortality in the United States before1900." Table 1.

[37] See Bengtsson and van Poppel. "Socioeconomic inequalities in death from past to present: An introduction"; Bengtsson and Dribe "The late emergence of socioeconomic mortality differentials"; Link and Phelan. "Social Conditions as Fundamental Causes of Disease" and Link and Phelan. "McKeown and the Idea That Social Conditions Are Funda-

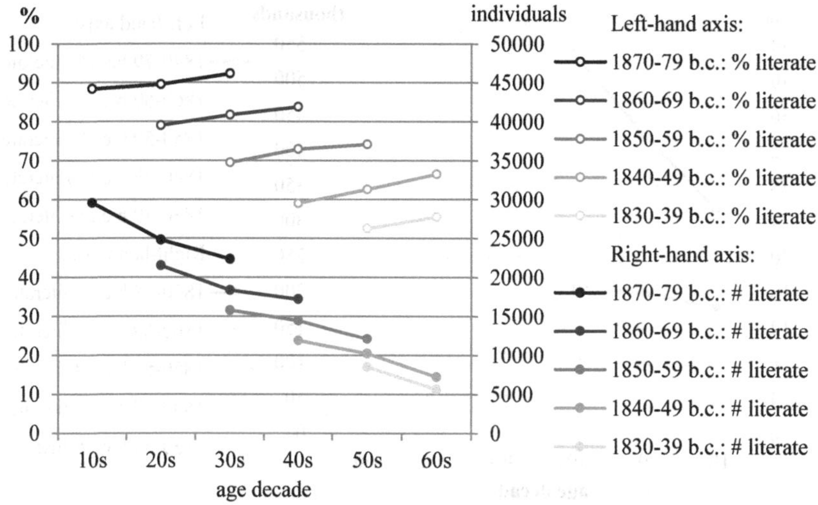

Figure 6.1: Education creep among Carinthian men
Note: "b.c." stands for birth cohort
Source: Österreichische Statistik

link between mortality and illiteracy is not directly relevant – even if the two were only spuriously correlated, it would be enough to produce an education creep in the data.

Consider Figure 6.1, which contains all of the available census-based literacy statistics pertaining to five cohorts of Carinthian men: the absolute number of literate men and the percentage literate. Each cohort appeared in three censuses (1890, 1900, 1910) except for the oldest one, for which the 1910 census did not supply a separate entry. The cohort born in the 1870s were in their teens (11.0–21.0 years old) when the 1890 census inquired about their literacy and found 29569 of them capable of both reading and writing. This amounted to 88.3% of all Carinthian males in that age range. By 1900, the number declined to 24801 but apparently the total number of Carinthian men in the cohort (now in their 20s) declined even more because the literacy rate increased to 89.5%. The same pattern reappeared between 1900 and 1910: the number of literate men in the 1870s generation dropped to 22366 but the percentage literate rose to 92.3%. So, over the two decades, the education creep amounted to four percentage points – not much but still an upward bias. Moreover, the figure shows

mental Causes of Disease." Bengtsson and van Poppel argue strongly that the social gradient in mortality, widely observed today in developed societies, did not emerge until well into the 20th century – countering Link and Phelan's notion of constant or at least persistent social gradient. Bengtsson and van Poppel's argument is that in an environment where death was frequently caused by exposure to virulent infectious diseases, which medicine was then powerless to cure, richer strata could not really "buy" better resistance.

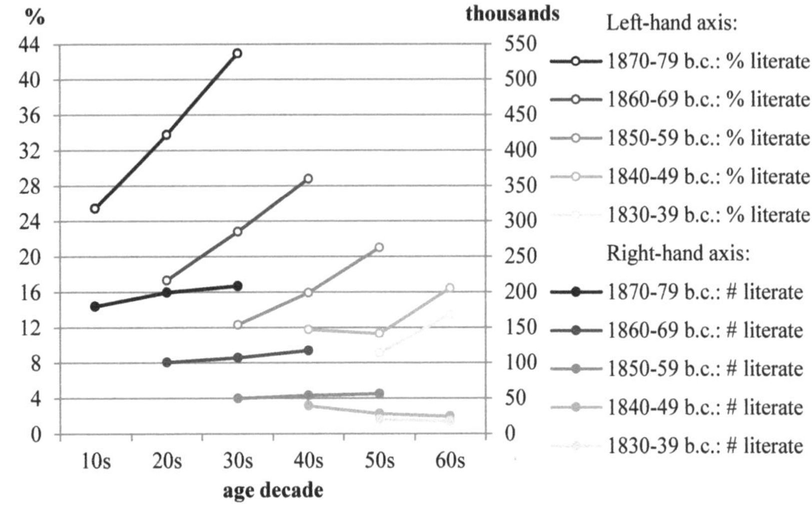

Figure 6.2: Education creep among Galician women
Source: Österreichische Statistik.

that the same process was also at work in other cohorts; sometimes with much more pronounced consequences. The literacy rate of the 1840s birth cohort rose from 59.0% to 66.6% between 1890 and 1910, to say nothing of the (unknown) creep that probably took place over the preceding thirty years from when this cohort were in their teens to 1890. Unadjusted for the upward bias, the 1890 reading on the 1840s cohort's (mid-life) literacy would give an overly rosy picture of the effectiveness of elementary schools. In other words, what is needed for a proper assessment is an estimate of a cohort's teen literacy rate, cleaned of the education creep.

Carinthian men are a fairly straightforward case in this regard: the education creep occurred at a similar rate and pace in every cohort, so one can obtain an estimate of the teen literacy rate through a simple extrapolation, using the fourteen cohort-age rates depicted in the figure. It is a rather thin evidentiary base and the implicit assumption of constant rate of education creep across decades becomes more problematic the farther back one extrapolates but it is probably the least bad option the available data can offer.

Other demographics did not always behave in as neat and predictable a manner as Carinthian men. Figure 6.2 replicates the same graph but for Galician women. The first thing to notice is that the education creep was significantly more severe. The 1870–79 cohort's literacy rate went from 25.4% in 1890 to 42.9% in 1910; that of the 1850s cohort rose from 12.3% to 21.0%. Again, note that the 12.3% literacy rate pertains to when the 1850s cohort was already in their thirties – in terms of one's stage of life, it corresponds to the 42.9% literacy of the 1870s cohort in 1910. In other words, even the 12.3% reading is possibly quite substantially inflated over what that cohort's literacy would have been when they were in their teens. The second thing to notice is that, in contrast to Figure 6.1, even the absolute number of literates actually increased from one census to the next among those born between 1850 and 1879! This is quite striking: for example, the total number of all surviving Galician women born in 1850–59 fell from 405000 in 1890 to 338000 in 1900, an almost 17% decline mostly due to mortality and to a lesser extent due to net emigration. Yet, the number of literates among them grew from 50000 to 53700. Then, from 1900 to 1910, it grew again to 56200, even as the cohort lost another 21% mostly to death (they were in their forties and fifties by then). The pattern of the growing absolute number of literate women decades after they were past their school age appeared in the record of many cohorts across several other provinces, usually those where literacy levels were quite low.

What was going on? Lower relative mortality of educated people can explain why their share in the population might increase but cannot account for their growth in absolute numbers. Could it be migration? If Galicia was an attractive destination for literate women of a certain age, they could have swelled the literate ranks over the decades. This is unlikely to be the explanation, however. For example, between 1880 and 1890, the absolute number of literate Galician women born before 1870 increased from about 171000 to 224000 – an increase of 53000. According to the 1890 census, there were in Galicia at that time some 40000 women who had not been born there – they had immigrated. Even if all of these 40000 recent immigrants were literate, they would still not suffice to fully account for the 53000 gain in literate women.[38] Of course, the simpler explanation is that they were lying to the census takers. There is, finally, also the possibility that some – perhaps many – acquired their literacy later in life, as the returns to this skill increased in line with economic development. From the data that are available, it is not possible to discriminate between these various explanations. But no matter: whether the surplus literates invented their literacy outright or actually acquired it late in life, either way, they did not get it in school. Clearly, where education creep is sizeable, adult literacy rates are inaccurate measures of the elementary school's value-added. As with Carinthian men, what is needed here are teenage literacy rates.

The Galician data, however, offer a note of caution regarding extrapolation: the record of the 1840–49 cohort shows that education creep need not be monotonic across time. This is not all that unexpected: in provinces, such as Carinthia, where literacy was already relatively high among teenagers, the pool of potential liars or late learners was relatively limited and so death was the main force that shaped the statistics from the start, leading to a picture resembling Figure 6.1. In places with low straight-out-of-school literacy, which wo-

[38] *Oesterreichische Statistik Vol. 32 Heft 2*, Tabelle I. Anwesende und abwesende heimatsberechtigte Bevölkerung, p. 26.

Table 6.5: Literacy estimation for Carinthia and Galicia

	Carinthia		Galicia	
	Model 1	Model 2	Model 1	Model 2
Dep. variable:	literacy rate	# literate	literacy rate	# literate
Cohort fixed effects				
1840–49	0.150*	2553.8*	0.052*	13511.6
	[0.027]	[621.9]	[0.017]	[9380.2]
1850–59	0.262*	4323.8*	0.148*	44740.0*
	[0.032]	[743.5]	[0.020]	[11213.5]
1860–69	0.410*	7377.5*	0.282*	113272.7*
	[0.037]	[863.2]	[0.023]	[13019.4]
1870–79	0.543*	11284.3*	0.473*	211847.5*
	[0.042]	[994.1]	[0.027]	[14994.2]
1(men)	0.094*	1091.9*	0.131*	46560.4*
	[0.015]	[351.9]	[0.010]	[5308.2]
Age	0.002	-329.8*	0.016*	3955.4*
	[0.003]	[79.8]	[0.002]	[1203.5]
Age^2	0.000	1.3	0.0001*	-43.2*
	[0.000]	[0.9]	[0.000]	[14.0]
Constant	0.253*	20581.2*	-0.447*	-77147.3
	[0.081]	[1892.1]	[0.051]	[28537.6]
Adjusted R^2	0.942	0.982	0.961	0.969
N	28	28	28	28

Note: Star (*) denotes statistical significance at 1%.

uld be the Galician case, the room for misreporting and post-school learning is obviously larger, which can produce the increases, observed among the younger cohorts in Figure 6.2. At higher ages, mortality clearly overpowers all other factors, so that for both the 1840s cohort and the 1830s cohort, the absolute number of literates starts declining. So different forces are at play at different points in time. This is somewhat unfortunate because it means that filtering out education creep is most difficult and fraught precisely in those provinces where it is most needed. Consequently, it is better not to push the extrapolation too far, which is why I limit myself in the following analysis to estimating the teenage literacy rate only for the 1850–59 cohort, the last one to have gone to school under the *Politische Verfassung* of 1805.[39]

I use two specifications, which differ only in their dependent variable: one uses the cohort literacy rates, the other the absolute number of literates. I estimate them for men and women in all provinces. By way of example, the results

[39] In this light, Kuzmin's use of 1890 literacy data for extrapolations back even into the cohort of 1780s and 1770s, for which no literacy data exist whatsoever, cannot but yield entirely unreliable numbers. See Kuzmin. *Vývoj školství a vzdělání v Československu*, p. 65–66.

for Carinthia and Galicia are shown in Table 6.5. Clearly, the specifications are very bare-bones because the sole purpose of this rather vulgar curve-fitting is not to analyse or explain anything but merely to extrapolate the literacy rate of the 1850–59 birth cohorts as of 1870 when they were 11.0–21.0 years old. The cohort fixed effects are all strongly significant, as is the male dummy variable. The main difference between the two provinces, other than the scale of the coefficients in Model 2, is that the age variables are consistently significant in Galicia while they are irrelevant in Carinthia. Judging by the high adjusted R^2, the seven independent variables are able to capture most of the variation, which is not surprising given the low number of observations.

The resulting out-of-sample predictions are presented in Table 6.6. In many of the provinces, literacy was already so close to 100% that there was no room for education creep to begin with. In those cases, there is nothing to be gained from extrapolation. For example, using the specification from Table 6.5 on Bohemia would yield an estimated teenage literacy rate for the male 1850s birth cohort of 94.5% with a standard error of 1.9%, which means that the estimate is not really statistically different from all the reported values. The 1890 value reported for the cohort (when they were already in their thirties) was apparently already a fairly precise indication of what their literacy was at age 11.0–21.0. Similar argument can be made for all the other genders and provinces where the estimate columns are left blank. That leaves those where two estimates are available, with a star indicating which of the two I consider better. In most cases, the decision was straightforward: if an estimate produces an impossible prediction, i.e. a negative literacy rate, then it is clearly not good. This is why I choose estimates from Model 2 for Dalmatia and Galicia. My other criteria are precision (lower standard error) and consistency with the notion of education creep, i.e. that the estimate be lower than the 1890 reported literacy (this is why I choose Model 1 for Carinthia, for example). In many cases, such as Silesia and the Austrian Littoral, the choice of model does not make much difference, because the values are close to each other.

The ultimate purpose of this exercise is to confront the estimated literacy rates with the enrolment record of the children of the 1850s. Their school age as a cohort falls between the years 1856 and 1871. Formally speaking, the youngest among them (those born from 1857 onwards) were already subject to the post-reform extended school age of 6.0–14.0 but as Figures 5.2–5.4 showed, it took some time before this change was fully absorbed by the system, so most of the 1850s children attended schools only for six years. In Figure 6.3, the average enrolment ratio of this cohort is on the horizontal axis, the estimated literacy rate along the vertical one.

The dotted 45° line indicates what may be called perfect efficiency: where the percentage enrolled exactly equals the percentage literate at the end of school age. The Austrian schools were less than perfectly efficient: all the points of the scatterplot lie below the 45° line. But many provinces were very

Table 6.6: Estimated and reported literacy of the 1850–59 birth cohort (in %)

		Model 1		Model 2		Reported literacy rates		
		Age 11.0–21.0		Age 11.0–21.0		30s	40s	50s
		point est.	s.e.	point est.	s.e.	1890	1900	1910
Lower	M					94.9	94.6	95.2
Austria	F					92.2	91.9	92.8
Upper	M					95.4	96.2	96.0
Austria	F					95.2	96.0	96.4
Salzburg	M					89.3	92.2	91.8
	F					92.2	91.6	92.0
Styria	M					81.9	81.8	83.7
	F	69.4*	3.2	75.3	1.9	73.5	75.6	77.7
Carinthia	M	63.6*	4.2	71.0	3.2	69.5	72.9	74.2
	F	54.2*	4.2	66.9	3.2	54.7	61.3	63.2
Carniola	M	43.5*	3.9	57.0	5.2	56.9	66.1	69.3
	F	33.8*	3.9	55.4	5.0	43.9	54.4	58.1
Austrian	M	40.6	2.4	41.1*	2.4	53.0	59.9	61.9
Littoral	F	29.4	2.4	32.9*	2.5	41.4	47.0	48.3
Tyrol	M					94.0	95.6	95.3
	F					91.4	93.5	94.0
Vorarlberg	M					99.0	98.7	99.1
	F					99.0	98.7	98.9
Bohemia	M					95.4	96.3	96.3
	F					92.1	93.1	93.0
Moravia	M					92.5	93.0	94.4
	F					86.2	88.1	88.9
Silesia	M	87.1	3.7	85.8*	2.0	86.5	90.4	91.6
	F	80.5*	3.7	86.4	2.0	81.3	83.5	85.0
Galicia	M	4.5	2.6	12.2*	2.8	24.9	32.0	37.7
	F	-8.6	2.6	3.2*	2.7	12.3	15.9	21.0
Bukovina	M	10.8	2.3	14.4*	2.3	22.0	23.1	23.5
	F	1.1	2.3	7.4*	2.3	12.8	13.5	13.7
Dalmatia	M	10.2	4.2	13.4*	4.9	14.9	24.3	25.2
	F	-6.2	4.2	1.9*	5.1	10.5	9.5	9.8

Note: "Model 1" extrapolates the literacy rates from reported literacy rates for all decadal age cohorts in the 1890–1910 censuses. "Model 2" extrapolates the absolute number of literate men and women (by decadal age cohort), recorded in the same censuses – this is then divided by the total surviving individuals from the 1850–59 birth cohort in the 1869 census. "Reported literacy rates" are not regression estimates but rates calculated directly from the census data. Star (*) denotes the preferred estimates (see discussion in text). "M" and "F" stand for male and female literacy rate.
Source: Census data from Österreichische Statistik.

close. The small inset graph in the upper left corner, which magnifies the rather crowded upper decile of Figure 6.3, shows clearly that in Bohemia, Upper and Lower Austria, Salzburg and Tyrol and Vorarlberg, both enrolment and literacy percentages were close to 100% – here the school system largely achieved its

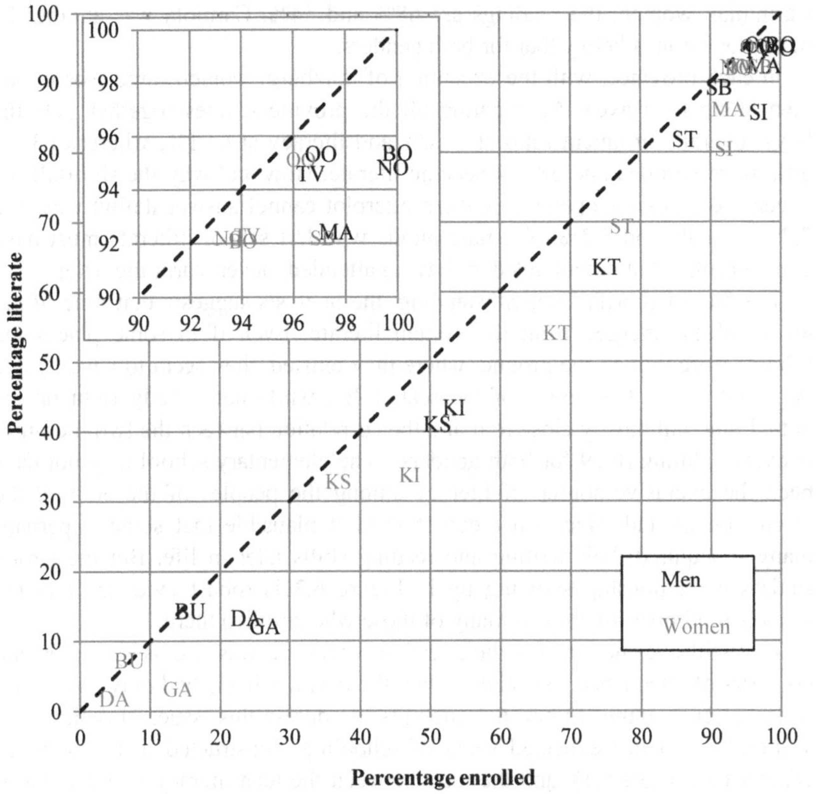

Figure 6.3: Enrolment-literacy scatterplot for the 1850–59 birth cohort
Note: Percentage literate (vertical axis) refers to the estimated literacy rates at ages 11.0–21.0 (see Table 6.6). Abbreviations denote provinces as follows: BO – Bohemia, BU – Bukovina, DA – Dalmatia, GA – Galicia, KI – Carniola, KT – Carinthia, KS – Austrian Littoral, MA – Moravia, NO – Lower Austria, OO – Upper Austria, SB – Salzburg, SI – Silesia, ST – Styria, TV – Tyrol & Vorarlberg

aims. At the other end of the spectrum were the perennial laggards, Galicia, Bukovina and Dalmatia. Of these, Bukovina can be said to have fared least poorly because, at least, those few who went to school actually came out literate at the other end. In Galicia, however, the distance between enrolment and literacy was quite large: more than half the enrolees seem to have left school unable to read and write. Finally, there is a group of provinces in the middle: Carinthia, the Austrian Littoral, Carniola and Styria. These areas reported some of the widest gaps between enrolment and literacy, indicating a large number of pupils who apparently enrolled in school in vain. Among Carinthian men, 75%

were enrolled but only 63.6% are estimated to have been literate.[40] For Carinthian women, the readings are 68% and 54%. Carniola was another 20 percentage points below that for both genders.

In each province, with the exception of Salzburg, women fared worse than men along both axes. Aggregating all the provincial rates together puts the boys' overall enrolment ratio at 71.8% and literacy at 64.1%, whereas 63.9% girls were enrolled and 58.2% became literate. How and why the shortfall between the two rates opened up, the scatterplot cannot answer definitively: the 7.7% of male and 5.7% of female pupils who left school illiterate must have either enrolled but not attended, or having attended, never learnt the letters.

The fact of shortfall notwithstanding, the analysis suggests that nine of out ten enrolees emerged from the system literate. Even if in some places the schools were thin on the ground, where they existed, they seem to have by and large delivered. The points of the scatterplot, while not exactly right on the dotted line, fall mostly close to it and the correlation between the two measures is overwhelming (0.99 for both genders). The elementary school may not have been the exclusive source of literacy among the peoples of the empire: the discussion around education creep showed it plausible that some – perhaps many – acquired their writing and reading skills later in life. But the strong statistical relationship showing up in Figure 6.3 is robust evidence that the schools did impart literacy to many of those who enrolled there.

That still does not answer the question whether it was necessary to demand six years of attendance, especially when the trivial schools had only two years' worth of curriculum. Figure 6.4 attempts to address this issue. This time, the scatterplot matches expected years of schooling, constructed in the previous chapter (see Table 5.1), and the ratio between the teen literacy rate and enrolment ratio from Figure 6.3.[41] This ratio can be interpreted as the proportion of enrolees who successfully acquired literacy in school. If all the six years were necessary, then this figure should show a positive relationship between the two statistics – provinces that cut corners, resorting to half-day and half-year schooling, should report lower literacy attainments. Instead, the three highest readings along the vertical axis belong to places where children spent the least time in the classroom: Tyrol and Vorarlberg, Lower Austria and Upper Austria. In Tyrol and Vorarlberg, almost 80% of all pupils attended schools with only half-year teaching (see Table 2.2), although they usually did so for seven years, instead of six. In Upper Austria, almost half were in half-day schools. Yet, this did not seem to put them at a disadvantage relative to Salzburg or Bohemia.

---

[40] Note that even the estimate from Model 2 in Table 6.6 would imply a shortfall, albeit a smaller one.

[41] Unfortunately, the *Detail-Conscription* of 1865, which is the source of data for the construction of the expected years of schooling, did not cover Galicia, Bukovina and Dalmatia in the same detail, which is why they are missing from Figure 6.4.

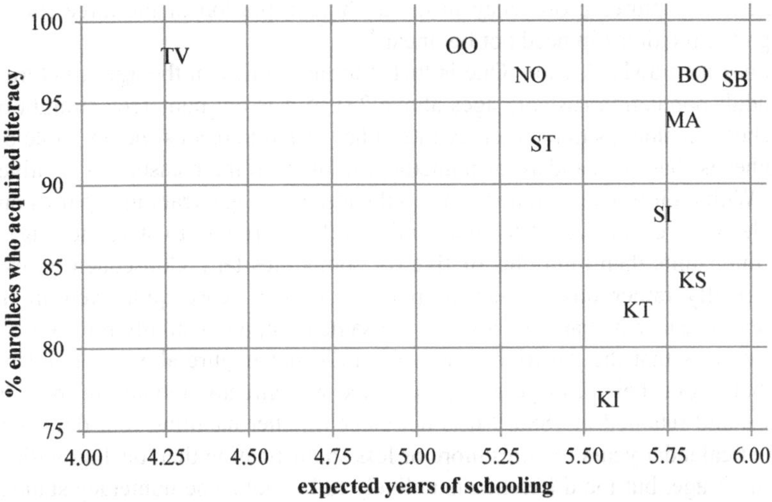

Figure 6.4: Scatterplot of expected years of schooling and literacy acquisition for the 1850–59 birth cohort
Source: For expected years of schooling, see Table 5.1; for percentage of enrolees who acquired literacy in school is Figure 6.3.

The achievement of the majority of the 150000 Tyrolean boys and girls who, in the 1860s, apparently mastered literacy in mere seven winter semesters implies that those skills could be learnt in a substantially shorter period than six years, mandated by the law, perhaps even in less than four, if class time were more continuous and not split into half-years as it was in Tyrol. The repetition of the same material in the trivial schools' second grade thus likely bore meager return. Of course, in contrast to Tyrol and Vorarlberg, the real embarrassment is the record south of the Alps – Carniola, the Austrian Littoral and Carinthia – where a substantial proportion of pupils left school illiterate and the literacy gap between male and female pupils, as Figure 6.3 showed, was at its widest.

Can similar analysis be conducted for numeracy? The short answer is "no" because there was never any effort to measure it systematically, perhaps due to the low priority accorded it in the curriculum. The more elaborate answer is that the only recourse would be proxy measures, such as the Whipple index of age heaping, which are inevitably even noisier than census literacy data.[42] The idea behind the Whipple index is that populations with lower numeracy will more likely report their ages inaccurately, rounding up to "attractive" numbers such as multiples of five. Its advantage is that it can be calculated from nothing more than the age structure reported in the census data, which by the late 19th century became relatively abundant. The index correlates with literacy, which

[42] A'Hearn et al. "Quantifying Quantitative Literacy: Age Heaping and the History of Human Capital."

suggests it captures proficiency in the arithmetic portion of the three Rs, although the relationship need not be linear.[43]

It has its drawbacks, too. One is that it usually relies on the age structure of the adult population (usually ages above 23) so it is not numeracy straight out of school, analogous to the literacy rates I have tried to reconstruct in Table 6.6. Another is that the standard of numeracy, implicit in the measure, is relatively low. With a bit of exaggeration, one could argue that age heaping captures only people who "cannot count to five" and therefore struggle to state their age in any finer units than multiples of five (or sometimes ten). Consequently, even numerically rather unsophisticated populations can score quite well in this measure because its bar is so low. At the same time, a potentially relevant consideration is that the Austrian census form did not inquire about respondents' age but about their birth year. This practice was already adopted in the 1869 census and retained in 1880.[44] It is not clear whether handling four-digit numbers of calendar years requires more or less sophistication than dealing with the two-digit age, but the difference is unlikely to be high. The numeracy standard embedded in the Austrian values of the index is rather low either way.

Jörg Baten and Ralph Hippe constructed their version of this index in such a way that the maximum value of 100 implies universal basic numeracy and the lower the index value, the lower the numeracy.[45] A value of 0 would mean that everybody rounded their age. Applied to the birth cohorts of 1808–1857 in the 1880 census, the index values for Imperial Austria ranged from 91 in eastern Galicia to 100 in Lower Austria. Recalculating the index by districts, the smallest administrative units for which age structure data are available, and smaller than those used by Baten and Hippe, yields a low of 80.3 for women in the Dalmatian district of Sinj, which was still higher than the average for all of Central and Eastern Europe at the time. To put that in context, even the least numerate district of Imperial Austria reported better results than most of Italy and much better than all of Eastern Europe from Poland and Hungary eastwards. Other provinces scored even higher than Dalmatia, with the Czech lands and Alpine lands on a par with Germany and Sweden.[46] About 90% of men and 65% of women lived in a districts where the index value was above 96. As mentioned above, all of this does not mean that the mathematical skills in the

---

[43] A'Hearn et al. "Rethinking Age-Heaping: A cautionary tale from Nineteenth-Century Italy," Figure 2.3.

[44] The 1880 census even asked for "day and month, if possible". See Verordnung des Ministeriums des Innern #103 von 6. August 1880. For the 1869 census form see Ficker. "Vorträge über die Volkszählung in Österreich. p. 38. or Verordnung des Ministeriums des Innern #142 von 15. August 1869.

[45] Baten and Hippe. "Geography, land inequality and regional numeracy in Europe in historical perspective."

[46] Baten and Hippe. "Geography, land inequality and regional numeracy in Europe in historical perspective", Figure 1.

Habsburg realms were on a stellar level but that the bar, inherent in the age-heaping measure, is low. Consider that in the least-numerate district of Sinj, the age-heaping index of 80.3 went hand in hand with a mere 1.5% literacy rate among women. Apparently, even illiterate women who had never gone to school could mostly count to five.

There is also the further problem that, in contrast to a straightforward census question about literacy, age heaping can be interpreted in more ways than one. Cultural factors such as lack of "respect for accuracy, or a more serious attitude towards time" could be the reason why people rounded their age.[47] Growing up in such a culture, even perfectly numerate persons may round their age. In other words, the low index values in Dalmatia or Galicia may be a consequence not so much of a lack of arithmetic skill but a lack of motivation. In the 1871 census of Italy, rounding of age appeared even among verifiably literate segments of the population in some regions, so that "the sparse educational elite of the South in provinces like Napoli, Reggio Calabria, and Bari reported age less accurately than the unschooled peasants and workers of the North."[48] If Dalmatians and Galicians had a similarly cavalier attitude towards accurate age reporting, it is possible that even the moderately high index values in fact still underestimate their actual numeracy. In all of this, the fact remains that, for the purposes of the Whipple index and its variants, numeracy requires very little knowledge of arithmetic but it is not designed to capture any skills even slightly more sophisticated than that. Overall, then, the age-heaping information tells us that the cohorts who went to school in the first half of the 19th century had in their overwhelming majority mastered this most basic numeracy but it does not tell us much beyond that.

As industrialization got under way, it was precisely the more advanced numeracy beyond the basics that could command a premium in some corners of the labour market. To be sure, the relationship between economic modernization and human capital was not straightforward. Evidence from Britain suggests that the First Industrial Revolution, epitomized by the textile mills of the North of England, was a time of retreating literacy and perhaps even more general deskilling.[49] Many of the new textile inventions "replaced skilled labour with a mixture of capital and unskilled labour."[50] On the other hand, new technologies did generate the demand for new kinds of expertise: after all, someone had to install and repair the new machinery. Those who had the requisite skills, which involved more than simple arithmetic and unit conversions, formed an upper tail of the skill distribution among workers and were the best positioned to

---

47 Mokyr. *Why Ireland starved*, p. 246.

48 A'Hearn et al. "Rethinking Age-Heaping", p. 7, Figure 2.4.

49 Lindert. *Growing Public*, p. 113.

50 Mokyr and Voth. "Understanding growth in early modern Europe", p. 29.

command a skill premium.[51] Rather than increasing returns to human capital across the board, industrialization in Britain had a negligible effect on average skill but a potentially sizeable effect among the best-trained and most skilled workers.

While lagging behind Britain, the Austrian economy, too, was not only becoming increasingly market oriented and economically integrated but, from the 1820s at least, also developing substantial modern industry.[52] Those skilled workers, who could read blueprints and understand technical instruction, came to enjoy similar opportunities as their counterparts did in Britain. Yet, advancing beyond the basics was scarcely possible in a trivial school: all the more useful content started from the third grade onward, which was the domain of the usually urban-situated major school. Here is that rural-urban contrast again: unambiguously a result of deliberate policy design, it nonetheless inadvertently highlighted the difference between what the Austrian school actually was and what it could have been. With a proper mix of useful content and a suitable teaching method, it could have served as an effective stepping-stone for a social and economic advance for a broad segment of the population, a pathway for children from poor families to become eligible for better paying jobs. This frames the question of the system's efficiency from a new angle: not as a question of whether the school achieved what it set out to do (teaching literacy and numeracy) but whether what it achieved had any further impact beyond the confines of the classroom.

The analysis of financing, enrolment and attendance in previous chapters uncovered some evidence that the support for schools from below was mostly lukewarm: extra classrooms were rarely built, teachers were poorly paid, school patronage rarely went beyond the absolutely necessary minimum and often stayed below it, especially in villages, and poor parents had good reasons for keeping their children out of school. And yet, there was a very definite popular demand for learning – at least for a certain kind of learning – which resurfaced in the explosion of the *Realschulen* after 1848 (Figure 1.1), the strong increase in the number of major schools at the same time (Figure 2.2), the apparent continued presence of *Winkellehrer*, the unlicensed tutors whom the education authorities ceaselessly struggled to stamp out, or the growth of private schools after 1848. Already in 1851, Vienna counted some 103 private schools educating over 3700 pupils.[53] They were quite small, averaging 36 pupils (the average Viennese public school had more than 400), and they did not necessarily cater

---

[51] Mokyr . "Long term economic growth and the history of technology", p. 1160.

[52] See Komlos. *The Habsburg Monarchy as a Customs Union* on the ongoing market integration within the Habsburg Empire and Good. *The Economic Rise of the Habsburg Empire* for a discussion of the onset of modern economic (and industrial growth). For the interaction between marketization and numeracy, see Emigh. "Numeracy or Enumeration? The Uses of Numbers by States and Societies."

[53] See Kaiser. *Lehrer-Schema*. Viennese public schools had a total 34000 pupils in 1851.

to the same age group as elementary schools, although there certainly was overlap. But they offered instruction in areas where the elementary school would not tread. One popular course was to combine women's housework and a foreign language, such as French. There were also numerous stand-alone language schools, drawing schools, music and singing schools, as well as finishing schools for bourgeois daughters, with dance and conversation lessons. It was a lively market with intense competition: by 1867, there were 101 private schools in Vienna and 70 of them were established just over the previous decade. Two thirds of these were girls' schools and many proudly advertised in their title their broad teaching scope (e.g. "*Weibliche Hauptschule mit Sprachen*" – girls' major school with foreign languages), lest someone mistook them for a lowly needlework class.[54]

In the public sphere, the majority of curricular innovations and amendments, such as they were, came in response to urban demand.[55] Efforts to extend the curriculum beyond the second grade were not, however, confined to the largest towns. These efforts increased in intensity particularly after 1848 but they had been around, in some form or shape, ever since public schooling first started. For example, at the time of the 1774 school reform, the long-standing piarist school in Brandýs nad Labem, a Bohemian town of about 3000 inhabitants, consisted of two grades. In 1778, a third grade was added, making this a major school. By 1806, a fourth grade was opened. The school building was big enough to accommodate separate classrooms for boys and girls and even to split the first grade into a beginners' section and an advanced section. In 1853, the Brandýs school added another two grades from the *Realschule* curriculum, which turned it into a civic school (*Bürgerschule*). Its curriculum was further extended by another grade in 1856.[56]

By 1865, more than half of all urban and a quarter of all rural pupils attended a school with a third grade or more.[57] And those were just the successful curriculum expansions, most of which surely took place over the previous decade and a half. There is no indication how much of that demand remained unmet or was outright rejected in the earlier years of the system – after all, any such extension had to be approved and officially sanctioned by the authorities, who sometimes took their sweet time. In Hlinsko, another Bohemian town, the third grade was granted only in 1824, even though the locals were ready to go ahead with it as early as 1809.[58] Where the public system could not deliver, private provision increasingly stepped in. In 1867, even small provincial towns,

---

[54] See K. k. Statistische Central-Commission. "Statistische Mittheilungen verschiedenen Inhalts." p. 38–42.

[55] Frank. "Kurzer Überblick", p. 18–20.

[56] Kneidl. *Paměti školského okresu karlínského*, p. 187–188.

[57] Cvrček and Zajíček. "The rise of public schooling in nineteenth-century Imperial Austria", Table 3.

[58] Adámek. *Paměti o školách v okresu hlineckém*, p. 13.

Table 6.7: Quantity and quality of schooling in country and city, 1865

Variable	Overall		District means		
	Mean	Std. Dev.	Urban	Rural	t-test
Full-time equivalent teachers (T_i)	1.205	0.474	1.327	1.191	-2.26
Full-time teacher requirement (FTR_i)	1.543	0.350	1.347	1.565	4.98
Third-grade exposure (GR_i)	0.283	0.221	0.528	0.256	-10.48
Proportion non-Catholic (NC_i)	0.027	0.067	0.069	0.022	-5.60
1(German majority district)	0.551	0.498	0.522	0.554	0.51
Literacy content index (LC_i)	0.198	0.069	0.281	0.189	-11.58
Average population in 1869 (in thousands)	20.1	25.4	42.3	17.6	

Note: T_i and FTR_i are normalized as rates per 1000 inhabitants. For a definition of the literacy content index of the local labour market (LC_i), see text. The definition of "urban" district is such where at least 5000 inhabitants lived in a town that had population of more than 3000.
Source: Cvrček and Zajíček. "The rise of public schooling", Table 3.

such as Judenburg in Styria or Račah in Carniola, both about the same size as Brandýs nad Labem, sported the occasional private school.[59]

In short, the public *was* interested in education, just not always in the type and the extent that the government deemed permissible. It is not easy to disentangle, how much of the school infrastructure grew out of a genuine demand among ordinary citizenry and how much was a product of the pressure from above. The artificial urban-rural divide in curriculum imposed by regulation offers an opening.[60] Table 6.7 shows several statistics that characterize the state of elementary education as of 1865. The first two are measures of quantity and they capture, by construction, how much schooling was in place relative to how much the government wanted. The full-time teacher requirement (FTR_i) measures how many teachers a district should have had by law, given the number of school-age children. It simply applies the parameters embedded in the law to the demographic situation in each district. The value is adjusted for population: the average district was supposed to have about 1.54 full-time teacher per 1000 inhabitants. The number of full-time equivalent teachers (T_i) is the number of teachers actually present per 1000 inhabitants.[61] These two variables measure the quantity of schooling offered. The exposure to third grade (GR_i) gauges the quality, i.e. the extent of the curriculum. It shows the share of the enrolled pupils who were in schools with three or more grades. In an average district, 28.3% of pupils attended such a school.

Among the broader social and economic measures, the proportions of non-Catholics (NC_i), namely Jews and Protestants, and an indicator variable for the

[59] K. k. Statistische Central-Commission. "Statistische Mittheilungen verschiedenen Inhalts." p. 43–44.

[60] The rest of this chapter draws substantially on the analysis in Cvrček and Zajíček. "The rise of public schooling in nineteenth-century Imperial Austria."

[61] The "full-time equivalent" adjective refers to the fact that not all teachers were teachers in "full-time" schools. Half-day and half-year teachers are weighted at 0.5.

German majority capture two usual socio-demographic correlates of higher demand for education, which in later analysis will reappear as controls. The index of literacy on the local labour market (LC_i) requires a more detailed explanation. It takes the 1869 census data on the occupational structure in each district and evaluates each of the 50 occupations listed in terms of their need of literacy, using David Mitch's categorization (already referred to in chapter 5).[62] The index is a weighted average of four categories of jobs, defined by Mitch, such that a value of 1 implies that all workers in a district worked jobs that absolutely required literacy while 0 means that all workers worked jobs that had no use for literacy.[63] An average value of 0.198 indicates that in the 1860s, most occupations in most districts still scored relatively low in terms of their use of literacy.

But the table also shows that there was a considerable variation between districts, especially between the urban and rural ones. The urban districts had more literacy-intensive labour markets by half and, not surprisingly, twice as many children went to school with a third grade there as did in the rural districts. The urban districts were also more likely to ensure that teacher numbers were close to the mandated levels. Rural districts were not only falling short of this mandate but had overall fewer teachers than urban districts. The reason why the teacher requirement was higher in the countryside was that the population was more spread out across various villages, requiring more schools and consequently teachers for a given number of pupils. The t-statistics in Table 6.7 show that the differences were systematic: all the t-tests turned out statistically significant at 5%, except in the case of the German majority indicator.

As mentioned earlier, the quality and quantity of schooling that a given community ended up with was a product of forces pushing both from above and from below. The teacher requirement, cited in Table 6.7, reflected what the government wanted. The curriculum extensions, mentioned earlier, pointed to the demands of the public (or at least some segments of it). Those pressures were all at work at the same time and any analysis of their relative importance needs to put them side-by-side in a horse race of sorts. I do that in the context of simultaneous equations estimation, where the quality of schooling (measured by the extent of the curriculum, GR_i), quantity of schooling (measured through teacher density, T_i) and their broader economic ramifications (proxied by use of literacy in the labour market, LC_i) are all modelled together. The model consists of three equations:

---

[62] Mitch. *The Rise of Popular Literacy in Victorian England*, p. 213–214.

[63] The four categories that Mitch uses are: occupations where literacy was indispensable, occupations where it was likely to be useful, occupations where the use of literacy was ambiguous and occupations which had no use for literacy. The weights assigned to these categories are 1, 0.7, 0.3 and 0 respectively. For example, a district where half the labour force worked "illiterate" jobs, a third worked ambiguously literate jobs and the remaining sixth likely literate jobs would have an *LC* index value of $\frac{1}{2}\times0 + \frac{1}{3}\times0.3 + \frac{1}{6}\times0.7 = 0.2167$.

$$\begin{array}{llll}
\text{Eq. 1} & T_i = \alpha_1 + \beta_1 LC_i & + \delta_1 FTR_i & + \theta_1 1_i(G) + \mu_1 1_i(U) + \varepsilon_{i1} \\
\text{Eq. 2} & GR_i = \alpha_2 + \beta_2 LC_i & + \delta_2 NC_i & + \theta_2 1_i(G) + \mu_2 1_i(U) + \varepsilon_{i2} \\
\text{Eq. 3} & LC_i = \alpha_3 \quad + \boldsymbol{Y_i}\gamma_3 & + \delta_3 GR_i + \zeta_3 T_i & + \mu_3 1_i(U) + \varepsilon_{i3}
\end{array}$$

In equation 1, the observed number of teachers, T_i, is a function of the labour market literacy content index, LC_i, and the full-time teacher requirement, FTR_i. The first term represents the extent to which the demand for more teachers was motivated by greater opportunities to use literacy in a job. The second term represents the pressure and enforcement of the regulation. If the learning in schools were genuinely useful for the labour market, it would be sensible to expect a strong popular demand for more teachers, as people would see the school as a conduit for social and economic advance. In such a case, β_1 will be positive and large while δ_1 will be insignificant, an indication that the presence of teachers was not driven by the letter of the law. On the other hand, if δ_1 turns out large and especially if it is close to 1, it will mean that the government was effective in enforcing its regulation. Such a constellation suggests the government commanded more education to be supplied than the economic realities called for, making the "extra" schooling wasteful, economically speaking. In that case, β_1 should be close to zero.

In equation 2, the quality of schooling, GR_i, depends on the labour market variable, LC_i, as well as another "popular" cultural determinant of demand for education, the proportion of non-Catholics, NC_i. Government regulation specified that three- and higher-grade schools should stay in the cities but by the 1860s, this position was not meticulously enforced anymore. To the extent that it was, it will show up in the coefficient μ_2 on the urban dummy variable, $1_i(U)$. Here, if the third-grade curriculum generated economically useful human capital, the coefficient β_2 will be high and significant. If, however, the demand had more cultural underpinnings (such as the greater stress on literacy historically associated with Jews and Protestants[64]) instead of economic ones, then δ_2 will be positive.

Equation 3 then accounts for the feedback into the economy: it models to what extent the literacy content of a district's labour market (LC_i) depends on the local provision of schooling, both its quantity (T_i) and its quality (GR_i). Other controls, entering as part of the matrix Y_i, include technological variables such as the number of steam engines and connection to railroad. They control for the possibility that some learning of literacy and numeracy takes place on the job, well after one leaves school. Thus, if γ_3 is large while δ_3 and ζ_3 turn out small, then the high literacy content observed on the labour market is primarily a result of on-the-job training.

The results are presented in Table 6.8. The unit of analysis is the civil dist-

[64] See Becker and Woessmann. "Was Weber Wrong?"

Table 6.8: Simultaneous equations estimation

Dependent Variable:	Eq. 1 T_i	Eq. 2 GR_i	Eq. 3 LC_i
Third grade exposure (GR_i)			0.191* [0.045]
Full-time equivalent teachers (T_i)			0.012 [0.016]
Literacy content of local labor market (LC_i)	-0.166 [1.728]	5.511* [1.113]	
Full-time teacher requirement (FTR_i)	0.451* [0.052]		
Proportion non-Catholic (NC_i)		0.034 [0.077]	
Steam engines per 1000 inhabitants			0.000 [0.003]
1(Railroad access in 1865)			0.001 [0.003]
1(German majority district)	0.309* [0.058]	-0.020 [0.041]	
1(Traditional urban centre)	0.076 [0.069]	-0.040 [0.048]	0.005 [0.008]
Constant	0.328 [0.296]	-0.412* [0.168]	0.059 [0.031]
N	688	688	688
257 political district fixed effects	Yes	Yes	Yes

Note: The unit of observations is the *Gerichtsbezirk*, civil or judicial district. Two to five *Gerichtsbezirks* added up to a *Bezirkhauptmannschaft*, or a political district, of which there were 258, hence the 257 local fixed effects. Square brackets report standard errors. Star (*) denotes statistical significance at 5%. "Traditional urban centre" is defined as a district with more than 5,000 inhabitants in towns of more than 3000 people.
Source: Cvrček and Zajíček. "The rise of public schooling", Table 4.

rict (*Gerichtsbezirk*), the smallest unit in the Austrian public administration. Table 6.7 showed that it had an average of 20000 inhabitants. An average district would have about 20 elementary schools. In equation 1, β_1 is small and negative while $\delta_1 = 0.451$. This implies that the labour market impact on demand for quantity was negligible. On the other hand, for every teacher demanded by the regulation, the schools in an average district hired 0.451 teacher, or almost one half-day teacher. Importantly, δ_1 is statistically different both from 0 and from 1, which implies that the regulation was neither toothless and irrelevant ($\delta_1 = 0$), nor fully enforced ($\delta_1 = 1$). Still, the conclusion emerging from Equation 1 is that the quantity of schooling depended more on the enforcement of the regulation, even if imperfect and incomplete, than on the local economic characteristics.[65] The pressure from above mattered more.

[65] Equation 1 also shows that the German-majority districts had systematically about 0.3

The situation is starkly different in Equation 2. The coefficient on LC_i is very high and very significant. With $\beta_2 = 5.511$, an increase in the literacy content index by 0.1, or roughly the difference between the average rural and average urban districts, would imply 55.1% more children attending a three-grade school or more. No other variable comes close to having a similar impact. In contrast, the coefficient on the proportion non-Catholics is negligible, implying that culturally motivated demand for literacy, such as would be associated with these religious communities, was unimportant.

Finally, the results for the third equation indicate that the impact of schooling on the literacy intensity of the local labour market was primarily linked to third-grade exposure rather than to the number of teachers present. Education influenced the sophistication of the labour force pretty much only through its quality, rather than quantity. Suppose that in an average district of 20 schools, five of the schools introduced a third grade, exposing an extra 25% of pupils to the more advanced curriculum. This jump in GR_i by 0.25 would lead to an increase in the literacy index of the local labour market by 0.048. That is equivalent to about 7% of workers moving from a job, which did not require literacy, to a job where the use of literacy was likely. In contrast, the number of teachers (T_i) did not exert much impact on LC_i within a realistic range of values: with $\zeta_3 = 0.12$, it would take an extra 4 teachers per 1000 inhabitants (or a total of 80 new teachers, given the size of an average district) – a massive increase – to achieve the same effect. The technological variables, such as the number of steam engines or the railroad connection, were also unimportant.

All these results together lend support to a coherent and unsurprising interpretation. The total number of schools, and by extension of teachers, was primarily driven by the enforcement of schooling law, with limited attention paid to their broader economic usefulness. That is why the regulation turns out significant in equation 1, while at the same time the number of teachers had no impact on the sophistication of the local labour market in equation 3. This in no way contradicts the earlier analysis, which showed that Austrian schools, regardless of curriculum, were by and large successful in imparting literacy (Figure 6.3) and that literacy-using jobs carried higher wages (Table 5.10). As a source of basic literacy, even the rural two-grade school offered a certain limited pathway for economic advance. But the regulation required pupils to stay in schools perhaps up to two years too long, which made it unnecessarily burdensome and costly. Under a two-grade curriculum, schooling was oversupplied by fiat beyond the level at which it made a positive contribution. If one wished to make the whole six years of compulsory schooling worthwhile, then introducing more new learning in the form of a third grade was a smart way of doing it. The push for a more extensive curriculum thus came from below, from

extra teacher per 1000 inhabitants, other things held equal, which is neither a negligible, nor an overwhelming difference.

the parents of school-age children, and it was especially strong in those districts, where the third and higher grade content could actually make a difference in a child's labour market prospects. The return-bearing skills acquired in those higher grades all rested on fully mastered literacy as the indispensable groundwork. Places that reported many workers from the upper tail of the skill distribution were also the districts with high literacy content (LC_i) of the local labour market because those extra skills presupposed literacy. Within the existing regulation framework, then, the population's preference ranking of all the schooling options that were realistically on the table could plausibly have run as follows: the most desirable was the high-cost/high-benefit three- or higher-grade school, followed by the no-cost/no-benefit option of defying the law and having no school (especially in the countryside), with the last place accorded to the medium-cost/low-benefit of the legally stipulated two-grade trivial school. It is telling that δ_l = 0.451 in equation 1 indicates far from a successful enforcement of the school provision mandate. When it was not entirely ignored, the least favourite option of running a trivial school could be made more palatable by effectively cutting the deadweight loss from mandated oversupply through limiting the local school to a branch or provisional status (see Table 2.1), half-day schooling (Table 2.2), overshooting the legal pupil-teacher ratio (Table 3.2) or avoiding enrolment or shirking attendance (Chapter 5).

Given that the people's least favourite was the government's top choice, did at least the rulers draw any benefit from the schooling policy? Francis I, quoted in Chapter 1, hoped to instil *Rechtschaffenheit* in his subjects – a well-disposed, conformist character, which makes one content in his social standing and therefore disinclined to demand reforms, strive for social advance or make any political waves, such as those that led to the French Revolution. If literacy is only imprecisely measured and numeracy must make do with a proxy, then gauging *Rechtschaffenheit* and the school's success in instilling it would almost certainly be a fool's errand. Perhaps the best one can do is to set the education policy's aims against the political events and trends that the school's ideological influence, properly wielded, was supposed to prevent.

If it aimed to prop up natural authority of feudal lords among serfs, it became moot after 1781 when serfdom was abolished. Feudal administration remained in place until 1848 and *robota* (corveé labour) was still demanded of peasants as a form of in-kind payment of land rent in places where it had not been monetized, but Austria's peasants were full-blown citizens at least since the adoption of the new Civil Code of 1811. If it aimed to uphold traditional Catholic morality and maintain the religious monopoly of the Roman Church, then the policy was certainly swimming against the currents. Liberal and secular ideas were seeping in to the country, not least by means of the printed word. Inevitably, the schooling policy, which sought to head off their influence through religious instruction, was simultaneously making them more accessible by teaching literacy. If it aimed to bolster the culturally German character of the empire, ensuring hegemony of Germandom, at least among the elites, then the empire's long-term track record is more than ample proof that the policy mostly failed. Before long, the school became a conduit for national agitation and one of the constant demands of all the empire's ethnic groups was for more schooling in their national language at all levels of the system.

Of course, in all these matters, one could counter that the schooling policy was nonetheless effective because without it, all of those undesirable political changes – undesirable, that is, in the eyes of the Habsburg monarchs – would have come even faster. The counterfactual history implicit in such a response is more involved than I can afford to reconstruct and evaluate in one book and so the challenge has to remain unanswered for now. But, perhaps, the most definitive indication, that the rulers and policy makers could not possibly have got what they wanted out of their schooling policy, was how far short of the mandate its enforcement remained for so long in so many areas.

Chapter 7

The Overhaul

Throughout Europe, the 1860s were the high watermark of 19th century liberalism. Great liberal causes, such as free trade, extension of suffrage, free labour and free press, were succeeding across a broad sphere of public policy.[1] Austria was part of that trend.[2] The disastrous military defeats in the Franco-Austrian War of 1859 made the continuation of the neo-absolutism untenable and, in February 1861, the emperor Franz Josef I granted a constitution.[3] The introduction of representative government and the accompanying electoral politics gave Austria's liberal-minded urban class a powerful new platform. Right away, they turned their reforming zeal to all areas of public life, including schooling, and by 1869 the existing system of elementary education was thoroughly reformed. The century-old structure of the *Politische Verfassung* and the *Allgemeine Schulordnung* came to an end. The political debate surrounding the liberal school reform of 1868–69 brought to the surface the long-standing dividing lines and conflicting interests that had permeated the school system almost from its inception.

To those actively involved in education, the writing had been on the wall for some time. In addition to the long-term dissatisfaction among teachers and other local stakeholders with the staleness of the teaching methods and the curriculum,[4] the 1848 abolition of the feudal, patrimonial administration created confusion and uncertainty within the financial and supervisory framework that held the system together. A major update was necessary and, as the 1848 revolution unfolded, things looked promising at first. In March 1848, a Ministry of Public Education replaced the out-dated and reform-averse Education Commission.[5] By autumn of the same year, undersecretary Ernst von Feuchtersleben produced a plan for the reform of elementary schooling, which argued in favour of the introduction of a third grade at every trivial school, for a longer

[1] See Komlos. *The Habsburg Monarchy as a Customs Union* on internal and external trade liberalization. Austria joined the Cobden-Chevalier network of bilateral free-trade treaties in 1867 through a treaty with France, having already abolished all internal tariffs back in 1851. See Lampe et al. "How much trade Liberalization was there in the World Before and After Cobden-Chevalier?"

[2] Kwan. "Austro-German Liberalism and the Coming of the 1867 Compromise", p. 64.

[3] See Taylor. *The Habsburg monarchy, 1809 – 1918* for a general overview.

[4] Engelbrecht. *Geschichte Des österreichischen Bildungswesens. Vol. 3*, p. 230.

[5] Engelbrecht. *Geschichte Des österreichischen Bildungswesens. Vol 4*, p. 515–516.

and more thorough teacher training and for the simplification of school financing through a shift of all responsibility onto the shoulders of the towns and villages.[6] Feuchtersleben resigned in November, however, the revolution was defeated the following spring and the plan remained just a proposal. Bits and pieces eventually became law during the ministry of Leo Thun (1849–1860), such as an extension of teacher training and a broader curriculum in urban schools. Still, in contrast to his far-reaching reforms in secondary and tertiary education, the aristocratic Thun's overall impact on elementary schooling was one of preserving the status quo and even turning the clock back before 1848 in some areas. He was the chief promoter of the Concordat of 1855 with the Holy See, which temporarily reintroduced church supervision into primary schooling.[7]

The real reform work had to wait for a different constituency, the rising urban middle class. It came about in three waves: the first abolished the *Schulpatronat*, the second secularised school administration and the third restructured school financing, rewrote the curriculum and reformed teacher training. Sizing up the diverse forces, whether cultural, political or economic, operating in the background of the three-act drama of the school reform is the central theme of this chapter. A proper understanding of the era's political economy, however, requires first a brief description of two key structures of the state which shaped both the interests and the agenda of the various constituencies as well as the channels through which they could influence policy: the electoral system and the system of taxation (especially at the local level).

The abolition of the *Schulpatronat* took place in the newly established provincial assemblies. Figure 7.1 depicts the complicated electoral system through which these assemblies were created under the 1861 constitution.[8] At both the provincial level and the central level, the defining principle of representation was the *Kurialsystem*: voters were split into four electoral colleges, *curias*, with highly unequal suffrage. The landowning *curia* included the most rarefied strata of Austrian aristocracy. In Bohemia, for example, a province of about 5 million inhabitants, a mere 471 individuals met the tax requirement for voting in this *curia*, set at an annual land tax bill of at least 250 fl. One would need an estate of about 1 km^2 or bigger to owe such a tax bill (the average landholding in Bohemia at that time was 0.07 km^2).[9] The threshold varied across provinces. In Lower Austria, it stood at 200 fl, yielding 201 voters, in Styria only 100 fl,

[6] Ficker. *Bericht über österreichisches Unterrichtswesen*, p. 37.

[7] Frankfurter. "Thun-Hohenstein, Graf Leo", p. 198; Aliprantis. "The afterlife of Enlightened Absolutism", p. 308.

[8] See *Staatsgrundgesetze der österreichischen Monarchie. Sammlung aller die Reichsverfassung und die Landerverfassungen betreffenden Gesetze, Verordnungen, Handschreiben und sonstigen Erlässe. 1. Bändchen.* 1861, for full detail.

[9] Cvrček and Zajíček. "The making of a liberal education", p. 4.

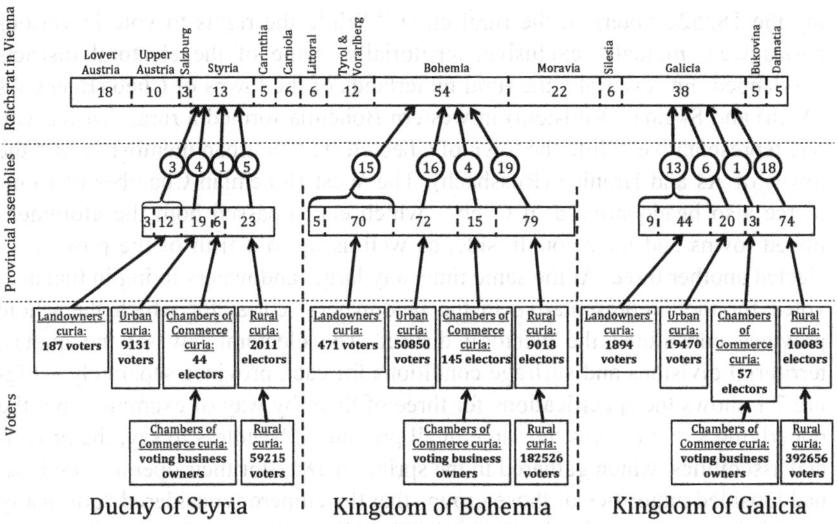

Figure 7.1: Electoral system of Imperial Austria, 1861–67
Source: Cvrček and Zajíček. "The making of a liberal education", Figure 1.

resulting in 187 landowning voters in 1867.[10] In the urban *curia*, the requirement for suffrage included permanent residency or place of business in a city and a specified minimum tax payment (e.g. business owners in the Styrian capital Graz qualified to vote if they paid at least 15 fl in direct taxes; in other Styrian towns, the threshold was 10 fl). Certain specified professions such as priests, public servants, military officers and academics, were also entitled to vote. The landowning and the urban *curias* elected their representatives directly. In the rural *curia* and in the Chambers of Commerce *curia*, the vote was indirect. All factory operators and business owners, large and small, had the right to elect Chamber of Commerce deputies, who then voted for their Chamber's representatives in the legislature. Voters in each rural district elected one elector per 500 voters, determined, as in cities, on the basis of residency and the tax census; the electors then chose the district's representative. The rural districts were where the majority of both the voters and the general population lived.

The inequality in the suffrage lay in the fact that different *curias* elected a different number of representatives. To use an example from Figure 7.1, the Bohemian provincial assembly's 241 members consisted of 70 representatives elected by the 471 landowning voters, 72 sent by the urban districts, 15 representing the five Bohemian Chambers of Commerce and 79 members represent-

[10] For comparison, in 1867, the day wage of an unskilled labourer in Bohemia was 0.68 fl (TSOM 1867).

ing the 182526 voters in the rural curia.[11] While the rights to vote in various *curias* were mutually exclusive, territorially, some of the electoral districts overlapped. For example, the rural hinterlands of the towns of Cheb (Eger), Aš (Asch) and Skalná (Wildstein) in western Bohemia formed a rural district with one representative, while the town of Cheb elected an urban member, as did the towns of Aš and Hranice (Rossbach). The West-Bohemian Chamber of Commerce also headquartered in Cheb – which encompassed both the aforementioned towns and their countryside, as well as up to a fifth of the province – elected another three. At the same time, any large landowners living in that area voted for their representative in the landowners' curia, for which the whole province constituted the electoral district. The electoral law set the quotas, territorial divisions and suffrage conditions for each province separately – Figure 7.1 shows the specifications for three of them by way of example – but the underlying structure was the same in all provinces. Needless to say, the provincial assemblies, which gathered in the spring of 1861 for their opening sessions, had lopsided majorities of those groups that the emperor considered "politically reliable": aristocrats, landowners, rich burghers, church representatives and Austrian Germans. This was the case even in the rural *curia*, which was the "most mass" of all, counting hundreds of thousands of rural voters, mostly small farmers. The separation of voters into such starkly delineated, economically defined constituencies is a far cry from modern democratic ideals but to the researcher it offers an unusually "clean" way to identify how particular economic interests approached various policy proposals. With Austria's *Kurialsystem*, there is little confusion about who represented the interests of the large landowners, of the cities or of the farmers: they each had their specially designated *curia*. So, where did each stand with respect to the schooling reforms of the 1860s?

The abolition of the *Schulpatronat* appeared on the agenda in 1863 out of the initiative of the central government. The government bill, which followed the same template in all provinces, declared all school patronage imposed by the Josephinian 1787 decree moot and also released former feudal lords from the last holdover of their pre-1848 patrimonial duties, the obligation to supply schools with firewood. All matters relating to school financing were transferred to towns and villages, except where private foundations and endowments were involved. The patron's right to have a say in teacher appointment, which had historically gone hand in hand with school patronage, was also transferred to the municipalities. Further, the law included provisions for those schools that catered to several villages, establishing school boards with representatives from each village.

[11] Another five members, called virilists, were representatives *ex offo*: the archbishop of Prague, the bishops of České Budějovice, Hradec Králové and Litoměřice and the Rector of the Prague University.

The shift towards more municipal involvement in schooling coincided with a broader society-wide conversation about matters of local government, a function both of administrative necessity and of the changing political atmosphere. In order to quickly fill the hole left by the 1848 abolition of the patrimonial administration, the emperor responded in March 1849 with a new, *pro tempore* decree on municipal self-government.[12] This was further updated in 1859 and again in 1862, so as to reflect the demands and preferences of the ascendant political constituencies among which the urban element was the strongest. The new powers granted to, and responsibilities imposed upon, municipalities also required establishing a sound fiscal basis for them. Both the 1859 and the 1862 laws viewed income from existing municipal property as the most important and most reliable source of revenue. Where it fell short of the expenditures, towns and villages could impose a surcharge on top of existing direct taxes and on the indirect consumption tax. Thus, rather than enact a new tax with a separate tax base, specifically earmarked for municipal revenue and levied independently of the central state, the lawmakers opted for a system where local government piggybacked on an already existing system of taxation and effective tax rates were allowed to vary locally, depending on the municipal surcharge.

The main direct tax was the land tax (*Grundsteuer*), introduced in 1817 and levied on an administratively estimated net income from all agricultural and wooded land.[13] The legal formula took into account the types of crops planted, the quality of the soil, the likely yield of timber in woodlands and local prices among other factors. The base rate started at 16% but another 5.3% was added in 1850 and a further temporary war surcharge of 2.7% came in 1859 (to pay for the Franco-Austrian war). Any municipal surcharge would be added on top of that combined 24% tax rate. The real estate in towns and cities was similarly subject to rent tax (*Hauszinssteuer*) on those houses that were generating rental income and a house tax (*Hausclassensteuer*) on the rest. They were levied at similar rates as the land tax. The profits of companies and small entrepreneurs were subject to an earnings tax (*Erwerbsteuer*). All these direct taxes formed the most important source of funds for the central government so that in 1868 they accounted for more than a third of all revenue and of that about 70% came from the land and house taxes.[14] Among the indirect taxes, the most important was the consumption tax (*Verzehrungssteuer*), which was applied to certain foodstuffs, such as wine, beer and meats.[15]

---

[12] This was part of a broader effort to introduce civil administration on all levels of government. See Urban. *Česká společnost*, p. 100–101.

[13] K. k. Finanzministerium. *Tafeln zur Statistik des Steuerwesens im Österreichischen Kaiserstaate*, pp. XX–XXIII.

[14] Jindra a Jakubec. *Dějiny hospodářských českých zemí*, p. 71; SJOM 1869, pp. 422–423.

[15] K. k. Finanzministerium. *Tafeln zur Statistik des Steuerwesens im Österreichischen

The abolition of school patronage was making its way through provincial legislatures just as these new fiscal and administrative details of local self-government were being put in place. In this context, the provisions giving towns and villages more responsibility for schools were not particularly controversial. The Lower Austrian assembly, for example, breezed through the second reading of the government's abolition bill in one day, introducing mostly cosmetic amendments.[16] The Carinthian assembly skipped the general debate altogether and in the special debate all but three articles passed in the exact form that had been approved in the committee without any discussion.[17]

The proceedings nonetheless revealed that representatives across all *curias* paid close attention even to the smallest financial consequences of the law. One telling example was the issue of firewood for schools. Back in 1848, as the feudal administration was being dismantled, a government decree reinstated the feudal obligation to supply firewood as an emergency measure. In order to forestall complaints from the aristocracy that their duties continued to be enforced even as their privileges were being cut, the decree acknowledged their right to claim, at some future date, compensation for the firewood from the (then still future) civil authorities. In spring 1863, this hitherto dormant clause became a live issue. In the Bohemian assembly, rural representatives, speaking for the villages, which were now becoming those very civil authorities against whom the compensation claims might be enforced, proposed an amendment rescinding the right to compensation.[18] With an average school consuming annually 6–7 fathoms of wood costing 10 fl each, the potential sums involved were not negligible but not exorbitant either.[19] The proposal engendered serious debate and two close votes, which split the Bohemian assembly, predictably, by material interest. All but one of the representatives of the landowner *curia* – the potential compensation claimants – voted against the rescindment, whereas rural deputies voted overwhelmingly for it. Members for the towns and cities, mostly indifferent to the issue since municipalities had usually served as patrons to their own schools and had to procure their own wood anyway, were split down the middle. The amendment was narrowly defeated and the right to

---

Kaiserstaate, pp. 291–295.

[16] Niederösterreichische Landtag. "41. Sitzung der niederösterreichischen Landtages vom 26. Marz 1863." *Stenographische Protokolle der niederösterreichischen Landtage. Zweite Session*, pp. 1048–1093.

[17] Kärntnerische Landtag. "Stenographisches protokoll der sieben und dreißigsten Sitzung des kärntnerischen Landtages zu Klagenfurt vom 21. März 1863." *Stenographische Protokolle der zweiten Session des kärntnerisches Landtages zu Klagenfurt*, pp. 895–920.

[18] Böhmische Landtag. "Stenographische Bericht über die XXVIII. Sitzung der dritten Jahres-Session des böhmischen Landtages vom Jahre 1861, am 2. Mai 1864" *Stenographische Protokolle des Böhmischen Landtages. Drittes Jahressession*. p. 7–25.

[19] For a further discussion of the physical amounts and cost of school firewood involved, refer back to Chapter 3.

compensation remained.[20] In Lower Austria on the other hand, where the aristocratic representation was weaker thanks to the clout of urban (particularly Viennese) representatives, the same kind of amendment passed.[21] The whole episode was a sign that in matters of school financing, even modest amounts were worth fighting over.

Around the country, the abolition of *Schulpatronat* was not always greeted with enthusiasm, given the increased fiscal burdens that this victory entailed for municipal self-government. While aristocratic patrons had, in the past, received a fair share of criticism for neglecting their obligations, e.g. in the press, now even rural representatives came to recognize that without the feudal lords, the school infrastructure would have likely been even sparser and poorer than it was.[22] By some estimates, towns and villages had usually contributed only about 20% to the construction of new schools, with the rest split between feudal lords and school patrons, who were often the same person.[23] Some local communities were fortunate enough that their long-standing school patron volunteered to continue in the role even after the abolition, simply out of a sense of *noblesse oblige*.[24] Some villages did not hesitate to take the initiative and petition the former school patron to keep his commitment, only to be rebuffed.[25] Where the new arrangements brought about tangible loss of school income, the new fiscal demands could lead to conflict over even the most trivial amounts. In the Bohemian village of Bělušice, for instance, a school was almost closed down because of the outrage over a levy to raise 19 fl among its 300 inhabitants in order to make good on the shortfall in teacher salary. In other places, teach-

---

[20] Böhmische Landtag. "Stenographische Bericht über die XXVIII. Sitzung der dritten Jahres-Session des böhmischen Landtages vom Jahre 1861, am 2. Mai 1864" *Stenographische Protokolle des Böhmischen Landtages. Drittes Jahressession.*, p. 25–28.

[21] Niederösterreichische Landtag. "41. Sitzung der niederösterreichischen Landtages vom 26. Marz 1863." *Stenographische Protokolle der niederösterreichischen Landtage. Zweite Session*, pp. 1053–1055.

[22] See for example, "Organisací národního učitelstva." *Škola a život. Pedagogický časopis.* (7) Sešit IV. 1861, p. 112; Böhmische Landtag. "Stenographische Bericht über die XXVI. Sitzung der dritten Jahres-Session des böhmischen Landtages vom Jahre 1861, am 28. April 1864" *Stenographische Berichte des Böhmischen Landtages*, p. 27.

[23] Böhmische Landtag. "Stenographische Bericht über die XXVI. Sitzung der dritten Jahres-Session des böhmischen Landtages vom Jahre 1861, am 28. April 1864" *Stenographische Berichte des Böhmischen Landtages*, p. 5; Böhmische Landtag. "Stenographische Bericht über die XXVII. Sitzung der dritten Jahres-Session des böhmischen Landtages vom Jahre 1861, am 29. April 1864" *Stenographische Berichte des Böhmischen Landtages*, p. 11.

[24] The law that abolished the patronage explicitly allowed for such voluntary agreements in the apparent expectation that they could soften the transition to purely municipal financing of schools. The villages had an obvious interest in accepting such largesse. See for example "První a poslední slovo", *Pěstoun, vychovatelský časopis* IV (3), 25th January 1865, p. 18.

[25] "Dopisy. Od Čáslavi." *Pěstoun, vychovatelský časopis* IV (15), 25th May 1865, pp. 119–120.

ers were pressured to accept reduced payments.[26]

The village elders quickly realized that they gained power to exert added pressure on teachers now that they controlled appointments – and they drove a hard bargain. Not surprisingly, teachers soon complained that the threat of job loss and the withholding of portions of salary were being used as leverage to make them comply with all kinds of demands, such as to alter the curriculum, to assess children of important parents more leniently and even to help out with agricultural labours in the village.[27] Within a year of the abolition of *Schulpatronat*, the Upper Austrian assembly received a petition of almost 700 teachers demanding a suspension of the municipalities' right of appointment.[28] Moravian teachers were considering a similar petition of their own.[29] It is telling, however, that one of their chief complaints targeted local governments' disregard of seniority when deciding teacher appointments, choosing younger and unmarried candidates over their older counterparts.[30] Such a strategy on the part of municipalities would have been consistent with the aim of reducing school-related outlays since single young teachers were less likely to demand high salaries compared to their older married counterparts. The municipalities may have also reasoned that the younger, more recently educated teachers, having gone through a two-year teacher training instituted in 1849, were better trained than the older teachers who had been certified after a mere three-month course in the pre-1848 era.[31] Clearly, their newly acquired power spawned both abuses as well as a sincere effort to improve local teaching. The dismantling of the decades-old institutional structure brought to the surface the whole tangle of competing interests, and there was not a stakeholder without a grievance.

It was also becoming gradually more apparent that the enhanced powers of municipalities in matters of schooling set them on a collision course with the Church. Teacher appointments could still be vetoed by the Catholic hierarchy, which remained in control of teacher training and teacher certification. The Church also continued to supervise the curriculum, as had been recently reaf-

---

[26] "Příběhy a zábavy školské. Z Bělušic." *Školník – Časopis katolického učitelstva* V (7): 1st March 1865, p. 54; "Příběhy a zábavy školské. Z Heřm. Městce." Ibid.

[27] See "Příběhy a zábavy školské. Od Jizery." *Školník – Časopis katolického učitelstva* V (34): 1st December 1865, p. 270; "Dopisy. Od Čáslavi." *Pěstoun, vychovatelský časopis.* IV (15), 25th May 1865, p. 120; "Was ist der nieder Clerus? (Die Schule. Was sie sein sollte. Was sie ist.)" *Der Publicist* II (10): 20th August 1865, p. 382.

[28] "Mittheilung aus dem oberösterreichischen Landtage des Jahres 1865, Schulangelegenheiten bettrefend (Schluß)" *Die Deutsche Volksschule: Monatschrift für Schule und Haus* 5, March 1866, p. 72–74.

[29] "Zprávy z blízka i zdaleka. Ze Znojma." *Pěstoun, vychovatelský časopis.* IV (14), 15th May 1865, p. 111.

[30] "Dopisy. Od Bečvy." *Pěstoun, vychovatelský časopis* IV (32): 15th November 1865, p. 253–255 and "Dopisy. Z Jičína." *Pěstoun, vychovatelský časopis* IV (33): 25th November 1865, p. 262.

[31] Engelbrecht. *Geschichte des österreichischen Bildungswesens, Vol. 4*, p. 108.

firmed by the Concordat of 1855. While schooling was not that treaty's main focus, it nonetheless gave the Church the power to exclude from the curriculum anything that was contrary to Catholic doctrine.[32]

That was about to change with the secularisation law of 1868, the second of the three reform waves. The immediate impulse was Austria's military defeat at Prussia's hands in 1866. As the finger pointing and the search for culprits (or scapegoats) inevitably set in after the loss, one school-related aspect that kept resurfacing the public debate was the stark difference in literacy between Austrian soldiers and those of other countries: apparently, only 31% of Austrian conscripts could read and write, compared to 96% for Prussia, 88% for Bavaria and 45% for Italy.[33] Austria's relative underperformance could not just be blamed on the southern and eastern provinces where the school network was sparse, for even soldiers from the Alpine provinces lagged behind their foreign counterparts. If the best that the schooling system, shaped by the *Politische Verfassung*, could achieve was a lag behind even Italy (as the liberal politicians argued), surely a reform was needed.[34]

The war also produced the political preconditions for the school reform: the definitive expulsion of Austria from German politics in consequence of the defeat engendered among other things the swift resolution of the empire's constitutional issue in the form of the 1867 Compromise with Hungary. The price that the Austrian urban liberals asked of the emperor in return for their support of the newly established Austro-Hungarian dualism was the creation of a new, liberal constitution, which was duly passed in December 1867.[35] Before the year was out, liberals reached the pinnacle of their power with the appointment of what came to be dubbed the *Bürgerministerium*, or Burgher Cabinet, in reference to the fact that most of its members were commoners as well as urban liberals.[36] It stayed in office for the next two years.

The newly approved constitution, enshrining the modern conceptions of liberal citizenship and civic freedoms, granted all citizens freedom of conscience, of teaching and of expression, and declared all religious creeds equal. This

---

[32] Engelbrecht. *Geschichte des österreichischen Bildungswesens, Vol. 4*, p. 109.

[33] Jellouschek. "Das Reichsvolksschulgesetz", p. 295.

[34] The liberals' emphasis specifically on literacy in this debate was probably more political spin than a genuine argument. First, it is doubtful that Italy was really ahead of Austria in literacy, outside the highly skewed and self-selected sample of army conscripts. Second, even Oskar Peschel, the author of the wisecrack cited in the Introduction (see fn. 9), argued that the Prussian educational advantage rested in subjects like geography and – even more importantly – mathematics, not literacy. See Peschel, Oscar. "Die Lehren der jüngsten Kriegsgeschichte." *Das Ausland: Ueberschau des neuesten Forschungen auf dem Gebiete der Natur-, Erd- und Völkerkunde* 29, 17th July 1866, p. 695.

[35] See Kwan. *Liberalism and the Habsburg Monarchy, 1861–1895*. pp. 46–64. See also Urban. *Česká společnost*, pp. 222–224.

[36] Urban. *Česká společnost*, p. 229.

clashed, if not in letter, then certainly in spirit, with the provisions of the 1855 Concordat.[37] When the controversy surrounding the bill to secularise schooling broke out in full in October 1867, for once the fight was not primarily about money but about control and cultural influence.[38] In some respects, the public debate was reminiscent of the discussions the Austrian policy establishment held a century earlier in the run-up to the 1774 *Allgemeine Schulordnung* of Maria Theresa: it was informed by fears of the erosion of the Catholic Church's cultural hegemony even as a humiliating loss to Prussia revealed the serious lack of basic skills among Austria's soldiers.[39] The fears among conservative Catholics were a predictable political response to the liberals' open anticlericalism. Liberal public opinion considered the Concordat an unacceptable cession of state sovereignty to a foreign power.[40] Consequently, liberal deputies in the *Reichsrat* insisted on returning full control over schooling back to the state whereas conservative deputies fought to preserve the privileges granted to the Catholic Church through the treaty. It was a strange sight: catholic conservatives clothing their arguments in the lofty notions of freedom of religion to fend off governmental power grab, liberals defending the supreme power and authority of the state.[41] On both sides, the arguments were convoluted in a self-serving way. The conservative line of attack against the state's appropriation of the school for its own political purposes (as the conservatives saw it) conveniently omitted that harnessing the school in service of ideological control so as to bolster a (mostly conservative) political status quo had been the purpose of all school-related legislation and policy making from the very beginning. Liberal complaints, that the Church had monopolized all of the power in school oversight at the expense of the state, never acknowledged that it had been the state that had outsourced this control to the Church in the first place.[42]

The secularisation bill proposed to open all public schools to all pupils and all teaching positions to all Austrian citizens, regardless of religion. Textbooks were to be approved only by the civil Ministry of Education, not by any religious authority. Religious supervision was restricted only to religious instruc-

[37] For example, Article 5 of the 1867 constitution granted ultimate control over all education to the state and Article 17 established the freedom of teaching and scientific research, together with the freedom to establish schools. Article 5 of the Concordat, on the other hand, gave the Catholic church the right to prevent the exposure of Catholic youth to anything contrary to the Catholic doctrine in any subject at any school, public or private. See *Staatsgrundgesetze der Österreichischen Monarchie*, p. 98.

[38] The constitution and the secularisation law were discussed almost concurrently: the former was approved in the third reading on 16th, the latter was debated 25th–29th October.

[39] Aliprantis. "The afterlife of Enlightened Absolutism," p. 311; Engelbrecht. *Geschichte Des österreichischen Bildungswesens, Vol. 4*, p. 112; Melton. *Absolutism*, p. 206.

[40] Engelbrecht. *Geschichte des österreichischen Bildungswesens, Vol. 4*, p. 112; Aliprantis. "The afterlife of Enlightened Absolutism," p. 309.

[41] Aliprantis. "The afterlife of Enlightened Absolutism," p. 311–312.

[42] Strakosch-Graßmann. *Geschichte des österreichischen Unterrichswesens*, p. 257.

tion. Next, the bill specified a new, civil structure of school oversight. In each province, the highest instance was to be the provincial school board, which reported directly to the Viennese Ministry of Education. Below it were district and local school boards, whose specific composition and election rules were to be determined by provincial legislation. The only provision with any fiscal consequence was that resources in the former *Studienfond* were made available to all schools regardless of their religious affiliation.

The stenographic record of the *Reichsrat* deliberations did not usually tally votes by name, except when a seemingly narrow voting margin had to be ascertained through a roll-call vote. In the single roll-call vote to have taken place in the secularisation debate, the vote on Article 2 in the second reading, the main opposition came from the landowners' *curia*. Article 2 barred religious influence from all school subjects other than religious instruction. The landowner representatives voted 12 in favour, 25 opposed, whereas urban representatives were 32 in favour and 5 against and Chambers of Commerce members 10 in favour, 2 opposed. The rural curia was split most evenly: 21 for, 22 against.[43] The tally was not all that surprising, given that representatives of the high Church hierarchy belonged in the landowner *curia* and that large landowners generally held conservative opinions on this question. The urban *curia* was overwhelmingly in favour because it was the main reservoir of liberal sentiment. Article 2 passed and the bill as a whole was approved by the end of October 1867. After the Upper Chamber of the Austrian *Reichsrat* inserted a few minor amendments, the emperor signed it into law in May 1868.

Unsurprisingly, the reaction from the Church hierarchy was ferociously negative. The Pope himself expressed his displeasure in June 1868.[44] His declarations against the law strengthened the Austrian Catholics' resolve to fight these changes.[45] In Upper Austria, the controversy escalated into a full-blown showdown between civil authorities and the bishop of Linz, Franz Josef Rudigier. In 1869, a civil court declared his pastoral letters against secularisation subversive and he was sent to jail for two weeks.[46] The trial turned into a spectacle, which more than anything else helped to rally popular opinion against the school legislation. In Tyrol, the locals were openly hostile to the new system of administration. Lay school inspectors, who were now supposed to take over from the

---

[43] Abgeordnetenhaus des Reichsrates. "44. Sitzung des 1. Session am 26. October 1867." *Stenographische Protokolle über die Sitzungen des Hauses der Abgeordneten des Reichsrathes*, p. 1189.

[44] Strakosch-Graßmann. *Geschichte des österreichischen Unterrichswesens*, pp. 259–260.

[45] Jellouschek."Das Reichsvolksschulgesetz," p. 301.

[46] He did not actually serve any prison time, thanks to an immediate pardon by the emperor. Voegler. *Liberalism and the Social Question in the Habsburg Hinterland*, p. 142–162. For a broader context of Rudigier's role in the Austrian "Kulturkampf", see Cole, Laurence. "Chapter II: The Counter-Reformation's last stand: Austria." pp. 299–306.

clerical ones, encountered threats and active opposition and at times even whole districts went without any school inspection for a year or more. In some areas, they required police protection to do their jobs.[47] The "Kulturkampf" was more vehement in Austria than in other German Catholic states, then also reforming their educational systems, partly because the Austrian law was more liberal and pushed secularisation farther than comparable laws in other Catholic countries, such as Bavaria or Baden.[48]

The opposition to the law continued in provincial assemblies, which were tasked with the necessary implementation legislation. As a member of the Upper Austrian assembly, bishop Rudigier declared any such legislation contrary to God's law and therefore not binding for Catholics. In practice, this meant that he expected faithful believers to boycott the newly instituted civic school boards.[49] Tyrolean assemblymen went even farther and tried to subvert the intent of the secularisation law by proposing an implementation legislation, which reinstated the power of the Church. Local and district inspectors were to be drawn exclusively from the ranks of the clergy and the three Tyrolean bishops were granted a veto in the provincial school board.[50] Even though this law passed in Innsbruck, it was immediately declared unconstitutional and Tyrol thus remained without the implementation legislation until 1892. At the same time, the liberal majorities in some other provinces, such as Lower Austria, decided to push the secularisation even further and denied the clergy any representation on school boards at all. The central government rejected such deviations in the opposite direction also, and the legislation did not receive the emperor's sanction until appropriately amended.

The provincial laws, passed between 1869 and 1873, ended up very similar across the provinces. They fleshed out the details of the three-tier administrative system, such as the number of board members, the election rules, the extent of participation of various religious representatives and they enumerated and specified the duties of each administrative layer. The only provincial deviations that received the imperial sanction were those that made allowances for various long-standing peculiarities of local ethnic or religious composition, so as to ensure the proper representation of all key stakeholders.[51]

The third and final round of the reform came in the spring of 1869 in the form of the *Reichsvolksschulgesetz* (Imperial Law on Primary Schools). The government bill was very ambitious in its scope. It enumerated new subjects to be taught in schools, such as history, geography, biology, music and physical education as well as home economics for girls (Art. 3). The law envisioned a

---

[47] Strakosch-Graßmann. *Geschichte des österreichischen Unterrichswesens*, pp. 266–267; Cole. "Chapter II: The Counter-Reformation's last stand: Austria." p. 294.

[48] Engelbrecht. *Geschichte des österreichischen Bildungswesens, Vol. 4*, p. 114.

[49] Strakosch-Graßmann. *Geschichte des österreichischen Unterrichswesens*, p. 261.

[50] Strakosch-Graßmann. *Geschichte des österreichischen Unterrichswesens*, p. 262.

[51] Strakosch-Graßmann. *Geschichte des österreichischen Unterrichswesens*, p. 264.

curriculum split into distinct yearlong grades, with pupils progressing from one to the next, and empowered the education minister to design the respective teaching plans (Art. 4 and 7). This innovation effectively implied the end of half-year teaching. With each grade reserved for exactly one year, pupils would also no longer have to suffer through the tedium of hearing the same content two, three or four times, as had been the practice in numerous rural schools. The Ministry of Education retained ultimate control over textbooks but within the approved list the law left the choice of teaching material to district school boards (Art. 8). The bill also retained the somewhat elevated status of the civic school (*Bürgerschule*), with a more extensive curriculum, which also allowed for classes in accounting and advanced mathematics.

Several provisions directly touched upon the financial requirements of the new school. By Article 11, a teacher was to be hired for every 80 pupils, with no more than a third of the staff consisting of uncertified teaching assistants or teaching candidates. The cost implications of this regulation were amplified by the extension of primary school age to 6–14 years (Art. 21). The demand for teachers and the related outlays were bound to increase significantly. Perhaps in view of the scale of the extra fiscal burden, Article 75 granted several provinces an exemption from this provision, and they made use of it: through their later provincial legislation, Galicia, Bukovina, Carniola and the Austrian Littoral reduced the school years back to six, as had been the case before 1869. The bill also pushed aggressively for a denser school network by mandating a new school for every 40 pupils who were unschooled and currently lived more than half an Austrian mile (≈ 3.8 km) from an existing school (Art. 59). The bill left unspecified how all these new demands were to be financed – provincial legislation was to fill in the details.

The ministry continued to press its secularising agenda through the proposal, devoting considerable attention to the situation of teachers. Teacher training courses were now extended to four years and open to all applicants over 15 years, regardless of confession (Articles 28 and 32). The government accepted financial responsibility for the training centres and reserved the right to appoint both their directors and the teaching staff (including the religious instructors!), thus effectively ousting the Church from teacher training throughout the empire (Art. 35 and 67). The training courses were to be tuition-free. Teaching was declared a public office and thus open to all regardless of religion. While the specifics of teacher pay and its sources were left to provinces to determine, the bill nonetheless entitled teachers and their widows to a pension and also gave them a measure of protection against arbitrary dismissal. Article 45 instituted regular teacher conferences in each district, which were empowered to make recommendations regarding textbook selection and the method of instruction. All in all, almost half the bill was devoted to teacher-related matters, with the clear intent of turning them into modern, professional public servants, with appropriate qualifications, prestige and morale-enhancing *esprit de corps*.

In a section that proved important in the subsequent development of the school network, the proposed bill acknowledged the existence of private schools and regulated their integration with the rest of the system. These schools could not deviate much from the official curriculum and their teachers had to be certified in the same way as all public school teachers. They were also subject to the same rules of supervision and inspection as state schools. But the private schools were granted complete autonomy in the language of instruction as well as the privilege of religious restriction in hiring and admissions, which proved so crucial in later decades.

When the bill came up for plenary debate in April 1869, the opposition criticized it on three grounds: federalism, clericalism and realism.[52] The federalist critique, formulated right from the debate's outset by Galician representatives, held that the Viennese government egregiously overstepped its constitutional boundaries with this bill. Within Austria's newly approved constitutional framework, the *Reichsrat* had the right to determine no more than "the basic underlying principles of elementary schooling" while everything else, including all details, were the preserve of provincial assemblies.[53] A bill that aimed to fix minute details such as the pupil-teacher ratios or the range of compulsory school age was surely over that line, they argued.[54] This argument split the vote in the chamber along geographic lines, with representatives from the core Austrian provinces, such as Lower Austria and Moravia, favouring centralistic tendencies, whereas representatives from provinces with the prospect or the tradition of autonomy, including Tyrol and Galicia, opposed them.

The clericalist opposition mostly recycled the objections presented already in relation to the secularisation law. Supporters of the Catholic Church invoked the liberal constitutional freedoms of religious expression and conscience as bulwarks against what they considered government intrusion into matters of faith. The Tyrolean representative Greuter asserted that "schooling is nothing more than family upbringing, organised on a societal level", from which he inferred that government had no business mandating secular education because it was the parents' sole prerogative to decide how they wanted their children brought up.[55] Even Protestants, such as the Silesian representative Schneider, who counted himself a liberal and ended up supporting the bill, spoke against the overarching and exclusive supervisory powers of the state. Pleading for the

---

[52] Jellouschek."Das Reichsvolksschulgesetz," pp. 299–302.

[53] The opposing speeches relentlessly referred to Article 11.i. of the 1867 Law on Representation from which the quoted formulation is taken. See *Staatsgrundgesetze der Österreichischen Monarchie*, p. 92.

[54] See for example, the speech of urban representative Sawczynski from Galicia. Abgeordnetenhaus des Reichsrates. "189. Sitzung der 1. Session am 21. April 1869." *Stenographische Protokolle des Abgeordnetenhauses des Reichsrates*. p. 5736.

[55] Abgeordnetenhaus des Reichsrates. "190. Sitzung der 1. Session am 22. April 1869." *Stenographische Protokolle des Abgeordnetenhauses des Reichsrates*. p. 5748.

autonomy of religious communities in matters of school oversight, Schneider argued that in a majority-Catholic country, such as Austria, even purportedly secular state supervision of Protestant schools would inevitably mean Catholic supervision in effect.[56]

Finally, the opposition grounded in "realism" raised the objection that the school reform was not practically enforceable and implementable. Many speakers alluded to the increased financial demands that the proposed requirements would place on the shoulders of the towns and villages.[57] The unofficial leader of the opposition to the whole school reform, the Tyrolean university professor Albert Jäger, presented his calculations of the expected cost increase, arguing that the Tyrolean elementary schooling outlays would rise from 203000 fl to 816000 fl, and warned that rural communities would have to "sweat blood" to meet such financial requirements.[58] It was not clear that the expanded elementary school could bring about extra benefits large enough to justify this increased spending. Professor Jäger claimed that elementary schooling was "overrated" and that in "our school-crazed times", government imposed parameters well beyond what was appropriate.[59]

It is not surprising that the Tyrolean representatives (not just Jäger) were particularly agitated about this: most of Tyrol's schools operated on a half-year basis, which was obviously cheaper than the full-year instruction that the bill demanded, and there were strong economic pressures to keep it that way, namely the widespread employment of children in cattle herding over the summer.[60] Moreover, the Tyrolean schools seemed actually rather effective in achieving what was considered their primary goal: teaching religion and literacy. As Chapter 6 showed, Tyrol had one of the best literacy records in the empire, with not much more than 4 years of effective school time per pupil (see Figure 6.4).[61] All that expansion along so many different dimensions seemed like yet

[56] Abgeordnetenhaus des Reichsrates. "189. Sitzung der 1. Session am 21. April 1869." *Stenographische Protokolle des Abgeordnetenhauses des Reichsrates*. p. 5727–28.

[57] They hailed from all parts of the empire: concerns about the costs were expressed by representative Pascotini from Trieste, Schneider from Silesia, Bauer from Carinthia, or the Upper Austrian assemblyman Huemer (when discussing the implementation legislation in 1870). See Abgeordnetenhaus des Reichsrates. "189. Sitzung", p. 5735, 5737; "190. Sitzung" p. 5744; Strakosch-Graßmann. *Geschichte des österreichischen Unterrichswesens*, p. 271.

[58] Abgeordnetenhaus des Reichsrates. "191. Sitzung" p. 5786.

[59] Abgeordnetenhaus des Reichsrates. "191. Sitzung", p. 5781.

[60] See Chapter 5 for details on the *Schwabenkinder*.

[61] This point was raised during the debate, when a proponent of the school reform, representative Ignaz Figuly von Szep, emphasised its urgency by quoting the mediocre-to-bad literacy rates, revealed by the recent conscription drive. Next to 96% literacy reported from Lower Austria and 89% in Upper Austria, he noted the mere 46% literacy among Moravian conscripts, 4% among Galician and Bukovinaer conscripts and 2% among Dalmatian ones. Challenged to quote the Tyrolean rate, Figuly von Szep conceded that, coincidentally, it "was

another wasteful liberal vanity project. Surveying the list of subjects that the government bill sought to introduce into the curriculum, Jäger asked rhetorically: how useful will any of these be in the remote Alpine valleys?[62]

They could be useful, however, in the industrializing cities. Without quite spelling it out, the Tyrolean representative touched upon an important way by which the rural communities were likely to be doubly hit by the bill's new demands. The increased educational standards in both rural and urban schools combined with the strong and persistent migration to the cities added up to an implicit subsidy that the country would pay to the city: if the law were fully enforced, the villages would end up paying for the schooling of productive young workers who would then have a strong incentive to move to the city to earn a return on their skill in the more skill-intensive urban labour market. This was more than just a theoretical possibility: these migration flows were quite apparent in the contemporary demographic record and, in fact, obvious to anyone who cared to visit the booming suburbs of Vienna, Trieste or Brno. As Table 2.5 in Chapter 2 illustrated, Vienna was the destination of throngs of young men (and quite a few young women), many of whom apparently set out for the city shortly after finishing their elementary education. The same pattern, although to a lesser degree, operated in other, smaller towns all around the monarchy. For example, the demographic record of Liberec, the North-Bohemian textile centre of over 20000 inhabitants, shows that of the 6700 boys and girls born in 1851–1860 around 3900 survived to school age.[63] But by 1869, the 1850s birth cohorts comprised 4700 of the city's inhabitants, which grew to 5400 by 1880 – a 15% increase in 11 years, and all through migration.

All things considered, the rural representatives had good reason to oppose the legislation on economic grounds: it brought potentially high costs to their constituents but doubtful benefits. Given the growing ease of migration and the boom in urban industry, the incentives regarding school expansion in the countryside were downright perverse: the more education the rural children would receive, the more likely they were to migrate. The most talented rural pupils were practically guaranteed to leave, if they decided to continue with their studies, because the secondary schools were all in the towns. Of course, in terms of population proportions, the rural-urban migration was a bigger boon to cities than it was a loss to the countryside. This implies that the countryside's

---

not available." He should have looked in the cabinet's initial report that motivated the whole reform effort: it put Tyrol's conscript literacy at 37% (next to Salzburg's 60%, Styria's 50% and Carinthia's 20%). The reliability of these figures as indicators of population-wide literacy was of course seriously compromised by the inevitable lack of representativeness due to selection. See Abgeordnetenhaus des Reichsrates. "191. Sitzung", p. 5777; Jellouschek. "Das Reichsvolks-schulgesetz", p. 295.

[62] Abgeordnetenhaus des Reichsrates. "191 Sitzung", p. 5781.

[63] Reichenberger Stadtrath. *Reichenberg in der Zeit der Selbstverwaltung vom Jahre 1850 bis 1900*. p. 101–103.

Table 7.1: Schooling situation and reform implications in rural and urban electoral districts in 1865

	Rural districts	Urban districts	t-test	p-value
Number of observations	70	49		
Average number of grades	2.05	3.40	-14.45	0.000
Proportion of schools teaching full-time	0.58	0.95	-7.43	0.000
Expenditure on teaching staff per pupil	2.13	4.64	-8.75	0.000
Pupils per teacher	72.80	64.36	1.61	0.110
Expected cost increase due to reform (*ECI*)	2.27	1.45	2.73	0.007
Literacy content of the local labor market (*LC*)	0.15	0.23	-6.27	0.000
Index of religious homogeneity	0.86	0.85	0.13	0.894

Source: Cvrček and Zajíček. "The making of a liberal education", Table 4.

bigger worry was the increased cost of schooling rather than the forgone benefits resulting from emigration.[64] The flipside of the rural opposition was, naturally, the eagerness of the urban constituency to impose better schooling across the board, especially if the financing would remain local. The Liberec example above shows that rural migrants, coming to the cities in their prime age, could form a sizeable portion of the urban labour market.

Available measures of both the cost hike implied by the legislation and the labour market demand for skill indicate that the difference between the city and the country was substantial. Table 7.1 compares the schooling situation in districts belonging in the urban curia in the *Reichsrat* against those in the rural curia. The first four variables cited in the table describe the situation as it was reported in the 1865 school census. It is clear that the urban schools already had a richer curriculum, were more likely to teach year-round and spent more mon-

[64] In 1869, about 2.12 million people lived in towns of 10000 inhabitants or more – about 10.3% of the total population of Imperial Austria, the western half of Austria-Hungary. By 1880, this share increased to 13.4%, or 2.97 million people. At the same time, about 13.3 million lived in villages of less than 2000 inhabitants in 1869, and 13.8 million did in 1880. (This leaves about 5 million in municipalities of 2000 to 10000 inhabitants). Even if the towns experienced no natural population growth at all and all of their 0.85 million gain came in the form of immigration from the countryside, such migration flow would imply a loss of only 6.4% of the rural population over a decade. The actual net migration inflow was lower; the precise estimate would depend on one's assumptions about the natural population increase in the urban areas. My best guess is that between 1869 and 1880 about a net 0.4 million people migrated from small (under 2000 inhabitants) villages to large (over 10000 inhabitants) towns. (The middle category of municipalities with 2000–10000 inhabitants grew roughly in line with the country's overall population increase, which implies that net migration was a minor factor.) This net 0.4 million migration represented a net loss amounting to 3.0% of the rural population and a gain equaling almost 20% of the population of the towns. See *Bevölkerung der Gemeinden mit mehr als 2000 Einwohnern*, 1881.

ey on a per-pupil basis. The overall provision was simply better in cities than in the countryside. The next two measures speak to the considerations implied by the reform. The expected cost increase (*ECI*) due to reform measures how much the staff costs would grow, if the reform bill were implemented and enforced. A value of 1.45 for urban districts means that, on average, the expenditure on teachers in those districts would increase by 45%. In the rural areas, it would more than double, increasing by 127%.

This cost measure is constructed using the parameters specified in the reform bill. It is a straightforward back-of-the-envelope calculation that the representatives could have conceivably made themselves, using the 1865 school data:

$$ECI = \left(\frac{\frac{\frac{4}{3}P_{6-12}}{80}}{T_{1865}}\right)\left[1 + 0.4\max\left(0, s - \frac{1}{3}\right)\right](1 + h)$$

To calculate the expected cost increase (*ECI*) due to reform, start with the number of children aged 6–12 in a district in 1865 ($P_{6\text{–}12}$), multiply by 4/3 to adjust for the extension of compulsory school years from six to eight. Then divide by 80, the newly proposed binding pupil-teacher ratio. That yields the number of teachers that would be required, once the reform passed. Divide that further by the number of teaching staff actually available in the district in 1865 (T_{1865}), obtaining the factor by which the teaching staff would have to grow in consequence of the reform. The square brackets of the formula reflect the stipulation that no more than a third of the teaching staff could be assistant teachers or teaching candidates. Since the gap between teacher salary and assistant salary amounted to about 40%, the predicted cost increase of the reform must account for the resulting cost of replacing assistants with certified teachers. Finally, the teacher expenditure would increase in consequence of converting half-year schools into full-year schools. So, if the proportion of teachers at half-year schools, h, were close to 1 (as it was in Tyrol, for example), the full-year conversion alone was going to double the outlays just by itself. To give a hypothetical example: if a representative came from a district where all schools were half-year schools and were just barely satisfying the existing regulation of 100 pupils per teacher, then the implementation of this reform would have implied that the costs would jump up (i) by one third to accommodate the extension of school years from six to eight, (ii) by another quarter on top of that to satisfy the more stringent pupil-teacher ratio of 80 and (iii) by a further 100% to convert all half-year schools into full-year schools – a combined (4/3)×(5/4)×2 = 3.33-fold cost increase. Note, however, that the formula makes no allowance for a change in teacher salaries – after all, the proposed law made no pronouncements on this issue, so the best approach was to calculate the expected cost hike taking salaries as fixed at the current level.

Overall, 165 of the 185 actively participating representatives in the *Reichsrat* represented districts with an *ECI* higher than one, meaning their teacher-related expenditures were bound to increase, but there was appreciable variation: 23 of them hailed from districts where the costs could be expected to rise more than threefold. Most of these were in Galicia, a large, sparsely schooled province.[65] At the extreme end of the spectrum stood the rural district of Dąbrowa and Żabno, where the school network was so thin on the ground, the full implementation of the reform would have meant a 14-fold cost hike. Its representative, Stanisław Morgenstern, did not support the reform. At the other end of the range were a few districts with *ECI* values lower than one, since their school network was already quite dense, e.g. Vienna, Graz or Krakow. But even here the values were generally above 0.9.

The next measure reported in Table 7.1 captures the potential benefits of the school reform. The index of literacy content of the local labour market (*LC*) takes on a value between 0 and 1, depending on how much local employers needed literate workers. It is the same measure as has already been used in chapters 5 and 6. It relies on David Mitch's classification of 19th century occupations into four groups on the basis of their use of literacy: those that definitely required literacy (e.g. teachers, preachers, clerks), those that likely required literacy, those where the use of literacy was ambiguous and those that definitely did not require literacy. The more literacy-based jobs in a district, the higher the value of the index: a value of 1 would imply that all the jobs in a district required literacy, while 0 means that no job did. Table 7.1 shows that there was a clear difference between the rural and urban districts and that the difference was quite large and statistically significant. The index – unsurprisingly – reached the highest values (above 0.3) in the metropolitan areas, such as Vienna, Trieste, Brno, Olomouc, Krakow.[66]

These two variables are constructed so as to reflect the economic arguments presented by the "realist" critics of the proposed school reform. Table 7.1 also reports a Herfindahl index of religious homogeneity, which speaks to the clericalist critique. It is another measure spanning the [0, 1] interval, such that the value of 1 implies a complete religious homogeneity of a district and the lower the value, the greater the fragmentation. The basis for this index is the infor-

[65] Interestingly, Jäger's protestations to the contrary, the expectable cost increase in Tyrol was unlikely to be as high: most Tyrolean schools were small and could easily absorb the extra two birth cohorts, resulting from the introduction of eight-year schooling, without running afoul the new pupil-teacher ratio. For Tyrol, the bigger cost issue stemmed from phasing out the half-year schools, but such move would at most double the outlays, not quadrupled as Jäger argued. Given the already dense extant school network, most Tyrolean districts faced a potential cost hike on the order of 30%.

[66] Note that the average and standard deviation of *LC* in Table 7.1 differs from that in Table 6.7. This is because the electoral districts (used in Table 7.1) and school districts (used in Table 6.7) were not always the same territorial units.

mation on religious composition of the population from the 1869 census. Table 7.1 shows that the degree of religious homogeneity was quite high in both city and country and that there was no sizeable rural-urban divide. The lowest values for this index were observed in Galicia, where Roman Catholics mingled with Orthodox believers as well as a sizeable Jewish minority.

While the table effectively documents certain important differences between the city and the country, it cannot say anything about how powerful they were in determining the vote on the reform. The curial electoral rules had built into the system specific sectoral interests, namely those of large landowners, those of big business etc. The allocation of representatives by province guaranteed that regional interests, too, would find their proper expression. But with respect to the school reform bill, there existed considerable variation in costs and benefits, both within *curias* and within provinces, which opened up the possibility of a breakdown of the strict voting along curial and provincial lines.

By a fortunate coincidence, the final vote on the school reform bill was a roll-call vote, meaning that the session's stenographic protocol preserved the voting record by name. On the 24th April 1869, after three days of heated general debate, the session's chairman opened the special debate about the bill's individual articles. Previous discussion had shown that the objections to the bill were numerous and strongly held, especially by representatives from Galicia, Tyrol and Carniola. The day before, the liberal representative Figuly von Szep who had steered the bill through the *Reichsrat*'s confessional committee hoped to defuse the tensions by inviting the opponents to propose amendments, so as to make the reform more palatable to them.[67] But as the special debate started, it became clear that his outreach effort fell on deaf ears. While the first article of the bill was being voted on, a large number of deputies walked out of the chamber in protest, ostensibly on constitutional grounds. To ensure that the votes of the remaining representatives were counted properly and to ascertain beyond doubt that the body was quorate after the walkout, the presiding officer ordered a roll-call vote in the third reading, taking place that same day. Thanks to this decision we know who voted which way. Thus, on that day, the law passed with the support of 111 representatives while 4 voted against and 70 were recorded as absent.

In Table 7.2, that final vote is analysed in the context of a probit analysis. The dependent variable is equal to 1 if a representative voted in favour of the reform and 0 otherwise. Columns (i) and (ii) report how much of the voting decision could be explained only through the *curia* membership. The rural *curia*, missing from the table, is the benchmark against which the others are compared. Column (ii) shows that the urban *curia* was the most supportive of the measure: urban representatives were, on average, 30.4% more likely to vote in favour than the representatives of the rural *curia*. Even the large landowners

---

[67] Abgeordnetenhaus des Reichsrates. "191. Sitzung", p. 5774.

Table 7.2: Probit model of voting on school reform, 1869

	Curial fixed effects only		Province fixed effects only		Cost-benefit variables only		Full specification	
	(i)	(ii)	(iii)	(iv)	(v)	(vi)	(vii)	(viii)
	Coeffs.	Avg. MFX	Coeffs.	Avg. MFX	Coeffs.	Avg. MFX	Coeffs.	Avg. MFX
Curial fixed effects								
Landowners' curia	0.306	0.121					0.295	0.071
	[0.228]	[0.090]					[0.306]	[0.074]
Chambers of Commerce curia	0.502	0.195					0.404	0.095
	[0.403]	[0.149]					[0.504]	[0.112]
Urban curia	0.829*	0.304*					0.781*	0.169*
	[0.249]	[0.084]					[0.385]	[0.080]
Province fixed effects (selected provinces)								
Galicia			-2.780*	-0.774*			-1.422	-0.407
			[0.482]	[0.068]			[0.727]	[0.231]
Carniola			-1.809*	-0.633*			-1.840*	-0.512*
			[0.649]	[0.165]			[0.723]	[0.162]
Tyrol & Vorarlberg			-1.095*	-0.400*			-1.605*	-0.456*
			[0.460]	[0.167]			[0.544]	[0.123]
Austrian Littoral			-0.842	-0.300			-1.093	-0.312
			[0.559]	[0.214]			[0.649]	[0.189]
Salzburg			-0.411	-0.133			-1.011	-0.287
			[0.782]	[0.279]			[0.864]	[0.249]
Cost-benefit variables								
Literacy content of local labor market (*LC*)					2.674	0.845	-0.711	-0.153
					[1.806]	[0.559]	[2.847]	[0.614]
Expected cost increase (*ECI*)					-0.325*	-0.103*	-0.642*	-0.138*
					[0.139]	[0.042]	[0.280]	[0.057]
Index of religious homogeneity					2.151*	0.680*	2.872	0.620
					[0.654]	[0.188]	[1.667]	[0.352]
Constant	-0.072		0.842		-1.431		-0.891	
	[0.150]		[0.226]		[0.842]		[1.574]	
N	185		174		185		174	
Log-likelihood	-118.6		-74.6		-102.8		-68.0	

Note: The dependent variable is equal to 1 if a representative voted in favour of the school reform, 0 otherwise. "Avg. MFX" is short for average marginal fixed effects. Of the 203 constitutionally mandated *Reichsrat* seats, 18 were unoccupied either due to a boycott of the institution (Czech nationalists) or a recent death or promotion of the representative, for whom no replacement had been sworn in yet: hence 185 observations in columns (i) and (v). Silesia (6 representatives) and Bukovina (5) voted unanimously in favour, meaning their probit coefficients could not be estimated and these 11 observations were dropped: hence 174 observations in columns (iii) and (vii). Standard errors are reported in square brackets. An asterisk (*) denotes statistical significance at 5%.

Source: Cvrček and Zajíček. "The making of a liberal education", Table 5.

and the Chamber of Commerce representatives were more supportive of the bill than the rural ones but the difference is not statistically significant. The result is consistent with the notion, explained earlier, that rural and urban representatives were likely to be the most "politically distant" on this issue across the four *curias*.

The specification reported in columns (iii) and (iv) considers the regional aspect, listing only those provinces that had the most negative attitude towards the reform. With Bohemia, one of the most pro-reform provinces, serving as a benchmark, the average marginal effects show how much less likely a particular province was to support the bill than Bohemia. (Provinces that are not listed in the table did not significantly differ from Bohemia, whether in the statistical or practical sense.) Among those where the opposition was strong, only in Tyrol & Vorarlberg, Galicia and Carniola was the difference statistically significant. Galician representatives were, on average, 77.4% less likely to support the bill than Bohemian ones. No province was unanimous in its opposition – at least one supporter was found even among the Tyroleans and the Galicians. On the other side, all Bukovina and Silesian representatives voted in favour. The variation in support across provinces therefore spanned a wide range.

So did the fiscal implications of the reform. The third specification, in columns (v) and (vi), brings in the costs and benefits. As predicted, representatives coming from districts with more sophisticated, literacy-intensive labour markets (higher *LC*) were more likely to support the reform. With a marginal effect of +0.845, a higher literacy content index by 0.1 would boost the probability of a representative's supportive vote by about 8.45% on average. That is a non-negligible impact in absolute value but the estimate's high standard error indicates that it is not very firmly or precisely estimated. In contrast, the expected cost increase (*ECI*) has a more definite and systematic negative impact. Here, a negative average marginal effect of -0.103 implies that a representative from a district where the schooling outlays were expected to double ($ECI = 2$) was about 10.3% less likely to vote in favour compared to a colleague representing a district that was likely to be fiscally unaffected ($ECI = 1$), other things equal. According to Table 7.1, the rural-urban gap in average *ECI* equalled 0.82: this would translate to about 8.4% difference in likelihood of support between the city and the country. The last in this batch of variables is the index of religious homogeneity, which is not a cost or benefit measure, strictly speaking, but a control variable accounting for the reform's consequences for the Church's power and prestige. There is no clear prior about which way the impact of this control should go: one could imagine that representatives of highly homogenous districts would be more likely to defend the religious and cultural hegemony of the Church and therefore be more likely to oppose the law. That should produce a large negative coefficient. On the other hand, it could be that districts where the Catholic faith was overwhelmingly dominant felt less insecure about the potential erosion of the Church's position, relative to districts that were more heterogeneous, and would therefore be more likely to vote for the reform. Moreover, more homogenous polities are generally more likely and more willing to engage in public expenditure with potentially redistributive consequences, which in the context of the 1869 school reform would mean that such districts would be more prepared to shoulder the burden of extra costs for the expanded schooling.[68] In such a case, the coefficient would be positive. As it turns out, the index of religious homogeneity has a high and positive coefficient and marginal effect. Consider two hypothetical districts, one with a 90% Catholic majority and 10% Orthodox minority and another with a 99% Catholic majority and only 1% Orthodox minority. The first, less homogenous one, would have a religious homogeneity index of 0.82; the second 0.98. With an average marginal effect of +0.680, the probit model in columns (v) and (vi) indicates that a representative from the more homogenous district would be on average 10.9% more likely to support the law, *ceteris paribus*. Of the three variables in this specification, the expected cost increase can explain the largest proportion of the extant political differences in the *Reichsrat* because it varied the most. As for the other two, most of Austria's districts were relatively homogenous religiously and rather unsophisticated in terms of their labour markets.[69] Even with large coefficients and marginal effects that these two variables have, little variation on the ground cannot but translate into rather small variation in political position.

In the last two columns in Table 7.2, the sectoral, regional and practical aspects are all brought together. If the cost-benefit considerations were the real cause behind the voting pattern, the cost-benefit variables should go some way towards explaining away the disparities between provinces and *curias* observed in columns (i) – (iv). That is, indeed, one of the conclusions emerging from columns (vii) and (viii). The average marginal effects of the *curias* all decrease from column (ii) to column (viii). Whereas in column (ii) the biggest gap – that between the rural *curia* and the urban *curia* – equals 30.4%, in column (viii) it falls to 16.9%. The chasm between the provinces also narrowed down between column (iv) and column (viii). The inclusion of the cost-benefit variables apparently both captured part of the political difference between the city and the country as well as accounting for some of the opposition coming from Galicia and Carniola. Conversely, the marginal effects of Salzburg, Tyrol & Vorarlberg and the Austrian Littoral increased in absolute size, suggesting that once the net effect of the fiscal matters is controlled for, there remained an even deeper wellspring of opposition arising from province-specific factors. Perhaps in contrast to Galicia and Carniola, the constitutional and cultural objections reso-

---

[68] See Alesina et al. "Public goods and ethnic divisions".

[69] Half of the representatives hailed from districts with an index of religious fragmentation falling between 0.92 and 1 and literacy content index between 0.12 and 0.17 – quite narrow ranges.

Table 7.3: Predicted probability of supporting the school reform, 1869

	ECI = 1	*ECI* = 2	*ECI* = 3
Bohemia			
Rural curia	0.840	0.638	0.387
Landowning curia	0.902	0.742	0.503
Chambers of Commerce curia	0.919	0.776	0.546
Urban curia	0.962	0.872	0.689
Salzburg			
Rural curia	0.494	0.256	0.097
Landowning curia	0.610	0.359	0.158
Chambers of Commerce curia	0.651	0.400	0.185
Urban curia	0.778	0.549	0.302
Carniola			
Rural curia	0.199	0.069	0.017
Landowning curia	0.292	0.117	0.033
Chambers of Commerce curia	0.330	0.140	0.042
Urban curia	0.475	0.240	0.089

Note: The imputation relies on coefficients from column (vii) of Table 7.2, assuming median values for the index of religious fragmentation (0.92) and for the index of literacy content of the local labour market (0.16). *ECI* stands for expected cost increase.

nated in these other three provinces more than the costs and benefits, which were not as important to them. All three were bastions of traditional Catholicism and homes to ancient bishoprics and archbishoprics.

The inclusion of curial and provincial fixed effects also affected the estimated impact of the cost-benefit variables. Both the literacy content index and the religious homogeneity index lost their statistical significance and decreased in size. The coefficient on literacy content, in fact, turns negative but since the marginal effect is so small in absolute size (-0.153), the implication is that the practical impact of this variable is effectively zero. In other words, the explanatory power of the literacy content index does not survive the inclusion of the *curia* and province fixed effects. Something similar can be said about the religious homogeneity index, whose impact also becomes less clear in column (viii). The average marginal effect of +0.620 is still relatively high but with a large standard error around it, one cannot reject, at reasonable levels of significance, the hypothesis that it was zero (or that it was twice its size, for that matter).

On the other hand, the marginal effect of the expected cost increase stays robustly negative in column (viii) and even increases in absolute size a little compared to column (vi). Since the probit model is a non-linear one and the average marginal effects therefore do not fully convey the varying sensitivity of the outcome to changes in the explanatory variables, Table 7.3 presents a series of imputed probabilities for several different hypothetical *Reichsrat* representatives, using the coefficients from column (vii) in Table 7.2. Holding everything else constant within each line, I allow the expected cost increase (*ECI*) to vary from 1 to 3 – roughly the 10th and 90th percentile of *ECI* observed across the representatives in the *Reichsrat*. The purpose of the exercise is to compare the impact of the cost consideration against the sectoral and provincial differences. Of the three provinces shown, Bohemia voted overwhelmingly in favour of the reform, whereas Carniola was strongly against and Salzburg stood somewhere in between the two. If the reform had no financial implications in his district (*ECI* = 1), a hypothetical rural representative from Bohemia could have been expected to support the reform with a probability of 0.840, i.e. a very likely vote in favour. In a similar situation, his Carniolan counterpart could offer no more than a 0.199 chance of support, or an almost equally likely vote against. That is a difference of 64 percentage points! But the table shows that the Bohemian rural representative would have moved from strong support to moderate opposition, if *ECI* rose to 3 – a decline in support probability by 45.3 percentage points. In the Salzburg urban *curia*, the same change in *ECI* could produce a swing from 0.778 probability of support to only 0.302 – a decrease of 47.6 percentage points. Apart from Carniola and Tyrol which were the real holdouts, the differences between the remaining provinces were smaller, whereas the *ECI* variation played out with equal force across all of them, meaning that the cost considerations generated much bigger movements in the predicted likelihood of support. This variation was also greater than any difference between the *curias*. In short, with the exception of the implacable resistance of a few provinces, the costs mattered more than any other factor.

This is an important conclusion because it reorders the usual ranking of what were perceived to be the prime movers on this issue. Recall that the larger part of the fiery rhetoric during the parliamentary debates dwelt on the constitutional and religious issues and most histories of the school reform, too, focus on the "Kulturkampf" aspect of it. Overall, of course, the probit models still bear out statistically what the primary sources revealed directly: constitutionally, the sharpest division opened up between centralizers and autonomists, which ran along provincial lines; socioeconomically, the main rift lay between city and country and an important reason behind it was money. But the value-added of the probit estimation is in gauging how much those cost issues drove overall political differences across the whole *Reichsrat*. It would be easy to treat the conflict of city and country as aligning neatly with the conservative and the progressive elements of Austrian society and interpret it as a clash of values or worldviews. Instead, the probit analysis puts their respective positions on school reform down to a more mundane economic calculus.

The economic explanation notwithstanding, the rural-urban cleavage signified an important shift in the politics of education over the course of the century since Maria Theresa's reform. In contrast to its beginnings, when elementary schooling was basically an elite imposition on the passive masses, the political debates in 1868–1869 showed that the old elites – the landed aristocracy – were actually on the sidelines of this debate and not all that interested. Chapter 3 showed that the landed elites had been unexceptional but certainly decent stewards of their duties in regards to schools. The school network, such as it was, owed its existence and sustained operation, to a considerable degree, to their patronage and largesse. By the 1860s, the aristocrats were glad to be rid of any direct financial responsibilities in this matter but they did not become active opponents of school expansion even though, as large landowners and employers of rural labour, they may well have shared the misgivings about the school as a gateway to city-bound migration. Instead, the landowner *curia*, which was the obvious vehicle of political influence for the traditional landowning elite across all Austria's elected bodies, struck out a position that was remarkably inconspicuous and middle-of-the-road. As a political constituency, the nobles had no strong opinion either way, were not prominent among the determined opposition as might be expected of a political constituency often viewed as a conservative bulwark and, in fact, ended up voting mildly in favour overall: with 32 out of 54 landowners supporting the 1869 law, their share of pro-votes (59%) was practically indistinguishable from the overall tally (60%). In column (viii) of Table 7.2, the marginal effect of the landowner curia is not statistically different either from the urban curia, or from the rural curia – they were almost perfectly in the middle. The Crown, too, was prepared to go along with the results of the *Reichsrat* deliberations. Clearly, by the late 1860s, the fight over education was no longer a conflict between the masses and the elites but between urban masses and rural masses: the two "most mass" *curias* were also the two most polarized.

As the law passed through the Austrian upper house and received the emperor's sanction, it was clear that the cities won this round. The conflict did not die down with the passage, however, precisely because the most disaffected constituency – the rural communities – was also the most populous. The resistance could rely on broad support. Treating all *Reichsrat* representatives as equals (which they were in the context of the parliamentary procedure) obscures the crucial feature of the electoral system, which is that they were not, in fact, representing comparable numbers of voters. Unequal suffrage was, of course, the whole point of splitting voters into *curias*, so that "politically reliable" constituencies could wield disproportionate influence. As of the 1867 elections, over 1 million voters elected their representatives in the rural *curia*, compared to 162000 voters in the urban *curia*, 4943 in the landowner *curia* and 587 in the Chambers of Commerce *curia*.[70] When it came to implementation – electing local school boards, approving local taxes, reconstructing and extending the village schools – an active cooperation of a large part of ordinary citizens was required. But those were also the ones most apprehensive about the new law.

[70] See Cvrček and Zajíček. "The making of a liberal education", Table 1.

Table 7.4: Consequences of the school reform, 1865–1880

	Districts with towns…		1865	1871	1875	1880
average grades per school	…under 5000	inhabitants	1.97	1.41	1.62	1.73
	…of 5–20000		2.06	1.62	1.88	2.06
	…over 20000		2.70	3.48	4.05	4.38
teachers per 1000 pupils	…under 5000	inhabitants	12.62	11.46	12.84	12.87
	…of 5–20000		11.77	11.13	12.39	13.04
	…over 20000		15.04	17.54	19.06	18.65
salary per teacher (fl per year)	…under 5000	inhabitants	171.20	352.77	437.23	540.90
	…of 5–20000		213.61	359.61	486.11	575.21
	…over 20000		309.79	412.75	770.67	899.68
salary expenditure per pupil (fl per year)	…under 5000	inhabitants	2.16	4.04	5.61	6.96
	…of 5–20000		2.51	4.00	6.02	7.50
	…over 20000		4.66	7.24	14.69	16.78
enrolment in public schools (% of 6–14 YO)	…under 5000	inhabitants	66.1%	69.1%	79.5%	84.6%
	…of 5–20000		65.5%	67.1%	76.4%	81.2%
	…over 20000		55.2%	53.2%	68.0%	73.8%
enrolment in private schools (% of 6–14 YO)	…under 5000	inhabitants	0.0%	1.2%	1.7%	1.5%
	…of 5–20000		<1.0%	2.5%	2.7%	2.3%
	…over 20000		<1.0%	9.7%	10.2%	7.6%

Note: All statistics refer to public schools, except the last three lines. Data pertain to 273 school districts across all Austrian provinces, except Galicia where the new civil school districts were not in place in time.
Source: Cvrček and Zajíček. "The making of a liberal education", Table 9.

The countryside adopted, to a lesser or greater degree, the same posture that it had resorted to on so many previous occasions: a posture of passive resistance, which hindered further development of the elementary school system. Table 7.4 offers some indication as to which aspects of the reform encountered most of that resistance. Here I divide the newly created civil school districts into three groups by the degree of urbanisation, measured by the size of each district's largest town.[71] The contrast between the most rural and the most urban districts is quite striking, as is the speed with which they diverged once the reform was approved. The reorganisation of the curriculum into separate yearlong grades failed entirely in the rural districts. By 1880 the schools in rural districts actually had fewer grades than they had before 1869. Even in the middle group of mid-sized towns, the average number of grades merely returned, by 1880, to where it had been in 1865. Note that only 15 of the 273 school districts fall in the most urbanized category, which means that in the majority of the country the curriculum part of the reform failed to make much progress more than ten

[71] The 1865 data come from the *Detail-Conscription*, which was conducted still under the old, pre-reform administrative system, based on Catholic vicariates. For better comparability, I have retrospectively reconstructed the post-1869 school districts in the 1865 by assigning each school as appropriate based on its location.

years after its passage. The quality of elementary education, in other words, remained mostly as it was before.

Quantitatively, however, certain areas experienced considerable change. Initially, the countryside struggled to expand the teaching staff in time for the influx of more pupils, which is why the teacher-pupil ratio fell in 1871 relative to 1865. By 1880, however, the villages had recovered and even ended up with a somewhat better teacher-pupil ratio than before the reform. In contrast to that, the large cities went from strength to strength, so that by 1880 their teacher-pupil ratio was on average 20% higher than it had been in 1865, the increase in the total number of pupils notwithstanding. Teachers were clearly among the biggest beneficiaries of the reform. Not only did the law create a higher demand for their services, it also led to higher salaries, which increased across the board. The table suggests that the fastest growth took place in the countryside where it was also starting from the lowest base. The strong demand drew a growing number of women into the teaching profession, who by 1880 made up 30.7% of the teaching staff in the urban districts and 12.5% in the rest.

All this hiring and pay increases inevitably showed up in the per-pupil salary costs. Even though the rural districts barely went beyond what was necessary to simply adjust to the higher pupil totals in hiring new staff, the per-pupil costs tripled. Clearly, the worries of the rural representatives had been justified. The cost hike in large cities was almost fourfold. The urban schooling sector was undergoing a genuine boom, with more money spent not only on teachers but also on new school construction and on repairs. And it still was not enough, so much so that next to the expanding public schools there emerged a lively private sector, which throughout the 1870s schooled anywhere between 7.6% and 10.2% of all school-age children.[72] The fledgling private schools of the 1860s blossomed into serious players on the urban education market. In contrast to that, there was little room for private schools in the countryside because the mandated levels of public provision more than satisfied the local demand for schooling.

These new financial burdens fell primarily on landowners generally and on small farmers specifically. One of the consequences of the reform, which played itself out in the early 1870s in the provincial assemblies, was the gradual elimination of the tuition fees, *Schulgeld*. Between 1871 and 1875, in one province after another this source of school income was curtailed which inevitably implied that more would have to come from the municipal coffers by way of the municipal surcharges on *Grundsteuer*, the land tax. Although on paper the tax rate was uniform across landholdings of all sizes, in its effect the tax was regressive. It was levied not on actual net income, generated by the land, but on an administratively determined income, generated by a formula, which assigned wooded areas lower value than agricultural land. Since large aristocratic

[72] Another single-digit percentage of city children were also attending secondary schools.

estates were more likely to include woodlands, the effective per-acre tax rate faced by the large landowners was lower than that facing small farmers, as even contemporaries readily recognized.[73] Moreover, thanks to the skewed electoral rules, the large aristocratic landowners had enough political clout to ease their own tax burden. In Galicia, for example, the nobles used their outsized presence in the Galician provincial assembly to vote themselves a discount when it came to school-related taxes.[74] Bearing the brunt of local taxation, the small farmers thus had an incentive to keep the fiscal needs of their villages in check. They also had the political leverage to affect the level of spending because they were the rural voters. Across the empire, the small farmers were the political force that, on the local level, pushed for a slower expansion of schools, putting a brake on teacher hiring as well as on school construction.[75]

While the educational progress in the countryside stalled, the political campaigning against the law continued unabated. Far from tapering out, the dissatisfaction with the secular nature of the school among traditional Catholics kept the education issue on the agenda throughout the 1870s, while the liberals continued to hold on to power. Then, in 1879, the conservative parties formed the "iron ring of the right", a parliamentary coalition that for the next fourteen years supported the cabinet of Eduard Taaffe. The ongoing political organising finally bore fruit, when in 1883 the 1869 law was amended, presumably in a manner more in tune with Catholic sensibilities.

The amendment did, in fact, include a few nods to the cultural demands of the traditionalists, such as reinstating a passing grade in religion as a necessary condition for graduating from elementary school (the 1869 law only demanded mastery of reading, writing and arithmetic). Also, district school boards lost the power to choose textbooks to provincial school boards, where the Catholic hierarchy could exert more influence. But the only serious breach of the secular nature of the school was the newly introduced provision that a school director or head teacher must be of the same faith as the majority of the school's pupils. Of course, many small village schools made do with only one teacher, who now had to be of the same religion as the village, so this amendment effectively closed off a large part of the teaching jobs in the countryside to non-Catholic candidates. But many of those teachers were already Catholic to begin with and the religious test imposed on teachers did not imply any direct supervisory powers for the Church. Indeed, school inspection and school board operation remained firmly in the secular sphere, all teacher training courses remained

[73] Jechl. *Statistische Nachweisungen über den land- und lehentäflichen Grundbesitz im Königreiche Böhmen*, p. XXVIII estimated that large landowners paid on average 1.39 fl per Joch (about 5746.5 m^2) whereas small landowners paid 1.70 fl per Joch. He blamed the difference entirely on the wooded areas on aristocratic estates.

[74] Strakosch-Graßmann. *Geschichte des österreichischen Unterrichswesens*, p. 271.

[75] See Cvrček and Zajíček. "The making of a liberal education", Section 6 for a more detailed analysis.

open to all candidates regardless of religion and the curriculum, while curtailed somewhat by the amendment, did not revert to its pre-reform shape.[76] Conspicuously absent were any corrections that would address the erstwhile constitutional grievances – the amendment brought no devolution of powers from the Viennese Education Ministry to the provincial assemblies. Clearly, this side of the issue lost its appeal in the meantime, since by 1883 the great constitutional questions were considered settled for the time being.

But next to the mostly superficial religiously and culturally motivated amendments, one finds a number of inconspicuous but ultimately important changes that spoke to the financial side of the matter. Article 7 reintroduced the option to bring back half-day teaching and Article 21 allowed "parents in the countryside and urban parents of modest means" to request exemption from school attendance for children in their seventh and eight school year. This was a clear concession to children's very real contribution to agricultural labours but it also had the effect of potentially reducing the number of pupils in the classroom. Further, the new law relaxed the regulation on maximum allowable teacher-pupil ratio and slightly broadened the geographical radius within which a new school was to be built in as yet unschooled areas. All these changes worked in the same direction: towards lower staffing requirements, a sparser school network and a more spread-out use of existing resources – in short, towards lowering the financial burden of schooling. Far more than de-secularisation, the 1883 amendment effected a scaling down of the financially salient provisions of the 1869 school reform. As in 1869, the money mattered more than anything else.[77]

The acrimonious controversies of the 1860s, the rural passive resistance in the 1870s and the 1883 amendments all indicate that the secularising reforms of 1868–69 did not succeed in fully resolving the tensions that had been present in Austria's schooling from the system's very inception in the 18th century. On the one hand, the reform laws without doubt put the Austrian schooling on a new footing, bringing about a universal public schooling that was modern and secular, less explicitly ideological and less status- or class-conscious than its predecessor. Austria caught up with, and even pulled ahead of, other European countries. Britain passed its Elementary Education Act, creating a more unified nationwide schooling system and guaranteeing every child access to school, at about the same time (1870), while in France primary schools were not fully laicized until the Jules Ferry laws of 1881. From a distance of more than a

[76] The list of subjects to be taught in school, which representative Jäger considered so useless for the Alpine valleys back in 1869, reappeared in the 1883 amendment with only small changes: arithmetic was combined with geometry, physical education was made voluntary for girls and home economics, a subject reserved for girls in the 1869 law, was dropped.

[77] In the words of one historian: "To put it bluntly, what was the right thing to do in 1869 needed to become the cheap thing to do by 1883." Lechner. "Die Revision des Reichsvolksschulgesetzes (1869) im Kronland Kärnten (1883). Meinungen und Maßnahmen", p. 3.

century, modern education historians have judged the liberal reform mostly positively.[78] If the quality of a law should be judged by its durability, then the 1869 reform certainly stood the test of time. After all, it survived even the Austro-Hungarian Empire itself. In the Austrian republic, after 1918, the majority of its provisions remained in force until 1962 and in Czechoslovakia, too, it served as the basic legislative framework for elementary schooling throughout the interwar period.[79]

On the other hand, even with the (ostensibly liberal) reform, the Austrian schooling legislation somehow never escaped a certain pattern of regulatory overkill, which the *Allgemeine Schulordnung* of 1774, the *Politische Verfassung* of 1805 and *Reichsvolksschulgesetz* of 1869 all had in common. Chapter 6 showed that the general public, both rural and urban, understood the value of a higher quality curriculum. Seizing that value required moving beyond the basic two-grade school. The 1869 law delivered on this aspect but then fell back into that century-old pattern of fixing in the law a number of one-size-fits-all parameters with a direct bearing on the costs and organisation of the school. Owing to its passage during one of the most spectacular booms in Austrian economic history, the reform's authors were apparently optimistic about the country's ability to meet the financial burdens.[80] Instead, the boom turned first into a severe depression in 1873 and then into a protracted agricultural slump in the 1880s. The fixed parameters of the law left no room for adjustment, which ended up undermining the expansion effort especially in the countryside throughout the 1870s. If, in 1869, Austria's schooling law successfully parted with *Standesmässigkeit* – the notion that education must be appropriate for one's social station – it certainly did not let go, to everyone's detriment, of its other preoccupation, *Gleichförmigkeit* – uniformity. The reform was not liberal enough.

[78] Engelbrecht. *Geschichte des österreichischen Bildungswesens*, p. 116 goes so far as to argue that it took Germany until 1918 and Britain until 1944 to achieve the same level of equality of access, regardless of status and wealth, as Austria achieved in 1869. Fischer. *Ernst von Feuchtersleben. Pädagogische Schriften*, p. 160 believed the reforms made Austria's elementary schooling "in one fell swoop among the most modern in Europe."

[79] One exception were the main schools, for which the regulations were updated by means of the 1927 *Hauptschulgesetz*. See Jellouschek. "Das Reichsvolksschulgesetz", p. 304; Jaroš and Job. *Rozvoj československého školství v číslech.* p. 23.

[80] Elmar Lechner dubbed it a "fair-weather law" on account of the auspicious economic circumstances, in which it was passed. See Lechner. "Die Revision des Reichsvolksschulgesetzes (1869) im Kronland Kärnten (1883). Meinungen und Maßnahmen", p. 2.

Conclusion

The first Austrian schooling system, especially in the form left behind by emperor Francis I, never had a very good reputation to start with. In 1873, a mere four years after its demise, a prominent Austrian statistician and analyst of education, Adolf Ficker, had this to say about it:[1]

"The established system of administration of public schooling was a fitting tool of paternalistic policing by the state and it rested on the principle of absolute standstill and intellectual isolation, for which it in turn furnished most powerful support."

Similar criticisms had appeared while the system was in operation, especially among those who worked within it.[2] In modern times, the *Politische Verfassung* of 1805 has been described, with some justification, as a "reactionary document", which could not but produce a stagnant and backward education system.[3] Throughout the 20th century, academic literature has shown sharp awareness of the system's shortcomings, as it asserted again and again a familiar litany of legitimate complaints: the status of teachers was low, they were miserably paid, the teacher training was inadequate, the approved methods were stale, the curriculum too narrow, the enrolment stayed below target, attendance was sparse, the administration resisted all change, the financial base was rickety and available resources were insufficient. The list goes on.

Methodologically, such observations have mostly rested on qualitative evidence, gleaned from government reports, contemporary polemical treatises and archived school reports.[4] The cited *quantitative* evidence, if any, usually did not go beyond a few select descriptive statistics, used for illustration: an enrolment ratio here and there, a ballpark figure of a teacher's salary, maybe a table of school totals by province. While such numbers were often effectively placed into their historical context, they were also quoted uncritically

---

[1] Ficker. *Bericht über österreichisches Unterrichtswesen*, p. 9.

[2] See, for example Prausek. *Die Verbesserung der Volksschule mit besonderer Rücksichtigung Österreichs* or Herrmann. *Denkschrift über die Zustände des Volksschulwesens in Böhmen*. Prausek was a school inspector in Lower Austria, Herrmann a teacher from Varnsdorf (then Warnsdorf) in Bohemia.

[3] Veselá. "Příspěvek k historii učitelského vzdělávání", p. 18.

[4] A few studies making a serious effort to grapple with the Austrian educational statistics have also appeared, e.g. Kuzmin, *Vývoj školství a vzdělaní v Československu* or Heiler and Lebmann. "Die Entwicklung der allgemeinbildenden Pflichtschulen in Österreich."

due to a lack of "statistical context", i.e. without considerations of plausibility, internal consistency or measurement reliability. Part of the reason was technological: some checks only become possible when a critical mass of data from a critical mass of sources is gathered literally in one spreadsheet. This constraint has been lifted only in the last few decades thanks to the progress of computing and the Internet. The other part was possibly a simple case of "why bother": after all, the qualitative evidence seemed to paint the picture fairly accurately and convincingly.

As it turned out, a systematic look at the reams of statistical material generated by the school administration yields new insights, some of which would probably surprise even the contemporaries who collected the data. Among other things, checks of internal consistency revealed how inadequately and incompletely they measured the very schooling system they worked in, which necessarily imposed a limit on what they could know about it. In almost all such cases, no matter how searing their own criticism, correcting for that ignorance and mismeasurement invariably shows that the reality was in fact worse than they had thought.

In practically every respect, my analysis of the statistical evidence revises the official record down. As Chapter 2 showed, school coverage was far from complete even decades after the law was promulgated and even in places where it was considered close to full. Long distances and difficult terrain rendered it at best nominal in many places. Because of this imperfect coverage, the government had biased information about enrolment ratios, which bias was unambiguously upwards, painting a rosier picture than was the reality – sometimes by more than 20 percentage points. In many areas, the government never even managed to form an accurate idea of how many school-age children were actually around to be schooled. Moreover, except in the 1865 *Detail Conscription*, the reported annual enrolment figures made no distinction between "full-time" schools and those operating on a half-year or half-day basis, further undercutting the usefulness of the enrolment ratio as a measure of effective exposure to education. Systematic aggregate data on actual attendance were not even collected. The majority of pupils attended schools that did not have sufficient classroom space and staff to accommodate all the school-bound children in their precinct. Often, the only way such schools could hope to comply with regulations on pupil-teacher and pupil-classroom ratios was by relying on less than full attendance, as I argued in Chapters 3 and 5. To put it bluntly, many teachers found themselves in a situation where any instruction was physically viable only if some non-negligible proportion of enrolled pupils did not show up for it. Official pressure, such as it was, to make the physical infrastructure and staffing more adequate ran into the reluctance of school patrons, parents and village elders to pay for it. The rural masses – the majority of the empire's population – showed the most impervious passive resistance of all these groups and this obstinacy was rooted in the hardnosed realisation that the investment of time and money was probably not going to bear returns. Indeed, outside the towns, the curriculum was very constrained and this distinction between city and country was consciously written into the law. But even within the countryside, the content varied widely because of the half-year and half-day teaching, so that "six years of school" meant different things in different places. In addition to all of this, the government had no way of actually assessing the efficacy of their educational model because, as I showed in Chapter 6, no "outcome statistics", not even basic literacy rates, were collected until 1880, except (occasionally) among conscripts who are a notoriously unrepresentative sample of the general population.[5] In short, while plenty of past scholars described the Austrian schooling as quite inadequate and bad, the confrontation of this assessment with the statistical evidence indicates that it was actually even worse than bad.

And yet, underneath all the criticism from researchers, both past and modern, one can also detect a layer of certain goodwill towards the original authors of the school reform, and especially towards Maria Theresa, as if to say: the schooling was deeply flawed, but kudos for trying.[6] Frequently, this atti-

---

[5] See Bodenhorn et al. "Sample-Selection Biases and the Industrialization Puzzle", p. 172–173.

[6] Frank called the 1774 reform "a glorious leaf in the laurel wreath of our great Empress" before going on to criticize intellectual and spiritual staleness of the early 19th century elementary education. According to Strakosch-Graßmann: "The reform effort was not error-free but it rested on a durable, lasting foundation." Engelbrecht concludes that "the fundaments of the reform were so deeply and firmly anchored that the inevitable further expansion was only a matter of time." In Kuzmin's estimation, the reform was "of great […] significance" and "quickly proved to be very effective." Scheipl and Seel allow that "the reform efforts of Maria Theresa and Joseph II were not without their flaws" but, noting the resulting "improvements in the quality of teaching through rudimentary training of teachers, unification of guidelines and cheaper textbooks", they conclude that "the reorganization of the school system would not have succeeded, had not the absolutist power of the state effected its implementation." Similar view informs the work of Beer and Hochegger, Helfert's compendious study and many others. Most remarkably, even Miroslav Riedl, who is otherwise unflinchingly critical of the "reactionary" methods of the Theresian school, concludes his disparaging chapter on Felbigerian pedagogy with the verdict that "once we add to the shortcomings of the Felbigerian method also aristocracy's refusal to support the school to the extent that the law required and the Catholic Church's appropriation of it after the Josephinian era as a buttress for the pulpit, we are able to understand, why we observe such paltry educational outcomes, especially in the countryside, *in spite of the Theresian reform's progressive and democratic nature*." [emphasis mine] Somehow – so Riedl – everybody else was to blame for the policy's failures except the policy itself. What unshakeable hold the empress has on the loyalty of these many researchers even two centuries after her death! See Frank. *Kurzer Überblick*, p. 61–2; Strakosch-Graßmann. *Geschichte des österreichischen Unterrichswesens*, p. 132; Engelbrecht. *Geschichte des österreichischen Bildungswesens*, p. 116; Kuzmin. *Vývoj školství a vzdělaní v Československu*; Helfert, *Die österreichische Volksschule*; Beer,

tude finds its expression in the starkly contrasting assessments of the two school laws of this period: whereas the *Politische Verfassung* of 1805 is spared no criticism for its apparent conservative thrust, the 1774 *Allgemeine Schulordnung* enjoys a most celebrated status as the foundational legislation, a statesmanlike act of reform, "a mighty cultural deed".[7] Yet, this contrast is more imagined than real as the two acts embodied the same fundamental principles and shared the same flaws, thanks to the underlying continuity between them, as I argued in Chapter 1. The unspoken assumption – and it usually is just an assumption – is that, for all its shortcomings, the Theresian reform deserves credit for having put the Austrian school on a firmer, stronger foundation which facilitated its further improvement. But given the relentless stream of downward revisions emerging from the statistical analysis, it is time to let go of this undue indulgence of the founders and instead to say more unequivocally that the policy implemented under Maria Theresa and her successors was probably, on the whole, a brake on education and its development in Austria.

How could such a verdict possibly stand? Surely, any assessment of the historical record must start from the basic acknowledgement that, for all the unfavourable statistical corrections, the Austrian school network *did* actually expand, teachers *did* really get trained and most pupils *did* come out of the trivial schools literate. The state built up an administrative apparatus dedicated to implementing the policy, by means of which it, without a doubt, pushed for schooling expansion at least to the extent that the law required. This is all true. But let us not forget how much of that policy was restrictive – even suppressive – in its disposition and impact. This side of it, the constricting side, must also be placed on the scales of the weight, just as the law's inducements, such as they were, are counted in its favour. Given how thoroughly the Habsburg school policy was informed by a conscious effort to prevent "unnecessary" and "undesirable" education from spreading through the realm, one must at least consider the unpopular but entirely plausible conclusion that, on balance, the inhibitory forces had the upper hand and that, more likely than not, the country's schooling system would have ended up in a better shape and the educational status of the population at a higher level, if the government had left it to its own devices.

An assertion like this invites the inevitable question: what would Austria's public education have looked like in the absence of the *Allgemeine Schulordnung*, the *Politische Verfassung*, the legally imposed *Schulpatronat*, the binding *Normallehrart*, the emphasis on *Standesmässigkeit*? Trying to reconstruct

Adolf and Franz Hochegger. *Die Fortschritte des Unterrichtswesens in den Culturstaaten Europas*; Scheipl and Seel, *Die Entwicklung des österreichischen Schulwesens*, 1750–1938, p. 19; Riedl. *Zavádění povinné školní docházky*, p. 55–56.

[7] Brezinka. *Pädagogik in Österreich.* Vol. 1, p. 10.

a century-long counterfactual would require tracking more moving parts and chasing more loose ends than is humanly doable and I do not have a model parallel universe in which to simulate that alternative history. But if one should try to speculate, the potential sources of that alternative educational development, that hypothetical could-have-been, were already in place in the concrete historical situation of the late 18th and early 19th centuries and there was nothing counterfactual or alternative about them. Time and again, various long-range time series showed an initial stagnation or a tepid upward trend conspicuously breaking into a sudden burst of growth right at the juncture of some reluctant and piecemeal liberalization, be it the explosion of the *Realschulen* after 1848 (Figure 1.1) and the embrace of major schools after 1850 (Figure 2.2) once the newly created Education Ministry relented in its opposition to both, the abrupt conversions of bilingual schools into Slavic and Italian ones at the various points when officialdom conceded to each nationality that instruction in its mother tongue would be more effective (Figures 2.6–2.8), the jump in educational spending and the growth of private schools after the liberal reform of 1869 (Table 7.4), the rise of women as public teachers after the same (Chapter 7) and so on. Each of these is a telltale sign of a pent-up demand, artificially suppressed by some regulation or other, which could have borne its fruit of learning long before it actually did, had the regulation not been in force in the first place. For many other areas, such as the proliferation of new textbooks once the censorship was relaxed in the Constitutional Era, the emergence of professional periodicals in the 1850s and the burgeoning post-1848 professional self-organising among teachers, the time series cannot even be accurately reconstructed but the anecdotal evidence leaves scarce doubt that they would show a similar pattern. All these factors, then, could have been the sources of that alternative, less regulated schooling history that never happened.

Its most obvious arena would have been the cities. Throughout the period, as the previous chapters have amply documented, the urban schools were constantly bumping up against the ceiling of regulation in matters of curriculum. The cities' persistent demand for more teachers drew in young teaching candidates from the countryside, as discussed in Chapter 4. The towns were willing to spend the requisite money both on public and on private education. By the late 1860s, the urban political representatives were in the driver seat of a reform aimed to make schools better and broader. The cities certainly offer the most compelling case that the existing policy was a constraint rather than a facilitator of educational development.

In the countryside, one could have reasonably expected some voluntary patronage from the aristocrats. As I discussed in Chapter 3, landowners usually receive criticism for having opposed mass schooling on account of their self-interest – the larger the estate, the stiffer the opposition, as the theory has it. But the Austrian record, as I also discussed in Chapter 3, presents a more complicated picture. There is scant evidence of any organised political opposition to the expansion of schools even though aristocrats were surely better placed than most constituencies to obstruct anything they did not like. When the expansion of elementary schools came up for a vote in 1869, they were moderately in favour, as Chapter 7 showed. Furthermore, many instances were documented of aristocrats actually standing on the frontier of the development of schooling, especially when they sought to be conscientious stewards of the estate in their possession.[8] The North-Bohemian Clam-Gallases assumed the role of school benefactors even before the institute of school patronage was written into the law.[9] In many cases, in fact, the aristocracy's efforts were foiled by the central authorities. The ups and downs of the various aristocratic attempts to establish *Realschulen* – in Styria, in Bohemia and elsewhere – were recounted in Chapter 1. The aristocratic interest in a forward-looking practically-minded education predated the Theresian school reform, as was the case, for example, with the proto-*Realschule* in Nový Bor (Haida), established already in 1761 with a view to spur the growth of the local glass industry by Count Kinský (and then cut down to size by an official decree in 1783).[10] Indeed, the most prominent champion of the whole concept of *Realschule* – a modern, skill-oriented educational institution – was the conservative Rottenhan whose main motivation was economic development. In other words, the aristocrats' self-interest in improving their estates' profitability combined with their own paternalistic self-image as traditional patrons of their local communities could well have been another source of support for schooling even in the absence of a centrally mandated policy.[11]

Such sensible educational efforts, rooted in the local economic situation and calibrated to the needs of the labour market, could plausibly have met with a positive response from the commoners. It would be a mistake to conclude from all the evidence of inadequate school provision, of a shortfall in coverage and of enrolment backsliding that the failures to launch schools originated in the peasants' blanket indifference or outright opposition to the very idea. On the contrary, there was a genuine popular demand for education, provided that it was of the right kind, shape and cost. Village schools had existed before 1774, some dating back centuries (although they were, admittedly, mostly very modest affairs).[12] The repeated attempts to stamp out the illicit *Winkellehrer* are another smoking gun: governments do not usually ban things that nobody is doing anyway. To the enforcers of public schooling,

---

[8] See Strakosch-Graßmann. *Geschichte des österreichischen Unterrichswesens*, p. 123.

[9] Hoffmann. *Geschichte der Haupt- und Mädchenschule in Reichenberg*, p. 41.

[10] See Pospíchal. "Piaristická škola v Boru (Heyde) 1763–1870".

[11] See Andersson and Berger. "Elites and the expansion of education in nineteenth century Sweden" for an example of similar role played by the landed elites in Sweden.

[12] For description and examples of pre-1774 village schools, see Šafránek. *Školy české I. svazek*, p. 136–139. Also Figure 2.1 in Chapter 2.

the threat of the *Winkellehrer* consisted precisely in his or her flexibility on curriculum, school time and cost.[13] Their customers' attitude to education was more nakedly instrumental, i.e. not swayed by the politicized, culture-war approach of the Court but instead focused on acquiring skills and knowledge that could lead to some improvement in one's lot. To the extent that they found such learning in school, the peasants sent their children there. But with a stale, mind-numbingly ideological curriculum, the time investment usually ran into diminishing returns quite quickly. The peasants' indifference was thus not inherent; it was conditional on the product on offer.

To see all these forces coalesce into a different and superior outcome (than actually obtained), Austria needed to do no more than to pursue a policy of "benign neglect", similar to that adopted by England at the time. At the outset of the 19th century, the English elementary school system relied strongly and exclusively on voluntarism and private charity.[14] In fact, when a bill was proposed to support parochial schools with public funds in 1807, it was defeated on the grounds that it would be costly for the public treasury (and also that it could lead to undue social and economic ambition among the lower classes).[15] In England, the state made practically no interference in the operation of the country's schools, which gave philanthropists, education enthusiasts as well as entrepreneurs a free hand to experiment with curricula and methods of instructions.[16] True, the English education inherited a number of elite "public schools" of ancient reputation – the Etons, Rugbys and Harrows of this world – but these were not "public" in the sense of being tax-financed and did not form the backbone of mass education at the time. The closest that England had to a public provision of primary education were the aforementioned parochial schools which operated under the wings of the established Church. But their financial sources were local and, as the example of the 1807 Whitbread bill showed, the political will to substantially buttress their material situation from the public purse was lacking.

Instead, early in the 19th century, two charitable societies, the National Society (of Anglican persuasion) and the British and Foreign School Society (a Non-Conformist one) arose with the aim to bring schooling to the working classes of England and beyond on a private, mostly self-financing, basis. Each had its own specific mode of operation. The British and Foreign School Society, for example, adopted the monitorial method, developed by Joseph Lancaster in 1798, which allowed one master teacher to conduct the instruction of hundreds of children at a time by delegating teaching of individual

[13] Engelbrecht. *Geschichte des österreichischen Bildungswesens* Vol. 3, p. 114–115.

[14] Benavot and Resnik. "Lessons from the Past: A Comparative Socio-Historical Analysis of Primary and Secondary Education", p. 154.

[15] Lindert. *Growing Public Vol. 1*, p. 100.

[16] Ramirez and Boli. "The Political Construction of Mass Schooling: European Origins And Worldwide Institutionalization", p. 8.

lessons to monitors, or pupil teachers.[17] Its manual came with specifications for classroom arrangements, a recommended timetable and practical advice on school organisation. The National Society worked out its own model, named sometimes after its author, Andrew Bell, sometimes after its place of origin (the Madras system).[18] In terms of curriculum, British educators were just as convinced about the need to inculcate proper religion in the masses as their Austrian counterparts, although practical considerations led them to assign it a more proportional place: out of 30 weekly hours of instruction in a British Society school, religion occupied not quite four. Arithmetic, both mental and written, received five, while geography, history, biology and other *realia* were allocated a combined six hours.[19]

This network of weekday schools was further supplemented by Sunday schools which started cropping up in England in the 1780s and which by 1833 apparently surpassed the enrolment of weekday schools.[20] Their name announced their chief advantage: the time of instruction did not interfere with children's potential employment during the week. Being restricted to a single day of teaching, their curriculum was correspondingly limited primarily to reading and religion with maybe a little bit of writing, if there was time. But that was the whole point of the trade-off: the curriculum was narrow but at least it reached its audience – the pupils who really physically showed up – because the Sunday school did not burden their families with the largest cost of schooling, the opportunity cost of forgone child earnings.

Last but not least, the education market accommodated small private schools, operated by enterprising individuals, known usually as dame schools where elderly matrons offered very rudimentary instruction for a fee. These likely came closest to what in the German cultural tradition were the *Winkelschulen*. They were, of course, of varying quality and some offered little beyond glorified baby-sitting. But they were also of varying costs, so it was up to the customer to decide what was the appropriate value for money. These single-person outfits were inevitably smaller than, say, a Society school, but this put them in a better position to offer individual attention.[21]

In 1833, Parliament approved a limited public support for schooling in the form of government grants, allocated on the basis of local petitions made

---

[17] British and Foreign School Society. *Hand-book to the Borough Road Schools*. p. 10–12.

[18] The substantial similarity of the two approaches, which also gave rise to the joint label "Bell-Lancaster method", did not get in the way of their partisans waging a fanatical, irreconcilable war on the pages of various British periodicals and pamphlets regarding the superiority as well as religious orthodoxy of each. See Jones. *The Charity School Movement*, p. 333–340.

[19] British and Foreign School Society. *Hand-book to the Borough Road Schools*. p. 123–125.

[20] Mitch. *The Rise of Popular Literacy in Victorian England*, p. 137.

[21] Ibid., p. 144–147.

through one of the charitable societies.[22] The idea was to build up, and speed up the extension of, the school network through a public subsidy, which in no way interfered with the robust private provision. Both manners of provision, public and private, coexisted side by side, competing and complementing each other. From plush boarding schools through ordinary parochial schools, cost-conscious Bell-Lancaster schools, convenient Sunday schools to ephemeral dame schools, the British education market offered the whole range of cost-benefit combinations so that there was something for everyone. Places that were entirely devoid of any school were both too small and too uninterested to sustain even a meager dame school.[23] As of 1851 across England and Wales, almost 46000 schools, two thirds of them private, competed to serve about 2.1 million pupils.[24] This put the parents, including working class parents, in the driver seat and they sure made use of their freedom of choice. They switched to a dame school when a parochial day school grew too irritating in demanding regular attendance; they pressured the Sunday schools to tone down the religion and dial up the writing classes; they picked up and left when a Society school turned too preachy on middle-class proprieties instead of focusing on the *realia*.[25] Numerous internal as well as parliamentary reports complained that the public apparently had their own ideas about how they wanted their schooling done – but in contrast to Austria, the English law did not compel them to accept any one specific package.

The English popular experience from early 19th century furnishes a convincing proof that, once the motivation to learn was present and the manner of instruction was open to market competition, acquiring literacy could be astonishingly cheap as well as effective.[26] Judging from the signatures on marriage documents, literacy among men went from 60% in 1780 to 65% in 1830, 67.3% in 1841 and 80.6% in 1871. For women, it was above 50% by 1830.[27] Numerous worker biographies bear witness to the changing method

---

[22] Ibid., p. 116.

[23] Mitch puts the critical village population at 500–600 inhabitants and notes that according to the 1881 census, around 10% of the English and Welsh population lived in parishes with fewer than 500 people. Even there, however, "private schools with their greater flexibility, may have met local needs better than public schools." See Mitch. *The Rise of Popular Literacy in Victorian England*, p. 149–150.

[24] See Long. "The Socioeconomic Return to Primary Schooling in Victorian England", Table 1. Comparable data for Imperial Austria were about 12900 public schools with 1.46 million pupils; for the Hungarian half of the monarchy, 11300 schools with 790 thousand pupils. See *TSOM* 1849-1851, II. Theil, Tafel 14, p. 51–52.

[25] Mitch. *The Rise of Popular Literacy in Victorian England*, p. 137, 146.

[26] Ibid., p. 136.

[27] See Mitch. "The Role of Education and Skill in the British Industrial Revolution", p. 243; Long. "The Socioeconomic Return to Primary Schooling in Victorian England", p. 1027. If, in the interest of a crude comparison with the cited 1841 English literacy rates, one should use the 1890 Austrian literacy data – inevitably upwardly biased due to education

of acquisition. As time went on, the "centre of gravity" gradually shifted in the direction of more sophisticated forms of instruction: late 18th century cohorts often relied on informal peer-to-peer tutoring, early 19th century generations learnt to read and write predominantly in Sunday schools, whereas by the 1850s the regular weekday school, whether of parochial or Society provenance, grew in importance.[28] After the Elementary Education Act of 1870, the tax-financed public school rose to permanently occupy a central position in the English schooling system. The gradual move towards a higher quality of instruction, greater sophistication of curriculum and a deeper time commitment occurred in response to the changing needs of the public demanding these services and, by extension, the changing needs of the economy. Importantly, attending a school actually increased one's chances of a real social advance, even if that increase was not very large.[29]

It is true that England did not score high on measures like enrolment ratio and expenditure per pupil in international comparisons – to the consternation of both contemporary and even some modern observers.[30] But a careful reader who followed the discussion around Tyrolean enrolment numbers in Chapter 5 will recall how fraught enrolment ratios are as indicators of exposure to schooling. To fall back on this example from the Austrian record: year after year, Tyrol reported miraculous enrolment ratios of more than 100% because their children enrolled in school beyond the legally prescribed school age in order to make up for the half-year instruction. Even so, they accumulated just over four years of actual school enrolment, which was less than in all other provinces (see column (iii) in Table 5.1). This example alone should disabuse anyone of any illusion that higher enrolment ratio constitutes conclusive statistical evidence of greater exposure to learning and that more years in school translate directly into more education. The example of England (as well as Tyrol) makes that distinction clear: all those measures are really just input measures. They alone tell us nothing about whether the school was an effective learning venue, whether it was cost-efficient or whether it was in demand, so it is a mistake to judge England on this basis. English parents sent their children to school to learn a particular skill and then they moved on. The pupils did not linger on in the classrooms well into their teen years so as to prop up national enrolment statistics. By the same token, no wonder Prussia

---

creep – then for the 1810–1819 birth cohorts, who would have been in a marriageable age by 1841, the uncorrected literacy rate of Austrian men was 64% and for women 51%. Correcting for the upward bias would make the Austrian rates unambiguously lower than the English ones. See *Oesterreichiche Statistik* XXXII. Band, 3. Heft, p. 178–185.

[28] Mitch. *The Rise of Popular Literacy in Victorian England*, p. 137–139.

[29] Long. "The Socioeconomic Return to Primary Schooling in Victorian England", Table 7.

[30] Lindert. *Growing Public* Vol. 1, Chapter 5 "The Rise of Mass Public Schooling before 1914."

bested England in enrolment rates among 5–15 year olds (see Table 5.2): it had instituted compulsory school attendance until 14 and apparently committed sufficient administrative muscle to enforce it.[31] But to what end? What precious gems of knowledge did the mid-century Prussian school have to offer that required it to compel peasant children to attend till age 14? Since Prussian schooling history is similar to the Austrian one – Prussia having served as Austria's template early on – it is entirely plausible to argue, as I do in the Austrian case, that Prussia likely overshot in school compulsion and enforcement, making the whole system appear splendidly attended and richly financed, when in fact it was more wasteful than the English one. It is a regrettable misunderstanding to criticize, say, the charitable Societies for low expenditure per pupil when bringing the costs down to a level sustainable for working class parents was the whole purpose of structuring their schools the way they did. Making them effective learning centres for less was a sign of success, not failure.

So, while in some quarters much is made of England's supposed lag behind other nations, such as Prussia and France, the country's record actually indicates a commendably balanced path. During the First Industrial Revolution, where literacy did not play much role, schooling was in hiatus and literacy mostly stagnated.[32] David Mitch has shown that the growth in human capital contributed only about one thirtieth to the overall rate of economic growth between 1780 and 1831.[33] In 1841, a mere 4.9% of male workers held jobs that required literacy while 46.9% were in occupations where it was useless. Then, with the onset of the Second Industrial Revolution, the sophistication of the British economy increased, so that by 1891 the first share grew to 11.1% while the second fell to 37.0%.[34] English educational attainment increased correspondingly. In other words, when England needed less schooling, she invested less, appropriately falling behind more rigid, less adaptable school systems in input statistics, and when she needed to catch up, she quickly caught up and "the gap was closed over the next two decades."[35] Such was the responsiveness and flexibility of the English educational system.

Austrian education was headed in a similar direction before the Theresian reform and had the basic preconditions in place for a similarly lively educa-

[31] Benavot and Resnik. "Lessons from the Past: A Comparative Socio-Historical Analysis of Primary and Secondary Education", p. 21.

[32] In the words of Joel Mokyr: "If England led the rest of the world in the Industrial Revolution, it was despite, not because of, her formal education system." See Mokyr. *Lever of Riches*, p. 240.

[33] Mitch. "The Role of Education and Skill in the British Industrial Revolution", p. 250–253.

[34] Mitch. *The Rise of Popular Literacy in Victorian England*, Table 2.1.

[35] Lindert. *Growing Public* Vol. 1, p. 114.

tional landscape: the tradition of the *Winkelschulen*, the readiness of major religious orders, such as the Piarists, to teach poor children on a sustainable basis, the judicious support of aristocrats for schooling that could aid economic development, the fledgling education market in the cities – all these were components that, absent the impositions from central government, could have produced a more flexible, effective and widespread schooling system. I do not delude myself that in the absence of the law, a dense network of sophisticated private schools would have somehow spontaneously sprung up in, say, rural Galicia or mountainous Carinthia. But neither should one fall into the opposite trap of assuming that had the government not forced it, nobody would have learnt anything. Let me emphasize again: the market demand for education was not zero; it was, admittedly, a demand for less education than the government demanded. But, more importantly, it was a demand for a different kind of education.

Left to themselves, places like Galicia would probably start from a market of itinerant instructors teaching limited but practical curriculum to a few voluntarily attending pupils in makeshift classrooms, and develop from there. In such a (counterfactual) world, the average village school could have gradually shaped up into something relatively modest, perhaps, but also resilient, viable and useful, consisting of, say, a mere two years of attendance, with less emphasis on religion and more on skills such as arithmetic, drawing and *realia*. School age would likely shrink to just 8–10 year-olds – the peak years of both enrolment and attendance according to Chapter 5 – so the average child would spend shorter but more effective time in school, and more families could potentially afford, and find it worthwhile, to send their child there. Less time and money would have been expended but more useful content would have been imparted. After all, if a particular set of skills can be imparted over a brief period of time, then short enrolment also means lower opportunity cost. One might have even encountered some readiness for classroom experimentation. After all, the famous Pestalozzi was active, right at that time, in Switzerland, his pedagogical ideas circulating all around Europe,[36] and the swift move by the Education Commission in 1820 (and again in 1837) to ban the Bell-Lancaster method from the Austrian classroom suggests that someone somewhere must have tried it out or at least proposed to try it out. And while it is possible, even likely, that such arrangements would have created a bigger gulf between the city and the country than actually occurred, such a divergence would have merely reflected the respective educational needs of the two locales which were genuinely different. The actual historical reality was that the countryside got more school than it bargained for while the city received less education than it needed. The rural-urban gap

[36] See, for example, Horlacher, "'Best Practice' Around 1800" on the operation of Pestalozzi's school in Burgdorf, Switzerland and its imitation elsewhere.

widened after 1869 accordingly, so if anything, the actual pre-1869 arrangements were simply postponing the inevitable.

Instead of such an open playing field, the Habsburg subjects were obligated to fashion their schools to the law's specifications, a challenge that was often greeted with scant enthusiasm. Throughout the 1820s, 1830s and 1840s, for example, provinces such as Styria, Carinthia and Bukovina added few new schools, even though they were far below full coverage and the number of school-age children grew over the same period by 23%, 12% and 16%. Between 1816 and 1847, the total number of Styrian schools, most of them small rural operations, fluctuated between 600 and 650, the period falling into a roughly equal number of years of school expansion and years of school contraction. Tellingly, in the meantime the number of teaching staff steadily increased moreless in proportion to pupils, with the overall result of more staff per school but not necessarily a geographic extension of the school network. Tracking schools individually reveals that, for example, in the diocese of Seckau with its roughly 450 schools, 41 operating in 1846 were no longer active by 1865 while 36 new ones sprang up in places where none had been twenty years before. Such movements betray evidence of local schools being founded and then abandoned either due to basic unviability or due to lingering doubts as to the merits of the whole enterprise. Indeed, many localities opted for lying low and doing nothing, if they could get away with it: that is how all the unenrolled children, uncovered villages, unbuilt schools, unhired teachers and absenting poor pupils show up (or not, rather) in the statistics.

The fundamental cause behind all this missing education and the biggest hindrance to its expansion was the sum total of the regulations. Intuitively, this charge runs into two closely related objections. One is the apparent contradiction of blaming under-provision of schooling on the very rules that demanded more of it. The second is to declare the policy a hindrance while also noting how widely ignored and under-enforced the law was. The obvious resolution of both paradoxes is that not all parts of the law were flouted in equal degree. Unfortunately, the strong enforcement of some aspects of the policy was in fact the cause of such widespread disregard of its other parts.

The government was most effective in enforcing the content side of the regulations. This was where it arguably also did the most damage. The responsibility here falls both on the Education Commission at the centre and on the numerous local overseers all around the country. The state practiced censorship over textbooks, specified the curriculum minutely and exercised tight and effective control over teachers through the Church-run training centres and through certification. The enforcement was especially strong in its preventive effect: recall, for instance, the Commission's near perfect record in rejecting calls for a longer and deeper training of teachers all the way until 1848! On the level of provinces and bishoprics, too, village petitions for curriculum extension were held up, German was pushed as a language of instruction in non-German schools (especially in the first third of the 19th century) and pressure was applied to convert half-day schools into all-day ones, so as to box them precisely into the shape the state wanted. On these points, the state often got its way. The archival record shows quite unambiguously that the teaching logs did follow the content regulations, the parish priests did teach the proper Catholic catechism, the lesson times did adhere to the prescribed timetables set out in the law, the vicariate supervisors did sign off on the examination protocols, thereby checking that students were indeed exposed to the prescribed content and not any other. If a village opened a school, then in matters of content and teaching method it was going to be a regulation school and nothing else.

The government was moderately, or intermediately, successful in enforcing enrolment and attendance once a school was built. The degree of that success depended on the interplay of two forces: on the one side, the presence and determination of the teacher and the local school supervisor in bringing in all school-age children, not least because they were an important source of the teacher's income; on the other, the economic reality of families, many of them poor and in serious need of their children's labour and earnings. The rural schools were hardly an avenue for social advance. Their deliberate inadequacy as a stepping-stone and preparatory stage for further education or training ensured that there was little tangible long-term benefit to set against the momentary cost of forgone child wages and tuition, and so the enrolment had to rely primarily on coercive incentives. These bore some fruit in that expansion of school coverage in an area usually correlated with quick and sizeable increases in enrolment. But most of the shortfall to full enrolment still came from a lack of enforcement rather than a lack of coverage (see Table 5.4). The policy's main bet was to combine the teaching and enforcement duties in the person of the schoolteacher once a local school opened, so that "if you build it, they will (have to) come." But this bet paid off only partially.

Many communities decided to not build a school, which was also the area where enforcement was arguably at its weakest. The law insisted on a school for every 90–100 school-age children living within half-hour of walking distance. But even by the late 1860s in large parts of Galicia, Bukovina and Carniola, that simply was not the case. Here, the fate of Austrian schooling serves as an abject lesson on the limits of social change by decree. So many at the Court laboured to legislate schools into existence! Yet, the intent of the policy was time and again undermined and thwarted wherever the local social and economic conditions were not ready for it. The perversely impressive track record of Dalmatia in holding out against the law's demands for most of the 19th century (see Figure 5.4) and the unceremonious climb-down from the bold ambitions of the 1869 liberal reform by way of the 1883 amendments are just two among many egregious examples of the fundamental inability of Austrian governments to simply will their desiderata into being.

This contrast in the degree of enforcement, namely that the government could not easily compel unschooled villages to open a school but could very easily supervise the teaching and content once a school was actually built, is the reason why the very law aimed at establishing mass schooling ended up discouraging it. The dilemma was inescapable: either follow the law and build a regulation school or ignore the law and have no school. There was no middle ground – nothing in between these two options – even though for many local communities, some such intermediate, halfway arrangement would have been optimal, as I argued above and in Chapter 5. Such is also the lesson offered by the exception that proves the rule – Tyrol, the province where the prevailing economic conditions were so strongly aligned against the legally sanctioned model of six full years of a repetitive two-grade curriculum that the most widespread solution was the half-year school, the closest example of such an intermediate setup that the Austrian record can offer. As the Tyrolean data show, the province had the densest network of schools, most extensive coverage, lowest pupil-teacher ratio, zero school tuition and one of the highest literacy rates in the empire.[37] The scaled-down half-year version apparently worked better for the Tyroleans, which is why they fought tooth and nail against the reform that outlawed it in 1869, imposing only costlier alternatives. Elsewhere in the monarchy, most villages did not have a handy excuse like Tyrol to deviate from the official blueprint. They had to face the unpalatable dilemma and many demurred, preferring to have no school at no cost rather than spend precious resources on a full-blown regulation school that brought them very little. So there it is: it was the government policy that cornered them into doing nothing.

Those that chose the other, legally mandated, path had to swallow the full complement of regulations. Since intermediate solutions were not an option, the government forced the communities to pay for everything the law required which in effect pushed at least some of them to spend beyond their optimal investment. This made the schools more costly and less beneficial than the communities would have liked. The implication is that the expense, the effort and the time that went into operating and expanding this system engendered unnecessary waste: true, the country spent relatively little on primary schools – a mere 0.34% of GDP in 1865 and surely less before that – but most of what it got out of this investment could have likely been had for

[37] Note that the argument is not that Austrian schooling should have adopted the Tyrolean arrangements across the board but that when Tyrol was allowed to escape from the straitjacket of the predominant legally sanctioned model in a way that took into consideration, and adjusted to, the local economic conditions, it ended up with outcomes superior to many provinces which were not afforded such luxury.

even less. The amount of waste would have been even greater had it not been for the effective passive resistance where locals, for example, stalled on classroom expansion or extra staff hires, discussed in Chapter 3, and cut back their enrolment and attendance, as described in Chapter 5. The central government contributed next to nothing from general tax revenue and instead, to add economic injury to the fiscal insult, billed the parents for the school through *Schulgeld*, which fell most heavily on the poorest. The same applies to the opportunity cost of time spent in school: it was deeply regressive in its impact and a good part of it was a waste. If Tyrolean children learnt as much literacy in, effectively, four years as Moravian children did in six, then the extra time spent in school in Moravia was apparently wasted. Furthermore, Chapter 6 uncovered substantial evidence both that some proportion of pupils failed to acquire literacy in school while at the same time a good number of people, especially in less schooled provinces, may have learnt to read and write somewhere else long after their school-age years. Either of these observations undermines the claim that the Austrian elementary school was the source of this important skill.

It should be clear, at this point, how and why the state's constraining and inflexible policy engendered the perverse incentives described above. The ultimate source of that policy was neither the indifferent peasantry, nor the self-interested aristocracy, nor the culturally conservative Catholic Church – although they all, willy-nilly, participated and contributed to the system. The main culprit was the centre, the Court, the Habsburg rulers. The guiding triad of the policy – *Standesmässigkeit*, *Gleichförmigkeit*, *Rechtschaffenheit* – reflected first and foremost their desires and preferences. They, by means of the policy expertise and the enforcement muscle of the Education Commission, breathed life into this unwieldy scheme and exerted all their power to crowd out all possible alternatives. As I argued in Chapter 1, the emperors had their own reasons for shaping education the way they did as well as their own expectations of what fruit it would bear. They, too, however, ended up largely disappointed, for it is doubtful that the Austrian *Trivialschule* really delivered as the inculcator of Catholic orthodoxy and dynastic legitimacy and, consequently, as the social stabiliser the way the Habsburgs had intended. Before long, it became a battleground of nationalisms, which at best slowed down, but certainly did not stop, the spread of liberalism. At the same time, the policy's inevitable by-product was such a degree of forced conformity that flexible adjustments to local conditions that could have made the system more viable were effectively prevented. It is against the backdrop of all these obtuse policy choices that even nothing – no specific policy at all! – would have been a better, more education-friendly alternative than what the Habsburgs actually instituted. Much of the misplaced goodwill towards the founders of Austria's public education rests on the comparison of the post-1774 school with the relatively sparse and rudimentary school network before. But the proper benchmark for the Austrian schooling system in 1869, after the Theresian policy had run its century-long course, is not the schooling system of 1769, which would have been an anachronistically low bar, but rather the system that realistically could have formed, if it had the chance to develop within a less suffocating institutional framework.

The root of that deep policy misjudgment lay in the reform's origin in the milieu of the gradually fading but still lingering serfdom, the basis of which was a particular conception of the ruler-subject relationship. As a product of the 1770s and 1780s, the golden years of Enlightened Absolutism, the reform naturally invites an uplifting interpretation: as a fruit of the Enlightenment, as a bold, "progressive and democratic" step towards modernization, as a commendably prescient, if imperfect, forerunner to the robust educational expansion of the 19th century. But appearances can be deceiving; the opposite is true. Its rationale, the manner of its implementation, its emphases and interdictions all put the Theresian school reform squarely "at home" within the broader framework of serfdom. Akin to any other feudal due, this was an imposition by a feudal ruler on her serfs to further her, not their, interests. The *Allgemeine Schulordnung* was one of the last policies to be so fundamentally steeped in, and informed by, that system of economic and social organisation. Seven years later, serfdom was abolished, making the new educational framework almost immediately anachronistic. It was not a harbinger of something modern but a vestige of something obsolete. The misfortune was that this last-gasp offspring of serfdom outlived its parent by almost a century.

Bibliography

Archival sources

Österreichische Staatsarchiv, *Studienhofkomission*, kartons 697–705, "Übersicht des Zustandes der Volkschulen ... im Jahre...", years 1809–1832

Státní okresní archiv Praha-východ, *Fond "Triviální škola Brázdim"*

–. *Fond "Triviální škola Čelákovice"*

–. *Fond "Triviální škola Dřevčice"*

–. *Fond "Triviální škola Horní Počernice"*

–. *Fond "Filiální škola Kamenice"*

–. *Fond "Farní škola Koloděje"*

–. *Fond "Triviální škola Kostelec u Křížků"*

–. *Fond "Národní škola Mukařov"*

–. *Fond "Triviální škola Panenské Břežany"*

–. *Fond "Triviální škola Říčany"*

–. *Fond "Triviální škola Sluštice"*

–. *Fond "Triviální škola Zvánovice"*

Státní okresní archiv Semily, *Fond "Národní škola Mříčná"*, "Denník přednešených učbozástojů", 1861–1872, inv # 18.

–. *Fond "Národní škola Bystrá nad Jizerou"*

–. *Fond "Obecní škola Jesenný"*

–. *Fond "Národní škola Loukov u Bystré"*

Státní okresní archiv Jičín, *Fond "Národní škola Úbislavice"*

–. *Fond "Národní škola Vidochov"*

Published primary statistical and documentary sources

ABC oder Namenbüchlein zum Gebrauche den Schulen in den kaiserlich-königlichen Staaten. Linz: Johann Michael Feichtingers Wittwe, 1786.

Abgeordnetenhaus des Reichsrates. *Stenographische Protokolle über die Sitzungen des Hauses der Abgeordneten des Reichsrathes. IV. Session*. Vienna: Kaiserlich-königliche Hof- und Staatsdruckerei, 1869.

Album. Herausgeben vom Lehrkörper der Oberrealschule in Reichenberg zur fünfundzwanzigjährigen Jubelfeier der Lehranstalt. Liberec: Heinrich Stiepel, 1862.

ALEX. Historische Rechts- und Gesetztexte Online. Österreichische Nationalbibliothek. Vienna, 2011, http://alex.onb.ac.at/

Allgemeine Schulordnung für die deutschen Normal- Haupt- und Trivialschulen in sämmtlichen kaiserl. königl. Erbländern. Vienna: Johann Thomas Edler von Trattner, 1775.

Berichte über die allgemeine Ausstellung zu Paris im Jahre 1867 erstattet von der für Preußsen und die Norddeutschen Staaten ernannten Mitgliedern der internationalen Jury. VII. Heft. Berlin: Königliche Staatsdruckerei, 1868.

Böhmische Landtag. *Stenographische Berichte des böhmischen Landtages. Dritte Jahressession.* Prague: Statthalterei Buchdruckerei, 1864.

British and Foreign School Society. *Hand-book to the Borough Road Schools; Explanatory of the Methods of Instruction adopted by the British and Foreign School Society.* London: British and Foreign School Society, 1856.

Demian, J.A. *Darstellung der Oesterreichischen Monarchie nach den neuesten statistischen Beziehungen. I. Band.* 1804.

Der Publicist II (1865). Vienna: Joseph Chowanetz.

Die Deutsche Volksschule: Monatschrift für Schule und Haus 15 (1866). Linz: Huemer's Witwe und Danner.

Druhá čítanka a mluvnice pro katolické školy v císařství rakouském. Vienna: C.k. školní knihosklad. 1860.

Engliš, Karel. "Příspěvky ke statistice národního školství." *Zprávy Zemského statistického úřadu království Českého* 7 (1905): sešit 2.

Felbiger, Ignaz. *Methodenbuch für Lehrer der deutschen Schulen in den kaiserlich-königlichen Erbländern/Kniha methodní pro učitelé českých škol v císařských královských zemích.* Prague: Verlag der k.k. Normalschulbuchdruckerey. 1777.

–. *Nachrichten von dem für die K.K. Staaten vorgeschriebenen Katechismus.* Vienna, 1977.

–. *Anleitung zur Rechenkunst.* Prague: Verlag der k.k. Normalschulbuchdruckerey. 1780

Gemeinderath der Stadt Wien. *Die Gemeinde-Verwaltung der Reichshaupt- und Residenzstadt Wien in den Jahren 1867–1870. Bericht des Bürgermeisters Dr. Cajetan Felder.* Vienna: Selbstverlag des Gemeinderathes des Stadt Wien. 1871

Gruber, Johann Leonhard. *Freymüthige Beurtheilung der Oesterreichischen Normalschulen und aller zum Behuf derselben gedruckten Schriften.* Berlin und Stettin: Friedrich Nicolai, 1783.

Handels- und Gewerbekammer Reichenberg. *Bericht über die materielle Lage der Arbeiter im B. Leipaer und Gitschiner Kreise Böhmens im Auftrage des hohen k.k. Ministeriums für Handel, Gewerbe und öffentliche Bauten.* Prague: Institut von C.W. Medau, 1852.

Hassel, Georg. *Statistischer Abriss des Östreichschen Kaisertums nach seinen neuesten politischen Beziehungen.* Nürnberg and Leipzig: Friedrich Campe, 1807.

Historische Statistik der Schweiz HSSO, 2012, hsso.ch

Huber, Franz. *Lehrer-Schema oder übersichtliche Zusammenstellung der in der Wiener Erzdiözese befindlichen öffentlichen und Privat-Lehranstalten und des an denselben angestellten Lehr-Personales.* Vienna, 1863.

Humpel, M.C. *Statistische Tableaus über die Bewegung der Bevölkerung, über die wichtigsten Lebensmittelpreise, über die Erwerb-, Einkommen- und Hauszinssteuer-Verhältnisse in der k.k. Reichs- Haupt- und Residenzstadt Wien, vom Jahre 1810 bis 1861.* Vienna: A. Hensinger. 1869.

Joanneum. *Jahresbericht des steiermärkisch-ständischen Joanneums zu Gratz für das Schuljahr 1846–1851. 35.–40. Jahresbericht.* Graz: 1847–1852.

Kaiser, Joseph. *Lehrer-Schema oder Ausweis des sämmtlichen, in der Erzdiöcese Wien und bischöfl. Diöcese St. Pölten befindlichen, und an öffentlichen und Privatschulen, an Lehr- und Erziehungs-Anstalten, welche der k.k. Landesschulbehörde von Nieder-Österreich unterstehen, angestellten Lehr-Personales mit Einschluss der weiblichen Arbeits-, Näh-, Musik-, Sprach- und Zeichnungsschul-Inhaber.* Vienna: A Pichler's Witwe & Sohn, 1852.

Kärntnerische Landtag. *Stenographische Protokolle der zweiten Session des kärntnerisches Landtages zu Klagenfurt.* Klagenfurt: Ferdinand von Kleimnmayr. 1863.

Katalog des an den Volksschulen der Lemberger lat. Erzdiözese angestellten Lehrpersonals, für das Jahr 1844. Lemberg: Peter Piller, 1844.

K. k. Böhmische Statthalterei. *Orts-Repertorum des Königreiches Böhmen. Mit Benutzung der von der k.k. statistischen Central-Commission zusammengestelltenene Ergebnisse der Volkszählung vom 31. Dezember 1869.* Prague: Verlag der k.k. Statthalterei. 1872.

K. k. Finanzministerium. *Tafeln zur Statistik des Steuerwesens im Österreichischen Kaiserstaate mit besondere Berücksichtigung der directen Steuern und des Grundsteuer-Katasters.* Vienna: K. k. Hof- und Staatsdruckerei, 1858.

K. k. Handels-Ministerium. Statistisches Büro der Rechnungs-Kontrollbehörde. *Versuch einer Darstellung der Oesterreichischen Monarchie in Statistischen Tafeln. I[ter] Jahrgang. 1828.* Vienna, 1829.

–. *Darstellung der Österreichischen Monarchie in Statistische Tabellen. II[ter] Jahrgang. 1829.* Vienna, 1830.

K. k. Handels-Ministerium. Direktion der administrativen Statistik. *Tafeln zur Statistik der Österreichischen Monarchie 1830–1848. Vol. 3–21.* Vienna: Kaiserliche-Königliche Hof- und Staats-Drückerei, 1831–1853.

–. *Tafeln zur Statistik der Österreichischen Monarchie. Vol. 1–5 Neue Folge.* Vienna: Kaiserliche-Königliche Hof- und Staats-Drückerei, 1856–1871.

K. k. Ministerium des Innern. *Statistische Übersichten über die Bevölkerung und der Viehstand von Österreich. Nach der Zählung vom 31. October 1857.* Vienna, 1859.

K. k. Österreichische Central-Comité. *Bericht über die Welt-Ausstellung zu Paris im Jahre 1867. I. Band: Einleitung (I). Die Kunstwerke und die Histoire du Travail (II). Instrumente für Kunst und Wissenschaft (III).* Vienna: Wilhelm Braumüller,1869.

K. k. Schulbucher-Verschleiß-Administration. *Politische Verfassung der deutschen Volksschulen für die k.k. österreichischen Provinzen mit Ausnahme von Ungarn, Lombardie, Venedig und Dalmatien. Neunte Auflage.* Vienna: Verlag der K.k. Schulbücher-Verschleiß-Administration, 1847.

K. k. Statistische Central-Commission. *Bevölkerung und Viehstand der im Reichsrathe vertretenen Königreiche und Länder, dann der Militärgrenze nach der Zählung vom 31. Dezember 1869.* Vienna: Kaiser-königliche Hof- und Staatsdrückerei, 1871.

–. "Bevölkerung der Gemeinden mit mehr als 2000 Einwohnern in den im Reichsrathe vertretenen Königreichen und Ländern nach der Zählung vom 31. December 1880." *Statistische Monatschrift* 4 (1881): Beilage.

–. *Österreichische Statistik Vols. 1–93.* Vienna: Kaiserlich-Königliche Hof- und Staats-druckerei. 1882–1916.

–. *Österreichische Statistik. Neue Folge. Vols. 1–18.* Vienna: Kaiserlich-Königliche Hof- und Staats-druckerei. 1912–1918.

–. *Detail-Conscription der Volksschulen in den im Reichsrathe vertretenen Königreichen und Ländern nach dem Stande vom Ende des Schuljahres 1865.* Vienna: C. Ueberreuter'sche Buchdruckerei (M. Salzer). 1870.

–. "Statistische Mittheilungen verschiedenen Inhalts." *Mittheilungen aus dem Gebiete der Statistik* 17 (1870): 19–78.

–. *Statistik der öffentlichen und Privat-Volksschulen in den im Reichsrathe vertretenen Königreichen und Länder. Nach den von den Bezirks-Schulbehörden für das Schuljahr 1870–1871 vorgelegten Erhebungen bearbeitet.* Vienna: C. Ueberreuter'sche Buchdruckerei (M. Salzer). 1873.

–. *Statistik der öffentlichen und Privat-Volksschulen in den im Reichsrathe vertretenen Königreichen und Ländern nach den von den Bezirks-Schulbehörden für das Schuljahr 1875 vorgelegten Erhebungen bearbeitet.* Kaiser-königliche Hof- und Staatsdrückerei, Vienna, 1876.

–. *Statistisches Jahrbuch der Österreichischen Monarchie für das Jahr 1863–1881.* 19 volumes. Vienna: Kaiserliche-Königliche Hof- und Staats-Drückerei, 1864–1882.

–. *Statistisches Jahrbuch für das Jahr 1880 – V. Heft: Volksschulen. Summarische Übersicht sämmtlicher Lehranstalten,* Vienna: Kaiserkönigliche Hof- und Staatsdrückerei, 1882.

Lehr-Personalstand der deutschen Schulen in der Seckauer- und Leobner-Diözese in Steyermark. Im Schuljahre 1846/47. Graz: J.A. Kienreich, 1847.

Lehr-Personalstand der deutschen Schulen in der Seckauer Diözese in Steiermark. Im Schuljahre 1861. Abgeschlossen 15. Dezember 1860. Graz: Jos. A. Kienreich, 1861.

Lehr-Personalstand der deutschen Schulen des Bisthums Seckau in Steiermark. Im Schuljahre 1864. Graz: Jos. A. Kienreich, 1863.

Lesebuch für die zweyte Klasse der Land-Schulen in den k.k. österreichischen Staaten. Graz: Verlag der samtlichen bürgerlichen Buchbinder & Jos. A. Kienreich, 1832.

Liechtenstern, Joseph Marx von. "Allgemeine Uebersicht des Standes der Bevölkerung im Erzherzogthum Niederöstreich unter der Enns im letzten Jahre des achtzehnten Jahrhunderts." *Archiv für Geographie und Statistik* 1 (1803): 203–206.

–. "Allgemeine Uebersicht des Standes der Bevölkerung im Erzherzogthum Niederöstreich ob der Enns im letzten Jahre des achtzehnten Jahrhunderts." *Archiv für Geographie und Statistik* 1 (1803): 208–210.

–. "Allgemeine Uebersicht des Standes der Bevölkerung im Herzogthume Steyermark im Anfange des 19. Jahrhunderts." *Archiv für Geographie und Statistik* 1 (1803): 326–328.

–. "Allgemeine Uebersicht des Standes der Bevölkerung im Herzogthume Krain im 1. Jahre des 19. Jahrhunderts." *Archiv für Geographie und Statistik* 1 (1803): 330–332.

–. "Allgemeine Uebersicht des Standes der Bevölkerung im Königreiche Böhmen im Anfange des 19. Jahrhunderts." *Archiv für Geographie und Statistik* 1 (1803): 388–391.

–. "Allgemeine Uebersicht des Standes der Bevölkerung im Marggrafthum Mähren mit Einschluss des damit verbundenen östreichischen Antheils an dem Herzogthum Schlesien, im Anfange des 19. Jahrhunderts." *Archiv für Geographie und Statistik* 1 (1803): 391–393.

Maresch, Johann. "Verzeichniss des gesammten an den Volksschulen der Leitmeritzer Diözese angestellten Lehrpersonals für das Jahr 1863." *Jahrbuch für Lehrer, Ältern und Erzieher* 27 (1863): Appendix.

Methodenbuch für Lehrer der deutschen Schulen in den kaiserlich-königlichen Erbländern. Vienna: Verlagsgewölbe der deutschen Schulanstalt, 1776.

Müllner, J. N. *Versuch einer statistischen Geographie von Böhmen.* Prague: Karl Barth, 1805.

Niederösterreichische Landtag. *Stenographische Protokolle des niederösterreichischen Landtages. Zweite Session 1863.* Vienna: K.k. Hof- und Staatsdruckerei. 1863.

"Österreich", *Allgemeine Zeitung München* 38, 7. Februar 1821.

Palacký, František. "Gradation der Bevölkerung Böhmens seit den letzten 60 Jahren." *Monatschrift des Gesselschaft des vaterländischen Museums in Böhmen* 3 (1829): 187–205.

–. *Popis království českého čili podrobné poznamenání všech dosavadních krajův, panství, statkův, měst, městeček a vesnic, někdejších hradův a tvrzí, též samot a zpustlých osad mnohých v zemi české, s udáním jejich obyvatelstva dne popisu r. 1843 vykonaného.* Prague: J.G. Kalve, 1848.

Pátek, Johann. "Katalog des gesammten Lehr-Personales an den Volksschulen der Brünner bischöflichen Diözese für das Jahr 1864." *Schul-Kalender für das Schalt-Jahr 1864* 7, pp. 129–168.

Peschel, Oscar. "Die Lehren der jüngsten Kriegsgeschichte." *Das Ausland: Ueberschau des neuesten Forschungen auf dem Gebiete der Natur-, Erd- und Völkerkunde* 29, 17th July 1866, p. 693–696.

Pěstoun, vychovatelský časopis IV (1865). Brno: J. Šnaidr.

Riegger, Joseph Anton von. *Archiv der Geschichte und Statistik, insbesondere von Böhmen. Zweyter Theil.* Dresden: Walterische Hofbuchhandlung, 1793.

–. *Materialien zur alten und neuen Statistik von Böhmen. VII. Heft*. Leipzig and Prague: Kaspar Widtmann, 1788.

–. *Materialien zur alten und neuen Statistik von Böhmen. X. Heft*. Leipzig and Prague: Kaspar Widtmann, 1790.

–. *Skizze einer statistischen Landeskunde Böhmens. II. Heftchen*. Leipzig and Prague: Kaspar Widtmann, 1795.

Schnabel, Georg Norbert. *Tafeln zur Statistik von Böhmen*. Prague: J.S. Calve'sche Buchhandlung, 1848.

Škola a život. Pedagogický časopis 7 (1861). Prague: Rohlíček a Sievers.

Školník – Časopis katolického učitelstva V (7) (1865). Hradec Králové: Ladislav Pospíšil.

Šrůtek, Josef A. "Soupis veškerého učitelstva národních škol v diecési Kralohradecké počátkem školního roku 1861." *Školník pro učitelstvo diecése kralohradecké a ostatních diecésí v Čechách a na Moravě* 10 (1861): Appendix

Staatsgrundgesetze der österreichischen Monarchie. Sammlung aller die Reichsverfassung und die Landerverfassungen betreffenden Gesetze, Verordnungen, Handschreiben und sonstigen Erlässe. 1. Bändchen. Vienna: Verlag von Friedrich Manz. 1861.

Staatsgrundgesetze der österreichischen Monarchie. Supplementheft. Vienna: Verlag der G. J. Manz'schen Buchhandlung. 1868.

Trajer, Johann. *Historisch-statistische Beschreibung der Diöcese Budweis*. České Budějovice: F. Zdarssa, 1862.

Vienna. Städtische statistische Bureau. *Die Bewegung der Bevölkerung in Wien im Jahre 1875. Trauungen, Geburten, Sterbefälle.* Vienna: Verlag des Städtischen statistischen Bureaus (M. Salzer). 1876.

Wilfling, Ignaz Richard. *Kalender für Aufseher, Katecheten und Lehrer der Nationalschulen in Königreiche Böhmen auf das Jahr 1790*. Prague: Caspar Widtmann. 1790.

Wiegand, Johann. *Versuch den Fleiß unter dem Landvolke einzuführen, zu verbreiten, und allgemein zu machen.* Vienna: Josef Kurzbock, k.k. illyrisch- und orientalischen Hof- wie auch N. Oest. Landschatfts- und Universitäts-Buchdruckern. 1772.

Secondary literature

A'Hearn, Brian, Jörg Baten and Dorothee Crayen. "Quantifying Quantitative Literacy: Age Heaping and the History of Human Capital." *Journal of Economic History* 69 (2009): 783–808.

A'Hearn, Brian, Alexia Delfino and Alessandro Nuvolari. "Rethinking Age-Heaping: A cautionary tale from Nineteenth-Century Italy." *University of Oxford Discussion Papers in Economic and Social History* #148, 2016.

Adámek, Karel Vácslav. *Paměti o školách v okresu hlineckém*. Velké Meziříčí: J. F. Šašek, 1890.

Aghion, Philippe, Xavier Jaravel, Torsten Persson and Dorothée Rouzet. "Education and Military Rivalry" *Journal of the European Economic Association* 17 (2019): 376–412.

Albisetti, James C. "The feminization of teaching in the nineteenth century: a comparative perspective" *History of Education* (1993): 253–263.

Alesina, Alberto, Reza Baqir and William Easterly. "Public goods and ethnic divisions" *Quarterly Journal of Economics* 114 (1999): 1243–1284.

Aliprantis, Christos. "The afterlife of Enlightened Absolutism: commemoration of Maria Theresa and Joseph II and the politics of liberal reform in nineteenth-century imperial Austria." *European Review of History: Revue européenne d'histoire* 26 (2019): 305–330.

Allen, Robert C. *The British Industrial Revolution in Global Perspective*. Cambridge: Cambridge University Press, 2009.

Andersson, Jens and Thor Berger. "Elites and the expansion of education in nineteenth-century Sweden" *Economic History Review* (2018): 1–28.

Bandiera Oriana, Myra Mohnen, Imran Rasul and Martina Viarengo. "Nation-building Through Compulsory Schooling during the Age of Mass Migration." *The Economic Journal* 129 (2019): 62–109.

Baten, Jörg and Ralph Hippe. "Geography, land inequality and regional numeracy in Europe in historical perspective." *Journal of Economic Growth* 23 (2018): 79–109.

Battista, Ludwig. *Die österreichische Volksschule: ihr Werden, ihre äusseren Arbeitsbedingungen und ihre Erziehungs- und Bildungsarbeit.* Vienna: Österreichische Bundesverlag, 1937.

Beales, Derek. *Joseph II: II. Against the World, 1780–1790.* Cambridge: Cambridge University Press, 2009.

Becher, Siegfried. *Statistische Übersicht der Bevölkerung der österreichischen Monarchie nach den Ergebnissen der Jahre 1830 bis 1840*. Stuttgart und Tübingen: J. G. Cotta'schen Buchhandlung, 1841.

Becker, Sasha, Erik Hornung and Ludger Woessmann. "Catch Me If You Can: Education and Catch-up in the Industrial Revolution" *CESifo working paper* #2816 (2009): 1–32.

Becker, Sasha and Ludger Woessmann. "Was Weber Wrong? A human capital theory of protestant economic history." *Quarterly Journal of Economics* 124 (2009): 531–596.

Beer, Adolf and Franz Hochegger. *Die Fortschritte des Unterrichtswesens in den Culturstaaten Europas. I. Band.* Vienna: Carol Gerold's Sohn, 1867.

Beltrán-Tapia, F., Martinez-Galarraga, J. "Inequality and education in pre-industrial economies: Evidence from Spain." *Explorations in Economic History* 69, (2018): 81–101.

Benavot, Aaron and Julia Resnik. "Lessons from the Past: A Comparative Socio-Historical Analysis of Primary and Secondary Education." Pages 123–230 in *Educating All Children: A Global Agenda*. Edited by Joel E. Cohen, David E. Bloom and Martin B. Malin. Cambridge, MA: MIT Press, 2007.

Benedikt, Heinrich. "Birckenstock, Johann Melchior Edler von." Page 254 In: *Neue Deutsche Biographie (NDB). Band 2*, Berlin: Duncker & Humblot. 1955

Bengtsson, Tommy and Martin Dribe. "The late emergence of socioeconomic mortality differentials: A micro-level study of adult mortality in southern Sweden 1815–1968" *Explorations in Economic History* 48 (2011): 389–400.

Bengtsson, Tommy and Frans van Poppel. "Socioeconomic inequalities in death from past to present: An introduction" *Explorations in Economic History* 48 (2011): 343–356.

Bidermann, Hermann Ignaz. *Die technische Bildung im Kaiserthume Oesterreich. Ein Betrag zur Geschichte der Industrie und des Handels*. Vienna: Carl Gerold und Sohn, 1854.

Binder, Ulrich. "State Official – Public Official – Pedagogic Official: Development of the Teaching Profession in Austria, France and Germany in the 18th Century" *Review of European Studies* 1 (2009): 76–82.

Black, Dan, Seth Sanders and Lowell Taylor. "Measurement of Higher Education in the Census and Current Population Survey" *Journal of the American Statistical Association* 98 (2003): 545–554.

Bodenhorn, Howard, Timothy W. Guinanne and Thomas A. Mroz. "Selection-Sample Biases and the Industrialization Puzzle." *Journal of Economic History* 77 (2017): 171–207.

Bolognese-Leuchtenmüller, Birgit. *Bevölkerungsentwicklung und Berufsstruktur, Gesundheits- und Fürsorgwesen in Österreich 1750–1918*. München: R. Oldenbourg Verlag, 1978.

Brezinka, Wolfgang. *Pädagogik in Österreich. Die Geschichte des Fachs an den Universitäten vom 18. Jahrhundert bis zum Ende des 20. Jahrhunderts. Band 1: Einleitung:*

Schulwesen, Universitäten und Pädagogik im Habsburger-Reich und in der Republik. Vienna: Verlag der österreichischen Akademie der Wissenschaften. 2000.

–. "Učitelské vzdělávání mezi státem a církví – rakouský příklad v letech 1774–1869." Pages 29–50 in *Učitel ve střední a jihovýchodní Evropě – Profesionalizace učitelského vzdělávání: historické a systematické aspekty*. Edited by Kasper, Tomáš, Markéta Pánková a kol. Prague: Academia and Národní pedagogické museum a knihovna J. A. Komenského. 2015.

Bukowski, Paweł. "How history matters for student performance: lessons from the Partitions of Poland." *Journal of Comparative Economics* 47 (2019): 136–175.

Carry, Alain. *Le compte satellite rétrospectif de l'éducation en France (1820–1996). Économies et societies*. Cahier de l'ISMÉA, Série AF, no. 25. Paris: ISMEA, 1999.

Cinnirella, Francesco and Hornung, Eric. "Landownership concentration and the expansion of education." *Journal of Development Economics* 121 (2016): 135–152.

Cinnirella, Francesco and Ruth Schueler. "Nation building: The role of central spending in education." *Explorations in Economic History* 67 (2018): 18–39.

Clark, Christopher. *Iron Kingdom: The Rise and Downfall of Prussia, 1600–1947.* London: Penguin Books, 2006.

Clay, Karen; Lingwall, Jeff and Melvin Stephens Jr. "Do schooling laws matter? Evidence from the introduction of compulsory attendance laws in the United States." *NBER working paper #18477*. 2012.

Cole, Laurence. "Chapter II – The Counter-Reformation's last stand: Austria." Pages 285–312 in *Culture Wars: Secular-Catholic Conflict in Nineteenth-Century Europe*. Edited by Clark, Christopher and Wolfram Kaiser. Cambridge: Cambridge University Press. 2003.

Cvrček, Tomáš. "Wages, Prices and Living Standards in the Habsburg Empire, 1827–1910." *Journal of Economic History* 73 (2013): 1–37.

Cvrček, Tomáš and Zajíček, Miroslav. "The making of a liberal education: Political economy of the Austrian school reform, 1865–1880." *Explorations in Economics History*, (2018): 1–17.

–. "The rise of public schooling in nineteenth-century Imperial Austria: Who gained and who paid?" *Cliometrica* 13 (2018)

Czoernig, Carl Joseph. *Topographisch-historisch-statistische Beschreibung von Reichenberg.* Vienna: Verlag bey Friedrich Volke. 1829.

Demian, Johann Andreas. *Darstellung der Oesterreichische Monarchie nach den neuesten statistischen Beziehungen. I. Band*, Austria, 1804.

Domej, Theodor. "Slowenisch als Unterrichtssprache in der Frühzeit des Kärntner Pflichtschulwesens (1774-1848)." *Wiener slawistischer Almanach* 22 (1988): 333–344.

Easterlin, Richard. "Why Isn't the Whole World Developed?" *Journal of Economic History* 41 (1981): 1–19.

Eklof, Ben. *Russian Peasant Schools: Officialdom, Village Culture and Popular Pedagogy, 1861–1914.* Berkeley and Los Angeles: University of California Press, 1990.

Emigh, Rebecca Jean. "Numeracy or Enumeration? The Uses of Numbers by States and Societies." *Social Science History* 26 (2002): 653–698.

Engelbrecht Helmut. *Geschichte des österreichischen Bildungswesens: Erziehung und Unterricht auf dem Boden Österreichs, Vol. 3. Von den frühen Aufklärung bis zum Vormärz.* Vienna: Österreichische Bundesverlag, 1984.

–. *Geschichte des österreichischen Bildungswesens: Erziehung und Unterricht auf dem Boden Österreichs, Vol. 4. Von 1848 Bis Zum Ende der Monarchie.* Vienna: Österreichische Bundesverlag, 1986.

Exner, Franz Wilhelm. *Das k.k. polytechnische Institut in Wien, seine Gründung, seine Entwicklung und sein jetziger Zustand.* Vienna: Friedrich Förster & Brüder. 1861.

Fialová, Ludmila, Zdeněk Pavlík and Pavel Vereš. "Fertility decline in Czechoslovakia during the last two centuries" *Population Studies* 44 (1990): 89–106.

Ficker, Adolf. "Vorträge über die Volkszählung in Österreich. Gehalten in dem vierten und sechsten Turnus der statistisch-administrativen Vorlesungen." *Mittheilungen aus der Gebiet der Statistik* 17 (1870): 1–142.

–. *Bericht über österreichisches Unterrichtswesen. Aus Anlass Der Welt-ausstellung 1873. I. Theil. Geschichte, Organisation und Statistik der österreichischen Unterrichtswesens.* Vienna: Alfred Holder, 1873.

–. "Ein weiterer Beitrag zur Organisierung der nächsten Volkszählung in Oesterreich." Statistische Monatschrift 4 (1878): 253–264.

Field, Alexander J. "Economic and Demographic determinants of Educational Commitment: Massachusetts, 1855" *Journal of Economic History* 39 (1979): 439–460.

Fischer K.G. *Ernst von Feuchtersleben. Pädagogische Schriften.* Paderborn: Ferdinand Schöningh Verlag. 1963.

Frank, Ferdinand. *Die Österreichische Volksschule von 1848–1898*. Vienna: Verlag von Pischler's Witwe und Sohn, 1898.

–. "Kurzer Überblick über die geschichtliche Entwicklung des österreichischen Volksschulwesens in den letzten fünfzig Jahren." Pages 60–78 In *Zur Geschichte und Statistik des Volksschulwesens im In- und Auslande*, Wien: Sonderausstellungs-Commission "Jugendhalle". 1898.

Frankfurter, Salomon. "Thun-Hohenstein, Graf Leo." Pages 178–212. In: *Allgemeine Deutsche Biographie (ADB). Band 38*. Leipzig: Dunkler & Humblot, 1894.

Friedrichs, Christopher R. "Whose House of Learning? Some Thoughts on German Schools in Post-Reformation Germany." *History of Education Quarterly* 22 (1982): 371–377

Galor, Oded. *Unified growth theory*. Princeton and Oxford: Princeton University Press, 2011.

Glaeser, Edward L., Giacomo A.M. Ponzetto and Andrei Shleifer. "Why does democracy need education?" *Journal of Economic Growth* 12 (2007): 77–99.

Go, Sun and Lindert, Peter. "The uneven rise of American public schools to 1850." *Journal of Economic History* 70 (2010): 1–26.

Goehlert, J. Vincenz. "Die Ergebnisse der in Osterreich im vorigen Jahrhundert ausgefuhrten Volkszahlungen im Vergleiche mit jenen der neuern Zeit." *Sitzungsberichte der philos.-histor. Classe der kais. Akademie der Wissenschaften* XIV (1854): 52–81

–. "Häuser und Volkszahl sowie Viehstand Oesterreichs in der Regierungsperiode Kaiser Josef's II." *Statistische Monatschrift* V (1879): 402–405.

–. "Die Entwicklung der Bevölkerung von Tirol und Vorarlberg." *Statistische Monatschrift* VI (1880): 52–64

Goñi, Marc. "Landed Elites and Education Provision in England: Evidence from School Boards, 1870–99." working paper (2017)

Good, David. *The Economic Rise of the Habsburg Empire, 1750 – 1914*. Berkeley: University of California Press.1984.

Green, Andy. *Education and State Formation: The Rise of Education Systems in England, France and the USA*. London: Palgrave Macmillan, 1990.

Hain, Joseph. *Handbuch der Statistik des Österreichischen Kaiserstaates. I. Band.* Vienna: Tendler & Compagnie, 1852

Hanushek, Eric A. and Ludger Woessmann. "Do better schools lead to more growth? Cognitive skills, economic outcomes and causation" *Journal of Economic Growth* 17 (2012): 267–321.

Heiler, Bernhard and Rosa Lebmann. "Die Entwicklung der allgemeinbildenden Pflichtschulen in Österreich." Pages 513–544 in *Geschichte und Ergebnisse der zen-*

tralen amtlichen Statistik in Österreich, 1829–1979: Festschrift aus Anlaß des 150jährigen Bestehens der zentralen Statistik in Österreich. Edited by Österreichisches Statistisches Zentralamt. Vienna: Oesterreichische Staatsdruckerei, 1979.

Helczmanovszki, Heimold. "Die Bevölkerung Österreich-Ungarns." Pages 369–402 in *Geschichte und Ergebnisse der zentralen amtlichen Statistik in Österreich, 1829–1979: Festschrift aus Anlaß des 150jährigen Bestehens der zentralen Statistik in Österreich.* Edited by Österreichisches Statistisches Zentralamt. Vienna: Oesterreichische Staatsdruckerei, 1979.

Helfert, Joseph Alexander. *Die österreichische Volksschule. Geschichte, System, Statistik. I. Band – Die Gründung der österreichischen Volksschule durch Maria Theresia.* Prague: Verlag von Friedrich Tempsky: 1860.

Herrmann, Franz Joseph. *Denkschrift über die Zustände des Volksschulwesens in Böhmen und treue Wünsche für die Hebung der Volksschulen im konstitutionellen Kaiserstaate Oesterreich.* Kroměříž: k.k. Hof- und Staats-Druckerei, 1849.

Hoffmann, Anton. *Geschichte der Haupt- und Mädchenschule in Reichenberg.* Reichenberg: Anton Schöpfer. 1868.

Hölzl, Sebastian. "Studien zum Pflichtschulwesen in Tirol 1774–1806" *Tiroler Heimat: Jahrbuch für Geschichte und Volkskunde* 38 (1974): 91–138.

Horlacher, Rebekka. "'Best Practice' Around 1800. Johann Heinrich Pestalozzi's Educational Enterprise in Switzerland and the Establishment of Private Pestalozzi Schools Abroad." *Encounters on Education* 12 (2011): 3–17.

Hoszowski, Stanislaw. *Ceny we Lwowie w latach, 1701–1914.* Lwow, Warsaw: Sklad glowny: Kasa im. Rektora J. Mianowskiego. 1934.

Humphries, Jane. "Childhood and child labour in the British industrial revolution" *Economic History Review* 66 (2013): 395–418.

Jakubec, Ivan and Zdeněk Jindra. *Dějiny hospodářských českých zemí: Od počátku industrializace do konce habsburské monarchie.* Prague: Karolinum. 2007.

Jaroš, Karel and Jan Job. *Rozvoj československého školství v číslech.* Prague: SEVT. 1961

Jechl, Johann. *Statistische Nachweisungen über den land- und lehentäflichen Grundbesitz im Königreiche Böhmen.* Prague: Verlag der J.G.Calve'schen k. k. Universitäts-Buchhandlung. 1868.

Jelinek, Carl. *Das ständisch-polytechnische Institut zu Prag. Programm zur fünfzigjährigen Erinnerungs-Feier an die Eröffnung des Institutes.* Prague: Gottlieb Haase Söhne. 1856.

Jellouschek, Friedrich. "Das Reichsvolksschulgesetz." *Erziehung und Unterricht* 119 (1969): 289–305.

Jones, Mary G. *The Charity School Movement: A Study of Eighteenth Century Puritanism in Action.* Cambridge: Cambridge University Press. 2013.

Kann, Robert A. *A Study in Austrian Intellectual History: From Late Baroque to Romanticism.* London: Thames and Hudson, 1960.

Kárníková, Ludmila. *Vývoj obyvatelstva v českých zemích, 1754–1914.* Praha: Nakladatelství Československé akademie věd, 1965.

Klein, Alexandr. "The Institutions of the 'Second Serfdom' and Economic Efficiency: Review of the Existing Evidence for Bohemia" working paper, (2014): 1–16.

–. "Did Children's Education Matter? Family Migration as a Mechanism of Human Capital Investment: Evidence from Nineteenth Century Bohemia." *Economic History Review* 64 (2011): 730–764.

Klingenstein, Grete. "Akademikerüberschuss als soziales Problem im Aufegklärten Absolutismus." Pages 165–204 in *Bildung, Politik und Gesellschaft: Studien zur Geschichte des europäischen Bildungswesen vom 16. bis zum 20. Jahrhunderts*. Edited by Grete Klingenstein, Heinrich Lutz and Gerald Stourzh. Munich: R. Oldebourg Verlag 1978.

Kneidl, František. *Paměti školského okresu karlínského. Soudní okresy: Karlín a Brandýs n. L. Od nejstarších časů, zvláště však od r. 1848 až do r. 1898.* Prague: J. Otta, 1898

Komlos, John. *The Habsburg Monarchy as a Customs Union: Economic Development in Austria-Hungary in the Nineteenth Century.* Princeton: Princeton University Press. 1983.

Kořalka, Jiří. *Češi v Habsburské říši a v Evropě 1815 – 1914: sociálně-historické souvislosti vytváření novodobého národa a národnostní otázky v českých zemích.* Prague: Argo. 1996.

Kuzmin, Michail N. *Vývoj školství a vzdělání v Československu.* Prague: Academia, 1991.

Kwan, Jonathan. "Austro-German Liberalism and the Coming of the 1867 Compromise: 'Politics Again in Flux'." *Austrian History Yearbook* 44 (2013): 62–87.

–. *Liberalism and the Habsburg Monarchy, 1861–1895.* London: Palgrave Macmillan, 2013.

Lampe, Markus, Felipe Tamega-Fernandes and Antonio Tena-Junguito. "How much trade Liberalization was there in the World Before and After Cobden-Chevalier?" *Journal of Economic History 72* (2012): 708–740.

Landes, William M. and Lewis C. Solmon. "Compulsory Schooling Legislation: An Economic Analysis of Law and Social Change in the Nineteenth Century" *Journal of Economic History* 32 (1972): 54–91.

Lechner, Elmar. "Die Revision des Reichsvolksschulgesetzes (1869) im Kronland Kärnten (1883). Meinungen und Maßnahmen." *Retrospektiven in Sachen Bildung* 7 (2012): 1–12.

Lenderová, Milena, Tomáš Jiránek and Marie Macková. *Z dějin české každodennosti: Život v 19. století.* Prague: Karolinum, 2009.

Liechtenstern, Joseph Marx von. "Ueber die Lage, Grösse, Bestandtheile und Bevölkerung der östrechischen Erb-Monarchie nach ihrem Zustande unmittelbar nach dem Friedensschulsse von Lüneville, oder im Anfange des XIXten Jahrhunderts." *Archiv für Geographie und Statistik* 1 (1802): 1–45

–. *Statistische Uebersicht des Oesterreichischen Kaiser-staats. Nach dessen Zustande in dem anfange des Jahres 1809.* Zweyte Auflage.Vienna, 1809

–. *Handbuch der neuesten Geographie des Österreichischen Kaiserstaates. I. Theil.* Vienna: B. Ph. Bauer, 1817.

Lindert Peter. *Growing Public: Social Spending and Economic Growth since the Eighteenth Century. Vol. 1.* Cambridge: Cambridge University Press, 2004.

Link Bruce and Jo Phelan. "Social Conditions as Fundamental Causes of Disease" *Journal of Health and Social Behavior* – Extra issue (1995): 80–94.

–. "McKeown and the Idea That Social Conditions Are Fundamental Causes of Disease" *American Journal of Public Health* 92 (2002): 730–732.

Long, Jason. "The Socioeconomic Return to Primary Schooling in Victorian England." *Journal of Economic History* 66 (2006): 1026–1053.

Lott, John R. Jr. "Public Schooling, Indoctrination, and Totalitarianism." *Journal of Political Economy* 107 (1999): S127–S157.

Margo, Robert. "Race, Educational Attainment, and the 1940 Census." *Journal of Economic History* 46 (1986): 189–198.

Mariscal, Elisa and Sokoloff, Kenneth L. "Schooling, Suffrage and the Persistence of Inequality in the Americas, 1800–1945." Pages 159–218 in *Political Institutions and Economic Growth in Latin America: Essays in Policy, History, and Political Economy*, Edited by Haber, Stephen. Hoover Institution Press, 2000.

Maynes, Mary Jo. *Schooling for the people: comparative local studies of schooling history in France and Germany, 1750–1850.* New York: Holmes and Meyer. 1985.
Melton, James Van Horn. *Absolutism and the eighteenth-century origins of compulsory schooling in Prussia and Austria.* Cambridge: Cambridge University Press, 1988.
Mincer, Jacob. "Investment in Human Capital and Personal Income Distribution." *Journal of Political Economy* 66 (1958): 281–302.
Mitch, David. *The Rise of Popular Literacy in Victorian England – The Influence of Private Choice and Public Policy.* Philadelphia: University of Pennsylvania Press, 1992.
–. "The Role of Education and Skill in the British Industrial Revolution", Pages 241–279 in *The British Industrial Revolution: An Economic Perspective*. Edited by Mokyr, Joel. (2nd Edition), Westview Press, 1999, pp. 241–279.
Mokyr, Joel. *Why Ireland starved A quantitative and analytical history of the Irish economy, 1800–1850.* London: Allen & Unwin, 1983.
_. *The Lever of Riches*. Oxford: Oxford University Press, 1990.
–. "Long term economic growth and the history of technology." Pages 1113–1180 in *Handbook of economic growth, vol 1B.* Edited by Aghion P, Durlauf S. Amsterdam: Elsevier. 2005.
Mokyr, Joel and Hans-Joachim Voth. "Understanding growth in early modern Europe." Pages 7–42 in: *The Cambridge economic history of Europe*. Edited by Stephen Broadberry and Kevin H. O'Rourke. Cambridge: Cambridge University Press. 2010.
Monaghan, J. "Some views on education and industrial progress a hundred years ago." *The Vocational Aspect of Secondary and Further Education* 20 (1968): 187–194.
Moody, J. *French Education Since Napoleon*. Syracuse: Syracuse University Press, 1978.
Mühlpeck, Vera; Sandgruber Roman and Hannelore Woitek. "Index der Verbraucherpreise 1800 – 1914: Eine Ruckberechnung fur Wien and den Gebietstand des heutigen Osterreichs" Pages 649–699 in *Geschichte und Ergebnisse der zentralen amtlichen Statistik in Österreich, 1829–1979: Festschrift aus Anlaß des 150jährigen Bestehens der zentralen Statistik in Österreich.* Edited by Österreichisches Statistisches Zentralamt, 649-99. Vienna: Oesterreichische Staatsdruckerei, 1979.
Nafziger, Stephen. "Did Ivan's vote matter? The political economy of local democracy in Tsarist Russia." *European Review of Economic History* 15 (2011): 393–441.
Organization for Economic Cooperation and Development. *Education at a Glance 2018.* OECD Indicators. OECD. 2018
Pacher, Lieselotte Maria. "Der elementare Rechenunterricht in deutschsprachigen Lehrbüchern Österreichs von Marie Theresia bis zum Ende der Monarchie." Unpublished dissertation, Vienna: University of Vienna. 2008.
Pietsch, Walter. *Die Theresianische Schulreform in der Steiermark (1775–1805).* Graz: Pädagogischen Institut in Steiermark, 1977.
Pospíchal, Vlastimil. "Piaristická škola v Boru (Heyde) 1763–1870" *Novoborský měsíčník – Městský zpravodaj* (2010): 27–28.
Prausek, Vinzenz. *Die Verbesserung der Volksschule mit besonderer Rücksichtigung Österreichs.* Vienna: Sallmayer & Komp., 1868.
Prechtl, Johann Joseph. "Geschichte des kaiserl. königl. polytechnischen Instituts." *Jahrbücher des kaiserlichen königlichen polytechnischen Institutes in Wien 20* (1839): V–XVIII.
Pritchett, Lant and Martina Viarengo. "The State, Socialisation, and Private Schooling: When Will Governments Support Alternative Producers?" *Journal of Development Studies* 51 (2015): 784–807.
Ramirez, Francisco O. and John Boli. "The Political Construction of Mass Schooling: European Origins And Worldwide Institutionalization." *Sociology of Education* 60 (1987): 2–17.

Reichenberger Stadtrath. *Reichenberg in der Zeit der Selbstverwaltung vom Jahre 1850 bis 1900. Ein geschichtlicher Rückblick und Verwaltungsbericht*. Reichenberg: Rudolf Gerzabek & Comp., 1902.

Riedl, Miroslav. *Zavádění povinné školní docházky na území současného Jihomoravského kraje. I. díl*. Brno: Univerzita J.E. Purkyně, 1981

Rohrer, Joseph. *Uiber der Tiroler: Ein Beytrag zur Oesterreichischen Völkerkunde*. Vienna: Verlag der Dollischen Buchhandlung, 1796.

Rottenhan, Heinrich Franz von. "Gutachten über den Gesichtspunkt und den Wirkungskreis der Studien-Revisions-Commission" Pages 23–80 in *Nachrichten von der beabsichtigten Verbesserung des öffentlichen Unterrichtswesens in den österreichischen Staaten mit authentischen Belegen*. Edited by Christian Ulrich Detlev von Eggers, Tübingen: J. G. Cotta'schen Buchhandlung, 1808.

Šafránek, Jan. *Školy české. Obraz jejich vývoje a osudů. I. svazek R. 862–1848*. Prague: Matice česká, 1913.

Sbor pro oslavu stoletého jubilea reálky rakovnické. *Sto let reálky rakovnické; památník vydaný k stému výročí založení reálky v Rakovníku. Díl 1. Dějiny, vzpomínky, význam*. Prague: Státní tiskárna, 1933.

Scheipl, Josef and Helmut Seel. *Die Entwicklung des österreichischen Schulwesens von 1750–1938*. Graz: Leykam Verlag, 1987.

Schimmer, Gustav A. "Mortalität und Vitalität der im Reichsrathe vertretenen Königreiche und Länder der Österreichischen Monarchie." *Mittheilungen aus dem Gebiete der Statistik* 14, IV. Heft. (1868): 1–93.

–. "Anzeige von: Die Bewegung der Bevölkerung in Wien im Jahre 1874" *Statistische Monatschrift* 1 (1875): 347–350.

–. "Frenquenz der Lehranstalten Oesterreich's von 1841 bis 1876, in Vergleichung zur Bevölkerung" *Statistische Monatschrift* 3 (1877): 53–74.

–. "Gedanken über die Durchführung der nächsten Volkszählung in Österreich." *Statistische Monaschrift* 4 (1878): 153–178.

Schmick, Ethan J. and Allison Shertzer. "The Impact of Early Investments in Urban School Systems in the United States." *NBER working paper* #25663 (2019): 1–49.

Schulze, Max-Stephan. "Patterns of growth and stagnation in the late nineteenth century Habsburg economy." *European Review of Economic History* 4 (2000): 311–340.

Seebauer, Renate. *Lehrerbildung in Porträts: von der Normalschule bis zur Gegenwart. Band 2. Schul- und Hochschulgeschichte*. Vienna: Lit Verlag, 2011.

Šišma, Pavel. *Matematika na německé technice v Brně*. Prague: Prometheus. 2002.

Smith, Daniel S. "Differential Mortality in the United States before1900" *Journal of Interdisciplinary History* (13): 735–759.

Sonnenfels, Joseph von. *Gesammelte Schriften: Reden. Achter Band*. Vienna: mit von Baumeisterischen Schriften. 1786.

Soysal, Yasemin N. and David Strang. "Construction of the First Mass Education Systems in Nineteenth-Century Europe." *Sociology of education* 62 (1989): 277–288.

Spener, Philip Jacob. *Pia desideria*. Fortress Press, 1964.

Steckel, Richard H. "The Quality of Census Data for Historical Inquiry: A Research Agenda." *Social Science History* (15): 579–599.

Stohr, Christian. "Multiple Core Regions: Regional Inequality in Switzerland, 1860–2008", *Research in Economic History 34* (2018): 135–198.

Strakosch-Graßmann, Gustav. *Geschichte des österreichischen Unterrichtswesens*. Vienna: Verlag von A. Pichlers Witwe & Sohn. 1905.

Šustová, Magdaléna. "Význam Aleše Vincence Pařízka v přípravě učitelů elementárních škol" Pages 101–112 in *Učitel ve střední a jihovýchodní Evropě – Profesionalizace učitelského vzdělávání: historické a systematické aspekty*. Edited by Kasper, Tomáš,

Pánková Markéta a kol. Prague: Academia and Národní pedagogické museum a knihovna J. A. Komenského. 2015.

Staffler, Johann Jakob. *Tirol und Vorarlberg, statistisch und topographisch, mit geschichtlichen Bemerkungen. I. Theil.* Innsbruck: Felician Rauch. 1839.

Taylor, Alan J.P. *The Habsburg monarchy, 1809–1918: a history of the Austrian Empire and Austria-Hungary.* London: Hamish Hamilton. 1948.

Tribe, Keith. "Cameralism and the Science of Government." *Journal of Modern History* 56 (1984): 263–284.

Uhlig, Otto. *Die Schwabenkinder aus Tirol und Vorarlberg*. Innsbruck: Universitätsverlag Wagner. 2016.

Urban, Otto. *Česká společnost 1848–1918*. Prague: Svoboda. 1982.

Veselá, Zdenka. *Vývoj české školy a učitelského vzdělávání*. Brno: Masarykova Univerzita, 1992.

–. "Příspěvek k historii učitelského vzdělávání." *Pedagogická orientace* (2005): 16–30.

Voegler, Max Herbert Religion, *Liberalism and the Social Question in the Habsburg Hinterland: the Catholic Church in Upper Austria, 1850–1914*. PhD dissertation, New York City: Columbia University, 2006.

Vollrath, Dietrich. "Inequality and school funding in the rural United States, 1890." *Explorations in Economic History* 50 (2013): 267–284.

Vondra, Roman. *České země v letech 1705–1792: Věk absolutismu, osvícenství, paruk a třírohých klobouků*. Prague: Libri, 2010.

Wandycz, Piotr Stefan. *The Lands of Partitioned Poland, 1795–1918*. Seattle: University of Washington Press, 1984.

Wangermann, Ernst. *Aufklärung und staatsbürgerliche Erziehung: Gottfried van Swieten als Reformator des österreichischen Unterrichtswesens 1781–1791*. Wien: Verlag für Geschichte und Politik, 1978.

Weiss, Anton. *Geschichte der österreichischen Volksschule 1792–1848. I. Band. Die Entstehungsgeschichte des Volksschul-Planes von 1804.* Graz: Verlagsbuchhandlung "Styria", 1904.

–. *Geschichte der österreichischen Volksschule 1792–1848. II. Band. Geschichte der österreichischen Volksschule unter Franz I. und Ferdinand I. 1792–1848.* Graz: Verlagsbuchhandlung "Styria", 1904.

–. *Geschichte der Theresianischen Schulreform in Böhmen.* Vienna and Leipzig: K. u. k. Hof-Buchdruckerei und Hof-Verlags-Buchhandlung Carl Fromme. 1906.

Winckler, Johann. *Die periodische Presse Oesterreichs. Eine historisch-statistische Studie.* Vienna: Leopold Sommer & Co., 1875.

Würzbach, Constant von. *Biographisches Lexikon des Kaiserthums Oesterreich, enthaltend die Lebensskizzen der denkwürdigen Personen, welche seit 1750 in den österreichischen Kronländern geboren wurden oder darin gelebt und gewirkt haben. 31. Theil: Schnabel–Schröter.* Vienna: Verlag der k.k. Hof- und Staatsdruckerei, 1876.

Zeps, Michael Joseph. *The Politics of Education in Austria: Church, State and the Reform of Education 1765–1962*. PhD dissertation, Stanford: Stanford University, 1979.

Subject Index

1848 revolution 1, 8, 39, 40–41, 54, 57–58, 86, 89, 92–93, 98, 108, 119, 140, 157, 161, 206, 224, 225, 233–234, 237, 238, 268, 276

Allgemeine Schulordnung (1774) 8, 18, 19, 25–30, 31, 32, 34, 35, 36, 37, 39, 42, 43, 51, 63–64, 88, 200, 201, 202, 205, 233, 242, 263, 267, 280 *see also* Theresian school reform
Altenwörth, Lower Austria 158
Arbesbach, Lower Austria 158
arithmetic 17, 26, 27, 28, 33, 36, 48, 202, 205, 222, 223, 261, 262, 271
Aš (Asch), Bohemia 236
Attendance sample 14, 180–190, 193–194, 196, 198, 206
attendance rate 15, 31, 179–190, 195–197, 209, 220, 264
Augsburg, Bavaria 166
Ausgleich see Austro-Hungarian Compromise
Austria 5, 7, 8, 9, 10, 17, 21, 22, 23, 24, 29, 39, 50, 54, 60, 66, 69, 70, 86, 100, 121–123, 126, 127, 128, 135, 136, 162, 170–172, 173, 177, 196, 199, 209, 211, 222, 233, 244, 246, 247, 249, 263, 267, 270, 272
- Lower 10, 14, 43, 52, 55, 59, 62, 63, 65, 66–68, 70, 71, 93, 94, 96, 97, 107–112, 115, 120, 128–135, 136, 148–150, 157–158, 161, 163, 165, 168, 169, 170, 171, 172, 174, 176, 196, 218, 219, 220, 221, 222, 234, 235, 238, 239, 244, 246, 247, 264
- Upper 39, 55, 56, 59, 65, 71, 94, 115, 134, 136, 164-165, 168, 169, 170, 171, 172, 174, 176, 196, 218, 219, 220, 221, 235, 240, 243, 244, 247
Austrian Littoral 17, 39, 53, 55, 59, 65, 71, 76, 77, 78, 93, 94, 115, 136, 137, 138, 164, 165, 168, 169, 170, 172, 173, 174, 175, 176, 178, 217, 218, 219, 221, 235, 245, 253, 255
Austro-Hungarian Compromise (1867) 241
Austro-Prussian War (1866) 4, 7, 123, 241
Austro-Turkish War (1788–1791) 51
Austrian Statistical Commission 13, 66, 165, 195, 211

Baden, Germany 244
Basedow, Johann Bernhard (1724–1790) 42
Bauer, Karl L. F. (1834–1895) 247
Bavaria, Germany 50, 97, 171, 241, 244
Belgium 5, 128, 132, 174
Bell-Lancaster method (monitorial system) 40, 42, 270–271, 272, 275
Bělušice, Bohemia 239
Bible 20, 21, 27, 202, 203, 205, 206
Birkenstock, Johann Melchior (1738–1809) 43
Bohemia 10, 11, 14, 21, 48, 52, 55, 56, 57, 59, 61, 62, 63, 65, 66, 68, 69, 71, 73, 74–76, 79–81, 86, 88, 93, 94, 96, 97, 103–104, 115, 120, 122, 126, 134, 136, 138, 156, 157, 158, 159, 168, 169, 170, 171, 174, 176, 182, 191, 196, 198, 200, 208, 217, 218, 219, 220, 221, 225, 234, 235, 236, 238, 239, 248, 254, 256, 257, 264, 269
Bohnice, Bohemia 90–92, 95, 107, 113
Bohosudov (Mariaschein), Bohemia 200

branch school (*Filialschule*, *Excurrendo-Schule*) 54, 55, 56, 87, 107, 114, 231
Brandýs nad Labem, Bohemia 146, 225, 226
Brázdím, Bohemia 181
British and Foreign School Society 270, 274
Brno, Moravia 45, 49, 96, 103, 114, 136, 163, 248, 251
Brody, Galicia 46
Budweis *see* České Budějovice
Bukovina 10, 13, 17, 53, 55, 59, 63, 65, 66, 71, 73, 113, 114, 115, 136, 148, 150, 160–161, 169, 172, 173, 174, 176, 196, 218, 219, 235, 245, 247, 254, 276, 277
Bürgerschule *see* civic school
Bystrá nad Jizerou, Bohemia 181

Čakovice, Velké, Bohemia 145, 146, 147
cameralism 20–21, 36, 43
Campo Formio, Treaty of (1797) 54
Carinthia 11, 39, 45, 55, 59, 63, 65, 66, 71, 76, 77, 93, 94, 115, 136, 138, 164, 165, 168, 171–172, 174, 176, 196, 210, 213–214, 215, 216, 217, 218, 219, 220, 221, 235, 238, 247, 248, 275, 276
Carniola 39, 53, 55, 59, 65, 66, 71, 76, 77, 94, 115, 136, 137, 138, 160, 164, 168, 172, 173, 174, 176, 196, 218, 219, 220, 221, 226, 235, 245, 252, 253, 254, 255, 256, 257, 277
Čáslav, Bohemia 74
Čelákovice, Bohemia 181
České Budějovice (Budweis), Bohemia14, 17, 79–86, 96, 127, 148, 236
Chamber of Commerce 14, 191, 192, 235, 236, 243, 253, 254, 256, 258
Cheb (Eger), Bohemia 236
Chernivtsi (Czernowitz), Bukovina 150
child labour 3, 88, 165–167, 177, 192–193, 197, 209, 247, 262, 277
Chrudim, Bohemia 74
civic school (*Bürgerschule*) 40, 41, 58, 81, 114, 225, 245
compulsory schooling 4, 5, 23, 28–29, 65, 95, 164, 199, 246, 250
Concordat (1855) 41, 79, 234, 241, 242
Constance, Lake 166
constitution 41, 100, 233, 234, 241, 242, 246, 262
consumption tax *see Verzehrungssteuer*
coverage *see* school coverage
Czech
– language *see* language of instruction, Czech
– provinces (Czech lands) 24, 70, 71, 74, 93, 120, 138, 139, 158–159, 160, 161, 170, 171, 211–212, 222
– Republic 70, 123
Czechoslovakia 10, 263

Dąbrowa, Galicia 251
Dalmatia 10, 13, 17, 39, 53, 54, 55, 59, 65, 70, 71, 73, 78, 113, 114, 115, 136, 160, 164, 169, 173, 174, 175, 176, 178–179, 196, 198, 217, 218, 219, 222, 223, 235, 247, 277
Dědová, Bohemia 122
Denmark 29
Detail-Conscription 13, 55, 56, 65, 66, 67, 73, 76, 77, 94, 100, 101, 102, 103, 113, 115, 120, 128, 135, 136, 138, 142, 144, 145, 148, 164, 176, 180, 181, 182, 185, 220, 259, 265
Dithmar, Justus Christoph (1678–1737) 20
Dřevčice, Bohemia 181

earnings tax see *Erwerbsteuer*
Education Commission (*Studien-Hof-Commission*, *Studien- und Büchercensurs-Hofcommission*) 14, 22, 28, 31, 33, 35, 39, 40, 43, 44, 45, 57, 64, 71, 86, 88, 126, 147, 166, 233, 275, 276, 279
education creep 212–217, 220
electoral system of Austria *see Kurialsystem*
emigration *see* migration
Enlightenment 42, 43, 280
England 3, 16, 29, 128, 174, 223, 270–274 *see also* Great Britain

enrolment ratio 12, 15, 16, 59, 61–62, 69, 81–86, 163, 164, 168, 170–174, 179, 195–198, 217, 219, 220, 259, 264, 265, 269, 273
Erwerbsteuer (earnings tax) 237
Excurrendo-Schule see branch school

Fassion (*Fasse*) 145–148, 153
Felbiger, Johann Ignaz (1724–1788) 23, 24, 25, 27–28, 30, 31, 32, 42, 52, 58–59, 74, 163, 200, 203, 204, 266
Ferry, Jules François (1832–1893) 4, 5, 6
Feuchtersleben, Ernst von (1806–1849) 233, 234
Ficker, Adolf (1816–1880) 264
Figuly von Szep, Ignaz Karl (1807–1875) 247, 252
Firmian, Leopold Ernst von (1708–1783) 1, 21, 22, 24, 42
First World War (1914–1918) 4, 5, 9, 70, 77, 175, 211
France 4, 5, 6, 29, 33, 123, 174, 233, 262, 274
Francis I, emperor of Austria (1768–1835) 9, 33–34, 47, 231, 264
Francis Joseph I (1830–1916) 40, 47, 233, 243, 244, 258
Francke, August Hermann (1663–1727) 20
Franco-Austrian War (1859) 233, 237
Frederick II, King of Prussia (1712–1786) 4, 23
French Revolution 231
French Wars *see* Napoleonic Wars
Friedrichshafen, Germany 166
Fünfhaus, Lower Austria 135

Galicia 10, 13, 17, 53, 55, 59, 63, 65, 66, 71, 73, 113, 114, 115, 120, 136, 148, 149, 150, 153, 156, 160–161, 169, 172, 173, 174, 176, 195, 214–216, 217, 218, 219, 222, 223, 235, 245, 246, 247, 251, 252, 253, 254, 255, 259, 261, 275, 277
Gall, Joseph Anton (1748–1807) 32–33, 42, 204
Gasser, Simon Peter (1676–1745) 20
Gaya, Philippides von 23
gender gap
– in school coverage 71–73, 177–179
– among teachers 15, 128, 131–132, 135, 137, 139, 150, 155–156
– in enrolment 174–179
– in attendance 182, 184–186, 190, 193–195
General Reglement (1763) 23
General School Ordinance (1774) *see Allgemeine Schulordnung*
Germany 5, 6, 22, 128, 162, 166, 222, 263
germanization 73–74, 78–79, 143, 276–277
Gerstner, Franz Joseph (1756–1832) 37
girls' school (*Mädchenschule*) 71, 116, 131, 132, 149, 150, 151, 155, 225
Gleichförmigkeit (uniformity) 27, 32, 33, 203, 263, 279
Gorica (Görz), Austrian Littoral 136, 137, 172, 196
Gradisca, Austrian Littoral 172, 196
Graz, Styria 45, 46, 108, 136, 235, 251
Great Britain (*see also* England) 5, 29, 40, 99, 128, 174, 193, 223, 224, 262, 263, 274
Great Turkish War (1683 – 1699) 50

Greece 29, 174
Greuter, Josef (1817–1888) 246
Grundsteuer (land tax) 237, 260
Gymnasium 36, 37, 44, 47, 73, 88, 171, 200, 202

Habsburgs 1, 7, 8, 16, 19, 63, 232, 267, 279
Hägelin, Franz Karl (1735–1809) 43
Halle, Germany 20
Hasner von Artha, Leopold (1818–1891) 9, 41
Hauptschule see major school
Hauszinssteuer (rent tax) 237
Hausclassensteuer (house tax) 237
Herbart, Johann Friedrich (1776–1841) 42
Hernals, Lower Austria 135
Hlinsko, Bohemia 122, 225
Hollenstein, Lower Austria 158
Horní Počernice *see* Počernice, Horní

house tax *see Hausenclasssteuer*
Hradec Králové (Königgratz), Bohemia 74, 96, 236
Hranice (Rossbach), Bohemia 236
Huemer, Franz (1836–1918) 247
Hungary 17, 19, 52, 127, 174, 211, 222, 241

illicit teachers *see* teachers, illicit
immigration *see* migration
Imoski, Dalmatia 198
Industrial Revolution 3, 170, 223, 274
Innsbruck, Tyrol 136, 137, 166, 244
Ireland 174
Istria 70, 137, 196
Italian *see* language of instruction, Italian
Italy 17, 174, 222, 223, 241
itinerant school *see* branch school

Jäger, Albert (1801–1891) 247, 248, 251, 262
Japan 4,
Jesenný, Bohemia 181
Jesuits 23, 24, 25, 31, 88, 200, 210
– dissolution (1773) 25, 30, 44
Jirny, Bohemia 92
Joseph II (1741–1790) 12, 31, 38, 43–44, 51, 52, 53, 58, 62, 71, 74, 80, 86, 88, 90, 93, 145, 203, 236, 266
Judenburg, Styria 226

Kaiser, Joseph (1807–1880) 14, 161, 162
Kamenice u Jílového, Bohemia 181
Karlín, Bohemia 122, 146
Kindermann, Ferdinand (1740–1801) 63
Klagenfurt, Carinthia 136, 137
Klosterneuburg, Lower Austria 135
Kolín, Bohemia 48
Koloděje, Bohemia 181
Königgratz *see* Hradec Králové
– Battle of *see* Sadová, battle of (1866)
Korneuburg, Lower Austria 135
Kostelec u Křížků, Bohemia 181
Krakow, Galicia 251
Krems, Lower Austria 135
Kurialsystem 234–236, 252, 258

Laibach *see* Ljubljana
Laic Laws (1881) 4, 5, 6, 263
land tax *see Grundsteuer*
language of instruction 15, 40, 73–79, 81–86, 137–138, 140–143, 206, 246, 268, 276
– Croatian 77, 139
– Czech 73–76, 81–84, 138, 139, 140, 146
– German 73–74, 79, 81–84, 136, 137, 140, 206, 276–277
– Slovenian 76–77, 139
– Italian 74, 77–78, 137, 138, 139, 268
Lavant, Carinthia 77
Lemberg *see* Lviv
Leopold II (1747–1792) 33
Letňany, Bohemia 146
Lex Hasner (1869) *see* liberal school reform of 1868-69
liberal school reform (1868–1869) 1, 2, 7, 8, 9, 14, 16, 26, 28, 39, 41–42, 53, 58, 64, 79, 87, 88, 122, 162, 170, 173, 233, 241–248, 252, 253, 258–262, 263, 268, 277, 278
Liberec (Reichenberg), Bohemia 17, 45, 57, 157, 191, 248, 249
Linz, Upper Austria 136
literacy 2, 3, 7, 16, 20, 21, 26, 54, 81, 200, 201, 203, 205, 207, 208, 209, 210–221, 223, 224, 226, 227, 230, 231, 241, 247, 251, 272, 274, 279
– rate 13, 16, 210–211, 212–221, 222, 241, 247, 266, 278
Litoměřice, Bohemia 96, 236
Littoral *see* Austrian Littoral
Ljubljana (Laibach), Carniola 47, 136
Lombardy, Italy 16, 39, 126
Lorenz, Martin 53–54
Loukov-Háje nad Jizerou, Bohemia 181, 182
Lower Austria see Austria, Lower
Lutheranism 23, 201, 204
Lviv (Lemberg), Galicia 14, 17, 45, 127, 131, 148–156, 157

major school (*Hauptschule*) 17, 26, 27, 28, 35, 37, 38, 40, 44, 47, 51, 54, 55, 57–58, 73, 78, 86, 88, 90, 100–101,

114, 115, 117, 118, 119, 124, 125, 128, 129–130, 135, 136, 140, 149, 150, 151, 154–155, 157, 200, 201, 205, 206, 207, 208, 209, 224, 268
Mann, Horace (1796–1859) 193
Maria-Dreieichen, Lower Austria 131
Mariaschein *see* Bohosudov
Maria Theresa (1717–1780) 8, 19, 22–25, 29, 36, 43, 44, 48, 86, 169, 257, 266, 267
Martini, Karl Anton von (1726–1800) 33
Meiji restoration (1868) 4
Mělník, Bohemia 114
Messmer, Joseph (1731–1804) 23
Methodenbuch 27, 125, 126
methods of instruction *see* teaching methods
migration 5, 66–68, 99, 107, 133-135, 149-150, 165–167, 212, 215, 248
Ministry of Education (Education Ministry) 9, 40, 41, 54, 58, 64, 93, 162, 233, 242, 243, 245, 262, 268
Mirovice, Bohemia 146
Morgenstern, Stanisław 251
monitorial system *see* Bell-Lancaster method
Montenegro 17
Moravia 11, 45, 49–51, 52, 53, 55, 59, 65, 71, 74–75, 93, 94, 96, 115, 120, 134, 136, 138, 156, 157, 158, 159, 163, 168, 169, 170, 171, 174, 176, 196, 210, 218, 219, 221, 235, 240, 246, 247, 279
Mörtersdorf, Lower Austria 131
Mříčná, Bohemia 208
Mukařov, Bohemia 181, 182
Myškovice, Bohemia 145, 146

Napoleonic Wars (French Wars) (1792 – 1815) 1, 4, 7, 16, 39, 44, 53, 70, 86, 126, 127, 160, 170, 171
National Society for Promoting Religious Education 270, 274
nationalism 3, 6, 15, 73–79, 279
Netherlands, the 174
Niederkreuzstetten, Lower Austria 158
Normal school (*Normalschule*) 17, 23, 25, 27, 28, 43, 90, 108, 201, 207, 209
Norway 174
Nothschule see provisional school
Nový Bor (Haida), Bohemia 269
numeracy 2, 3, 201, 202, 203, 205, 207, 208, 209, 211, 221–223, 224, 231

Olomouc, Moravia 251
Opava, Silesia 136
Ottakring, Lower Austria 135

Panenské Břežany, Bohemia 181
Papacy (Holy See) 21, 25, 41, 234, 243
Pardubice, Bohemia 114
Parhammer, Ignaz (1715–1786) 23
Paris World Expo (1867) 4
parish school (*Pfarrschule*) 21, 55, 87, 108, 146
Pařízek, Aleš Vincenc (1748–1822) 63, 74
Pascotini von Ehrenfels, Carlo (1797–1879) 247
Passau, Germany 22
patronage of schools *see Schulpatronat*
Patronage sample 95–102
peasant uprising (1775) 21, 88
Pergen, Johann Anton von (1725–1814) 24–25, 43
– Pergen plan 24–25
Pestalozzi, Johann Heinrich (1746–1827) 42, 275
Piarists 23, 24, 88, 200, 275
pietism 19–20
Pillichsdorf, Lower Austria 158
Počernice, Horní, Bohemia 181, 182
Poděbrady, Bohemia 48
Poland 10, 222
Politische Verfassung (1805) 7, 18, 34–39, 41, 42, 43, 44, 46, 53, 58, 63–64, 87, 90, 91, 94, 102, 103, 112, 115, 125, 127, 145, 148, 157, 171, 179, 180, 183, 205, 206, 207, 211, 216, 233, 241, 263, 264, 267
Potato War (1778) 50
Prague, Bohemia 16, 37, 45, 46, 91, 114, 122, 136, 145, 146, 236

Präparanden 126 *see also* teacher training
private school 6, 40, 108, 123, 127, 130–131, 163, 195, 224–225, 226, 242, 246, 259, 260, 268, 271, 272
Probstdorf, Lower Austria 158
Prosek, Bohemia 146
Protestantism 23, 24, 227, 228
– underground, in Austria 21, 22, 24
– Protestant schools 114, 148, 247
provisional school (*Nothschule*) 54, 55, 56, 101, 103, 107, 117, 231
Prussia 4, 5, 7, 20, 21, 23, 26, 28, 29, 99, 174, 241, 242, 273–274

Račah, Carniola 226
Rakovník (Rakonic), Bohemia 45
Ratio Educationis 19
Realschule 17, 34, 37, 45–47, 58, 98, 171, 224, 225, 268, 269
Reichsrat 17, 235, 242, 243, 246, 249, 252, 253, 255, 256, 257, 258
Reichsvolksschulgesetz (1869) 244, 263 *see also* liberal school reform (1868–1869)
Religionsfond 90, 97, 101–103, 105, 106, 107, 108, 110, 114, 118, 147
Reichenberg *see* Liberec
rent tax *see Hauszinssteuer*
returns to schooling 16
review school *see Wiederholungsschule*
revision commission (1795–1799) *see* Rottenhan commission
Říčany, Bohemia 181, 183
robota 21, 90, 93
Romania 17
Rosenburg-Mold, Lower Austria 131
Rottenhan, Heinrich Franz von (1738–1809) 33, 34, 37, 42, 43, 45, 269
Rottenhan commission 33–34, 37, 39, 42, 43, 204
Roztoky, Bohemia 91
Rudigier, Franz Josef (1811–1884) 243, 244
rural-urban divide 26–27, 37, 97, 100–101, 103, 104–105, 111–112, 114, 117–118, 129–130, 131, 137, 141, 191, 201, 206, 208, 224, 226, 227, 248, 249–250, 254, 257, 258–260, 266, 268, 275–276
Russia 57, 100, 174

Sadová, battle (1866) 4
Sadská, Bohemia 48
Sagan, Prussian Silesia 23
Salzburg 39, 54, 55, 59, 65, 71, 94, 115, 136, 137, 168, 169, 170, 171–172, 174, 176, 196, 218, 219, 220, 221, 235, 248, 253, 255, 256, 257
Sankt Christophen, Lower Austria 158
Sankt Pölten, Lower Austria 96, 103, 133, 135
Schneider, Karl Samuel (1801–1882) 246–247
Schöller, Alexander von (1805–1886) 145, 146, 147
school age 23, 27, 28, 29–30, 38, 40, 52, 60–62, 63–69, 80, 162, 164–167, 168, 170, 172, 176, 189, 245, 246, 250, 273, 276
school coverage 15, 48, 53, 55, 56, 58–73, 79–87, 146, 164, 174, 176–179, 193, 265, 269, 277, 278
Schule-Kirche-Gesetz see liberal school reform (1868–1869)
Schulgeld see tuition fee
Schulpatronat (school patron) 32, 38, 39, 40, 41, 52, 86, 89–98, 100–113, 119, 127, 145, 146, 147, 224, 234, 236, 238, 239, 265, 267, 269
Schwabenkinder 165–167, 247
Scotland 174
Seckau, Styria 21, 22, 77, 89, 95, 96, 107, 276
Sedan, battle (1870) 4
Sedlec, Bohemia 91, 92
serfdom 21, 88, 99, 280
Šestajovice, Bohemia 92–93
Seven-Years War (1756–1763) 4, 7, 50
Šibenik, Dalmatia 73
Silesia 23, 52, 55, 59, 65, 71, 74–76, 86, 94, 114, 115, 120, 136, 137, 138, 156, 158, 159, 163, 167, 168, 170, 171, 174, 176, 177, 196, 217, 218, 219, 221, 226, 235, 246, 247, 254
Sinj, Dalmatia 222, 223
Skalná (Wildstein), Bohemia 236

Slomšek, Anton (1800–1862) 77
Slovenia 123
Slovenian *see* language of instruction, Slovenian
Sluštice, Bohemia 181
Sonnenfels, Joseph von (1733–1817) 20, 43
Spain 99, 174
Spendou, Joseph (1757–1840) 42, 74
Spener, Philip Jacob (1635–1705) 20
Styria 11, 21, 51, 52, 53, 55, 59, 60–62, 63, 65, 68, 71, 73, 76, 77, 89, 94, 95, 96, 103–104, 107–108, 115, 136, 137, 138, 156, 168, 170, 171, 172, 174, 175, 176, 178, 196, 218, 219, 221, 234, 235, 269, 276
Standesmässigkeit 24, 26, 34, 42, 263, 267, 279
Studienfond 25, 57, 97, 101, 102, 105, 124, 145, 146 147, 242
Studien-Hof-Commission see Education Commission
Studien- und Büchercensurs-Hofcommission 22, 43, *see* also Education Commission
suffrage 7, 99–100, 233, 234–236
Swabia 166–167
Sweden 222, 269
Swieten, Gerhart van (1700–1772) 52, 71
Swieten, Gottfried van (1733–1803) 31, 44
Switzerland 5, 123, 275

Taaffe, Eduard (1833–1895) 261
tabulation method 28, 32, 203, 204, 205
tax system 237
teachers 4, 9, 14, 15, 24, 27, 28, 32, 33, 35–36, 38, 40, 48, 49, Chapter 4, 176–177, 186, 203, 204, 207, 208, 224, 226, 233, 236, 240, 242, 245, 246, 250, 260, 264, 267, 268, 276, 277
– gender gap *see* gender gap among teachers
– illicit (*Winkellehrer*) 36, 44, 163, 224, 269–270, 271, 275
– training 8, 26, 27, 35, 40, 41, 47, 51, 54, 57, 74, 100, 125–126, 128, 129, 133-134, 155, 158–159, 161, 203, 204, 234, 240, 245, 261, 264, 266, 276
– salary and remuneration 30, 32, 37, 88, 112, 115–117, 118–120, 125, 126, 138, 142, 143–156, 157, 245, 250, 259, 260, 264
– women 15, 128, 129, 132, 133, 135, 136, 137, 138, 139, 150, 155–156, 163, 260, 268 *see also* gender gap among teachers
teaching methods 25, 27–28, 30, 32–33, 35, 39, 40, 42, 51, 125, 163, 200, 203, 204, 210, 224, 233, 245, 264, 266, 267, 270
technical school *see Realschule*
textbooks 25, 27, 31, 35, 40, 51, 74, 77, 177, 200, 203, 204, 206, 208, 242, 245, 261, 266, 268, 276
Theresian school reform (1774) v, 7, 11, 18, 22–31, 36, 48, 51, 53, 58, 86, 88, 163, 200, 201, 211, 225, 257, 266, 267, 269, 274, 280 *see also Allgemeine Schulordnung*
Thun und Hohenstein, Leopold von (1811–1888) 9, 234
Třeboratice, Bohemia 145–147
Trient (Trentino), Tyrol 137, 170
Trieste, Austrian Littoral 45, 46, 136, 137, 160, 172, 196, 247, 248, 251
trivial school (*Trivialschule*) 17, 26, 27, 43, 51, 54, 55–58, 74, 81, 84, 87, 100–101, 117, 125, 128, 149, 154–155, 157, 200, 201, 205, 206, 207, 208, 209, 220, 221, 224, 231, 233, 267, 279
Troppau *see* Opava
Trója, Bohemia 91, 92
tuition fee (*Schulgeld*) 30, 31, 32, 37, 38, 39, 40, 44, 54, 56, 71, 81, 83, 84, 88, 112–118, 120, 124, 126, 145, 146, 147, 148, 177, 183, 185, 186, 187, 191, 193, 199, 260, 277, 278, 279
Tyrol 11, 31, 39, 45, 55, 56, 59, 63, 65, 66, 68, 70, 71, 77–78, 93, 94, 114–115, 120, 126, 136, 137, 138, 139, 144, 164, 165–167, 168, 169, 170, 171, 172, 173, 174, 176, 196, 218,

219, 220, 221, 235, 243, 244, 246, 247, 248, 250, 251, 252, 253, 254, 255, 257, 273, 278, 279

Úbislavice, Bohemia 181
Ukraine 17, 148
Unigenitus, papal bull (1713) 21
United States 4, 5, 29, 99
Upper Austria *see* Austria, Upper
urban-rural divide *see* rural-urban divide

Varnsdorf (Warnsdorf), Bohemia 264
Veleň, Bohemia 146
Velké Čakovice *see* Čakovice, velké
Venetia 16, 39, 44, 126
Verzehrungssteuer (consumption tax) 237
Vidochov, Bohemia 181
Vienna, Lower Austria 16, 22, 23, 25, 27, 35, 39, 43, 45, 46, 66–68, 70, 86, 96, 97, 108, 109, 114, 127, 129–135, 136, 150, 161, 163, 166, 167, 170, 171, 204, 206, 224–225, 235, 239, 243, 246, 248, 251, 262
Vorarlberg 11, 39, 55, 59, 65, 66, 68, 71, 78, 94, 115, 136, 137, 165–167, 168, 169, 171, 172, 174, 176, 196, 218, 219, 220, 221, 235, 253, 254, 255

Wales 128, 174, 272
War of Spanish Succession (1701–14) 50
War of Austrian Succession (1740–48) 7, 23, 50
Whitbread bill (1807) 270
Whipple index 221–223
Wiederholungsschule (also review school) 40
Wiener-Neustadt, Lower Austria 133
Winkellehrer see teachers, illicit
Women *see* gender gap, teachers-women

Żabno, Galicia 251
Zaingrub, Lower Austria 131
Zell, Carinthia 201
Zurich, Switzerland 123
Zvánovice, Bohemia 181, 183